*Winner of the Buddhist S*
*Christmas Humphreys Memoria*



This beautiful book ... captures so well the s
whole range of Buddhist canonical literatur ... a great deal of depth and subtlety in presentation together with that gentle sense of irony that is so characteristic of Buddhist canonical texts.

*Lama Shenpen Hookham*

A clear and comprehensive survey of the entire body of Buddhist canonical literature.... Not only will this book provide the general student of Buddhism with a concise survey of the Buddhist scriptures, but its chapters on the Mahayana sutras will enable the Theravadin reader to acquire a capsule knowledge of the sacred texts followed by his Mahayana compeers.

*Ven. Bhikkhu Bodhi, BPS Newsletter*

A remarkable book.... succeeds brilliantly ... in offering a comprehensive, accessible guide to the teachings, organization, style and status of all the Theravada and Mahayana canonical texts.

*The Middle Way*

Of great value to almost anyone working in Buddhist studies or living in the Buddhist tradition.... An indispensable reference book and compendium.

*Tibet Society Bulletin*

A mine of information even for scholars who are not well versed in all traditions of Buddhism.

*The Tibet Journal*

A handy reference guide ... intended for the reader without sufficient language skills to gain access to the scriptural sources at first hand.

*Buddhist Studies Review*

Dedicated to
the memory of
WILLIAM GEMMEL
and
WONG MOW LAM

Shakyamuni renounced nobility and devoted his life to
Preventing others from falling into ruin.
On earth eighty years,
Proclaiming the Dharma for fifty,
Bestowing the sutras as an eternal legacy;
Today, still a bridge to cross over to the other shore.

*Ryōkan*
(Japanese hermit monk, *circa* 1758–1831)

*One Robe, One Bowl: The Zen Poetry of Ryōkan*
translated and introduced by John Stevens
Weatherhill, 1977

Also by Sangharakshita

*Books on Buddhism*
A Survey of Buddhism
The Ten Pillars of Buddhism
The Three Jewels

*Edited Seminars and Lectures*
The Bodhisattva Ideal
Buddha Mind
The Buddha's Victory
Buddhism for Today – and Tomorrow
Creative Symbols of Tantric Buddhism
The Drama of Cosmic Enlightenment
The Essence of Zen
A Guide to the Buddhist Path
Human Enlightenment
The Inconceivable Emancipation
Know Your Mind
Living with Awareness
Living with Kindness
The Meaning of Conversion in Buddhism
New Currents in Western Buddhism
Ritual and Devotion in Buddhism
The Taste of Freedom
Tibetan Buddhism: An Introduction
Vision and Transformation
What Is the Dharma?
What Is the Sangha?
Who Is the Buddha?
Wisdom Beyond Words
The Yogi's Joy

*Essays*
Alternative Traditions
Crossing the Stream
Forty-Three Years Ago
The FWBO and 'Protestant Buddhism'
Going for Refuge
The History of My Going for Refuge
The Priceless Jewel
Was the Buddha a Bhikkhu?

*Memoirs and Letters*
Facing Mount Kanchenjunga
From Genesis to the Diamond Sutra
In the Sign of the Golden Wheel
Moving Against the Stream
The Rainbow Road
Travel Letters
Through Buddhist Eyes

*Art and Poetry*
The Call of the Forest and Other Poems
Complete Poems 1941–1994
In the Realm of the Lotus
The Religion of Art

*Miscellaneous*
Ambedkar and Buddhism
A Stream of Stars

# THE ETERNAL LEGACY

## An Introduction to the Canonical Literature of Buddhism

SANGHARAKSHITA

WINDHORSE PUBLICATIONS

Published by
Windhorse Publications Ltd
11 Park Road
Birmingham
B13 8AB
United Kingdom


Originally published by Tharpa Publications, 1985

Cover image: Devamitra
Cover design: Marlene Eltschig
Printed by Cromwell Press Ltd, Trowbridge, England

*A catalogue record for this book is available from the British Library*
ISBN-10: 1 899579 58 3
ISBN-13: 978 1 899579 58 7



The publishers gratefully acknowledge the invaluable assistance of Dhivati and Dharmashura in preparing this edition for press.

# CONTENTS

# ABOUT THE AUTHOR

Sangharakshita was born Dennis Lingwood in South London, in 1925. Largely self-educated, he developed an interest in the cultures and philosophies of the East early on, and realized that he was a Buddhist at the age of sixteen.

The Second World War took him, as a conscript, to India, where he stayed on to become the Buddhist monk Sangharakshita. After studying for some years under leading teachers from the major Buddhist traditions, he went on to teach and write extensively. He also played a key part in the revival of Buddhism in India, particularly through his work among followers of Dr B.R. Ambedkar.

After twenty years in India, he returned to England to establish the Friends of the Western Buddhist Order in 1967, and the Western Buddhist Order (called Trailokya Bauddha Mahasangha in India) in 1968. A translator between East and West, between the traditional world and the modern, between principles and practices, Sangharakshita's depth of experience and clear thinking have been appreciated throughout the world. He has always particularly emphasized the decisive significance of commitment in the spiritual life, the paramount value of spiritual friendship and community, the link between religion and art, and the need for a 'new society' supportive of spiritual aspirations and ideals.

Sangharakshita has now handed on most of his responsibilities to his senior disciples in the Order. From his base in Birmingham, he is now focusing on personal contact with people, and on his writing.

# PREFACE TO THE FIRST EDITION

The student of Buddhism will naturally want to know about the sacred books of Buddhism. He will want to know what their names are, how they came into existence, and what they actually contain. Unfortunately, even though Buddhism itself is beginning to be quite well known in the West, no book exists in any Western language able to meet this vital need. There is a history of Indian literature, published more than fifty years ago, and there are several histories of Pāli literature, but there is no one work that gives the student of Buddhism a straightforward and comprehensive account of the Buddhist canonical literature as a whole. There is no one work devoted exclusively to what tradition terms the Buddhavacana or word of the Buddha.

It is this state of affairs that is responsible for the appearance of *The Eternal Legacy*. Like its predecessor *The Three Jewels* (1967), it began life as a series of articles for the *Oriya Encyclopedia* that, in the process of writing, considerably outgrew the purpose for which they had been commissioned. During the last few years copies of the English draft of these articles have circulated in typewritten form among my own students under the title *The Word of the Buddha*. Some of these students, finding the work of great help to them in their study of Buddhism, repeatedly urged me to revise it and publish it in book form. For a long time I resisted their friendly importunity. I resisted it for two reasons. Firstly, I was extremely busy, and did not really have time to give the work the thorough revision it needed. Secondly, I was conscious of the shortcomings of the work and hoped that, if I only waited long enough, someone better qualified than myself would produce a work more worthy of its great subject. Since no such work has appeared, and since an introduction to the canonical literature of Buddhism is more urgently needed than ever, I have at last decided to give this sequel to *The Three Jewels* such revision as I could and send it forth into the world.

In so doing I would like to make it clear that *The Eternal Legacy* is not meant for scholars, who in any case will have access to the Sanskrit, Pāli, Chinese, Tibetan, and Khotanese texts on which it is ultimately based. Though not (I hope) unscholarly, the work is meant primarily for the student of Buddhism who is not in a position to explore for himself a canonical literature fifty times more extensive than the Bible and two-hundred-and-fifty times more extensive than the Koran. Obviously it has not been possible for me to deal with so vast a mass of material in the way it deserves. It has not even been possible for me to deal with the different canonical texts at a length proportionate to their comparative historical and spiritual significance, with the result that within the limited perspective of this work some of the grandest monuments of Buddhist canonical literature may appear strangely foreshortened. It has also not been possible to indicate the special connections existing between certain Mahāyāna sūtras and certain Far Eastern schools of Buddhist thought and practice. (I have done this, to a limited extent, in *A Survey of Buddhism*, chapter 3.) Despite these and other deficiencies, however, I hope that until such time as it is superseded by a more adequate treatment of its subject *The Eternal Legacy* will be of use to all students of Buddhism, as well as to students of Religion and students of Literature. Even though one cannot actually enter the Cave of Treasures, the fact that one is able to run a few of its diamonds and rubies through one's fingers will give one at least an idea of the inexhaustible riches it contains.

Since *The Eternal Legacy* is a book about Buddhist canonical literature, I have not thought it necessary to give much information about translations from that literature, whether ancient or modern, or in the languages of the Orient or the Occident. Information about the great 'classical' Chinese and Tibetan translations has been given only to the extent necessary to determine the age of the original texts, or as a matter of general interest. For the benefit of the more serious student, however, I have compiled for each chapter of the book a short bibliography of works pertaining to the subject-matter of that chapter and/or modern translations (mainly English) of canonical texts belonging to the class of texts dealt with therein. Such students will, however, notice that the translations listed in the bibliography are not always the same as the ones actually used in *The Eternal Legacy*. This is because in the case of certain texts, notably the *Saddharma-Puṇḍarīka* and the *Vimalakīrti-Nirdeśa*, the old translations are in some respects better than the more recent ones – at least so far as the passages actually quoted are concerned.

Sanskrit and Pāli proper names and technical terms have been transliterated in accordance with the prevailing system. In the case of proper names in Chinese and Tibetan, no such uniformity has been attempted, since no single system of transliteration yet prevails for these languages.

An understanding of Buddhism cannot be divorced from a knowledge of the Buddhist sacred books. It is therefore with great satisfaction that I see *The Eternal Legacy* at last available in book form.

*Sangharakshita*
Padmaloka
Norfolk
1985

# PREFACE TO THIS EDITION

Since the publication of *The Eternal Legacy* in 1985 interest in Buddhism has grown steadily in the West. Centres and groups affiliated to this or that branch of the Buddhist tradition have multiplied, and more and more people are practising meditation in one form or other. Enterprising publishing houses on both sides of the Atlantic have moreover continued to bring out books on Buddhism – both popular and scholarly – in ever-increasing numbers.

Much of this secondary literature is of a higher standard than would have been the case forty or fifty years ago. Nonetheless, for the serious student of the Dharma an acquaintance with the Buddhist scriptures remains indispensable. The difficulty is that the Buddhist scriptures are vast in extent and varied in content and exist in several canonical languages. Where shall the student begin? How is he to gain an overview of the whole field of what is known as the Buddhavacana or word of the Buddha?

It was with such questions in mind that I wrote *The Eternal Legacy*. In the preface to the first edition of the work I expressed the hope that it would soon be superseded by a more adequate treatment of its great subject by someone better qualified than myself. Though I have now waited twenty years, that hope has not been fulfilled. I have therefore decided to bring out this new edition of *The Eternal Legacy*.

Since the original publication of the work, translations of many Buddhist texts have appeared. Among the more important of these are Bhikkhu Bodhi's *Middle Discourses of the Buddha* (1995) and *Connected Discourses of the Buddha* (2000), Thomas Cleary's *The Flower Ornament*

*Scripture*, and some of the volumes published in the *Bukkyō Dendō Kyōkai* English translation series.

I would like to thank Windhorse Publications for agreeing to bring out a new edition of *The Eternal Legacy*, and Dharmachari Shantavira in particular, for his help in correcting errors and regularizing diacritics. May this work help awake students of Buddhism to the unparalleled riches of that legacy!

*Sangharakshita*
Madhyamaloka
Birmingham
14 October 2005

# 1

# BUDDHISM AND LANGUAGE

Before essaying a rapid survey of Buddhist canonical literature we must briefly discuss our principal terms. By canonical literature is meant the written records of the Buddhavacana or living word of the Buddha, or what purports to be such, whether original or translated, or what is traditionally regarded as such by the Buddhist community or any section thereof. The whole of the vast derivative literature, in the form of commentaries and expositions, is thus excluded from our purview.

Now the term 'word of the Buddha', and therefore the expression 'canonical literature' also, can be understood either in a wider primary sense, or in a narrower secondary one, depending upon our definition of the word 'Buddha'. If we mean by Buddha simply the state of Supreme Enlightenment by whomsoever experienced, then by Buddhavacana is to be understood any expression, or better reflection, of this transcendental state in the medium of human speech. If, on the other hand, Buddha means the historic Buddha Gautama, the initiator of the spiritual movement now known as Buddhism, then Buddhavacana will be confined to the literary record of the sayings of this teacher. Buddhism as a whole tends to oscillate between the two extremes. Even the Theravādins, who are committed to a pedantically narrow and rigid doctrine of Buddhavacana, include in their Tipiṭaka discourses which, though delivered by disciples, are regarded as Buddhavacana inasmuch as the Master had approved them, thus making them, as it were, his own. Conversely, the Mahāyāna, which in principle maintains that 'Whatever is well said is a word of the

Buddha',[1] in practice certainly hesitates to accept as such any teaching that conflicts with the scriptures.

In whichever way it may be interpreted, Buddhavacana consists of an assemblage of words in a particular language or languages. This introduces the extremely important question of the relation of Buddhism to language in general which, also, can be understood in various ways. Philosophically, the question is that of the relation between the purely spiritual import of the teaching – ultimately coinciding with the transcendental state of Enlightenment itself – and its conceptual-cum-verbal formulations: historically, that of the language spoken by Gautama the Buddha. It will be convenient to deal with these two senses in reverse order, proceeding from the narrower to the broader one.

Modern Theravādins are fond of making such statements as 'the Buddha taught in Pāli' or 'Pāli is the language of the Buddha'. The problem of what linguistic medium the Buddha adopted in communicating his teaching to mankind does not, however, admit of so straightforward a solution. To begin with, Pāli is not the name of a language at all. The word means, literally, 'a line, a row (of letters)' and thus, by extension of its meaning, 'the (canonical) text'. Early Western students of Theravāda literature, finding in the commentaries expressions such as *pālinayena*, 'according to the (canonical) text', took the word for the name of the language of the texts and, through their writings, gave currency to this misunderstanding. According to Theravāda tradition the Buddha spoke Māgadhī which, since the Tipiṭaka is regarded as a verbally faithful record of his teaching, for them also designates the language of the canonical texts. In uncritical usage, therefore, Pāli and Māgadhī have become synonymous, both of them now being applied by the Theravādins indiscriminately to the Buddha's personal language and the language of the Tipiṭaka.

But even to say that the Buddha spoke Māgadhī does not really help us. Māgadhī is the language of Māgadha just as Spanish is the language of Spain, and, in the absence of independent literary records in that tongue, to tell us that the Buddha spoke Māgadhī leaves us no wiser than we were before. Though born among the Śākyas, who were feudatory to the kingdom of Kośala, the Buddha spent much time after his Enlightenment in the adjacent kingdom of Māgadha. The language of Māgadha, or 'Māgadhī', was therefore undoubtedly his normal means of communication within that area. When in Kośala he must have spoken Kosalese. Being enlightened, he was exempt from linguistic prejudice, and his attitude, exemplified by a well-known episode, was tolerant and practical:

> Two monks [it is related] of fine (cultivated) language and fine (eloquent) speech, came to the Buddha and said: Lord, here monks of various (names, clan-names, races or castes, and families) are corrupting the Buddha's words by (repeating them in) their own dialects. Let us put them into Vedic (*chandaso āropema*). The Lord rebuked them: Deluded men, how can you say this? This will not lead to the conversion of the unconverted.... And he delivered a sermon and commanded (all) the monks: You are not to put the Buddha's words into Vedic. Who does so would commit a sin. I authorize you, monks, to learn the Buddha's words each in his own dialect [*sakkāya niruttiyā*].[2]

As Edgerton points out, it is clear from this passage that in addition to Sanskrit, the language of the upper classes, there existed a number of popular and more or less mutually intelligible Middle Indic dialects (among them Māgadhī and Kośalese), in one or more of which the Buddha himself was accustomed to preach, and that it was in those dialects, therefore, that the monks were to learn, recite, and (according to the Chinese versions) to disseminate the Buddhavacana.[3] In this way the teaching, instead of being confined to a Sanskrit-educated elite would, as befitted its universal character, be accessible to all. There was no question of compiling a single standardized version of the teaching in a learned tongue, such a procedure being expressly prohibited. The freedom which the Buddha had allowed his followers promoted, after his *parinirvāṇa*, the growth of parallel versions of the teaching, first in different local vernaculars and afterwards in different languages. The oldest and most authentic portions of the 'Pāli' Tipiṭaka are based, ultimately, on one of these versions, being a literary recension of a Middle Indic version originating not in Māgadha but somewhere in western-central India.

The insistence of the Theravāda that the Buddha spoke Pāli, the language of the Tipiṭaka, stems less from ignorance of historical facts than from a doctrinal misunderstanding. This misunderstanding, which is of the essence of the Theravāda, consists in the belief that the import of the teaching is inseparable from its original conceptual-cum-verbal formulations, or what is believed to be such. Hence sweeping pronouncements such as 'It is impossible to understand Buddhism properly without studying Pāli,' or 'How can the Tibetans be real Buddhists? They don't know Pāli.'

Reinforced by the belief that in the Tipiṭaka they possess the only complete and accurate record of the *ipsissima verba* of the Buddha, this literalistic attitude has given rise to that spirit of bigotry, exclusiveness, and dogmatic authoritarianism for which some modern Theravādins are notorious. Yet such an attitude is clearly incompatible with a number of passages in the Tipiṭaka itself, including the one quoted. From the latter it is, indeed, obvious that according to the Buddha the spirit of his teaching, far from being dependent on any particular form of words, could be given equally valid expression in languages other than the one in which it had originally been propounded.

Buddhavacana was not to be identified exclusively with any one of its linguistic versions. Hence for Buddhists there can be no scripture, no canon, in the sense of a single finally definitive, universally authoritative text of the teaching such as the Bible constitutes for Christians and the Koran for Muslims. The word of the Buddha, it must be emphasized, has from the beginning been extant in a multiplicity of alternative versions – some more and some less complete – no one of which is *a priori* more reliable than the rest, or can claim superiority over them on any grounds other than that of greater depth and comprehensiveness of content. This is not to deny that early versions of the teaching, especially when their language approximates to the language used by the Buddha (assuming this to be known), will always possess a special historical significance. They will obviously be of greater help, moreover, in reconstructing the original form of his teaching than the later versions. What we deny, and deny emphatically, is that by an extraordinary coincidence the language used by the Buddha (whatever it may have been) happens to be intrinsically more capable of conveying his meaning than any other and that, therefore, a knowledge of the letter of the Dharma is indispensable to an understanding of its spirit. Indeed it has been suggested, by a close and critical student of the Tipiṭaka, that the Buddha found the linguistic resources of his day inadequate, being in particular hard pressed for want of a stronger word for 'will' than the feeble *cetanā*.[4]

Taking this as a starting point, one might even argue that classical Chinese, or modern English, being more highly developed languages, are intrinsically more capable of giving expression to the spirit of Buddhism than ancient Middle Indic or medieval Pāli. Some do, of course, maintain that it is impossible to translate Buddhist texts satisfactorily into modern European languages. This is to confuse fidelity to the spirit with capacity to reproduce the letter of the Buddha's teaching. Moreover, were it in reality impossible to disengage the former from the latter and give it an independent expression it would mean, in effect, that the Buddha's spiritual experience, far from transcending thought and speech, had on the contrary been conditioned by them. Thus his Enlightenment would be no enlightenment at all.

Contradictions of this sort can be precluded only by recognizing, once and for all – as the Mahāyāna has done – that the spirit of the teaching is capable of expressing itself in a variety of forms, no one of which, however authentic or however excellent, is perfect or final, or can possibly exhibit in full the infinite riches of its transcendental content. The Buddha himself, as one might have expected, was as keenly aware of the limitations of words in respect of spiritual reality as the poet Marlowe was in respect of sensuous beauty:

If all the pens that ever poets held
Had fed the feeling of their masters' thoughts,
And every sweetness that inspired their hearts,
Their minds, and muses on admired themes;
If all the heavenly quintessence they still
From their immortal flowers of poesy,
Wherein, as in a mirror, we perceive
The highest reaches of a human wit;
If these had made one poem's period,
And all combined in beauty's worthiness,
Yet should there hover in their restless heads
One thought, one grace, one wonder, at the least,
Which into words no virtue can digest.[5]

Evidence of the Buddha's awareness is provided by the list of ten 'inexpressibles' (*avyākṛtavastuni*, Pāli *avyākatavatthuni*), according to which it is impossible to declare (1) whether the world is eternal or not, (2) whether the world is finite (in space) or infinite, (3) whether the

Tathāgata exists after (physical) death, or does not, or both, or neither, and (4) whether the soul is identical with the body or different from it.[6]

Moreover, in communicating his spiritual experience even a mediocre religious teacher has a definite advantage over the poet, however gifted. By virtue of the very conditions of his art the poet is entirely dependent upon words. The religious teacher, on the other hand, can supplement any deficiencies of language – whether intrinsic or due to his own inadequate command over that medium – by the direct impact of his personality on the hearts and minds of his auditors, whether through looks and gestures, or in ways still more subtle and indefinable. In the case of the Buddha, the perfectly enlightened Teacher of teachers, this impact is out of all proportion to either the number or the actual import of the words spoken. It may, indeed, be entirely independent of words. The Dhyāna (Ch. Ch'an, Jap. Zen) School, which claims to represent 'a special transmission outside the scriptures',[7] is believed to have originated from an unverbalized communication of this kind. According to a late Chinese legend:

> Śākyamuni was once engaged at the Mount of the Holy Vulture in preaching to a congregation of his disciples. He did not resort to any lengthy verbal discourse to explain his point, but simply lifted a bouquet of flowers before the assemblage, which was presented to him by one of his lay-disciples. Not a word came out of his mouth. Nobody understood the meaning of this except the old venerable Mahākāśyapa, who quietly smiled at the master, as if he fully comprehended the purport of this silent but eloquent teaching on the part of the Enlightened One. The latter perceiving this opened his gold-tongued mouth and proclaimed solemnly, 'I have the most precious treasure, spiritual and transcendental, which this moment I hand over to you, O venerable Mahākāśyapa!'[8]

The Tibetan branch of the Vajrayāna, no doubt following Indian traditions, reckons three different 'lineages' of the Dharma corresponding to the three different planes on which its transmission may take place. On the highest, the purely spiritual plane, that of the mind-lineage of the Jinas (or Buddhas), the transmission consists in a communication of spiritual experience directly from the heart or mind of the enlightened master to the heart or mind of the disciple without recourse to language or gesture. On the intermediate plane, that of the sign-lineage of the Vidyādharas or 'Tantric initiates of high spiritual attainment', it takes place by means of gestures only (according to some, through study of the written, as distinct from the spoken, word). It was in this way, apparently, that the Dharma was transmitted to Mahākāśyapa. Finally, on the third and lowest plane, that of the word-lineage of the *ācāryas* or 'teachers profoundly versed in the scriptures', the Dharma is transmitted orally by means of language. The treasure handed over to Mahākāśyapa and the two higher Vajrayāna lineages represent, in different ways, the living spirit of the Dharma which, unless it vivify the letter, the letter is dead.

In studying the canonical literature it is important to remember that Buddhism is not to be understood by words alone, not even when those words are authentically the Buddha's. If misunderstandings are to be avoided, it must be studied, not in isolation, but with reference to the tradition of spiritual experience out of which it sprang, to which it returns, and to which it all the time belongs. Moreover, besides the fact that the teaching expresses itself in a multiplicity of forms, it should also be remembered that before its reduction to writing the canonical literature existed in the form of oral tradition.

# 2

# THE ORAL TRADITION

Whatever differences of opinion there may be about the relative authenticity of the various canonical texts, it is at least agreed that the Buddha himself wrote nothing. The records are unanimous that, so far as its expression in words is concerned, his teaching was imparted entirely through the medium of conversations and discourses. When accretions are cleared away, and the subject matter of the scriptures is seen in historical perspective, it is an attractive and moving picture that emerges – like a distant landscape framed by clouds – from the welter of traditions partially recorded and imperfectly understood. In fact there emerges a series of pictures:

The Buddha, having finished his morning meal, is sitting beneath a tree not far from the highway. Attracted by his dignified and serene appearance, a party of travelling merchants stop their bullock-carts, alight and greet him, and make the usual polite enquiries. A religious discussion then ensues.

Clasping the dead body of her infant son, a young woman stumbles, mad with grief, into the Master's presence and flings herself at his feet. Compassionately, but with an understanding that eventually opens her eyes to the Truth, he consoles her.

It is the night of the autumnal full moon, when the lotus blooms. In a clearing of the jungle the Buddha and five hundred disciples are seated in silent meditation. Hour after hour goes by, but no sound is made, no movement. Not so much as a leaf stirs. Suddenly, like a pebble dropped into a pool, there comes a disturbance; a visitor has arrived. It is the king, his mind troubled this peaceful night by the recollection of a fearful deed. What tangible fruit, he asks, accrues to a man living the religious life? Patiently, the Lord explains, leading him step by step, and progressing from the known to the unknown, until in grand sequence and with majestic sweep the fruits of all the successive stages of the path, even up to Nirvāṇa, the supreme fruit, have been revealed.

A brahmin whose house the Master has approached for alms pauses in the midst of his devotions and, with sacrificial ladle uplifted, angrily abuses him as bald-pate and outcaste. Gently, but not without irony, the Master enquires if he really knows what makes an outcaste. From the discourse that, having received an astonished negative, the Buddha now delivers, it is clear that the arrogant brahmin himself is morally and spiritually an outcaste.

Moved by an impulse of compassion, the Buddha abruptly sends for all the monks in the neighbourhood. They come, and standing in the doorway of his lodgings he exhorts them in eloquent and earnest words not to relax their efforts until they have achieved, through wisdom, unshakeable deliverance of mind. So saying, he dismisses them to the forest to meditate at the roots of trees.

Pictures such as these, wherein, against a background now of forest and river, now of city mansion or village street, the Buddha imparts his teaching, might be multiplied indefinitely. In all of them, shining with a luminous beauty of its own, there appears the same unique central figure, a figure pre-eminently that of an infinitely wise and boundlessly compassionate Teacher. As the venue, so the form, of the teaching shifts and changes. Discourses, enlivened with anecdotes and embellished with similes, alternate with keen 'Socratic' dialogue, lengthy expositions with apophthegms, and inspired spontaneous utterance with rigorous cross-examination. At times, under the stress of some profound spiritual excitement, or because of the unusual solemnity of the occasion, the Buddhavacana, becoming rhythmical, orders itself according to metre and assonance, and prose bursts into bloom as poetry. As we saw in the Chapter 1, Māgadhī might alternate with Kośalese. But in whatever language or literary form the teaching was imparted, its substance remained unchanged.

> Just as the great ocean, O monks, has one taste, the taste of salt, so my Dharma has one taste, the taste of liberation.[9]

After the *parinirvāṇa* the Buddha's disciples naturally felt that their first duty was to preserve his teaching intact for the benefit of humanity. In those days writing, though already introduced from Babylonia by the merchant community and widely practised, was still considered too profane an art to be utilized for religious purposes. They had, therefore, to preserve the Buddha's sayings, or what they remembered of them, solely by word of mouth, transmitting the teaching from master to disciple in an unbroken line of oral tradition. During his lifetime the Buddha, aware of the transcendent value of his message, had encouraged the monks to commit it to memory, and to repeat at least the main headings of his discourses, as well as to reflect and meditate upon them. This was made easier for them when, probably in the latter part of his pastoral career, his discourses on the more important spiritual topics tended, by dint of constant repetition, to become increasingly standardized in form.

Poetry being more easily remembered than prose, there existed also a long-standing tradition of versification. Encouraged by the Master, Vaṅgīsa more than once reproduces the substance of the Buddha-vacana in embellished stanza form.[10] Such Dharma-stanzas, which by the inclusion of narrative elements were sometimes expanded into ballads, the monks recited as they went about, not for their personal edification only but as a means of propaganda. It is with a stanza that Aśvajit answers Śāriputra's enquiry as to the Buddha's teaching. By arranging the Dharma-stanzas in groups, according to topic, little collections could be gradually built up. Thus at the Master's bidding the young monk Soṇa recites in the congregation the entire *Aṭṭhaka-vagga* or 'Chapter of Eights', a title now designating an ancient collection of sixteen poems in 210 stanzas comprising chapter 4 of the *Sutta-Nipāta*, but which then consisted, in all probability, of the four poems of eight stanzas each which constitute the nucleus of the collection.[11]

Besides solo recitations of this sort, there were also congregational chantings (*saṅgīti*), by means of which the teaching could be fixed in the collective memory, and thus preserved. Already during the lifetime of the Master, the recitation of a *prāṭimokṣa* or verse summary of the Dharma formed, as I have explained elsewhere, part of the *poṣadha* or fortnightly congregational service.[12] According to the *Saṅgīti-sutta* of the *Dīgha Nikāya*, the death of Mahāvira, the restorer of Jainism, was the occasion of so much wrangling among his followers that Śāriputra, apprehensive of a similar outbreak among the bhikshus, organized what is called a *saṅgīti-paryāya*, or 'round of congregational chantings', in order that, in the words attributed to him, 'this holy life may persist and be well maintained'. Since the great disciple predeceased the Buddha, this incident, which bears the stamp of historicity, must have occurred during the latter's lifetime.

After the *parinirvāṇa*, congregational chanting of the Buddhavacana naturally became a popular practice, assuming as time went on a solemn liturgical character. Eventually, towards the end of the first century BCE, when there was no personal disciple of the Buddha living, the congregational chanting of a 'text' or collection of texts came to be regarded, in the absence of other criteria, as guaranteeing its authenticity. All the texts were not, of course, equally authentic. The degree of authenticity depended on the size and influence of the congregation. Absolute authenticity could be guaranteed not by any local sangha, but only by a kind of general council of all the bhikshus.

On this idea, never fully realized in practice, the Theravādins later on attempted to base the claim that their own version of the scriptures was the only complete and authentic one. According to *khandhakas* 11 and 12 of the *Cūḷa-vagga*, which are appendices to their recension of the Vinaya Piṭaka, this version of theirs was recited at *saṅgītis* held, first at Rājagṛha immediately after the *parinirvāṇa* by all the bhikshus and afterwards at Vaiśālī by the 'orthodox' *sthavīras* (Pāli *theras*) or senior monks after the secession of the Mahāsaṅghikas. These legends, which are clearly manufactured as a means of asserting the sectarian claims of the Theravādins, are on the internal evidence of the Pāli canon itself quite unacceptable. Neither immediately after the *parinirvāṇa*, nor at any subsequent period, was any such *saṅgīti* held in which all the bhikshus in north-eastern India participated. The most that can be said is that during the first century BCE the bhikshus of the Middle Country,[13] remaining in close contact with one another, transmitted orally at their various local centres versions of the Dharma-Vinaya which, developed from a common stock of tradition under identical conditions, did not greatly differ one from another. Surviving the Vaiśālī schism, and the subsequent division of Buddhism into schools, the tradition of oral transmission, with a continually expanding content, continued for four or five centuries and, in the case of certain teachings, for not less than a full millennium.

Where and when the practice of committing the oral tradition to writing was introduced, and under what circumstances, we have no certain means of knowing. The transference of the canon from word of mouth to written text is marked, however – as S. Dutt points out – by a legend of the *Divyāvadāna* or 'Divine Glorious Deeds', in which a casual reference is made to the *reading* of the word of the Buddha: 'The ladies of the house are said to peruse, after the day's household labours are over, the *Buddha-vacana* by lamp-light and take notes therefrom, for which *bhūrja* (birch-bark) leaves, ink and pen, as well as oil (for the lamp) and cotton (for the wick) are required.'[14]

Since the *Divyāvadāna* belongs, in all likelihood, to the first century BCE, written texts of the Buddha's sayings must have become, by that time, sufficiently numerous to circulate among the laity. Even so, this solitary reference affords no clue as to how much of the Buddhavacana had then been committed to writing. The *Mahāvaṃsa*, or 'Great Chronicle' of Sri Lanka, which was composed about the beginning of the sixth century CE, records a tradition that: 'The text of the three piṭakas and the aṭṭhakathā thereon did the most wise bhikkhus hand down in former times orally, but since they saw that the people were falling away (from religion) the bhikkhus [of the Mahāvihāra] came together, and in order that the true doctrine might endure, they wrote them down in books.'[15]

Though no direct inference from events in Sri Lanka to those in India is permissible, it is not without significance that the *Mahāvaṃsa* assigns this work of redaction to the reign of King Vatthugāmini, who belongs, like the composition of the *Divyāvadāna*, to the first century BCE. Two centuries earlier than either, Aśoka had, of course, recommended the monks to study seven scriptural passages, all of which have now been identified;[16] but this circumstance, though indicating that at least one school possessed a definitive collection of the Buddha's sayings, does not establish the existence of this collection in written form.

As was natural, the scriptures tended, when reduced to writing, to preserve in the newly-acquired literary medium the distinctive characteristics of the old oral method of transmission. This circumstance is responsible, in part at least, for what Eliot characterizes as 'the wearisome and mechanical iteration of the Pāli Canon'[17] which, like its Sanskritic counterpart, abounds in repetitions. If the Mahāyāna sūtras are comparatively free from such blemishes – as they must appear from the literary point of view – it is because they concentrate on preserving the spirit and feeling of the Buddha's teaching rather than its exact original wording. The scriptures also tend to reproduce, as literary forms, the various styles and types of composition assumed by the Buddhavacana in the course of centuries of oral transmission. As these are traditionally nine in number, the scriptures themselves frequently characterize the teaching, in respect of its form, as the *navaṅgabuddhasāsana* or 'Nine-Membered Message of the Buddha'. The nine *aṅgas* or members are:

(1) *Sūtra* (Pāli *sutta*). According to usage a dialogue or discourse, and meaning literally 'a thread', the word suggests a series of topics strung on a common thread of argument or exhortation. By implication, therefore, a sūtra is of considerable length, systematic in form, and substantial in content. It is the best known, and in some ways the most characteristic, of all Buddhist literary genres. According to the Theravāda commentator Buddhaghosa, who in some cases appears uncertain of the meaning of the *aṅgas*, this type of composition includes the Vinaya, certain *suttas* in verse, and 'other utterances of the Tathāgata named *suttas*'.[18] The Vinaya is certainly out of place here, the reason for its inclusion not being at all evident.

(2) *Geya* (Pāli *geyya*), mixed prose and verse, is a sūtra which contains *gāthās*, especially the first chapter of the *Saṃyutta Nikāya*.

(3) *Vyākaraṇa* (Pāli *veyyākarana*). This means answer, explanation, exposition, elucidation, especially of questions put. It is technically of four kinds, *ekāṅśa-*, *vibhajya-*, *paripṛcchā-*, and *sthāpanīya-*, according to whether a question can be answered with an absolute affirmative, or only after analysing or distinguishing, or by putting a counter-question, or whether, being wrongly put, it is to be passed over as unanswerable. As his replies to questions were frequently of the second type, the Buddha, it is said, was known to his contemporaries as a *vibhajyavādin* or analyser, a title afterwards appropriated by the Vibhajyavādins, an early Buddhist school patronized by Aśoka and nowadays sometimes identified with the modern Theravāda of Sri Lanka. Theravāda tradition, in the person of Buddhaghosa, identifies *veyyākarana* with the Abhidhamma Piṭaka and other utterances of the Buddha not included in the remaining eight *aṅgas*. For the Sarvāstivādins, and following them the Mahāyānists, *vyākaraṇa* is the prediction, that is to say the elucidation by the Buddha, in response to an enquiry, of the future career of a disciple, especially of his attainment of Enlightenment, as well as the canonical and non-canonical literary works embodying such predictions; but this extended application of the word is late.

(4) *Gāthā* or 'verses' are the *Dhammapada*, *Thera-* and *Therī-gāthā*, and those verses of the *Sutta-Nipāta* not called *sutta*.

(5) *Udāna*, literally 'breathing out', is defined as 'exulting cry, i.e. an utterance, mostly in metrical form, inspired by a particularly intense emotion, whether joyful or sorrowful'.[19] In the Buddha's case, such 'breathings-out' were generally expressive of a mood of intense spiritual exultation.

(6) *Ityuktaka* (Pāli *itivuttaka*), 'sayings' – or in its more common wrongly Sanskritized form *itivṛttaka*, 'happening' – beginning with the phrase 'Thus (*iti*) it has been said (*uktam*) [by the Buddha]'.

These last two *aṅgas* correspond with the canonical works bearing their respective names.

(7) *Jātaka*. This literally means 'belonging to, or connected with, what has happened'. As an *aṅga*, it designates the *canonical* stories of the previous births of the Buddha as a wise man of old. These must be clearly distinguished from the much later *non-canonical* stories of the Theravāda Jātaka book, in which only the verses supposed to be uttered by the future Buddha are canonical and not the stories themselves. It is these stories, which form the commentary on the verses, and which are peculiar to the Theravādins, that relate the Buddha's previous lives as an animal.

(8) *Adbhutadharma* (Pāli *abbhutadhamma*) consists of the sūtras that describe the wondrous, extraordinary, supernatural, or miraculous events or phenomena manifesting at different periods, or on special occasions, in the earthly life of the Tathāgata. As to what it comprises, according to Buddhaghosa, 'All Suttantas connected with wonderful and marvellous things spoken in this wise: "There are, bhikkhus, four wonderful and marvellous things in Ānanda," should be understood as *Abbhuta*'.[20] Once again, however, the great commentator has erred, his choice of illustration being here particularly inept. In the *Acchariyabhutadhamma Sutta*[21] the wonderful and marvellous qualities enumerated are those of the Buddha himself, not of Ānanda, and comprise the various extraordinary phenomena that occurred at the time of his conception and nativity. Descriptions of this sort, it seems, were eventually reduced to a standard list of the Twelve Principal Acts of the Buddha.[22] The latter, in turn, provided a skeleton, or framework, for biographies such as the *Mahāvastu* and the *Lalita-vistara*. In however rudimentary form, *adbhutadharma* is therefore biography.

(9) *Vaidalya* (Pāli *vedalla*). Buddhaghosa, making the best of a bad job, describes it as 'all Suttantas in the form of questions asked through repeated attainment of delight and understanding' and gives a list of six *suttas*, two of which have the title *vedalla*.[23] Thomas's suggestion that *vidala*, 'split open, expanded', would mean fragmentary, and *vedalla* a sūtra of fragments, is more acceptable. 'This would suit', he observes, 'the fact that those suttas are of a miscellaneous character and as it were made up of fragments.'[24] The *Mahāvyutpatti* lists a *Sarvavaidalyasaṃgraha* which is, apparently, a collection of such miscellanies.[25]

These nine *aṅgas* were increased to twelve by the Sarvāstivādins, who added to the original list three forms of composition peculiar to their own school. The three additional *aṅgas* are *nidāna*, 'statement of subject matter', 'table of contents', or 'summary' of a work; *avadāna*, 'glorious deed', 'heroic achievement', of the Buddha and his disciples in their present and past existences; and *upadeśa*, 'instruction'. As Thomas points out, the importance of the list of twelve *aṅgas* lies in the fact that it shows the growth of other types of scripture which could not be placed in the Piṭakas.[26] Among the three extra *aṅgas* the most important is the *avadāna*. Though a crystallization of ancient floating traditions it represents a form of composition perhaps literary rather than oral. It will be considered in a separate chapter.

Besides having no certain means of knowing where and when the oral tradition was first committed to writing, or by whom, we are ignorant of the order in which the various types of composition were transferred from the old medium to the new. The *Mahāvaṃsa*, as we have seen, assumes that the whole Tipiṭaka was recorded simultaneously; but this, though possibly the case with the Mahāvihāravāsins of Sri Lanka, was not necessarily what happened in other regions and with other schools.

Even accepting the hypothesis of a general writing down of oral traditions in the first century BCE, the possibility that individual works were recorded both before and after this period cannot be excluded. Some traditions, indeed, survived in oral form much longer than others. They are not on that account the less genuine. The point is important because only too often do we allow ourselves, in dealing with the canonical literature, to be influenced by the uncritical and largely unconscious assumption that of two different texts, one committed to writing in the first century BCE and the other 200 years later, for example, the former must be genuine and the latter, if not actually spurious, at least of dubious authenticity. Yet this is by no means invariably the case. Indian memories were extraordinarily retentive, and no arbitrary limit can be set to the length of time for which a work could be preserved and handed down by purely oral means.

For this reason alone, if for no other, the Theravādin view that the existing canonical literature comprises two independent blocks, consisting in one case of a verbally faithful recension of the entire oral tradition, and in the other of forgeries which were 'put into the Buddha's mouth' at a much later date, cannot possibly be entertained. Whether earlier or later in respect of their original reduction to writing, the scriptures in fact represent a millennium-long series of literary deposits, or crystallizations, from the reservoir of an orally transmitted spiritual tradition that may not be exhausted even now. This is not to confuse the literary form of a canonical work with its essential content, nor to overlook the fact that even when the latter originated with the Buddha the former may be very much of its age. Neither is it to exclude *a priori* the possibility of textual interpolation and even forgery. In dealing with the Mahāyāna sūtras, especially, it is necessary to bear in mind that the great spiritual movement which produced these documents was concerned less with the reproduction of the original letter of the teaching than with fidelity to its inner spirit and meaning.

That some traditions should have been committed to writing before others is due partly to the accidents of history, and partly to the fact that they pertained to different levels of religious life and spiritual experience. Conze suggests:

> What in the history of Buddhist thought seems to be doctrinal innovation may very often be nothing but the gradual shifting of the line between esoteric and exoteric teachings. At first, even up to Aśoka, the bulk of the doctrine, except for some moral maxims, and so on, was esoteric. By the time of the Tantra ... even the most esoteric doctrines were written [down].[27]

Doctrinal innovation was usually associated with the appearance of a 'new' sūtra or group of sūtras. To the extent that 'esoteric' coincides with 'oral', and 'exoteric' with 'committed to writing', the above remarks are applicable *mutatis mutandis* to the canonical literature.

There was a tendency, but perhaps no more than a tendency, for the readiness with which a work was given literary form to be in inverse ratio to the profundity of its content. Broadly speaking, the order in which the canonical works appear as literary documents corresponds to that of their spiritual progression. Though not unmindful of the impossibility of assigning not only to each canonical work, but even to every class of works, its exact place in a strictly chronological sequence, this is the order to which we shall generally adhere in the following chapters. In the spiritual, though not in the ecclesiastical, sense, the most exoteric group of works is that containing the Monastic Code.

# 3

# THE MONASTIC CODE

The canonical literature is often referred to collectively as the Tripiṭaka (Pāli Tipiṭaka) or 'three baskets'. This designation, which is an ancient one, is of uncertain origin. It may derive from the custom of assigning different types of manuscript to separate receptacles, or from the practice, common in India, of passing earth or other excavated material from hand to hand in baskets along a line of workmen. In the latter case it would signify transmission by tradition. The 'three collections', as the term is often rendered, are those of Vinaya, Sūtra (Pāli Sutta), and Abhidharma (Pāli Abhidhamma). All three belonged, originally, to the oral tradition, though the compilation of the first and second preceded, while that of the third succeeded, the division of the Sangha into schools. There are also scattered references to a Bodhisattva Piṭaka and to a Dhāraṇī Piṭaka, which were, apparently, collections respectively of Mahāyāna and Vajrayāna works.

The separation, in respect of the two older Piṭakas, of Sūtra from Vinaya, corresponds to the even older distinction, in the Buddha's teaching itself, between Dharma, in the sense of a coherent body of spiritual teachings, and Vinaya, or those teachings practically applied, especially their ideal exemplification in the Buddha's own life. As I have pointed out elsewhere, during the century that succeeded the *parinirvāṇa*, the term *vinaya* came to acquire a predominantly monastic and coenobitical connotation.[28] In accordance with this later usage, which is now the standard one, the Vinaya Piṭaka is regarded as treating essentially of the rules to be observed by the members of the bhikshu sangha, and as such the title of this Piṭaka continues to be translated, and its contents described, in uncritical accounts of Buddhist literature.

From the days of Csoma de Körös (1784–1842CE), who was the first European to explore, in Tibetan translation,[29] the treasures preserved in this vast repository of ancient Buddhist lore, it has, however, been known to modern scholarship that the (Tibetan) Vinaya records are not only the regula of monastic life but, in the great Hungarian pioneer's own words, 'the manners, customs, opinions, knowledge, ignorance, superstition, hopes, and fears of a great part of Asia especially of India in former ages'.[30] To an extent even greater than the Sūtra Piṭaka, it is our richest contemporary source of information on the civilization and culture, the history, geography, sociology, and religion, of India during the axial period which includes at one extremity the glorious figure of the Buddha and at the other the splendid one of Aśoka. Scholars have therefore laid it increasingly under contribution. Besides being our most important original source for the Buddha's biography, it is moreover an important source of doctrinal statements such as the 'First Discourse' and the 'Fire Discourse'.

The Vinaya Piṭaka consists essentially of two great divisions, the *Prāṭimokṣa* (Pāli *Patimokkha*) or Monastic Code proper, and the *Skandhakas* (Pāli *Khandakas*) or 'Chapters'. The first is contemporaneous with, and corresponds to, the eremitical type of monastic life which originated during the Buddha's lifetime and came to an end, or at least ceased to be generally followed, during the first century of the Buddhist era, while the second is related to, and reflects the prevailing conditions of, the coenobitical type of monastic life by which it was succeeded or which, to be exact, supervened upon it. Owing to the fact that, like the rest of the Tripiṭaka, the Vinaya Piṭaka has been preserved in different versions by different schools, the number and order of the 'Chapters', as well as the relative priority of the Monastic Code and the 'Chapters' within the Piṭaka, varies from one version to another.

At present there are extant in the Buddhist world seven complete recensions of the Vinaya, one in Pāli and six translated from Sanskrit. The Pāli version is that of the Theravādins, which in the Pali Text Society's roman script edition comprises five printed volumes. The Chinese Vinaya Piṭaka contains two sections, one devoted to Mahāyāna and one to Hīnayāna works. The latter, which according to Nanjio's Catalogue (nos. 1107–1166) in turn contains sixty works belonging to various schools, comprises five very substantial recensions of the whole Vinaya, besides extracts, compendiums, and manuals. The five recensions are those of the Sarvāstivādins, the Mūlasarvāstivādins, the Dharmaguptas, the Mahīśāsakas and the Mahāsaṅghikas. In China itself the first of these, the *Shih-sung lü*, was regarded as the most important and attained the greatest influence. Translated from Sanskrit by Puṇyatara and Kumārajīva in 404CE, the *Daśādhyāya-vinaya* or 'Vinaya in Ten Readings', as it was originally known, comprises in their version sixty-five *chüans* or Chinese fascicules. The Tibetan version of the Vinaya, which, having been translated (during the ninth century CE, by various hands) from the Sanskrit of the Mūlasarvāstivādins, corresponds to the second Chinese recension listed above, consists of thirteen xylograph volumes divided into seven parts and comprising more than 6,000 folios. Not a single complete text of any Sanskrit version of the entire Vinaya seems to have survived; but many important fragments, including the *Prāṭimokṣa-sūtra* of the Mūlasarvāstivādins, have been discovered during the twentieth century in eastern Turkestan, Nepal, and Tibet, as well as at Gilgit in Kashmir (Pakistan).

Both the Sarvāstivādins and the Mūlasarvāstivādins arranged their Vinaya Piṭaka in four main divisions: (1) *Vinaya-vibhaṅga*, (2) *Vinaya-vastu*, (3) *Vinaya-kṣudraka-vastu*, and (4) *Vinaya-uttara-grantha*.

(1) *Vinaya-vibhaṅga*. This consists of two parts, the *Prāṭimokṣa-sūtra* or text of the Monastic Code proper, and the *Sūtra-vibhaṅga* (Pāli *Sutta-vibhaṅga*) or commentary on this text. While the former embodies the various categories of rules binding upon members of the Sangha, the latter gives a word-for-word explanation of each rule and narrates the circumstances in which it came to be promulgated. For example the first *pārājika* rule is introduced, in both the Sanskrit and the Pāli versions, by the stories of the monk Sudinna having sexual intercourse with his former wife and of another monk having sexual intercourse with a female ape. The Buddha, on being appraised of these facts by the other bhikshus, rebuked the offenders and framed the rule that a monk having intercourse with anyone, down to a beast, should be permanently expelled from the Sangha.

The *Prāṭimokṣa-sūtra* and the *Sūtra-vibhaṅga* are themselves each divided into two sections, one for the bhikshus or monks, the other for the bhikshunis or nuns. Thus the *Prāṭimokṣa-sūtra* is divided into the *Bhikṣu-prāṭimokṣa-sūtra* (Pāli *Bhikkhu-patimokkha-sutta*) and the

*Bhikṣuṇī-prāṭimokṣa-sūtra* (Pāli *Bhikkhunī-pāṭimokkha-sutta*), and the *Vinaya-vibhaṅga* into the *Bhikṣu-vinaya-vibhaṅga* or *Vinaya-vibhaṅga* proper, commonly known as the *Mahā-vibhaṅga* or 'Great Commentary', and the *Bhikṣuṇī-vinaya-vibhaṅga.*

The Sanskrit *Vinaya-vibhaṅga,* which makes up 'Readings' 1, 2, 3, 7, and 10 of the *Daśādhyāya-vinaya,* corresponds to the Pāli *Sutta-vibhaṅga,* the first of the three divisions of the Theravāda Vinaya Piṭaka.

(2) *Vinaya-vastu.* In the Tibetan Vinaya Piṭaka this work stands first. It contains the *Skandhakas* (Pāli *Khandakas*) or the 'Chapters'. In the Sarvāstivādin version, as preserved in Tibetan, and in the Mūlasarvāstivādin version, as represented by 'Readings' 4 and 5, and part of 6, of the *Daśādhyāya-vinaya,* there are in all seventeen of these. They correspond to the first ten chapters of the Pāli version, known collectively as the *Mahā-vagga* or 'Great Section', plus chapters 1–4 and 6–9 of the *Cūḷa-vagga* or 'Small Section'.

Without taking the historical and other non-historical material into account, the resemblance appears greatest between the Tibetan and the Pāli, though the first ten chapters, in practically the same order, together with several of the remaining chapters, are common to all three versions. That chapter 11 in the former corresponds to chapters 1 and 2 of the 'Small Section' in the latter, as well as the first part of chapter 8, makes the resemblance more striking still. In the resultant seventeen chapters, comprising the complete institutes of the fully developed coenobitical system, the *Vinaya-vastu* deals with the following important topics, the order of the chapters being that of the Tibetan version of the Mūlasarvāstivādin recension:

(a) Ordination;

(b) the *Poṣadha,* or fortnightly meeting, and the recitation of the *Prāṭimokṣa;*

(c) the *Pravāraṇa* or ceremony concluding the rains residence;

(d) the *Varṣāvāsa* or rains residence.

In the *Mahā-vagga* the order of the last two is reversed, which is obviously the more logical arrangement.

(e) The use of leather for shoes; rugs, carriages. The number of monks required for conferring ordination in the border regions.

(f) Medicine and food.

(g) Material for robes, sleeping regulations, and rules for sick monks. Disposal of a deceased monk's personal effects.

(h) The *Kaṭhina* or 'difficult' ceremonies for the annual making and distributing of robes.
(i) Proceedings in case of dissensions.
(j) The modes of executing official acts of the Order, especially the minimum number of monks required for each type of act.
(k) Suspension and reinstatement.
(l) Special cases not covered by (k).
(m) Duties of monks under suspension.
(n) Exclusion from the recitation of the *Prāṭimokṣa*.
(o) Dwellings, furnishings, lodgings, order of precedence among bhikshus.
(p) Settlement of disputes.
(q) Schism.

(3) *Vinaya-kṣudraka-vastu*. This corresponds in name to chapter 5 of the *Cūḷa-vagga*, the *Khuddaka-vatthu*, which also means 'The Minor Relation (of the Vinaya)', but in respect of contents to the whole of the remaining portion of the *Cūḷa-vagga*, that is to say to chapters 10, 11, and 12 as well. The subjects dealt with are, principally, the rules relating to bathing, the ordination and instruction of nuns, the history of the First Council at Rājagṛha, and the history of the Second Council at Vaiśālī, to each of which the Pāli version devotes a separate chapter. Though definite information is wanting, the present division would seem to correspond to that portion of 'Reading' 6 of the *Daśādhyāya-vinaya* which has no counterpart in the 'Chapters'.

(4) *Vinaya-uttara-grantha*. This division is a kind of appendix to the Vinaya. Like the *Parivāra-pāṭha*, the third of the three main divisions of the Pāli Vinaya Piṭaka, to which it corresponds, it is in dialogue form and briefly recapitulates the subject matter of the first three divisions in such a way as to form a kind of abstract of the entire contents of the Vinaya. Whereas the Tibetan version contains twelve, the Pāli version contains nineteen subdivisions. The last of these in Tibetan is the *Upāli-paripṛcchā*, or 'Questions of Upāli', a more or less independent work corresponding to the fifteenth in the Pāli series, the *Upāli-pancaka*. In intention, though apparently not in design, this abstract has its counterpart in a portion of 'Reading' 8 of the *Daśādhyāya-vinaya*, one section of which, under the heading of *Ekottara-dharmas*, arranges the various groups of monastic rules in the order of the ascending numerical value of their constituent items.

As noted above, the Chinese Vinaya Piṭaka comprises two sections, one for Mahāyāna and one for Hīnayāna works. The *Daśādhyāya-vinaya*, while belonging to the latter, contains in 'Reading' 9 a section dealing with the Mahāyāna Vinaya, that is to say, with the additional rules to be observed by novice Bodhisattvas. Though bearing the title *Upāli-paripṛcchā* this work has, apparently, no connection with the Mūlasarvāstivādin text of that name already mentioned. Indeed it has no counterpart anywhere in the Hīnayāna canon. Like the *Brahmajāla-bodhisattva-śīla Sūtra*,[31] it comprises both disciplinary precepts and devotional practices, and deals *inter alia* with such topics as offences (*āpatti*), non-offences (*anāpatti*), confession of faults (*pāpadeśanā*), going for refuge to the Three Jewels (*śaraṇagamana*), entreating the Buddhas to turn the wheel of the Dharma (*adhyeṣanā*), dedicating one's merits to the cause of universal good (*pariṇāmanā*), and arousing the Will to Enlightenment (*bodhicittotpāda*).

With the exception of Mahāyāna incorporations such as the above, the Pāli and the various Sanskrit versions of the *Prāṭimokṣa* and the 'Chapters' are in substantial agreement. They represent different recensions, by different schools, of what is basically a common stock of traditions. It is in respect of their non-legalist contents, and more especially of the nature and relative importance of those contents, that the divergencies between one Vinaya Piṭaka and another are most numerous and striking.

Many of the narratives by which the monastic rules are introduced, as well as some of the historical, biographical, and sociological material incidental thereto, are common to both the Pāli and the Sanskrit versions. Broadly speaking, while the Theravādins tended to exclude, the Sarvāstivādins tended to include, material of this kind. The former is therefore the more homogeneous. On the other hand the latter, in its Mūlasarvāstivādin form, is according to Przyluski, 'a sort of reservoir into which have flowed all the currents of the Sarvāstivādin literature'.[32] Besides the monastic rules and other, cognate material, it includes a mass of works which strictly belong to the Sūtra Piṭaka. Among these are the *Sthavira-gāthā* or 'Psalms of the Elder Brethren' and a whole *Mahā-parinirvāṇa Sūtra*, as well as various *jātakas*, *avadānas*, *vyākaraṇas*, and *udānas*. Which of these two recensions of the Vinaya Piṭaka is, by and large, the more ancient, it is difficult, and perhaps unnecessary, to determine. Both seem to have evolved, in different ways, from a common original nucleus consisting of a primitive

Buddha-biography corresponding to the *adbhutadharma* into which the earliest monastic rules have been inserted.

As, in theory, only the 'founder' himself could legislate for the Sangha, biographical episodes were manufactured to explain the introduction of new rules. Thus the 'biographical' and the monacho-legalist contents of the Vinaya Piṭaka increased *pari passu*. Once this stage had been reached the different schools might, according to their individual predilections, exclude or include, reduce or augment, other types of material. But as we shall see in a later chapter, at least one school preserved an important Vinaya work which has nothing to do with the Monastic Code.

# 4

# THE DIALOGUES

Like the works comprising the Vinaya Piṭaka, the contents of the Sūtra Piṭaka are of two kinds, Mahāyāna and Hīnayāna, and as such are they classified in Chinese editions of the Tripiṭaka. The Mahāyāna sūtras are dealt with separately below. More or less complete recensions of the Hīnayāna sūtras were made in at least two languages, in Pāli by the Theravādins and in Sanskrit by the Sarvāstivādins: other schools – such as the Mahāsaṅghikas, who are credited with a canon in Prakrit – may have compiled recensions of their own in other languages. Whereas the Pāli version has been preserved intact in Sri Lanka, the Sanskrit version has survived complete only in Chinese translation. Individual sūtras were, however, translated into Tibetan and included in the fifth section of the Kangyur or Tibetan edition of the Tripiṭaka; fragments of the original texts have also been discovered in eastern Turkestan. In both versions the sūtras are arranged in four great collections, known as Āgamas in Sanskrit and Nikāyas in Pāli, to which a fifth was added subsequently. As between the first two collections the principle of division is simply that of length. All the long dialogues are grouped together in the *Dīrghāgama* (= Pāli *Dīgha Nikāya*) or 'Long Collection', and all those of medium length in the *Madhyamāgama* (= Pāli *Majjhima Nikāya*) or 'Middle Collection'. The two remaining collections are anthologies.

Since both the original texts of the *Dīgha* and *Majjhima Nikāyas* and their translations into modern languages are much more easily accessible than their Chinese counterparts, it is upon the Pāli version that the present account will draw for information. Comparative studies already conducted in this field reveal no major doctrinal differences between the two versions, and though both in order and classification the arrangement of sūtras may vary, and though numerous sūtras occurring in one version do not appear in the other, the familial resemblance between the two sets of texts is unmistakable, so much so, indeed, that by giving an account of one it is possible to exhibit the general character of both.

In deference to a distinguished precedent, the *suttas* contained in these two 'collections' have been termed dialogues. They might with almost equal justification be described as discourses; some are, in fact, speeches with short introductions setting forth the circumstances in which they were delivered and conclusions describing what effect they had upon the hearer or hearers. Sometimes the Buddha speaks on his own initiative, sometimes in response to a specific incident or enquiry. But even when, as in the majority of *suttas*, there is an interlocutor throughout, the result, though indisputably dialogue, is not dialogue in the brilliant and nimble Platonic manner. Besides the immense difference in style between the Greek and the Indian productions, there is with the latter no question of a living interplay of minds engaged in a common quest for truth. Ignorance, or at best partial knowledge, stands confronted by spiritual Omniscience, and though the spectacle of the contrast is impressive, even awe-inspiring, it is hardly dramatic. Like their counterparts in traditional Buddhist art, the interlocutors in these dialogues, though possessing a definite life of their own, in comparison with the majestic figure of the Buddha are of pigmy size; they ask questions that are immediately answered, raise problems that are at once resolved, as through a labyrinth of difficulties, to the rhythm of constant repetitions, like a Bach fugue the dialogue marches triumphantly, and with absolute assurance, to its predestined conclusion.

The differences between the Platonic and the Buddhist dialogues must not, however, be exaggerated. Both make extensive use of dialectic, by means of which the opponent, under skilful cross-examination, eventually finds himself admitting the opposite of what he had originally asserted; both allow free play, when having recourse to this method, to a spirit of refined and gentle irony, and in both the tone of debate, especially as exemplified by the principal speaker, is invariably good-humoured, courteous, temperate, and urbane.

In any case, the Buddhist dialogues, though 'skilfully constructed and couched in language of restraint and dignity',[33] are not literary compositions at all but oral redactions of the Doctrine. They were composed, in Winternitz's pointed words, 'for Buddhist hearers, and not for Western readers',[34] and cannot be judged, therefore, by purely literary criteria, especially when these are of occidental origin. Their appeal is through the ear to the heart rather than through the eye to the intellect. Chanted congregationally, as throughout the Theravāda world they are still, in the sonorous and harmonious Pāli language, they create an extraordinary impression. The repetitions, blemishes in the texts when read as literature, are transformed into beauties, possessing not only a mnemonic but a musical value. One might even argue that the texts were compiled in their present form for purposes of liturgical meditation, wherein the grave rhythm of the chanting serves to calm and concentrate the mind, while the recurrence, at regular intervals, of certain key words and phrases, enables it to penetrate, with each repetition, ever deeper into the truth which these formulas represent.

The *Dīgha Nikāya* consists of thirty-four dialogues and discourses, as against thirty in Chinese; each of them deals, at considerable length and in great detail, with one or more aspects of the teaching, and therefore may well have existed originally as an independent work. The whole collection falls into three parts (there are four in Chinese), the first comprising thirteen, the second ten, and the third eleven *suttas*. Though differing from one another in contents and character, all these divisions embody earlier and later strata of tradition. According to Winternitz, the earliest stratum is represented principally in the first part, and the later one mainly in the third part, while the second part is composed of the longest *suttas*, some of which he says have grown to their present bulk owing to interpolations.[35] These conclusions are vitiated to some extent by the assumption that the more 'rational' *suttas*, in which the Buddha appears as a human teacher, must be earlier than the 'mythical' and 'legendary' ones, which present him also as a wonder-worker, or display a tendency to glorify him, and it is therefore impossible to accept them unreservedly. All the *suttas* in Part 1, and a number in Parts 2 and 3, are in prose. The rest are a mixture of prose and verse, including two composed almost entirely in the latter medium.

Part 1, known as the *Sīlakkhanda-vagga*, is concerned mainly with ethical and spiritual topics, especially with Morality (*sīla*), Meditation (*samādhi*), and Wisdom (*paññā*), the three groups of practices which, cultivated in succession, enable the disciple to attain the state of absolute spiritual freedom. It is so called because under the heading of Morality its component *suttas* all introduce three lengthy sections wherein the Buddha enumerates an immense number of wrong occupations, conversations, modes of life, and ways of thought current among contemporary *réligieux* from which his bhikshus are to remain aloof.

In the first dialogue, that of the 'Perfect Net' (*Brahmajāla-sutta*), wherein are caught and held all conceivable 'views', he further enumerates, in connection with Wisdom (here termed *vijjā*), a total of sixty-two idle philosophical speculations that, far from helping, actually hinder the attainment of emancipation. The second dialogue, the *Sāmaññaphala-sutta*, deals with the fruits (*phala*) of asceticism (*sāmañña*), concerning which the Buddha is able to convince the king Ajātasattu that they are no whit less tangible than those which, by the exercise of their calling, accrue for example to the potter or goldsmith. Four *suttas*, the *Ambaṭṭha, Soṇadanda, and Kūṭadanta*, so named from their principal interlocutors, together with the *Tevijjā* or 'Three Knowledges', with gentle but deadly irony ridicule the social and religious pretensions of the brahmins, and expose the absurdity of their beliefs and practices compared with the saner and more spiritual ideals recommended by the Buddha. In the other *suttas* the Buddha refuses to answer questions not conducive to Enlightenment, criticizes the practice of self-mortification, deplores the exhibition of miraculous powers, which are in any case inferior to the 'miracle of instruction', and declares that the best spiritual teacher is one who, having himself realized the truth, out of compassion reveals it to mankind.

Part 2, the *Mahā-vagga* or 'Great Section', is so called because it consists mainly of titles bearing the prefix *mahā-* or 'great'. This epithet serves either to distinguish them from shorter treatments of the same topic elsewhere in the canon, as with the *Mahā-satipaṭṭhāna-sutta* or 'Greater Discourse on the Foundations of Mindfulness', or to indicate their length, or signalize the importance of their contents, as in other cases. There are purely philosophical dialogues, such as the *Mahā-nidāna-sutta*, which deals with the twelve *nidānas* or 'links' in the process of conditioned co-production, as well as dialogues rich in 'legendary' and 'mythological' elements, both symbolical and otherwise. Longest and most important is the *Mahā-parinibbāṇa-sutta*, which for united pathos, sublimity, and beauty is unexcelled even in Buddhist literature. It describes the Buddha's last days, his attainment of final Nirvāṇa, the funeral ceremonies, and the distribution of his bodily relics. Owing to its importance, it has been subjected to interpolation to so great an extent as to have become a 'veritable mosaic' of earlier and later material.[36]

While Part 1 tends to be predominantly ethical and spiritual, and Part 2 predominantly 'legendary' in content, the miscellaneous character of the *suttas* making up Part 3, known from the title of its opening dialogue as the *Pātika-vagga*, precludes a corresponding generalization. Subjects dealt with include cosmogenesis, the two kinds of asceticism, the coming of Maitreya the future Buddha, and the thirty-two marks of a *mahā-purisa* or 'superman'. In one *sutta* the Buddha repeats to the monks a protective spell he had received from the Four Great Kings; in another, the celebrated *Sigālaka-sutta* or 'Advice to Sigālaka', he expounds the whole duty of the Buddhist layman. The last two *suttas* are highly analytical and scholastic discourses by Sāriputta.

The *Majjhima Nikāya* consists of 152 *suttas* divided into a First, a Middle, and a Final 'Fifty', the two supernumerary *suttas* being included in the third division. Each 'Fifty' contains five sections and each section ten (in one case twelve) dialogues or discourses. Though the difference between the *suttas* making up the two 'collections' is mainly one of length – those of the *Majjhima* being, on the whole, shorter than those of the *Dīgha Nikāya* – the fact that the former contains a much larger number of *suttas* enables it to encompass an even greater variety of content. As if in conformity with this characteristic, the individual *suttas* of which it is composed are even more of the nature of independent works than those of the 'Long Collection'. Yet, with the possible exception of one *vagga*, its divisions and subdivisions are mechanical, not organic, and apparently do not correspond to any process of historical development. The compilers of this Nikāya have not even adopted, in making up their fourteen decads and one duodecad of *suttas*, any single principle of classification. It is not astonishing, therefore, that the first and second *vaggas*, as well as the eleventh, twelfth, and thirteenth – all of which are named simply after their opening *sutta* – should be rather miscellaneous in composition, though it is true the first is concerned mainly with different aspects of the spiritual training of the monk.

The third *vagga*, which owns no other title, at least possesses formal unity inasmuch as its dialogues and discourses either centre upon, or simply elaborate, a single striking parable or simile. Thus in the 'Simile of the Saw' the monks are exhorted not to cherish ill will even when being sawn in two, and in the 'Simile of the Water-Snake' they are warned against the danger of grasping the Doctrine wrongly. The only *sutta* not constructed in this manner is the *Ariya-pariyesana*, or the 'Noble Quest', an important autobiographical discourse wherein the Buddha reminisces about his renunciation of the household life, his practice of self-mortification, and his eventual attainment of *sambodhi*.

Next come two *vaggas* of paired *suttas*, so arranged because of identity of titles, or similarity of content, or both, the first being the more common. Like the two *vaggas* themselves, *suttas* bearing the same title are distinguished by the prefixes 'greater' (*mahā-*) and 'smaller' (*cūḷa*). In form these dialogues range from the lyrical to the controversial, from the analytical to the autobiographical, and their content is by turns ethical, spiritual, psychological, and 'legendary'.

The sixth, seventh, eighth, ninth, and tenth *vaggas* possess greater unity of interest. Their *suttas* are classified, not without exceptions, as it were sociologically, according to the social status of the principal interlocutor, and the *vaggas* themselves are so denominated. Thus there are *vaggas* devoted respectively to householders, monks, non-Buddhist 'wanderers', kings, and brahmins. In the *Gahāpati-vagga*, or 'Section on Householders', we encounter, among other personalities, an elephant-trainer, a citizen, a kinsman of the Buddha, a physician, a Jain devotee, and a prince. It is significant that the *Jīvaka-sutta*, in which the Buddha is represented as permitting the consumption of three kinds of 'pure' meat, has no counterpart in the Chinese version. In the *Bhikkhu-vagga* the Buddha addresses various individual monks and groups of monks, including Rāhula and Māluṅkyā(putta), after each of whom two *suttas* are named. The 'Lesser' *Māluṅkyā-sutta* contains one of the most celebrated parables in the entire canon, that of the man wounded by a poisoned arrow, wherewith the Buddha enforces the point that for those stricken by suffering self-salvation is the immediate task, not speculation about the origin of suffering. The *Paribbājaka-vagga*, or 'Section on Wanderers', consists of vigorous and lively dialogues with non-Buddhist sectaries. Three of them trace the spiritual evolution of the naked ascetic Vacchagotta, who is finally converted and becomes an Arhant. The *Rāja-vagga*, or 'Section on Kings', introduces various royal personages, both of the past and the present, especially King Pasenadi of Kośala, the gradual development of whose faith in the Buddha is traced through no fewer than five *suttas*. Several of the 'dialogues' are in fact racy narratives, one of which describes the dramatic conversion of the notorious bandit Aṅgulimāla. Each of the ten *suttas* in the *Brāhmaṇa-vagga* is called after the name of a brahmin. In most cases the brahmin concerned is old, wealthy, and learned, with a large following, and after much or little discussion he generally takes refuge in the Buddha, even if he does not become a monk. Thus even more vividly than the rest, perhaps, this group of five 'sociological' *vaggas* not only preserves the Buddha's teaching but depicts it in its original social, political, and religious framework as part of the variegated pattern of ancient Indian life.

The five remaining sections comprise three miscellaneous ones named after their opening *sutta*, as already noted, and two of a more homogeneous type. These latter, the fourteenth and fifteenth of the whole collection, are the *Vibhaṅga-vagga* or 'Section of Analyses', and the *Saḷāyatana-vagga* or 'Section on the Sixfold Sense-Field'. The first contains twelve *suttas*, each one consisting of an original brief doctrinal statement of the Buddha and its subsequent elaboration, in rather formal style, by the Buddha himself or by a prominent disciple. In the second the interest tends to be psychological, though other matter, such as discourses to sick persons and an exhortation to the nuns, is by no means lacking.

The dialogues of both the *Dīgha* and the *Majjhima Nikāya* are richly embellished with similes, metaphors, and parables. As we have seen, it is possible for an entire *sutta* to be spun out of one such figure of speech. This is not just a literary device or empty rhetorical flourish, but an integral part of the Buddha's teaching method. It represents an attempt to communicate his vision of Reality, not merely in abstract and conceptual terms, but by means of concrete images, appealing not to the understanding alone, but to the total psyche, including those unconscious but powerfully operative forces that are hardly to be reached in any other way. As such the metaphors, similes, and parables of the Dialogues have their counterparts, on an infinitely grander scale, in some of the 'myths' and 'legends' likewise embedded in the Buddha's teaching and, to an even greater and more significant extent, in some of the 'legendary' episodes of his biography.[37] As might have been expected, they are of an extraordinary variety, singularly apt, and of rare poetic beauty, and seemingly cover all aspects of the spiritual life:

The brahmins and their teachers, who falsely profess to know the way to union with Brahmā, are compared to a chain of blind men, of whom neither the first nor the middle one, nor yet the last one can see.

The happiness of a monk freed from all mundane fetters is like that of a debtor who, after discharging his debt, has enough on which to live and maintain a family; or of an invalid who has recovered from a severe illness; or of a slave set free; or of one who, having wandered lost in the forest, eventually reaches a village.

Sensual pleasures are able to satisfy a man no more than a meatless bone a dog.

As the strings of a lute should be neither too tight nor too slack, so should a monk exert energy in an even manner.

The disciple cannot reach his goal by a wrong means any more than silk can be obtained from the horn of a cow, or sesamum oil by churning a mixture of water and sand.

Whether kindled by a priest, a warrior, a trader, or a serf, from whatsoever type of fuel, a fire will emit light and heat; even so, all men, regardless of caste, are equally capable of the highest spiritual attainment.

So abundant are such comparisons that modern scholars sometimes append to their translations of these Nikāyas a separate Index of Similes. The use of figurative expressions, however, far from being confined to the Dialogues, extends also to the Anthologies, particularly to the poetical books.

# 5

# THE ANTHOLOGIES

Apart from the two great collections described in Chapter 4, the Sūtra Piṭaka consists of the *Saṃyuktāgama* (= Pāli *Saṃyutta Nikāya*) and the *Ekottarāgama* (= Pāli *Aṅguttara Nikāya*). In the case of the Pāli Sutta Piṭaka there exists a further collection known as the *Khuddaka Nikāya*, or 'Little Collection', which has, however, *as a collection* no Sanskrit, and therefore no Chinese or Tibetan, counterpart. What we call the Anthologies comprises the whole of these two together with parts of the third. Though the Āgama and Nikāya versions of the third and fourth collections consist of much the same materials classified in accordance with the same principles, the correspondence between them is less close than that between the Pāli and Sanskrit recensions of the first and second collections. Nevertheless, the similarity is neither remote nor obscure so that, in this section as in the last, portions of the Sūtra Piṭaka of which several versions are extant (such as three of the *Saṃyuktāgama* in Chinese) fall to be considered in terms of the contents of the one most readily accessible.

An anthology is defined as 'a collection of flowers of literature, that is, beautiful passages from authors; a collection of poems or epigrams'. The *Saṃyutta-* and the *Aṅguttara Nikāya* are anthologies in a wider sense. Both in the main consist of material anthologized, in accordance with their respective principles of classification, from the previous two Nikāyas; of original archaic material – often of first-rate importance – not existing elsewhere in the canon, and later material inserted or added after the main body of the work had been compiled. As between the two Nikāyas themselves there is probably a certain amount of overlapping, some material being common to both; but the question has not been systematically investigated, and cannot be pronounced upon with certainty. In the case of their respective principles of classification, there is a radical difference.

As its name suggests, the *Saṃyutta Nikāya* is a collection of dialogues, discourses, and sayings, in prose and verse, grouped or 'bound together' (the literal meaning of *saṃyutta*) in accordance with the doctrinal topic with which they deal, the class of gods, demons, or men to which they refer, or the prominent personality appearing in them as hearer or speaker. There are fifty-six of these groups, named after and comprising respectively *suttas* connected with the gods, the sons of the gods, the kingdom of Kośala, Māra the Evil One, the nuns, the Brahmās, the brahmins, Vaṅgīsa, the forest, the Yakkhas, Sakka the king of the gods, the *nidānas* or 'links' in the process of conditioned co-production, *abhisamaya* or 'realization', the twelve *dhātus* or 'elements' of perception, the *anamatagga* or 'worlds without end', Kassapa, gain and honour, Rāhula, Lakkhana, similes, the monks, the *khandhas* or 'aggregates' of conditioned existence, Rādha, views, Stream Entry, genesis, the *kilesas* or 'corruptions', Sāriputta, the Nāgas or serpent-deities, the harpies, the heavenly musicians, the cloud-spirits, Vacchagotta, *jhāna* (or *samādhi*), the sixfold sense-field, women, the wanderers Jambukhādako and Sāmaṇḍaka, Moggallāna, Citta, the headman, the unreckonable things, the undeclared topics, the Way, the conditions favourable to Enlightenment, the four Foundations of Mindfulness, the five Spiritual Faculties, the Best Efforts, the Spiritual Powers, the Bases of Psychic Power, Anuruddha, the Gangā-repetition, mindfulness of respiration, Stream Entry again, and the four Truths. These fifty-six groups are distributed into five parts, each of which is named after its opening *saṃyutta*. The groups themselves are divided into sections, each containing a number of short *suttas*. According to a modern breakdown, the total number of *suttas* in the *Saṃyutta Nikāya* is 2,889, some of which are, however, identical except for a single word or phrase.

Among the five parts, or *vaggas*, there is a marked difference between the first part, known as the *Sagātha-vagga* or 'Part with Verses', and the four remaining parts:

> Whereas these latter treat, for the greater part, [observes Govind Chandra Pande] of points of metaphysics and

> psychology in a set formular style, the former is concerned mainly with the ethical regulation of conduct, events out of Buddha's life, and other much simpler but more picturesque material. The conspicuous part that verse and narrative play in the first vagga is in striking contrast to the very prosaic prose formulae which dominate the rest. Although quite a number of later pieces are to be found in the first vagga, yet, on the whole it has a greater proportion of early suttas than the other vaggas.[38]

The compilation of the *Sagātha-vagga* is in fact thought to have preceded that of *Dīgha Nikāya* Parts 2 and 3. For a general account of its contents it would be impossible to better the brilliant impressionism of C.A.F. Rhys Davids:

> The mass of these little Suttas, slight and concise sketches, with the verses which sum them up, or which they, the Suttas, explain – many of them very poor poetry as such – dealing with legends of fairies, gods and devils, with royal and priestly interviewers of the sublime teacher, may seem a tantalizing jungle to the traveller bound for hills of thought more austere. But let him enter not as hurried and unseeing, but leisurely, with open mind and sympathetic imagination awake. So will he wander not unrewarded. He will find himself for the most part in a woodland of faṣrie, opening out here on a settlement of religious brethren, there on scenes of life in rural communities such as might well be met in the India of to-day, or indeed in other countries. Devas he will see; sons and daughters of 'the gods', one may call them, yet let him ever remember that, for the Indian, they are neither as the god nor the angel of Western cults. They (that is, certain of their antecedent individualities) have been men and women, with the memory of at least one such former life abiding. Now, possessed of greater power over matter, and in some cases only of improved wisdom, most of them are shown greatly concerned with the central fact of the book:– the wonderful period of incarnate wisdom and service that has broken over one favoured realm of earth, and the opportunity, within their reach, of benefiting by it. They are not here to consult our traveller, but they will enchant the eye of his imagination with

> a glory of colour, and while minor forest devas will show concern in his spiritual welfare, those of this or that heaven will welcome him to celestial mansions. He will hear riddles and saws in doggerel metre, current in ancient Indian folk-philosophy, and pressed into a veritable canon that mothered efforts at thinking seriously, however rudimentary they might be. The prince of darkness – of life-lust and of recurring death – will startle him in odd and fearsome shapes and ways. Grave and noble Sisters will show him a serene peace, and a grasp of truth won at the cost of much that life holds dear. The incorrigible if amiable despot, and the priest, often no less incorrigible, will give themselves away as they talk before him. Mysterious aboriginal creatures, in process of being merged into the stock of folk-myth, will come forth from the abandoned shrines of dead deities to listen or to menace. And the gods of to-day will contend before him with the gods of yesterday, become the Titans of to-day.
>
> And ever, as he wanders on, there will move before him, luminous and serene, the central figure of the great-hearted Gotama, bringing him to the wood's end braced and enlightened by the beneficient tension of listening to so many wise sayings. In these he will hear the lesser gods instructed and the higher gods brought low, the devil swept aside and the demons fearlessly confronted; the king given simple, practical, secular advice, not too high or unworldly for his limited intelligence, and the priest's rites and dogmas tested by a new and higher Norm; the disciples' talents evoked and appreciated, and the earnest lay inquirer made welcome.[39]

The transition from *Saṃyutta Nikāya* Part 1 to *Saṃyutta Nikāya* Parts 2–5, from the ethico-spiritual-cum-'legendary' to the analytico-psychological, has already been apparent, to some extent, in the list of titles of the fifty-six *saṃyuttas*. Though more or less homogeneous in respect of their difference from Part 1, Parts 2–5 are nevertheless internally heterogeneous. For instance, Part 2 contains a stratum of archaic *suttas* corresponding to those which are most characteristic of the *Sagātha-vagga*, while isolated deposits of the same type of material exist embedded in the midst of the most wearisomely repetitive and drily epistemological disquisitions.

Broadly speaking, Part 5 represents an earlier stage of tradition than Parts 2–4. It mainly treats of various standard groups of spiritual exercises, especially those later collectively known as the thirty-seven *bodhipakkhiyā-dhammā* or 'conditions favourable to Enlightenment', as well as with the Way, Stream Entry, and the Truths. Though repetitions abound, similes and parables yet more abound for the delectation of hearer or reader; many of them being, in fact, not only excellent illustrations of the topic in hand, but of great intrinsic beauty.

Parts 2–4 handle their material in the markedly scholastic manner of a much later period. They are concerned, on the whole, with the statement, exposition, and correlation of doctrinal formulas such as the twelve *nidānas*, the five *khandhas*, and the six *āyatanas*, which along their several lines of development represent the highest point of metaphysical elaboration in the four Nikāyas. Narrative is minimal or non-existent, and often the predication of a succession of attributes of one or more subjects is spun out into a whole series of separate, artificially manufactured '*suttas*', in each of which one attribute is predicated of one subject. Thus the fact that the sight, hearing, smell, taste, touch, and the organ of thought, together with their respective objects and sense-perceptions, are impermanent, painful, and insubstantial, comes to be adumbrated throughout the 207 *suttas* of the *Saḷāyatana-vagga*. That this tedious multiplication of *suttas* had its origins in the requirements of liturgical meditation may be doubted. The *saṃyuttas* of these three parts are really Abhidhamma works, and as such belong less to the second than to the third Piṭaka, or represent, perhaps, a transitional stage between the two.

In the *Aṅguttara Nikāya* the principle of classification is numerical. The *suttas*, of which there are more than 2,300, are divided to begin with into eleven *nipātas* or sections according to the ascending numerical value of the topics with which they deal, the progression (*uttara*) from one to eleven being at the rate of a single factor (*aṅga*) at a time. Section 1 treats of things of which only one exists, Section 2 of which there are only two, Section 3 of things of which there are three, and so on, up to Section 11, treating of things of which there are eleven.

Each *nipāta* is divided, this time generally according to subject, into ten or more *vaggas*. Section 4, which is the bulkiest, contains twenty-seven, all of which are subdivided. Thus, for instance, in the Section of Monads there are *suttas* on the one sight, the one sound, the one scent, etc., that can occupy the mind of a man or woman, and so on; in the

Section of Duads, *suttas* on the two things one must avoid, on two dark and two bright things, two reasons for living in the forest, two kinds of Buddha, and so on; in the Section of Triads, *suttas* on the threefold division of man into body, speech, and thought, three kinds of monks, the three messengers of the gods (old age, disease, and death), three kinds of silence, three things which lead women to hell, and so on; in the Section of Tetrads, *suttas* on the four things leading to liberation from conditioned existence (Morality, Meditation, Wisdom, and Emancipation), the four purities of a gift, the four kinds of thoroughbred, the four *jhānas*, the four Sublime Abidings (*brahma-vihāras*), the four wonderful and extraordinary qualities in Ānanda, the four blessings, the four clouds, the four postures, and so on; in the Section of Pentads, *suttas* on the five resemblances between a Tathāgata and a Universal Monarch, the five Spiritual Faculties, and so on.

From the sixth *nipāta* begins the practice, continued for the rest of the collection, of sometimes making up the requisite number of topics by combining two groups of smaller numerical value between which there is, at times, no obvious doctrinal correspondence. For example, the three kinds of craving (*taṇhā*) are enumerated together with the three kinds of conceit (*māna*) to make up a sextet, and the five mental stiffnesses (*cetokhila*) with the four Foundations of Mindfulness (*sati-paṭṭhāna*) to make up an ennead. Apart from these rather forced combinations, however, there are in the Section of Septads *suttas* on the seven requirements for meditation, seven miracles, seven kinds of wife, and so on; in the Section of Octads eight things by which the wife binds the husband and the husband the wife, eight kinds of alms, eight qualities which women must possess in order to be reborn as divine beings, eight causes of an earthquake, and so on; in the Section of Decads, *suttas* on the ten Powers of a Buddha, the ten Fundamental Questions (a summary of the whole teaching), ten reasons for the institution of the *Pāṭimokkha*, ten kinds of rich people, and so on. The eleventh *nipāta*, which is lacking in Chinese, is probably a much later appendix to the collection proper. Besides containing the smallest number of *vaggas* it is deficient in originality.

However adequate such an outline may be as showing on what principle the anthology is compiled, or as illustrating its range of topics, it cannot do justice to the individual quality of the constituent *suttas*. In the case of the present Nikāya, however, these *suttas* are often short enough to be allowed to speak for themselves. A few examples will therefore be given from the Section of Tetrads, where there is a difference not only among the topics but in the style of treatment, though all deal, of course, with a group of four things. As an example of compelling earnestness, with a ring of urgency in it, we may take the *sutta* wherein the Buddha reminds the monks of the true aim of the holy life:

> O brethren, this holy life is not practised with a view to deceive people, nor to seek their favour, nor for the purpose of gain, benefit, or fame, nor with the intention of getting out of difficulties in controversy, nor that one may be known as such and such by men. Indeed, brethren, this holy life is practised for the controlling (of body and speech), the cleansing (of corruptions) and the detachment from and cessation (of craving).[40]

Advice to the laity is homelier and less exalted in tone. To the father and mother of Nakula, who told him that, having lived happily together since their youth, they desired to rejoice with each other both in this life and the next world, the Master replied:

> House-holders, these two, husband and wife, should indeed desire to rejoice with each other in this life and also to rejoice with each other in the next world. Both should be equally faithful, equally virtuous, equally generous and equally wise.[41]

Occasionally there appears to be a subtle trace of humour, as though we detected on the Buddha's lips the shadow of a smile:

> [Brethren,] there are four very distant things. What are the four? [Brethren,] the sky and the earth – this is the first pair of very distant things. [Brethren,] the hither shore and the further shore of an ocean – this is the second pair of very distant things. [Brethren,] the place where the sun rises and the place where the sun sets – this is the third pair of very distant things. The doctrine of the righteous and the doctrine of the unrighteous – this is the fourth pair of very distant things.[42]

A number of *suttas* are doctrinal in content, and a number deal with a group of four types of persons. Both these features are combined in an important discourse which emphatically proclaims, in effect, the superiority of what afterwards came to be known as the Bodhisattva ideal. Preserved as it is in the canon of the Theravādins, a Hīnayāna school, yet bearing witness to the ideas of the Mahāyāna, this *sutta* is of more than ordinary interest.

> There are these four persons, [brethren,] to be found existing in the world. What four?
>
> He who has not striven for his own welfare nor that of others: he who has striven for others' welfare, but not his own: he who has striven for his own welfare but not others': he who has striven for both his own welfare and that of others.
>
> Just as, [brethren,] a torch from a funeral pyre, lit at both ends, and in the middle smeared with dung, kindles no fuel either in village or in forest, – using such a figure of speech do I describe unto you this person – one who has striven neither for his own welfare nor for that of others.
>
> Then again, [brethren,] in the case of the person who has striven for the welfare of others but not his own – of the two he is the more excellent and eminent.
>
> Then again, [brethren,] in the case of the person who has striven for his own welfare, but not that of others – of these three he is the most excellent and eminent.
>
> Then again, [brethren,] in the case of the person who has striven both for his own welfare and for that of others – of these four persons this latter is best and chief, topmost and highest and supreme.
>
> Just as, [brethren,] from the cow comes milk, from milk cream, from cream butter, from butter ghee, from ghee come the skimmings of ghee, and that is reckoned best of all – even so, monks, that person who has striven for his own welfare and for that of others is, of these four persons, best and chief, topmost and highest and supreme.
>
> These are the four to be found existing in the world.[43]

While the Dialogues and that part of the Anthologies with which we have already dealt are conterminous with a particular collection

(= Āgama/Nikāya), this is not true of the rest of the works with which this section is concerned. From their very inception these shorter pieces, some of them real anthologies in the modern sense, were essentially independent works that, even after their subsequent inclusion in one or another division of the canon, retained their separate identities, being forcibly embedded rather than organically incorporated in the surrounding material.

With the exception of the last, the *Sūtra of Forty-Two Sections*, all these anthologies exist (or existed) in both Sanskrit and Pāli, while for one there is a Prakrit recension too. The Sanskrit texts, or their translations in Chinese and Tibetan, do not occur all together in one division of the canon as a complete collection; some are scattered in different parts of the Vinaya Piṭaka, others in the Sūtra Piṭaka – in the latter case either as included in the Āgamas or outside them. In the Pāli Tipiṭaka, however, all of them except the *Sūtra of Forty-Two Sections* have been included, along with other miscellaneous works, in what is styled the *Khuddaka Nikāya* or 'Minor Collection'.

Though the term *Kṣudraka-Āgama* is indeed not unknown, it would appear that none of the Sanskrit canons ever contained, as a fifth Āgama, a collection of works corresponding to the contents of this Nikāya. Whether the *Khuddaka* is so called because of the supposed minor importance of its component texts, or for any other reason, it has not yet been possible to ascertain. Winternitz suggests that from the Buddha's disparaging reference to 'profane Suttantas proclaimed by disciples, made by poets, poetical, adorned with beautiful words, beautiful syllables' we might conclude that the poetical pieces were not at first generally recognized, that their claim to canonicity was contested, and that only later on were they combined into a separate collection.[44] But these observations apply only to the Theravāda Pāli Tipiṭaka: there is nothing to suggest that the Sarvāstivādins, for example, ever doubted the authenticity of these anthologies.

The celebrated historian of Indian literature is right, however, in pointing out that the chief contents of the *Khuddaka Nikāya* are works of poetic art – collections of aphorisms, songs, poems, fairy tales, and fables – and that the collection itself was probably concluded at a late date. It may, indeed, have consisted originally of the more ancient anthologies only, in which case it could have been termed *Khuddaka* at an earlier period, when small in comparison with the existing Nikāyas, and have retained the designation even when, by the accession of large quantities of much later and more obviously apocryphal material, its proportions had considerably exceeded theirs.

As it now stands the *Khuddaka Nikāya* comprises fifteen independent works; four more, which are included by the Buddhists of Burma, are not regarded as canonical in other Theravāda countries. The *Dhammapada, Udāna, Itivuttaka, Sutta-Nipāta, Thera-gāthā,* and *Theri-gāthā,* which are the Pāli versions of the works that make up the remaining portion of the Anthologies, occur as the second, third, fourth, fifth, eighth, and ninth items of this collection, and they will be considered, though briefly, in the same order.

So far as texts still extant in the original language are concerned, there are three *Dhammapadas*, one in Pāli, one in Sanskrit, and one in Prakrit. The Chinese Tripiṭaka is said to contain four texts of this name, all translated from different Sanskrit originals. Comparative studies so far made reveal no basic discrepancies among the various recensions. All consist of the same type of material organized in the same way, that is to say, of verses embodying ethical and spiritual precepts grouped more or less according to subject under various sectional headings. Though the total number of verses is not the same, and though the selection of verses, as well as the number and nature of the sections into which they are classified, differ considerably from one text to another, all the *Dhammapadas* have certain blocks of verses in common. Some of these blocks are found elsewhere in the Sūtra Piṭaka; others appear to be peculiar to the *Dhammapada* literature. It would seem, therefore, that taking these blocks, which together constituted the basic text, as a nucleus, each of the early schools composed a *Dhammapada* of its own. Sanskrit Buddhist tradition mentions in this connection the name of Dharmatrāta, whom Tibetan sources credit with the compilation of the *Udānavarga*. This celebrated work, which is sometimes referred to as a Sanskrit *Dharmapada*, contains in the Tibetan translation not only 375 verses corresponding to verses of the *Dhammapada* but also the greater part of the verses of the *Udāna*, and numerous verses which have parallels in the *Sutta-Nipāta* and other portions of the Pāli canon.

Largely as a result of historical accident, the Pāli *Dhammapada* is at present by far the best known example of this class of canonical texts. Since its appearance in a Latin version in 1850 it has been repeatedly translated into the principal European and Asian languages, the depth and universality of its doctrine, the purity and earnestness of its moral teaching, and the sublimity of its spiritual ideal, combined with the refined simplicity and pellucid poetical beauty of its language, winning for it an honoured place in world literature.

The *Udāna* and the *Itivuttaka* both correspond, as we have already noticed in Chapter 2, with particular types of oral composition. Both are short independent works of relatively ancient date, and both consist of a mixture of prose and verse. So far as the Pāli text is concerned, the first of these anthologies comprises eight sections containing ten *suttas* each. Most of the *suttas* are quite short, and practically all of them can be divided into two parts, one consisting of a verse or verses 'exhaled' by the Buddha in a mood of intense spiritual exaltation, and the other of a prose narrative purporting to explain the circumstances under which he uttered them.

The verses, to which alone the term *udāna* properly applies, constitute a single homogeneous stratum of great antiquity. For the most part they give expression, in direct and simple language, to the loftiest spiritual insights and ideals, being concerned especially with the realization of Nirvāṇa, and strike a note that is at once profound, solemn, impassioned, and serene. Such are the verses said to have been spoken with reference to Bahiya Daruciriya, with which Section 1 concludes:

> Where water, earth, heat, air no footing find,
> There burns not any light, nor shines the Sun,
> The Moon sheds not her radiant beams,
> The home of Darkness is not there.
>
> When in deep silent hours of thought
> The holy sage to Truth attains,
> Then is he free from joy and pain,
> From Form and Formless worlds released.[45]

Though later than the verses, and relatively heterogeneous, the prose portion is still early. A few of the narratives might, indeed, have been attached to their respective verses from the beginning; but many, if not most, either have little or no connection with the verses they purport to explain or give the impression of having been manufactured to order afterwards. In some cases the narrative has obviously grown out of a figure of speech in the *udāna* proper. All the same, the narratives on the whole reflect an early, even a pre-coenobitical, stage of development, and preserve a number of interesting and important traditions, both biographical and doctrinal. It is this anthology that contains, among other treasures, the celebrated 'Parable of the Blind Men and the Elephant'[46] and the less celebrated affirmation of an unconditioned without which escape from the conditioned would not be possible.

The Pāli version of the *Itivuttaka* or 'Logia' consists of four sections containing, in all, 112 *suttas*, most of them quite short. The fourth section, which has no counterpart in Chinese, is probably the latest portion of the work. Like the *Udāna*, the *Itivuttaka* consists of a mixture of prose and verse, but in the case of this anthology the relation between the two elements is closer: about fifty *suttas* give expression to the same ideas in both mediums, while in many of the remaining pieces one supplements the other. On occasions the prose is more poetical than the verse, as in the following passage, which may be allowed to represent the spirit of the whole collection:

> None of the means employed to acquire religious merit, O monks, has a sixteenth part of the value of loving-kindness (*maitrī*). Loving-kindness, which is freedom of heart, absorbs them all; it glows, it shines, it blazes forth.
>
> And in the same way, O monks, as the light of all the stars has not a sixteenth part of the value of the moonlight, but the moonlight absorbs it and glows and shines and blazes forth: in the same way, O monks, none of the means employed to acquire religious merit has a sixteenth part of the value of loving-kindness. Loving-kindness, which is freedom of heart, absorbs them; it glows, it shines, it blazes forth.
>
> And in the same way, O monks, as at the end of the rainy season, the sun, rising into the clear and cloudless sky, banishes all the dark spaces and glows and shines and blazes forth: in the same way again, as at night's end the morning star glows and shines and blazes forth: so, O monks, none of the means employed to acquire religious merit has a sixteenth part of the value of loving-kindness. Loving-kindness, which is freedom of heart, absorbs them: it glows, it shines, it blazes forth.[47]

So far as the Pāli canon is concerned, the *Sutta-Nipāta* contains what is undoubtedly the earliest recorded version of the Master's teaching. The value of this oldest and greatest of the anthologies as a source not only of basic material for the scientific study of Buddhism, but perpetual inspiration for its understanding, practice, and realization, cannot therefore be overestimated. In it we encounter the Master face to face and enjoy, with greater confidence than usual, the unique privilege of hearing the Message of Enlightenment conveyed, if not in its original form, at least in words closer to those actually used than almost all others.

Resting as it does on evidence both internal and external, the fact of the *Sutta-Nipāta*'s antiquity is particularly well attested. Internally the work is marked not only by archaic vocabulary and grammatical irregularities but by the loose syntax characteristic of very primitive literatures. Metaphorical references to psychological and spiritual experiences have not yet hardened into the precisely defined technical terms of a well-thought-out system, but are still fluid and alive; doctrinal formulas, including the four Truths, the five *khandhas*, and the eightfold path, are conspicuous by their absence; neither is there any sign of the existence of nuns. External evidence is mainly twofold. In the first place, the two concluding *vaggas* of the *Sutta-Nipāta*, which are even older than the rest, are cited by name in six other passages of the Tipiṭaka itself, the *Pārāyana-vagga* once in the *Saṃyutta* and three times in the *Aṅguttara Nikāya*, the *Aṭṭhaka-vagga* once in the *Saṃyutta Nikāya* and once in the Vinaya Piṭaka. Secondly, there is the fact that even a commentary on part of the *Sutta-Nipāta*, known as the *Niddesa*, is of sufficient antiquity to have been accorded canonical status by the Theravādins, it being included in the Tipiṭaka as the eleventh book of the *Khuddaka Nikāya*.

No Sanskrit version of the complete *Sutta-Nipāta* anthology appears to have existed; but individual sūtras occur embedded in the text of the *Mahāvastu* and the *Lalita-vistara*, while the Chinese Sūtra Piṭaka contains, apart from odd single discourses, complete translations of the two concluding sections, that is to say, of the oldest portions of the entire Pāli work. The first of these sections was rendered from a text known, apparently, as the *Arthapāda Sūtra*, the verses of which differ from those of the *Aṭṭhaka-vagga* only in being embedded in lengthy, semi-commentarial prose narratives of much later date.

As handed down in Pāli, the *Sutta-Nipāta* is divided into five *vaggas* or sections, the first and third containing twelve, the second fourteen, and the fourth sixteen *suttas* each, while the fifth *vagga* is a long independent poem consisting of sixteen shorter parts. All of them bear marks of careful composition and editing, the juxtaposition of *suttas* being at times highly dramatic, while the verse, with its frequent change of metre, its consistently elevated tone, its richness of imagery, and its outbursts of ecstatic devotion, rises on occasions to sublime poetic heights.

So great is the unity of impression produced in particular by the *Uraga-vagga* or 'Snake Section', named thus from its opening *sutta*, that it is thought to have been the work of a single highly gifted poet-author who had sat at the Master's own feet. While the first *sutta* exhibits the spiritual ideal, describing how the true monk sloughs off all bonds as the snake his old and worn-out skin, the second, the *Dhaniya*, contrasts the ideal with the business of secular living, the contrast being heightened by the fact that the *sutta* is in dialogue form. In the next, the extremely ancient *Khagga-visana* or 'Rhinoceros Horn' *sutta*, the ideal is asserted still more strongly, emphasis being placed on the spiritual value of solitude, after which we again return to society for a dispute with a haughty brahmin farmer who contemns the homeless life. The following *sutta*, however, concedes, in effect, that all that glitters is not gold, and describes for the benefit of a lay devotee four different types of monk. This leads, naturally, to a dialogue with a female deity on the factors leading to spiritual deterioration, after which the Buddha again attacks the pretensions of the brahmins, roundly declaring that deeds not birth determine whether a man is outcaste or brahmin. As though to strengthen the sense of social and cosmic solidarity, he then teaches, in the beautiful *Karanīya-metta-sutta*, how one should cultivate towards all sentient beings the same love that a mother feels for her only son. In the next *sutta* two deities chant the praises of the Master in alternate verses, and he instructs them. The *Āḷavaka-sutta* witnesses the conversion of a fierce demon who, far from chanting any praises, had threatened the Master with destruction unless he could answer his riddling verses. The penultimate *sutta*, on self-control, stresses the repulsiveness of the physical body, while the last, as though to correct a one-sided emphasis, gloriously returning to the theme of the opening *sutta*, presenting, in its description of the sage, the living image of a lofty spiritual ideal.

The *Cūḷa-vagga* or 'Minor Section' is no less rich and varied in content, though perhaps as a work of art less unified. It opens with the *Ratana-* or 'Jewel' *sutta*, probably the latest *sutta* in the whole anthology, a ward-rune, and much used in Theravāda countries for protective purposes.

The *Mahā-vagga* or 'Great Section' is unique in that it contains three biographical ballads describing, respectively, in a vigorous and highly poetic style, the Buddha's going forth from home, his striving for Enlightenment, and temptation by Māra. It is also remarkable for encounters with brahmins, two of whom adore the Master in verses of exceptional force and beauty, for a lengthy characterization of the true brahmin that reappears in the *Dhammapada*, and for a graphic description of the torments of hell.

The sixteen *suttas* of the *Aṭṭhaka-vagga* or 'Section of Eights' are arranged not according to any artistic or religious principle, but strictly with regard to length, the first of them containing six and the last twenty-one stanzas. The nuclear part consists of *suttas* 2–5, from which, as they consist of eight stanzas each, the whole section is evidently named. The titles of these *suttas* – 'The Cave', 'Of Ill Will', 'Of the Cleansed', and 'Of the Yondermost' – give little indication of the spiritual significance of their contents, and no summary could do them justice. The tenor of the whole section, in particular its firm grasp of fundamentals and its profundity, is, however, well illustrated by a passage from the fourteenth *sutta*, 'The Quick Way'. Asked how a monk, having seen, becomes 'cool' and unattached to any worldly thing, the Buddha, going directly to the point, makes reply in five tremendous verses:

Let him by insight break the root of this,
Reckoned as hindrance: all the thoughts 'I am';
Whatever craving there may be within,
Let him train ever mindful that to oust.

Whatever thing he comes to know in full,
Be it a thing within or thing without,
Let him not firmly be convinced by that:
Not that is called the cool state of calm men.

Let him not think by that, ''Tis better this',
''Tis lacking worth', nor yet ''Tis equal this':

Touched by the contact of diversity,
Let him not stay therein, misleading self.

Then should the monk indeed grow calm within;
Let him not from another seek that calm:
And verily as he grows calm within,
Naught is assumed, how then rejected aught?

As in the mighty ocean's midmost depth
Riseth no wave but all stays ever poised,
So let the monk stay poised and ever still
And nowhere then form thoughts of 'Prominence'.[48]

The concluding *vagga*, entitled 'The Way to the Beyond', consists of sixteen short dialogues, in each of which the Buddha resolves the doubts of a brahmin questioner. Though the teaching is here more 'metaphysical' in form, there is no question of any descent from the transcendental heights of the *Aṭṭhaka-vagga*; the difference between the two sections being, indeed, no more than that between the snow peaks of the Himalaya in the dazzling purity of their noonday whiteness and the same peaks transformed, at sundown, into a glittering mass of apricot-gold. There is also a Prologue and an Epilogue, probably of later date. In the former, which contains what for the Sutta Piṭaka is a rare reference to the South, the sixteen questioners are represented as disciples of the brahmin Bāvarin, or 'the Babylonian', on whose instructions they all journey North to interview the Master. In the latter, after reporting the success of their mission, the oldest of the questioners proclaims his fervent devotion to the Buddha, with an ecstatic paean on whom the *Pārāyana-vagga*, and therewith the *Sutta-Nipāta*, most fittingly closes.

The poems of the next two anthologies are attributed, not to the Buddha, but to certain of the more spiritually advanced and poetically gifted among his disciples. Both Pāli and Sanskrit versions are known, the former being included in the *Khuddaka Nikāya*, the latter in the Vinaya Piṭaka of the Sarvāstivādins.

The *Sthavira-* (Pāli *Thera-*) *gāthā*, or 'Verses of the Elder Monks', for example, are introjected into chapter 5 of the Tibetan *Vinaya-vastu*, dealing with the use of leather for shoes (see above p.21). Fragments of the original text have been recovered from Gilgit in Kashmir. As preserved in Pāli, the 'Verses of the Elder Monks' comprises 264 poems by

259 different authors, arranged according to length in twenty-one books, the first of which contains poems of one verse only, the second poems of two verses, and so on up to the last book, which consists of a single poem of seventy-one verses.

The 'Verses of the Elder Nuns' (*Sthaviri/Theri-gāthā*) comprises 73 poems by 71 authors, two poems having been composed by the followers of Patācārā collectively. In this collection, too, the poems are arranged according to length, there being here sixteen books, the last two consisting each of a single poem, one of forty-seven and one of seventy-four verses, and each narrative rather than lyric in style. On the whole, however, the poems of the *theris* (Sanskrit *sthavirīs*) are not only fewer in number but also shorter, on the whole, than those of the monks.

The spiritual temper of the two collections is identical. Both celebrate, with varying degrees of pathos and exultation, release from secular cares and mundane attachments and the achievement, here and now, of imperturbable serenity of mind. As literature, both rank with the best productions of Indian lyric poetry. At the same time there is a marked difference of idiom and accent. The poems of the nuns strike a more personal note, and are frequently anecdotal. Those of the monks, though more preoccupied with the inner life, tend to revel in descriptions of scenic beauty. If the monk makes much of the essential repulsiveness of the feminine form, the nun rejoices at her new-found freedom from masculine domestic tyranny. Moreover, whereas the former is fluent in expression, the latter sometimes falters. Differences such as these, without detracting from the spiritual, enhance the human interest and value of the two anthologies, and help place the *Thera-* and *Theri-gāthā* among the best-loved books of the Pāli canon.

The *Sūtra of Forty-Two Sections*, the last of our anthologies, has no Pāli counterpart. It may indeed have been compiled in China. We know that it was translated, whatever that may mean, by Kāśyapa Mātanga, a monk from central India, at Loyang, the capital of the later Han dynasty during the first century CE. A collection of extracts from various sūtras, it is, though in prose, an anthology in the strict sense. Apart from its historical importance as the first canonical text to be rendered into Chinese, it possesses considerable ethical and spiritual value, and has enjoyed great popularity in China. Each of the forty-two sections consists of a single extract, each introduced – probably in imitation of the Lun-yu or Confucian Analects – by the words 'The

Buddha said'. As now extant the text contains several Mahāyāna, particularly Ch'an, interpolations. Typical of the spirit of this little collection, which appeals no less to the modern European than to the ancient Chinese reader, is Section 38:

> The Buddha said to a Sramana [novice]: 'How long is the span of a man's life?' 'It is but a few days,' was the answer. The Buddha said: 'You have not understood,' and asked another Sramana, who replied: 'It is (like) the time taken to eat (a single meal).' To this the Buddha replied in the same way and asked a third: 'How long is the span of a man's life?' 'It is (like) the time taken by a (single) breath,' was the reply. 'Excellent,' said the Buddha, 'You understand the Way.'[49]

# 6

# THE JĀTAKAS AND AVADĀNAS

## The Birth Stories and Glorious Deeds

Though our definition of 'canonical' was a broad one, the class of Buddhist texts now falling to be considered qualifies for it to a limited extent only. Like the Christian *Apocrypha*, their proper function is to illustrate faith and morals rather than to define doctrine. Humanity has ever loved a story, and the people of India have been, perhaps, even more addicted to this form of entertainment than those of other lands. Dialogues and Anthologies could hardly be expected to vie with them in popularity. Quite early in the history of the religion, therefore, the followers of the Buddha lighted, either by design or by accident, on the happy idea of appropriating the entire wealth of ancient Indian folklore, including fables, proverbs, fairy tales, anecdotes, ballads, riddles, humorous stories, jokes, novels, romances, moral narratives, and pious legends, and incorporating them *en bloc* in their own rapidly growing oral-cum-literary tradition as the simplest and most effective means of propagating the truths of the Dharma among the common people. In this way the Jātakas and Avadānas came into existence.

Genuinely canonical precedents for the class of literature thus created were not wanting. As we have seen in Chapter 2, the *Jātaka* or 'Birth Story' is one of the nine types of proto-literary composition mentioned in the Āgamas/Nikāyas while the *Avadāna* (Pāli *Apadāna*) is the foremost of the three supplementary *aṅgas* of Sarvāstivāda tradition. There is no essential difference of meaning between the two. Both consist of narratives illustrating the workings of the law of karma from one life to another, the experiences of the present life being represented as the outcome of, or as having been foreshadowed by, actions committed in a former existence. Their moral, as one collection reminds us at the end of every tale, is that the fruit of white deeds is white, of black deeds black, and of mixed mixed, so that, giving up the black and mixed deeds, one should take pleasure only in the white. As such they document for the ordinary man the pictorial 'wheel of life'.[50] Whereas the Jātakas are devoted, mainly, to former lives of the Buddha, the Avadānas generally deal with the pre-natal (sometimes, in the form of Vyākaraṇas, with the post-mortem) careers of his immediate disciples and of other illustrious Buddhist personages. Sometimes, however, as when Āryaśūra's *Jātakamāla* or 'Garland of Birth Stories' is also styled the *Bodhisattvavadāna* or 'Glorious Deeds of the Bodhisattva', the former is treated as a species of the latter.

In the canonical Jātakas, that is to say, those which occur independently elsewhere in the Sūtra Piṭaka or in the Vinaya, the Buddha is invariably depicted as a wise ruler or famous teacher of ancient times. Thus in *Majjhima Nikāya* 81, the *Ghaṭīkāra-sutta*, the Buddha goes back to the days of Kassapa Buddha and relates the tender and affecting story of the potter Ghaṭīkāra and his friend the brahmin youth Jotipāla. Having told the story, he says:

> It may be, Ānanda, that this will occur to you: 'Now, at that time the brahman youth Jotipāla was someone else.' But this, Ānanda, should not be thought of in this way. I, at that time, was Jotipāla the brahman youth.

According to this pattern, and with the riches of Indian folklore for raw materials, the non-canonical Jātakas were produced as though to a regular formula. Each story consists of four parts:

(1) an introduction, technically known as the 'story of the present', relating on what occasion the Buddha told his disciples the Jātaka in question;

(2) a longer or shorter prose narrative, known as the 'story of the past', i.e. the 'Jātaka' proper;

(3) the *gāthās* or verses, which form, as a rule, part of (2);

(4) the *samodhāna* or 'connection' wherein the Buddha identifies the personages in the 'story of the present', including himself, with those in the 'story of the past'.

By encasing it within the Buddhist framework represented by (1) and (4), it was possible to transform any piece of ancient folklore, represented by the two middle parts, into a 'Birth Story'. The homiletic advantages of such a method are obvious. While the narrative and other traditional elements arrest the attention of the audience, the concluding identification, linking them with the Bodhisattva and the Buddha, reinforces the general moral teaching contained in these elements, and adds to their often very worldly wisdom the catalyst of a specifically Buddhist spiritual principle. Thus the audience is simultaneously amused, instructed, and inspired.

Sometimes the spiritual interest is intrinsic to the story, in which case the identification, although adding to it a higher dimension, is felt to be hardly needed. Such true Jātakas, as they may be called, are either stories that, though derived from folk sources, have been remodelled in accordance with Buddhist ideals, or, even, stories specially composed by Buddhist authors. Since they usually illustrate the practice of one or another of the *pāramitās* or 'perfections' necessary to the attainment of Buddhahood they possessed greater unity of interest than the rest and could, therefore, easily constitute a separate collection of their own. The Sanskrit Jātaka collections, as distinct from the numerous single Birth Stories occurring independently in the Sūtra and Vinaya Piṭakas, are uniformly of this type.

The biggest collection of Birth Stories that has come down to us is the Pāli Jātaka book described by Rhys Davids as 'the most reliable, the most complete, and the most ancient collection of folklore now extant in any literature in the world.'[51] According to the Theravāda tradition the verses only are strictly canonical, the stories themselves being contained in the commentary, known as the *Jātakāṭṭha-vaṇṇana*. This tradition indicates the relative textual stability of the verses, which were preserved all the time in Pāli, as compared with that of the stories, which were rendered first into Sinhalese and then from Sinhalese back into Pāli.

Some of the verses are in fact non-canonical and some of the stories canonical. Not all the Birth Stories current in the various parts of the Sutta and Vinaya Piṭakas have, however, been utilized in the compilation of the Jātaka book. That of Ghaṭīkāra and Jotipāla, for instance, has been omitted. Others, though found in the canonical literature, occur there simply as moral apologues, no identification of characters being attempted. Such is the deeply moving story of Prince Dīghāyu, who makes every effort to avenge the murder of his parents, but who, at the very moment the murderer, King Brahmadatta of Benares, is at his mercy, suddenly remembers his father's last advice, and instead of striking off his enemy's head sheathes his sword and forgoes revenge.[52] Jātakas nos. 371 and 428 relate the same story and identify the Buddha, as Bodhisattva, with the hero. Similarly the parable of the partridge, the monkey, and the elephant, told by the Buddha in connection with the introduction of rules of precedence among the monks, reappears as Jātaka no.37, the Bodhisattva being identified this time as the partridge.

Canonical Jātakas, and Jātakas that are canonical as stories only, are comparatively rare. In the main the Jātaka book consists of narratives that appear to derive directly from folk sources. The whole collection, constituting the tenth book of the *Khuddaka Nikāya*, consists of 547 Birth Stories arranged in twenty-two sections or *nipātas*, theoretically according to the number of verses contained in them. In fact the number of narratives is even greater, as sometimes one of the characters in a Jātaka tells a story. The first section comprises 150 stories supposedly of one verse each, the second 100 stories of two verses each, the third 50 stories of three verses each, and so on. Actually there are many discrepancies. The verse portion, which towards the end of the book assumes larger and larger proportions, is on the whole earlier than that in prose. In some of the longest stories, especially the universally popular *Vessantara Jātaka*, with which the collection concludes, the verse portion is in reality a regular Alexandrian 'miniature epic' consisting, in the case of the *Vessantara* itself, of no fewer than 786 stanzas.

The stories themselves are of numerous types. Among the animal fables of the first *nipātas*, which contain the shorter Jātakas, there are several that parallel those of Aesop – the stories of the ass in a lion's skin and the jackal who, to get some fruit, praised the crow for her fine voice, are examples. Who borrowed from whom we do not know. The fairy tales, of which there are many genres, include tales of grateful animals and ungrateful human beings, of strange adventures with ghostly women and lovely cannibal demonesses, of superhuman beings of various types, both quaint and monstrous, as well as tales of mystery and magic. Humorous sketches, satires, and tales in which the Bodhisattva, as hero, exhibits his ready wit, good judgement, cleverness, and skill by answering riddles, resolving dilemmas, and accomplishing all kinds of seemingly impossible tasks, are also plentiful. Of great interest from a sociological, and even from a literary, point of view, are the picaresque tales in which robbers, vagabonds, gamesters, and courtesans play the principal roles, as well as the sometimes coarse, but evidently highly popular, stories dealing with feminine frailty in general and uxorial infidelity in particular.

Besides material of this sort, the connection of which with Buddhism is at times obscure, the Jātaka book contains, as might be expected, a good number of patently didactic moral tales. Much the greater part of the work, however, especially in its later sections, is taken up by various types of legend. These are often of great beauty. Some of them occur in that ancient Indian epic-cum-encyclopaedia the *Mahābhārata*. They inculcate the old grave moral virtues, such as service to one's parents, truthfulness, and chastity, and teach the impermanence of all worldly things and the happiness of renunciation. To this class belong the purely Buddhist stories, especially those illustrating the practice of the *pāramitās*. As Winternitz observes, they are characterized by 'exceeding kindness and gentleness, and self-sacrifice transcending by far the bounds of what is natural.'[53] The King of the Śivis sacrifices his eyes; Prince Kaṇha, renouncing all he possesses, goes to the Himalayas as a hermit; Khantivādin, the 'Preacher of Patience', remains free from anger even when barbarously mutilated by an enraged potentate; Prince Vessantara gladly gives away not only the palladium of his father's kingdom but his wife and two young children. The superiority of the golden rule is also inculcated. In spirit if not in form, some of the tales of grateful or heroically virtuous animals belong to the same category. The monkey-chief, in order to save his retinue, makes himself into a bridge; the Banyan deer, moved by the plaints of the pregnant doe, offers his own life to the king as a ransom for hers.

Popular as the whole of the Jātaka book undoubtedly is, it is the legends of sublime self-abnegation and absolute altruism that have most deeply and decisively influenced the religious outlook of the Buddhist peoples of South-East Asia. So much might be said, indeed, of China, Japan, and Tibet; for, as we are about to see, there exist Sanskrit collections of Jātakas which, in translation, are no less familiar to the followers of the Mahāyāna. Whether told by monk or minstrel, or enacted in dramatic form, the story of Vessantara is as well known to the Tibetan nomad as to the Burmese farmer, and moves both equally to tears. Most of the finest Bodhisattva stories are, in fact, the common heritage of the entire Buddhist world, and one of its greatest unifying influences.

Whether the Sanskrit canon ever contained a complete separate collection of Birth Stories corresponding to the Pāli Jātaka book is doubtful. Individual Jātakas occur mostly in the Vinaya Piṭaka, which, as we have seen, includes a large admixture of narrative and other nonmonastic elements. Drawing on these and any other available sources there were compiled various select anthologies of the type known as *Jātakamālas* or 'Garlands of Birth Stories'. These consisted of a limited number of stories illustrating the Bodhisattva's practice of the Ten Perfections.

The most famous such collection, in fact the *Jātakamāla* proper, is that of the poet Āryaśūra, who lived probably about the fourth century CE. If the Pāli Jātaka book be compared with a mass of unrefined auriferous ore containing, here and there, veins of pure metal, the *Jātakamāla* of this poet is a reliquary of solid gold most exquisitely wrought, burnished, and sparkling with precious stones. Āryaśūra was, in fact, a 'court poet', and the thirty-four stories in mixed prose and verse of which his work consists are retold from the old legends in ornate, elegant language, the style being that of the *kāvya* or classical epic, 'but lofty and refined, more artistic than artificial'.[54] According to the Chinese pilgrim I-tsing, the *Jātakamāla* was among the works which, at the time of his visit, enjoyed the greatest popularity in India. It was also honoured by the finest artists, there being among the frescoes of the Ajanta Caves illustrations to the *Jātakamāla* with verses by Āryaśūra in inscriptions. The fact that it is the production of an individual poet, working upon and embellishing traditional materials, just as Milton, in *Paradise Lost*, refurbishes the Bible narratives, is indicative of the quasi-canonical status of the whole Jātaka and Avadāna literature.

Its Pāli counterpart, which bears the interesting title of the *Cariya-piṭaka* or 'Basket of (the Bodhisattva's) Conduct', is, however, like the Jātaka book, firmly included in the Theravāda Tipiṭaka as the last book of the *Khuddaka Nikāya*. This is a piece of real monkish hackwork, its thirty-five verse tales being told in a clumsy, tasteless, and uninspired manner. Twelve of the stories of the *Jātakamāla* appear, also, in the *Cariya-piṭaka*, and most of the others are found in the Jātaka book. Among the few with no Pāli equivalent is the famous story of how the Bodhisattva, when living in the forest as a hermit, sees in a rock cave a young tigress who, exhausted by hunger, is about to devour her own cubs. Moved by compassion, as Mount Meru by an earthquake, he flings himself from the precipice down before her, and dies in order to provide her with food.

Apart from the fact that they generally celebrate the past lives not of the Buddha but of his disciples, the Avadānas do not differ greatly in intention from the Jātakas. We have seen that the *Jātakamāla* is also styled the *Bodhisattvavadāna*. At the same time the Avadāna narratives would appear to be by and large less dependent on folk sources and more of the nature of original Buddhist compositions. In Sanskrit they had, moreover, an even longer and richer literary history, and so far as the later collections are concerned move more definitely in the direction of the Mahāyāna. As in the case of the Jātakas, there are canonical Avadānas that occur sporadically in different parts of the Sūtra and Vinaya Piṭakas, as well as a number of both deuterocanonical and purely literary collections.

Undoubtedly the most important of the deuterocanonical collections are the *Avadāna-śataka* and the *Divyāvadāna*. The first, which belongs to the second century CE, is the older of the two, and as its name denotes it contains 100 (actually 103) narratives distributed into ten decades. Each decade deals with a particular subject.

The first four decades contain narratives purporting to show the various kinds of actions by which one can become a Buddha or a Pratyeka-Buddha. Some are in the form of *vyākaraṇas* or 'predictions': a brahmin, a rich merchant, a gardener, a king, a ferryman, a little girl, and so on, worship the Buddha with flowers, or perfumes, or gold; a miracle ensues, and the Buddha thereupon smilingly predicts their attainment of Buddhahood or Pratyeka-Buddahood, as the case may be, in a future world-period. Others are in reality Jātakas, for they describe the 'glorious deeds' of the Buddha himself in a previous existence.

The last four decades are made up of Avadānas illustrating the kind of deeds one must perform in order to become an Arhant. Individual sections are devoted to Arhants of the Śākya tribe, women Arhants, Arhants who had been men of blameless conduct and Arhants who, after committing evil deeds and suffering for them, had attained Arhantship by means of the glorious deed in question.

The middle two decades illustrate, respectively, the various kinds of evil deed leading to rebirth as a *preta*, or hunger-tormented ghost, and the various good actions resulting in a happy heavenly rebirth among the gods. They are analogous to, without being the Sanskrit canonical counterparts of, two late Pāli works, the *Petavatthu* and *Vimānavatthu* of the *Khuddaka Nikāya*.

Besides being compiled in accordance with a definite scheme, the tales of the *Śataka* are narrated after a single stereotyped pattern, and moreover abound in stock descriptions. Yet they are not devoid of interest. From one of them, no.54, Rabindranath Tagore has adapted the plot of his famous drama *Natir-Puja* or 'The Dancing-Girl's Worship'. A few tales appear also in the Pāli *Apadāna*, the thirteenth book of the *Khuddaka Nikāya*, a voluminous but, from the literary point of view, mediocre work the main two portions of which, entitled *Thera-apadāna* and *Theri-apadāna*, contain respectively 550 *apadānas* devoted to the glorious deeds of eminent monks and forty devoted to those of eminent nuns.

The *Divyāvadāna* or 'Divine Glorious Deeds' is a much less unified work than the *Avadāna-śataka*. Though compiled as late as the fourth century CE it contains passages written before the third century BCE. A variety of literary styles reflects the heterogeneous nature of its sources. Twenty out of a total of thirty-eight stories are derived from the Vinaya Piṭaka of the Mūlasarvāstivādins, while nearly all the remaining ones have been located in other Sanskrit works. Many of them also occur in different parts of the Pāli canon. Yet despite its composite nature, or perhaps even because of this, the *Divyāvadāna* contains much valuable material. Avadānas 26 to 29 narrate, partly from ancient sources now available only in Chinese translation, a series of legends centering upon the person of the good King Aśoka. Several deal with the career of Aśoka's preceptor Upagupta. Among them is the well-known story of Upagupta and the courtesan Vāsavadattā, upon which more than one modern poet has seized, together with the extraordinary episode in which Māra, converted by Upagupta, assumes at the latter's request the glorious form of the Buddha.

The *Divyāvadāna* also contains the highly popular story of Ānanda and Prakṛti. The latter, an outcaste girl from whom Ānanda had once begged water, falls deeply in love with the noble monk, and with the help of her mother, an enchantress, draws him to her house by means of spells. At the critical moment he is saved by the miraculous intervention of the Buddha. Prakṛti eventually becomes a nun. This gives rise to fresh complications, as the Hindu public strongly objects to a despised outcaste being given ordination, and complaints are made to the king. Through the medium of a 'story of the past', with whose characters he identifies, the Buddha vindicates his own universalist outlook and severely criticizes the whole theoretical basis of the brahminical caste structure.

Other deuterocanonical collections, both of them now extant only in Tibetan translation, are the *Karma-śataka* or 'Hundred Karma Stories' and the *Damamukha* or '(Tales of) Wise and Foolish (Deeds)'. The former is an old work resembling the *Avadāna-śataka* with which it possesses, in fact, a number of narratives in common. Purely literary collections, as well as single Avadānas retold in verse by individual poets, have really no pretensions to canonicity and need not be discussed here. Nevertheless, just as *Paradise Lost* was once acceptable Sabbath reading in stern Nonconformist households that otherwise admitted only the Bible, so the popularity of these works was such that, along with the corresponding Jātaka collections, they in practice enjoyed among all sections of the Buddhist community quasi-canonical authority. The production of such collections continued for well over a millennium, the last being the *Avadāna-kalpalatā* of Kṣemendra, a prolific and versatile Kashmirian poet of the eleventh century CE.

The greatest of the Avadānas, however, and one that enjoys full canonical status, has not yet been mentioned. This is the *Mahāvastu-avadāna*, which describes itself as a work of the Vinaya Piṭaka of the Lokottaravādins, a branch of the Mahāsaṅghikas. Though as a whole it belongs only nominally to this branch of the canonical literature, it contains a sufficient number of Jātakas and Avadānas to justify a brief reference to it at the close of this section. It is, in fact, a biography of the Buddha. Why a biography should choose to call itself a Vinaya work, which usually means a work dealing principally with the Monastic Code, is a question on which scholars have not yet sufficiently exercised their minds. The original, nuclear Vinaya Piṭaka was probably, if not identical, at least closely connected, with the primitive Buddha-biography as represented by the *adbhutadharmas*. With the rise of coenobitical monasticism, pseudo-biographical incidents fabricated to justify the introduction of the more elaborate new regulations were incorporated into the primitive 'legendary' biography to produce the partly biographical and historical, partly disciplinary work that is the Vinaya Piṭaka as preserved, for example, in the Theravāda Pāli canon.

The *Mahāvastu* is probably the sole surviving example of a primitive biography that has been made to incorporate not disciplinary rules tricked out with pseudo-biographical introductory narratives but legends in the form of Jātakas and Avadānas. As such its significance is enormous. It constitutes one of the most important links in the chain of evidence establishing not merely that the original Vinaya was far more than a code of monastic discipline, but that the Buddha's teaching itself, as a whole, cannot be equated with its formation in terms of the ideals and practices of post-*parinirvāṇa* coenobitical monasticism.

As now extant, in the shape it finally assumed after five centuries of accretion upon the original biographical nucleus, the *Mahāvastu* is an extremely bulky and richly composite work consisting of various literary strata. Yet though great in quantity, subsidiary and even extraneous interpolated matter has not been able wholly to obscure the grandeur of the biographical outline. Volume 1, which opens with an account of Maudgalyāyana's visits to various worlds, and describes the ten *bhūmis* or 'stages', centres upon the Bodhisattva's existences at the times of the former Enlightened Ones, and relates how, as the young brahmin Megha, he was predicted to Supreme Enlightenment by the Buddha Dīpaṅkara. The second volume tells of the wonderful and extraordinary phenomena that accompanied his conception, his birth, his departure from home, his victory over the hosts of Māra and his final attainment of the highest transcendental realization under the bodhi tree. The third volume, dealing with the initial phases of the Buddha's propagation of the Dharma, relates the history of the first conversions and the rise and consolidation of the primitive, pre-coenobitical Sangha.

Written entirely in Mixed Sanskrit, with a strong admixture of verse, this stratum gives the impression of following all these incidents of the Buddha's career with breathless loving interest. It exhales, indeed, an aroma of the most exalted devotion which, informing every part, gives it a joyous animation akin to that of the sculptures which quicken into rhythmic processional movement on the stones of the Great Stupa at Sanchi. Here, moreover, all is radiant with light and aglow with colour. At intervals the text breaks out into ecstatic paeans that celebrate at great length, and often with striking poetical beauty, the glorious attributes of the Buddha. Devotional practices such as the decorating and worshipping of stupas are enthusiastically recommended and extravagantly praised. Teaching of the doctrinal type is minimal, but no opportunity is lost of reminding us of the Lokottaravādins' distinctive tenet, afterwards inherited by the Mahāyāna, that the Buddha is in reality a purely transcendental (*lokottara*) being who, projecting himself into the world out of compassion, undergoes in appearance only the experiences of life.

Into this glittering biographical-cum-devotional structure are inserted the Jātakas and Avadānas. For the most part they are introduced in order to explain occurrences in the present by means of similar ones in the past. When King Suddhodana was told that the Bodhisattva had died as the result of his austerities he did not believe the report. Questioned by the monks, the Buddha declared it was not the first time such a thing had happened. He then relates the *Śyāmaka Jātaka*, in which the blind parents of the young hermit Śyāmaka, refusing to believe that he has really been killed by the poisoned arrow shot by the king of Kāśi, restore him to consciousness by means of an incantation. The story is told first in prose and then in verse. Similarly, in order to explain the routing of Māra and his host at the foot of the bodhi tree, the Master is made to narrate the lengthy story of how, as King Kuśa, he had subdued seven kings and their armies with a terrible shout. As it was apparently the intention of the compilers to 'load every rift with ore', fully half of the *Mahāvastu* is made up of such stories. Most of them probably belong to the later rather than to the earlier strata of the work.

Sūtras have also been inserted at various places. Among them is an archaic version of the First Discourse, as well as other material paralleled in the Āgamas and Nikāyas, including a whole section of the *Dhammapada* and portions of the *Sutta-Nipāta*. The *Mahāvastu*'s version of the *Khadgaviṣāna* or 'Rhinoceros Horn' Sūtra, and the *Aṭṭhaka-* and *Pārāyana-vaggas*, which are the oldest part of the *Sutta-Nipāta*, and possibly of the entire Theravāda canon, is believed to be even earlier than the Pāli version. Thus despite repeated accretions, the foundational substratum of the *Mahāvastu*, consisting principally of primitive 'legendary' biography, and archaic versions of early texts, must be numbered among the very oldest Buddhist documents we possess. For this reason, as well as on account of its intrinsic spiritual value, the work as a whole is one of the most significant so far encountered.

# 7
# THE FUNDAMENTAL ABHIDHARMA

With the class of texts now falling to be considered, we leave that part of the canonical literature which is universally accepted as such and enter the regions of disputed canonicity.

Originally, in the Āgamas/Nikāyas, the word *Abhidharma* (Pāli *Abhidhamma*) denoted not any particular type or style of composition but simply what pertained to, or was connected with, the Buddha's teaching. This usage is illustrated by a passage in the *Mahā-gosiṅga-sutta* of the *Majjhima Nikāya* where the elder monks are said to have an *Abhidhamma-kathaṃ*, meaning a talk or discussion about the Dharma. Carried beyond a certain point, however, all discussion inevitably becomes technical. For this reason, unmistakable as its initial spiritual emphasis might have been, every higher religious tradition sooner or later gives birth to a scholasticism.

In the case of Buddhism such a development started quite early and seems to have been associated with the growth of the *mātṛkas* (Pāli *mātikās*) or 'tables of contents'. These latter, the original function of which was probably mnemonic, were a kind of abstract or summary of the principal headings under which the Dharma was expounded. They coincide to some extent with the various numerical lists of doctrinal categories. In the later *Majjhima* and *Aṅguttara*, though not in the earlier *Dīgha* and *Saṃyutta, Nikāyas*, a class of monk known as *Mātṛkadharas*, who specialized in memorizing and reciting the tables of contents, are mentioned along with the specialists in the discourses and in the Monastic Code.

Discussion of the Dharma being often conducted in question and answer form, the incipient Abhidharma was moreover associated with the ninth *aṅga*, the *vaidalya* (Pāli *vedalla*), which although really signifying a sūtra made up of fragments can also be understood in the sense of a catechetical sūtra. The earliest 'Abhidharma' was thus simply a technique of abstracting the various subject-topics of the Dharma from their original homiletic context and subjecting them, frequently in *vaidalya* form, to a process of analysis and amplification.

In the canonical literature this stage is represented by the *Vibhaṅga-vagga* of the *Majjhima Nikāya*, and by Parts 3 and 4 of the *Saṃyutta Nikāya*, the *suttas* of which, though comparatively late, were still compiled early enough to be included in the Sutta Piṭaka. Noteworthy and perhaps of significance is the fact that out of the twelve discourses of the *Vibhaṅga-vagga* – all except the last of which are expansions of statements the Buddha is said to have made in brief – four are delivered by disciples. Ānanda and Sāriputta are responsible for one each, while Mahākaccana, elsewhere described by the Buddha as the most eminent expounder in full of what had been stated in brief, is responsible for two. It is, however, the name of Śāriputra (Pāli Sāriputta) that tradition particularly and persistently connects with the rise of the tendencies now under discussion.

As the Abhidharma technique was perfected, and the process of analysis and amplification carried to its logical conclusion, the word came to connote a more detailed, systematic, and precise elucidation of the same doctrinal topics which, in the Dialogues and Anthologies, are normally dealt with in a general, comparatively disconnected, and free manner.

Among the literary monuments of this second stage are the *Niddesa* and the *Paṭisambhidā-magga*, both in Pāli, and probably the *Śāriputra-abhidharma-śāstra*, originally composed in Sanskrit but now available only in Chinese translation. All three are traditionally ascribed to Śāriputra.

The *Paṭisambhidā-magga* or 'Path to Analysis', as it is significantly called, is a collection of thirty different treatises on important psychological and ethical topics arranged in three parts. These topics, most of which are taken from the Nikāyas, include knowledge (*ñāṇa*), emancipation (*vimokkha*), sphere of existence (*gati*), mental perversity (*vipallāsa*), amity (*mettā*), the transcendental (*lokottara*), psychic power (*iddhi*), conduct (*cariya*), and establishment of mindfulness (*satipaṭṭhāna*). Though the treatises are all in question and answer form, the work is not devoid of narrative and other literary elements characteristic of the sūtras rather than of the Abhidharma. The Theravādins were in fact long uncertain whether it should be relegated to the second Piṭaka or to the third. At present it constitutes the twelfth book of the *Khuddaka Nikāya*.

The composition of the *Śāriputra-abhidhamma-śāstra* is attributed, as its title states, to the Buddha's chief disciple, for which reason it cannot be held canonical. In reality the author is unknown, likewise the school to which he belonged, though the work is said to reflect both Sammitīya and Mahāsaṅghika views. It consists of four parts, dealing respectively with questions (*praśna*), non-questions (*na-praśna*), assimilation and association (*saṅgraha-samprayoga*), and origins (*prasthāna*). Among the topics dealt with in the second part, which is the earliest, and which perhaps alone belongs to this stage of development, are the eighteen psychophysical elements (*dhātu*), *karma*, persons (*pudgala*), knowledge (*jñāna*), the links (*nidānas*) of conditioned co-production, the establishment of mindfulness (*smṛti-prasthāna*), the bases of psychic power (*ṛddhi-pada*), concentration (*dhyāna*), the path (*marga*), and the defilements (*kleśa*).

By the time of Aśoka, in the middle of the third century after the *parinirvāṇa*, the Abhidharma had reached practically its apogee of development and crystallized into a more or less self-contained and independent system. This third stage is represented by a work, or rather collection of works, constituting what is termed the fundamental Abhidharma, namely the Abhidharma Piṭaka.

Herein not only do the characteristics of the Abhidharma in its earlier stages appear fully developed but certain new characteristics emerge. To begin with, the earlier Abhidharma's preoccupation with the precise definition of terms led to the development at this stage of a special type of language. As contrasted with the vivid concreteness of the sūtras which generally employed the expressions of ordinary life, and called things by their ordinary names, this new Abhidharma language is not only more precise but highly abstract and rigorously 'scientific' in character. It attempts to describe existence, not in terms of unreal 'things' to which permanence and substantiality have been wrongly attributed, but in terms of impersonal psychophysical events and processes. In the sūtras, for example, popular terms such as *pudgala* or man, *puruṣa* or person, and *sattva* or sentient being, are freely employed, despite the fact that it is taught, at the same time, that in reality no entity corresponding to them exists. Such terms have no place in the Abhidharma. What is commonly referred to as a man or person is here discussed exclusively in terms of *skandhas*, *āyatanas*, and *dhātus*, etc. In other words the Abhidharma sought to create for itself a special Buddhist language less liable to misinterpretation than the one in ordinary use.

This attempt was connected with developments which, for want of a more suitable expression, may be called philosophical. Whereas ordinary language denotes appearances only, that of the Abhidharma purports to denote realities. These realities, which are conceived of as the ultimate elements of existence, are technically known as *dharmas*. It is with the eminently practical task of the enumerating and classifying of these dharmas, as well as with the analysis of the various combinations and permutations into which they may enter, that the fundamental Abhidharma and its dependent exegetical literature is mainly concerned. As the number of dharmas is limited, there being 170 (with subdivisions, 202) in all according to the Theravādins, and 75 according to the Sarvāstivādins, what the Abhidharma really attempted to do was to compile a gigantic card-index of the universe. For the execution of this ambitious project it employed the method not of deduction but of induction, so that its system on the whole appears 'scientific' rather than speculatively metaphysical in character. Unlike modern science, however, which is merely descriptive, the Abhidharma besides being dominated by an intense spiritual concern possessed at the same time a positive normative aspect. The psychical ultimate elements of existence were enumerated and classified not 'objectively' but according to their place in a hierarchy of ethical and religious values, for which reason a modern exponent of the Abhidharma has termed it the 'psycho-ethical philosophy of Early Buddhism'.[55] Moreover, whereas in the sūtras the successive stages of the path were not always delineated in a comprehensive manner, the Abhidharma attempts to catalogue them in detail and systematically, though here, too, in keeping with its general principles, it is concerned not with the experiences of a real psychical entity, but only with an impersonal normative series of psychophysical events.

Despite this predominantly practical orientation, however, the fact that the fundamental Abhidharma aimed, in its description of existence, at exhaustiveness, could not but stimulate the emergence of purely theoretical, not to say speculative, interests. Though it never discussed how many angels could dance on the head of a pin, it undoubtedly gave serious thought to a number of questions having no direct bearing on the attainment of emancipation. Thus it came about that the Abhidharma eventually assumed, at least partially, the lineaments of a philosophy.

The development of these characteristics, representing the acquisition by the Abhidharma of an independent subject matter, is reflected in the changed interpretation of the word itself. The preposition *abhi*, meaning 'about', 'connected with', or 'pertaining to', can also signify 'supplementary', 'special', or 'superior'. At this stage, therefore, the Abhidharma as a system of thought, and especially that system as embodied in the works of the Abhidharma Piṭaka, came to be regarded not as merely connected with the Dharma as taught in the Dialogues and Anthologies, but as constituting in itself a Higher Doctrine distinct from, and even superior to, the teaching of the Sūtra Piṭaka.

According to Theravāda tradition their own Pāli Abhidhamma Piṭaka had been taught in its present literary form by the Buddha himself and was therefore canonical. Buddhaghosa, in the introductory verses to his *Atthasālinī*, a commentary on the first book of this Piṭaka, says that the Muni taught the Abhidhamma when, after performing the Twin Miracle, he sojourned in the Heaven of the Thirty-Three Gods. Among the auditors was his own deceased mother, who had been born as a deity there. What had been taught among the gods during the day he afterwards repeated in concise form to Sāriputta in the evening, when the latter waited on him at Anottata Lake, and Sāriputta taught it to the monks.[56]

The Sarvāstivādins are less dogmatic. Though maintaining that the Abhidharma was taught by the Buddha on a variety of occasions, they nevertheless concede that the books constituting their Abhidharma Piṭaka are the work not of the Master himself, but of his personal disciples and their followers. In practice there was little if any difference between the respective attitudes of the adherents of the two schools. The Abhidharma was for both the highest Buddhist wisdom, the very quintessence of the teaching, and both, therefore, not only accorded it the utmost respect, but invariably treated the Abhidharma Piṭaka as possessing at least equal canonical authority with the Vinaya and Sūtra Piṭakas.

It was indeed the Sarvāstivādins who exhibited the most ardent devotion to the Abhidharma, and among whom the most important of its subsequent developments took place. Other schools were less enthusiastic. Some, like the Sautrāntikas, refused to accept the Abhidharma as the word of the Buddha and rejected the Abhidharma Piṭaka outright. The debate continues down to the present day. The consensus of informed scholarly opinion sees in the Abhidharma a historical development which not only presupposes the Dharma but which, in its 'fundamental' form, cannot possibly be attributed to the Buddha, being compiled at least two centuries after the *parinirvāṇa*. This by no means implies that the Abhidharma is worthless. On the contrary, it was not only a natural, but perhaps even a helpful, development, into which, for half a millennium at least, flowed the creative energies of the greater part of the Sangha. As such it possesses permanent historical interest, besides being, even at the present day, an invaluable adjunct to our own understanding and practice of the Dharma.

That the Abhidharma Piṭaka, despite the impressiveness of its achievement, is not really the word of the Buddha, is not only manifest from the circumstances already adduced but also disclosed by a fact that is bound to strike us the minute we start investigating its actual contents. The Pāli and the various Sanskrit versions of the Vinaya Piṭaka, consisting ostensibly of the Monastic Code, and of the Sūtra Piṭaka, consisting of the Dialogues, the Anthologies, the Birth Stories, and the Glorious Deeds, though differing in many respects, are nevertheless patently all recensions of what was, broadly speaking, the same general body of primitive traditions. All schools therefore accept them as canonical, those of the Mahāyāna with the reservation that, though undoubtedly the word of the Buddha, they are merely introductory to the profounder sūtras handed down in their own tradition but rejected by the Hīnayāna. In the case of the Abhidharma Piṭaka the position is different. Not only was it not accepted as canonical by all the early schools but the two surviving examples of such a Piṭaka, that of the Theravādins and that of the Sarvāstivādins, are not two different literary versions of the same, or even of related, material, but independent collections of almost entirely different treatises. The fact that the number of works is in each case seven is merely a coincidence. From this we can only conclude that the final compilation of the third Piṭaka, or rather of the two third Piṭakas (there may have been even more), took place after the separation of the Sthavīravādins and the Sarvāstivādins shortly before the time of Aśoka. Despite its tremendous prestige and enormous historical influence it therefore stands on a somewhat different footing from the Vinaya and Sūtra Piṭakas.

The seven Pāli and the seven Sanskrit texts of the fundamental Abhidharma were composed not all at the same time but over a period of something like three centuries. Some are comparatively primitive, showing a resemblance to the later, Abhidharma-type sūtras, while others, in respect of both form and content, are the more sophisticated products of a much later generation. Broadly speaking, the works belong to three different periods which, for the purpose of this section, may be designated the pre-Aśokan, the Aśokan, and the post-Aśokan. Each period will be dealt with separately, and the works belonging to it, both Pāli and Sanskrit, briefly characterized. As this will involve, not only the simultaneous treatment of the Theravādin and the Sarvāstivādin works, but several dislocations in the traditional order of texts, the contents of each Piṭaka had best be listed separately, first according to the accepted enumeration.

The Theravāda Abhidhamma Piṭaka consists of the *Dhamma-saṅgaṇī*, the *Vibhaṅga*, the *Dhātu-kathā*, the *Puggala-paññatti*, the *Kathā-vatthu*, the *Yamaka* and the *Paṭṭhāna*. The Sarvāstivāda Abhidharma Piṭaka contains the *Saṅgīti-paryāya*, the *Dharma-skandha*, the *Prajñapti-śāstra*, the *Vijñāna-kāya*, the *Dhātu-kāya*, the *Prakaraṇa-pāda*, and the *Jñāna-prasthāna*.

(1) The *pre-Aśokan period* saw the production of the greatest number of works, six in all, each of the two schools being responsible for three. Of the Pāli works undoubtedly the most important is the *Dhamma-saṅgaṇī*, or 'Enumeration of Elements', which according to the Theravāda tradition constitutes the foundation, even as the great *Paṭṭhāna* the pinnacle, of the whole mighty soaring edifice of the Abhidhamma Piṭaka. As its name indicates, it is an enumeration of the ultimate elements of existence, these elements being throughout considered from the ethical, or better from the karmic, point of view, which is to say according to the karmic results produced now or hereafter in the so-called individual psychophysical continuum.

The elements or *dhammas*, comprising, according to the fundamental Abhidharma, consciousness (*citta*), mental concomitants or coefficients (*cetasika*), and form (*rūpa*), are therefore trebly divided into those which are karmically wholesome (*kusala*), in the sense of being dissociated from greed, aversion, and delusion, and productive of happiness; those which are karmically unwholesome (*akusala*), or associated with greed, aversion, and delusion, and productive of misery; and those which are 'undetermined' (*avyākata*) or karmically neutral. They are also classified according to the plane of existence on which they occur. Thus there are eight wholesome *cittas* belonging to the sensuous plane (*kāmāvacara*), four to the plane of form (*rūpāvacara*), four to the formless plane (*arūpāvacara*), four to the 'unrelated' or transcendental (*lokottara*) plane, and so on. In all, 89 *cittas*, 52 *cetasikas*, and 28 *rūpas* are enumerated. These are all 'constituted' (*saṅkhata*) or conditioned in nature. Together with the one 'unconstituted' (*asaṅkhata*) or unconditioned element recognized by the Theravāda, namely *nibbāṇa*, they make up the 170 ultimate elements which, according to this school, between them exhaust the whole content of reality, both mundane and transcendental.

From the psychological point of view the work consists of four main parts, (a) an analysis of states of consciousness and their concomitant mental factors, (b) an analysis of form, (c) an analysis of neutral elements, and (d) the catechetical summary. However clearly such an analysis may exhibit the formative principles of this seminal work, it is unable even to illustrate the extraordinarily detailed manner in which they are applied and worked out. Yet this is perhaps no great loss, for while the principles of the *Dhamma-saṅgaṇī* are undoubtedly of permanent relevance and validity, some of the details may have to be revised in the light of modern psychological knowledge.

Though presupposing the *Dhamma-saṇgaṅī*, in the sense of being based partly on the categories and classifications which it is the business of that work to establish, the *Vibhaṅga* is cast in the comparatively primitive form of a collection of independent treatises on different doctrinal topics. In this respect, as well as in certain of its contents, it resembles the *Paṭisambhidā-magga*.

There are in all eighteen *vibhaṅgas* or treatises. The first three break new ground in that they are devoted, respectively, to exhaustive investigations of the five aggregates of existence (*khandha*), the twelve psychophysical bases (*āyatana*), and the eighteen elements of perception (*dhātu*), which although categories of the first importance are not, as such, dealt with in the *Dhamma-saṅgaṇī*. The remaining treatises deal with the four Noble Truths (*sacca*), the twenty-two faculties (*indriya*), the twenty-four modes of conditionality (*paccayākāra*), the four establishments of mindfulness (*satipaṭṭhāna*), the four great efforts (*sammappadhāna*), the four bases of psychic power (*iddhi-pāda*), the seven constituents of Enlightenment (*bojjhaṅga*), the eightfold path (*magga*), the four states of concentration (*jhāna*), the four unbounded states (*appamañña*), the five steps in moral training (*sikkhāpada*), the four analytical knowledges (*paṭisambhidā*), various types and degrees of knowledge (*ñāṇa*), and minor points (*khuddaka-vatthu*); while the last, entitled 'The Heart of the Doctrine' (*Dhamma-hadaya*), forms, in part, a summary recapitulation of the contents of the previous treatises together with innumerable searching cross-questions. As the word *vibhaṅga* itself suggests, these treatises are not dissimilar from the *suttas* of the *Vibhaṅga-vagga* of the *Majjhima Nikāya*. The latter, with one exception, each consist of a brief enunciation of a doctrinal topic followed by a detailed exposition, the latter being sometimes given, as we saw in Chapter 4, not by the Buddha himself but by a disciple.

As if by way of parallel, most of the eighteen *vibhaṅgas* consist of three parts, a Sutta-explanation, an *Abhidhamma*-explanation, and a summary. Whereas in the first part the topic in question is explained in the popular language of the *Suttas*, passages from which are quoted, in the second the explanation is given by way of the 122 *mātikās* or matrices of discussion of the fundamental Abhidharma. This enables us to see very well the difference between the two approaches. Thus in the *Āyatana-vibhaṅga* the eye-base (*cakkhu-āyatana*), for example, is described, following the *suttas*, simply as impermanent, miserable, insubstantial, and so on. The Abhidhamma explanation defines it as 'made up of sensitivity (*pasāda*), derived from the four primary physical elements, related to individual existence, invisible but reacting on sense impressions (*sappaṭigha*) – this invisible eye reacting on sense impressions by means of which one has seen, sees, will see, or may see the visible object – this is the eye ... etc.'[57]

Certainly the shortest and probably the oldest of the three works belonging to the pre-Aśokan period, and therefore of the entire Pāli Abhidhamma Piṭaka, is the *Puggala-paññatti* or 'Designation of Persons'. In fact it might equally well have been included in the *Khuddaka Nikāya* of the Sutta Piṭaka. As its title indicates, it does not deal, in the manner characteristic of the fundamental Abhidharma, with the real ultimate elements of existence, but with persons. Not only are these described, moreover, entirely in the conventional language used in the *suttas*, but there are many literal parallels with the *Saṅgīti-sutta* of the *Dīgha Nikāya* and various portions of the *Aṅguttara Nikāya*.

Like those of the latter collection, the contents of the work are arranged according to the ascending numerical value of the different groups dealt with. Section 1 describes single human types, Section 2 groups of two types, Section 3 groups of three, and so on up to Sections 6 to 10, each of which deals with one group of six, or seven, or eight, or nine, or ten human types. For example under Section 1, which describes fifty different *puggalas*, are included the worldling (*putthujana*), the āriya, the person incapable of progress, the learner (*sekha*), the possessor of the six superknowledges (*chaḷabhiñño*), the Fully Enlightened One and the Privately Enlightened One. In Section 4, containing twenty-nine groups, occur the four types of preacher of the Dharma, and so on. Each of the last four sections deals with a different group of Holy Persons (*āriya-puggala*).[58] From a literary point of view the work compares favourably with the rest of the Piṭaka, its descriptions being in many cases embellished with parables and similes.

The *Saṅgīti-paryāya*, or 'Method of Congregational Chanting', illustrates the interrelation between the latest parts of the second and the earliest parts of the third Piṭaka. In form it resembles the *Saṅgīti-sūtra* of the *Dīrghāgama*, corresponding to the *Saṅgīti-sutta* of the *Dīgha Nikāya* (no.33), but in respect of content there is a greater similarity to the *Dasottara Sūtra*. Like the *Puggala-paññatti*, which it also resembles in being the most ancient work in its own Piṭaka, it is arranged *Aṅguttara*-fashion according to the ascending numerical value of its constituent groups.

The work is divided into twelve sections. Section 2 deals with single doctrinal topics, Section 3 with groups of two, Section 4 with groups of three, and so on up to Section 11, dealing with groups of ten. For example, the groups of seven include the seven spiritual treasures (*dhana*), the seven constituents of Enlightenment (*sambodhyaṅga*), and the seven propensities (*anusaya*); the groups of eight the eight Noble Paths (*ārya-mārga*), the eight persons (*pudgala*), and the eight emancipations (*vimokṣa*). According to A.C. Banerjee's analysis, the total number of topics dealt with in the *Saṅgīti-sutta* is greater than that in the *Saṅgīti-paryāya*.[59] Yet according to Kōgen Mizuno the latter work contains more items than the *Saṅgīti-sūtra*.[60] The interesting hypothesis therefore presents itself that these texts represent three progressively more elaborate versions of what is in reality the same work, the first version being included in the Sanskrit Sūtra Piṭaka, the second in the Sanskrit Abhidharma Piṭaka, and the third in the Pāli Sutta Piṭaka.

The remaining two sections of the *Saṅgīti-paryāya*, namely the first and the last, consist respectively of a *nidāna* or *exordium* setting forth the circumstances leading to the composition of the treatise and an admonition by the Buddha concerning its recitation. According to the first of these former, it was occasioned by dissensions among the bhikshus of Pāva following the Second Council, the Council of Vaiśālī. Chinese sources attribute the work to Śāriputra, Yaśomitra and Bu-ston attribute it to Mahākausthila. It was translated into Chinese by Hsüan-tsang in the seventh century CE.

The *Dharma-skandha*, or 'Compendium of Doctrines', is characterized by Takakusu as 'the most important of the Abhidharma works, and the fountainhead of the Sarvāstivāda system.'[61] This is the position generally assigned to the *Jñāna-prasthāna*, which according to tradition stands to the six other treatises in the relation of trunk to legs. At the lowest estimate the *Dharma-skandha* is not only an original, independent work, but as regards both form and content in no way inferior to its more celebrated rival. Like the *Vibhaṅga*, to which it bears a distant resemblance, it is a collection of treatises on various doctrinal topics. The number of treatises constituting the different sections of the work is twenty-one. In the case of the *Dharma-skandha*, however, the predominant interest is not psychological or epistemological, less still metaphysical, but practical and religious. It covers, in fact, all aspects of the moral and spiritual – including the transcendental – life and experience of the disciple, and though the topics are not arranged strictly in progressive order, nevertheless constitutes, like the *Visuddhi-magga*, an exhaustive guide to practice of the successive stages of the path.

This is evident from a glance at some of the contents of the work. The first three sections are concerned mainly with the spiritual life of the layman, and deal with the five steps of moral training (*śikṣāpada*), the four constituents of Stream Entry (*srotāpattyaṅga*), and the four kinds of firm faith (*avetyāprasāda*) in the Three Jewels. Sections 4 to 15 are devoted to the higher spiritual practices and experiences, which, according to the Hīnayāna, are open only to the monks. Topics dealt with include the four noble lineages (*ārya-vaṃsa*) or types of the

Buddha's disciples, the six superknowledges (*abhijñā*), the four establishments of mindfulness (*smṛtyupasthāna*), the four degrees of concentration (*dhyāna*), the four unbounded states (*apramāṇa*), otherwise known as the Sublime Abodes (*brahma-vihāra*), the four degrees of formless concentrative attainment (*ārupa-samāpatti*), the three stages in the practice of meditation (*samādhi-bhāvanā*), and the seven constituents of Enlightenment (*bodhyaṅga*). Section 16 is a miscellany of various topics. The remaining five sections are more theoretical in character, being devoted, respectively, to an examination of the twenty-two controlling faculties (*indriya*), the twelve psychophysical bases (*āyatana*), the five aggregates (*skandha*), various worldly elements (*nānā-dhātu*), and conditioned co-production (*pratītya-samutpāda*).[62]

Though throughout based on the Āgamas, passages from which are cited and explained, the work is in style and manner of treatment scholastic. Like the *Saṅgīti-paryāya*, its authorship is uncertain, being ascribed to Maudgalyāyana by Chinese writers and to Ārya Śāriputra by Yaśomitra and Bu-ston. It too was translated by the indefatigible Hsüan-tsang.

Simpler in form and slighter in content, but based, like the first two treatises, on the Āgamas, is the *Prajñapti-śāstra* or 'Treatise of Designations'. As used here, the term stands for the conventional designations, or conceptual symbols of things, as contrasted with what they are in reality (*dravya*). Theravāda tradition speaks of six designations, one of them being the *Puggala-paññatti* or designation of human types. The present work consists of three sections, one dealing with cosmological (*loka*), one with causal (*kāraṇa*), and one with karmic designations. It is indicative of the haphazard way in which Buddhist texts have come down to us, and how dependent we are for what we possess on the merest accidents of transmission, that though only Section 3 was translated into Chinese, and that as late as the eleventh century CE, the whole work is available in Tibetan. This is all the more extraordinary inasmuch as, out of the seven fundamental Abhidharma works of the Sarvāstivāda, only the *Prajñapti* was ever rendered into that tongue. As in the case of the six remaining works the original Sanskrit text has, of course, been lost.

According to Chinese traditions, this treatise was composed by Kātyāyana, but according to Sanskrit and Tibetan sources by Maudgalyāyana. In the Tibetan version Sections 1 and 2 are both divided into seven subsections, and Section 3, translated into Chinese by Fâhu (Dharmarakṣa) and others, into five. Section 1, the *Loka-prajñapti*, dealing with the universe as envisaged by Buddhist tradition, describes the evolution and involution of the world-system, with its gods and men, its animals, revenants, and tormented spirits, in a manner reminiscent of the *Agañña Sutta* of the *Dīgha Nikāya*.[63] Its cosmogony is, in fact, said to be a development of that of the corresponding Āgama discourse.[64] Section 2, the *Kāraṇa-prajñapti*, expounds the causes of the seven treasures (*ratna*) of a universal monarch (*cakravarti-rāja*), the thirty-two marks of a superman (*mahā-puruṣa-lakṣana*), of the difference of mental faculties existing between the Buddha and his disciples, and of various natural and psychological phenomena. The last section, the *Karma-prajñapti*, elucidates the different types of volitional activity.

(2) The *Dhātu-kathā*, or 'Discussion of Elements', is based on the first three sections of the *Vibhaṅga* in much the same way that the *Vibhaṅga* itself, in common with the rest of the Abhidhamma Piṭaka, is based on the Nikāyas. Thus whether or not composed during the three decades of Aśoka's reign, it clearly belongs to that later middle period of development which we have termed the Aśokan period. As Nyanatiloka points out, it should really be called the *Khandha-āyatana-dhātukathā*, for it classifies doctrinal categories not only with reference to the eighteen elements of perception (*dhātu*), but also with reference to the twelve psychophysical bases (*āyatana*) and the five aggregates of existence (*khandha*).[65]

The work is divided into fourteen sections, in accordance with the number of times a given category is included or not included in, or associated or not associated with, the aggregates, or bases, or elements, or the number of times it is included or not included in, or associated or not associated with, the included or the unincluded, or the associated or not associated, and so on. Among the categories that are subjected to this rigorous treatment are form (*rūpa*), feeling (*vedanā*), consciousness (*viññaṇa*), the four Truths (*sacca*), the five spiritual faculties (*indriya*), and the seven constituents of Enlightenment (*bojjhaṅga*). The whole complex analysis is conducted in catechism form. For example the work asks itself, 'In how many aggregates, bases, and elements is the *rūpa-khandha* included?' To which the reply is given 'In one aggregate, in eleven bases, and in eleven elements.' 'In how many is it not included?' 'It is not included in four aggregates, in one base, and in seven elements.' Again, in response to similar enquiries, the truth of *dukkha* or suffering is said to be included in each and every one of them and unincluded in none.

More than any other Abhidhamma work, whether Pāli or Sanskrit, the *Kathā-vatthu* is more or less firmly embedded in a concrete historical context. While the other treatises are apt to seem, like Plato's Ideas to a modern English rationalist, 'a bloodless ballet of unearthly categories', in this one we get a glimpse of live issues and live men. Significantly, it is the only work to which Theravāda tradition attaches the name of an author. Yet even so the concession to history is more apparent than real. According to Buddhaghosa, the putative author of the *Kathā-vatthu* commentary, the Buddha himself, foreseeing the disputes that would arise in the Sangha after his *parinirvāṇa*, tabulated in advance the matrices of discussion for the work, and laid down the method of treatment to be adopted, leaving the details to be filled in by Moggalliputta Tissa. This was done, so the commentator asserts, in connection with the proceedings of the 'Third Council', that of Pāṭaliputta, when the Tipiṭaka was rehearsed, and the *Kathā-vatthu*, as compiled by Moggalliputta, incorporated in the Abhidhamma Piṭaka. Actually the work must have grown by a process of gradual accretion covering a period of centuries.

In the form in which it is now extant, as commented on in the fifth century CE, it consists of twenty-three sections each of which contains discussions (*kathā*) of eight to twelve different points that were the subject of disagreement among the early schools. There are 219 such points. In arrangement the work is quite unsystematic, the points of discussion being grouped with regard neither to their subject matter nor to the different parties supposed to be participating in the debate. For the names of the latter we are, indeed, indebted to the commentary, which being much later is not always reliable.

This lack of system is due to the fact that the *Kathā-vatthu*, far from representing a once-for-all filling in of previously tabulated matrices, simply grew by a process of accretion. As, with the emergence of new trends of thought and new schools, fresh points of discussion arose, additional sections went on being added to the work in order to scotch, one after another, what the Theravādins regarded as misrepresentations of the Buddha's teaching and to vindicate what was, for them, the orthodox tradition. Thus the work clearly reflects a process of historical development.

Most of the views dealt with are ascribed to schools which came into existence five or six centuries after the *parinirvāṇa*. Moggalliputta Tissa could therefore either have lived several centuries later than Aśoka and compiled the whole work or have been a contemporary of Aśoka and compiled the original nucleus of discussions only. The latter is the more likely alternative. In either case the Theravāda tradition collapses. Moreover, the point discussed in the first section, which is the longest and philosophically the most important, is whether a *puggala* or person exists as a real absolute fact. The origin of the work may, therefore, be connected with the rise of the Pudgalavādins or 'Personalists', who had separated from the Sthavīravādins before the accession of Aśoka. Whether the *Kathā-vatthu* was recited, even in nuclear form, at the 'Third Council', by Moggalliputta or anybody else, or whether there was any Third Council at all, are, however, quite different questions.

The points of discussion themselves cover practically the whole universe of early Buddhist discourse, and range in importance from the trivial to the fundamental. In a number of cases they represent misunderstandings of the Buddha's teaching which had arisen, as the Theravādins are able to demonstrate, out of one or another type of semantic confusion. Thus one party, identified by the commentary with the Hetuvādins, maintained that the worldling (*putthujana*) possesses no real knowledge.[66] This was due to a failure to distinguish between worldly (*lokiya*) knowledge and its transcendental (*lokottara*) counterpart.

Questions representing a real difference of opinion between the Theravādins and their opponents were less easily disposed of. Did the Buddha really preach the Doctrine on earth among men, or did he, remaining in the Tuṣita heaven, project for the purpose a specially created human form? Can an Arhant fall away from his attainment? Can he still possess ignorance, or doubt, or be excelled by others? Can the *sāsana* be 'made new' (*nāvakata*) or reformed? These are weighty questions indeed. Yet however serious the subject discussed, and however profound the differences of opinion disclosed, the discussion never becomes acrimonious. As C.A.F. Rhys Davids points out, 'The courteous mode of address on both sides, and the absence of any polemical asperities, is a pleasant feature in the dialogues. The opponent, moreover, is sometimes allowed to have the last word.'[67]

The discussion is also not without logical interest. As the differences of opinion were all within the *sāsana*, among parties that on certain basic issues were in full agreement, the Theravādins generally attempted to confute the opposite party by demonstrating that their thesis was inconsistent either with other views peculiar to themselves or with principles held in common by all. Symbolically, the line of argument was: if A is said to be B, C must be said to be D; but it is not admitted that C is D, therefore it cannot be maintained that A is B, and so on. This eventually led to the development of the three-membered syllogism.

Just as the *Kathā-vatthu* maintains the tradition of the Sthavīras against all comers, so in the two Sanskrit Abhidharma works of the Aśokan period we begin to see the emergence of specifically Sarvāstivāda ideas. One of them, indeed, resembles the Pāli work in that it enters into polemics with the thinkers of rival schools. This is the *Vijñāna-kāya*, apparently meaning a body (*kāya*) or group of subjects connected with consciousness (*vijñāna*), which according to the unanimous testimony of the Sanskrit, Chinese, and Tibetan sources was composed by the Arhant Devaśarman at Viśoka, near Śrāvastī, one hundred years after the *parinirvāṇa*. In view of the high degree of doctrinal differentiation it represents, the work must, however, be considered as belonging to a later period. The exact nature of its connection with Devaśarman is therefore uncertain.

It is divided into six sections. The first, which is philosophically the most important, after recording the views of one Maudgalyāyana (apparently not the Buddha's disciple of that name) on different philosophical, psychological, and ethical topics, devotes itself to the refutation of his doctrine that the present existence of things alone is real and not their past or future existence. As against this Devaśarman, or whoever else composed the work, advances the distinctive, indeed the characteristic, Sarvāstivādin thesis that the past, present, and future dharmas are all equally real. In the *Vijñāna-kāya*, however, the doctrine of a single entity really existent throughout the three periods of time, though implicit in its position, is not explicitly formulated as it is in the *Jñāna-prasthāna*. Indeed, as if by way of showing that there is no danger of his lapsing into substantialism, the author proceeds, in Section 2, to deny that there exists, as a substratum for the operations of karma, the *pudgala* or metaphysical person as a real existent fact. On account of the contents of these two sections, Kōgen Mizuno, indicating the historical importance of this treatise, says: 'Inasmuch as the real existence of phenomena in the three states of time and *anātma-vāda* (non-ego theory) constitute the cardinal points of the Sarvāstivāda doctrine, the *Vijñāna-kāya*, which emphasised these two points, laid the theoretical foundation of the school.'[68]

Sections 3 and 4 deal, for the first time, with another distinctive theory of the Sarvāstivādins, that of the four conditions (*pratyāya*). These are object (*ālambana*), the immediate antecedent (*samanantara*), the predominant condition (*adhipati*), and the co-operating condition (*sahakāri*). Section 5, entitled 'Miscellaneous' (*saṃyukta*), analyses the mental functions of a *saikṣa* or 'learner', that is to say of the four Holy Persons excluding the fourth, the Arhant, whose mental functions are analysed in the concluding section, entitled '(Spiritual) Endowment' (*samanvāgama*). The work was translated into Chinese by Hsüan-tsang.

Between the *Dhātu-kāya* and the *Vijñāna-kāya* there exists a correlation in that, while the latter deals with consciousness itself, the former analyses the mental states that are the concomitants of consciousness. Chinese sources attribute the composition of the work to Vasumitra, who flourished 300 years after the *parinirvāṇa*, but Yaśomitra and Bu-ston attribute it to Pūrṇa. On the grounds that its subject matter more or less coincides with that of Section 4 of the *Prakaraṇa-pāda*, a work unanimously attributed to Vasumitra, some scholars are inclined to favour the claims of this master to be considered the author of the treatise. In view of the close mutual interdependence existing between the various fundamental Abhidharma works, the evidence, such as it is, cannot be regarded as conclusive. Moreover in the *Prakaraṇa-pāda*, as we shall presently see, the same subject matter is treated in the more highly systematic manner characteristic of the latest period of development. Takakusu suggests that the Sanskrit text of the *Dhātu-kāya* probably existed in two or three recensions, long, short, and of middling length, the last being the one translated by Hsüan-tsang.[69] It has also been suggested that, containing as it does discussions on the association and dissociation between dharmas, the *Dhātu-kāya* is probably a source of the Pāli *Dhātu-kathā*.[70]

The work consists of two main sections. Section 1 is of great psychological interest. It attempts, for the first time in the history of the Abhidharma, to define and classify a class of elements (*dharmas*) known therein as the *caitasikas* (Pāli *cetasikas*) or concomitants of consciousness (*citta*). Though the term itself is unknown in the Vinaya and Sūtra Piṭakas, some of the *caitasikas*, such as the five moral defilements (*kleśa*), the five views (*dṛṣṭi*), and the five dharmas, are already described in the Āgamas/Nikāyas. In the *Dhātu-kāya* these groups are not only explained in greater detail but defined according to the Abhidharma method. The great originality of the present work, however, consists in the fact that it introduces an entirely new method of classifying the *caitasikas* which, in a revised and improved form, occupies a prominent place in the later scholastic developments. According to this classification the *caitasikas* may be divided into three groups consisting, respectively, of elements present in all types of consciousness (*mahābhūmika-dharmas*), defiled elements present in all types of unwholesome consciousness (*kleśa-mahābhūmika-dharmas*), and additional defiled elements present only in certain types of unwholesome consciousness (*upakleśa-dharmas*), there being ten *caitasikas* in each group. Section 2 is devoted to a detailed investigation into the relations subsisting between eighty-eight doctrinal categories divided into eighteen subsections.

(3) With the works of the last, post-Aśokan period, both Pāli and Sanskrit, we reach the highest point of doctrinal systematization in the literature of the fundamental Abhidharma. Originality of treatment, though not entirely lacking, is by no means conspicuous. More often than not the concern is with the elaboration of technicalities, or with the working out, in a more or less mechanical fashion, of a whole series of permutations of concepts. This is true in particular of the Pāli *Yamaka* or 'The Pairs'. C.A.F. Rhys Davids describes this treatise, with its ten sections, as the 'ten valleys of dry bones.'[71] Even so conservative an authority as Nyanatiloka is constrained to observe:

> To me it looks as if this book was composed for examination purposes, or to get versed in answering sophistical and ambiguous, or captious questions, on all the manifold doctrines and technical terms of Buddhist Philosophy. The questions of identity, subordination, and co-ordination, of concepts are playing a prominent part in our work, which tries to give a logical clearing up and delimitation of all the doctrinal concepts, as to their range and contents. It is a work of applied logic, just as Kathā-Vatthu, Netti-Pakaraṇa, etc. In my opinion, there would be no very great loss to the

> Abhidhamma literature, if this work were altogether not in existence. Many of its plays upon words, though uttered in the dignified tones of logics, must to any Westerner, at times, appear rather strange, if not silly.[72]

Though hardly literature, even examination papers have their uses, however. For some, the study of Formal Logic is a fascinating and absorbing pastime.

In the Thai edition the work consists of two volumes of more than 1,300 pages divided into twelve sections that investigate the elements of existence by referring them respectively to the wholesome, unwholesome, and neutral 'roots' (*mūla*), the five aggregates (*khandha*), the twelve bases (*āyatana*), the eighteen elements (*dhātu*), the four Truths (*sacca*), the bodily, verbal, and mental 'formations' (*sankhāra*), the seven propensities (*anusaya*), consciousness (*citta*), the elements themselves (*dhamma*), and the twenty-two faculties (*indriya*). Most of the sections are subdivided into three parts, which between them constitute the threefold method of investigation employed in this work.

The first part is concerned with the delimitation of terms. Thus in Section 1, for example, the first pair (*yamaka*) of questions runs: 'Are all karmically wholesome elements wholesome roots? And are all wholesome roots wholesome elements?' The second part deals with process (*pavatti*), that is to say, it investigates with regard to what person, or what place, or what person and place, the element or elements of existence under discussion, originate, or cease, or both originate and cease. Thus under Section 2, dealing with the five groups (*khandhas*), it is said that the *rūpa-khandha*, for instance, obtains in all planes of existence except the formless (*arūpa*) plane, and under Section 3, dealing with the bases (*āyatanas*), that for those beings who are in their last existence, none of the bases will arise again after the attainment of *parinirvāṇa*, but that, on the contrary, for them all bases will cease, and so on. The third part, dealing with penetration (*pariññā*), is analogous to the second, except that the elements are discussed with reference to persons only. For example, under Section 10, on the faculties (*indriyas*), the question as to whether the Arhant will penetrate the three transcendental faculties is answered in the negative because, of course, he has penetrated them already. This threefold method of investigation, though apparently the standard procedure for the treatise, is not rigorously followed in all the ten sections. Some consist of only one or only two out of the three parts, and even in these there may be modifications. Throughout its entire length down to the last subdivision, the treatise strictly adheres, however, to the catechetical method.

On account both of its size and its importance the *Paṭṭhāna* or *Paṭṭhāna-pakaraṇa*, the 'Treatise of Origination', a recondite and voluminous work considerably more than twice as long as the *Yamaka*, is often referred to as the *Mahā-pakaraṇa* or 'Great Treatise'. In Theravāda circles it has always enjoyed an enormous prestige. According to Buddhaghosa, when the Buddha, during the fourth week after his Enlightenment, contemplated the contents of the previous six Abhidhamma works, not a single ray of light issued from his body.

> but when, coming to the Great Book, he began to contemplate the twenty-four universal causal relations of condition, of presentation, and so on, his omniscience certainly found its opportunity therein. For as the great fish Timiratipiṅgala finds room only in the great ocean eighty-four thousand yojanas in depth, so his omniscience truly finds room only in the Great Book. Rays of six colours – indigo, golden, red, white, tawny, and dazzling – issued from the Teacher's body, as he was contemplating the subtle and abstruse Law by his omniscience which had found such opportunity.[73]

As its title suggests, the *Paṭṭhāna* is concerned, not with simple enumeration of the ultimate elements of existence, in the manner of the *Dhamma-saṅgaṇī*, but with the much more complex task of considering the origination of these elements, and the relations subsisting between them, in terms of a certain agreed number of causal factors or conditions (*paccaya*). Thus while the first work of the Abhidhamma Piṭaka presents a predominantly analytical and static picture of the universe, the latter reveals one which is, on the contrary, synthetical and dynamic – in fact, a motion picture. It is a card index in which every card dances. Nirvāṇa, as the eternal and unconditioned element, is of course excluded from the picture.

The twenty-four causal conditions, described by C.A.F. Rhys Davids as 'the one notable constructive contribution to knowledge in the Abhidhamma', are enumerated and explained in the first, introductory portion of the work. They comprise causal conditions which are such by way of root-cause (*hetu*), object (*ārammaṇa*), dominance (*adhipati*), contiguity (*anantara*), immediate contiguity (*samanantara*), co-nascence (*sahajāta*), reciprocity (*aññamañña*), dependence (*nissaya*), sufficing support (*upanissaya*), antecedence (*purejāta*), consequence (*pacchājāta*), recurrence (*āsevana*), intentional action (*kamma*), result (*vipāka*), nutriment (*āhāra*), controlling faculty (*indriya*), concentration (*jhāna*), means (*magga*), association (*sampayutta*), dissociation (*vippayutta*), presence (*atthi*), absence (*natthi*), abeyance (*vigata*), and continuance (*avigata*). Some of these had been discussed already in the *Paṭisambhidā-magga* and the *Kathā-vatthu*, but it was only in the present work that, for the first time, an attempt was made to draw up a comprehensive list of causal factors. The first three, together with the fifth, are identical with the four *pratyāyas* of the *Vijñāna-kāya*. Later Theravāda scholasticism reduced the list from twenty-four items to four.

The main body of the *Paṭṭhāna* is divided into four great sections in which the subject of origination is dealt with according to the positive (*anuloma*), the negative (*paccaniya*), the positive-negative, and the negative-positive methods respectively. Each of these sections deals, in accordance with its own distinctive method, with the origination of triplets (*tika-paṭṭhāna*), of doublets (*duka-paṭṭhāna*), of triplets and doublets combined, of doublets and triplets, of triplets and triplets, and of doublets and doublets. By triplets is meant the triple groups of doctrinal categories like those of the wholesome (*kusala*), the unwholesome (*akusala*), and the neutral (*avyākata*), and joy (*pīti*), happiness (*sukha*), and equanimity (*upekkhā*). Twenty-two such triplets are enumerated, and eighty-nine doublets. Thus each section consists of six subsections, one divided into twenty-two chapters, one into eighty-nine, and so on. Each of these chapters is divided into a number of identical sub-chapters. In accordance with the four methods which constitute the principle of division for the four great sections of the whole work, namely the positive method, each such sub-chapter, again, consists of four smaller sections. Finally, every one of these smaller sections, throughout the entire length of the treatise, is divided into 'paragraphs' corresponding to the twenty-four causal conditions. In this way the *Paṭṭhāna* attempts to construct, out of the materials collected in the previous six Abhidhamma treatises, and in accordance with the plan provided by its own list of causal conditions, a vast and intricate system of psycho-cosmic dynamics. Though tending somewhat to the reduction of the whole of conditioned existence to a gigantic mechanism, the result is not unimpressive.

In the *Prakaraṇarakaraṇ-pāda* or 'Auxiliary Treatise', unanimously attributed to Vasumitra, the topics descanted on in the Abhidharma books of the pre-Aśokan and Aśokan periods are brought together into a more complete arrangement. Further refinements of scholasticism are also introduced. Like the *Vijñāna-kāya* and the *Dhātu-kāya*, the work of which it may be said to continue, it is therefore of importance for the development of Sarvāstivāda thought. Despite its present title, which probably reflects the canons of a later age, the *Prakaraṇa* is not merely one of the *Jñāna-prasthāna*'s six feet (*pada*) but an independent treatise no whit inferior to its more celebrated counterpart. Strictly speaking, it is a collection of treatises. Twice translated complete into Chinese, once by Guṇabhadra and Bodhiyaśas in the fifth century and once by Hsüan-tsang in the seventh, the eight sections into which the book is divided seem also to have circulated independently, three of them having been translated separately as early as the second century CE.

The opening section is philosophically the most important. Herein for the first time in the history of Buddhist thought the ultimate elements of existence are distributed into five great categories: form (*rūpa*), mind or consciousness (*citta*), mental concomitants (*caitasika*), factors dissociated from mind (*cittaviprayukta*), and the unconditioned (*asaṃskṛta*). So far as the Sarvāstivāda is concerned, this classification, of aggregates, bases, and elements, henceforth replaces the older one. The development is of great significance. Whereas the older classification was intended to function as a support for the contemplation of the transitory, insubstantial, and unsatisfactory nature of conditioned things, the new grouping aims rather at facilitating 'the thinking consideration of things' as a whole, rationally and objectively, without reference to religious criteria. The introduction of this fivefold classification therefore marked a transition, in the Abhidharma, from the practical and scholastic to the theoretical and philosophical, and as such contributed to the determination of the whole course of its future development. Whether the change is regarded as constituting an advance or a decline depends, in the last analysis, on one's estimation of the relative merits of the religious and the scientific outlooks.

Sections 4 and 5 contain the *Prakaraṇa-pāda*'s contributions to Buddhist psychology. The first, which discusses not only the aggregates, bases, and elements, but also the new psychological categories established in the *Dhātu-kāya*, adds to the latter the ten *kuśala-mahābhūmika-dharmas* or mental factors present in all states of wholesome consciousness, thus raising the total number of factors according to the scheme from thirty to forty. The second discusses ninety-eight *anusayas*, or evil propensities, thirty-six of which obtain on the plane of sensuous desire (*kāmadhātu*), thirty-one on the plane of form (*rūpadhātu*), and thirty-one on the formless plane (*arūpadhātu*).

The five remaining sections, though not responsible for any startling innovations, are nevertheless all weighty contributions to Sarvāstivāda thought. Section 2 treats of the ten kinds of knowledge, culminating in the knowledge of non-origination (*anutpāda-jñānam*), which also form the subject matter of two subsections of the *Jñāna-prasthāna*. Sections 3 and 6 are respectively concerned with the acquisition of the knowledge of the bases (*āyatanas*) and with matters that can be the subject of inference (*vijñeya, anumeya*). Section 7, which discusses a thousand questions connected with various doctrinal categories, is identical in content with the *Saṅgīti-paryāya*, though its method of treatment is more exhaustive than that of the earlier work. Section 8 is a digest of the entire treatise.

Because it treats the Abhidharma topics as a whole, whereas the previous six treatises of the Sanskrit collection dealt with them only partially, the *Jñāna-prasthāna* or 'Establishment of Knowledge' is known as the *Kāya-śāstra* or trunk-treatise, and the rest as the *Pada-śāstras* or limb-treatises. Though unfair to the *Dharma-skandha* and the *Prakaraṇa-pāda*, the comparison reflects the great, indeed the unique, eminence of this work in the history of the Sarvāstivāda, and, through that school, in the development of the Abhidharma generally. According to tradition it was composed 300 years after the *parinirvāṇa* by Kātyāyanīputra, a great Sarvāstivādin teacher of Kashmir who, it is furthermore stated, was a contemporary of King Kaṅiṣka. As the latter flourished some two centuries later, there appears to be a discrepancy.

Two Chinese translations have come down to us. One generally known as the *Aṣṭa-grantha* or 'Eight Books', was executed in the fourth century by Gautama Sanghadeva and Ku Fu-nien, while the other, generally known as the *Jñāna-prasthāna*, was the work of the prince of translators, Hsüan-tsang. Despite the fact that the second is shorter by half than the first, the two versions each consist of eight sections divided into forty-four chapters. In the one translated by Hsüan-tsang, however, the titles of a few chapters are different.

Though encyclopaedic in content, the *Jñāna-prasthāna* is unsystematic in form. According to their titles, the eight sections into which it is divided deal respectively with miscellaneous topics (*saṃkīrṇa*), the fetters (*saṃyojana*), knowledge (*jñāna*), intentional actions (*karma*), the four great material elements (*mahā-bhūta*), the controlling faculties (*indriya*), meditation (*samādhi*), and views (*dṛṣṭi*), but this bare enumeration gives little or no idea of the depth and universality of the work, which in fact ranges over the whole field of Sarvāstivāda dogmatics. Yet the topics dealt with are so abstruse, and the manner of discussion so concise and technical, that the author's meaning is at times in doubt. Consequently, despite or perhaps even because of the high esteem in which the work was held as the principal textbook of Buddhism, a variety of different interpretations arose among its various exponents.

After accumulating for two centuries these interpretations were incorporated in the *Mahā-vibhāṣā*, the still more encyclopaedic 'Great Commentary' on the *Jñāna-prasthāna*. This work was in turn responsible for the production in the fifth century CE of Vasubandhu's monumental *Abhidharma-koṣa* or 'Treasury of the Abhidharma', wherein the Abhidharma, after practically a millennium of development, at last reaches the culminating phase of complete systematization. Long before this, however, there had begun to appear a group of canonical texts which not only exemplified a totally different type of approach to the Dharma but which, as the starting-point and basis of the Mahāyāna, eventually brought about the overthrow, or at least the revaluation and reconstruction, of the whole edifice of Buddhist scholastic thought.

# 8

# TRANSITION TO THE MAHĀYĀNA SŪTRAS

Reference has already been made to the fact that the Sūtra Piṭaka, or 'Collection of Discourses', is divided into two parts, one consisting of Hīnayāna, the other of Mahāyāna sūtras. Some account of the former was given in the chapters on the Dialogues and the Anthologies, as well as in that on the Jatākas and Avadānas. A survey of the latter must now be attempted. Before this can be done, however, it is necessary to take note, at least, of the fact that the Mahāyāna sūtras are not recognized as Buddhavacana by the Hīnayāna schools, including the modern Theravāda. For the Mahāyāna form of Buddhism, the Mahāyāna sūtras are not only Buddhavacana but, in a sense, Buddhavacana *par excellence*, inasmuch as the teachings they contain go far beyond the limited and provisional teachings of their Hīnayāna counterparts. According to modern Western scholarship the beginnings of the Mahāyāna are to be found among the Mahāsaṅghikas and other Hīnayāna schools, which means that the Mahāyāna sūtras are affiliated to the original, orally transmitted Dharma through the Mahāsaṅghikas and other schools in much the same way that the Hīnayāna sūtras are affiliated to it through the Theravāda and the Sarvāstivāda schools. Continuity of development as between what appear to be the older portions of the Āgamas/Nikāyas, on the one hand, and the early Mahāyāna sūtras (e.g. some of the sūtras of the 'Jewel-Heap' Collection), on the other, can be distinctly perceived by any impartial student of these texts. At the same time, the differences between them are sufficiently striking.

Passing from the Hīnayāna to the Mahāyāna sūtras, one is transported to a new plane of existence, finds oneself living in another world, and breathes a different atmosphere. Some hint of the nature of this transition is contained in the very designations of the two types or classes of sūtras. The Hīnayāna sūtras, or such of the Buddha's discourses as were preserved, compiled, and edited exclusively under coenobitical auspices, uphold as the highest spiritual goal the attainment of Arhantship or individual liberation from the bondage of conditioned existence. The Mahāyāna sūtras, on the other hand, advocate the supremacy of the Bodhisattva ideal, that is to say the ideal of a life dedicated to the attainment of Supreme Enlightenment not for one's own sake only but for the good and benefit of all sentient beings. Nevertheless, the difference is not absolute, and traces of the Mahāyāna ideal are discernible, here and there, in the Hīnayāna *suttas*, quite apart from the fact of its being fully exemplified in the Buddha's own life as depicted even by those sources. Similarly the Mahāyāna sūtras recognize Arhantship as a stage of spiritual development, though not as the highest stage.

Probably what first strikes one on turning, say, from a *sutta* of the *Majjhima Nikāya* to the *Saddharma-puṇḍarīka* or *Prajñā-pāramitā*, is their marked difference in amplitude of extension. While the former occupies not more than a dozen printed pages, each of the latter comprises at least a volume. The major Mahāyāna sūtras are, in fact, known as *vaipulya* sūtras, or discourses of great length, or expanded, amplified, and developed discourses. The cognomen is indicative of much more than the size of these texts, though a reference thereto is not excluded. It mainly serves to point out that, in principle at least, each of them embodies not merely this or that individual item of the Buddha's teaching but a comprehensive presentation of the total Dharma which, in respect of both theory and practice, is complete in itself without reference to any alternative formulation.

Each such presentation is made from a certain angle of vision, or in accordance with the needs of a particular type of mentality, and it is this circumstance which invests each vaipulya sūtra with its distinctive individual character. One treats the Dharma in terms of philosophic principles, one in terms of the personality of the Buddha, one in terms of practical religious ideals, and so on, but in each case it is the total Dharma which is so treated. Such an approach differs radically from that of the Abhidharma, and implies that the Dharma, far from being a closed list of lists, is a living spiritual principle capable of assuming, in its entirety, new aspects and new forms in accordance with the differing needs of sentient beings.

For this reason each vaipulya sūtra is also called a *dharma-paryāya*, a term which bears in this context almost the sense of *upāya-kauśalya* or 'skilful means', and which may therefore be rendered not simply as an exposition or elucidation of the Doctrine, its literal meaning, but as an exposition which for a certain type of religious person functions as sufficient means for a full realization of the import of the Doctrine. Containing as they did the whole Dharma, most of the great Mahāyāna sūtras eventually attracted their own groups of adherents who, without disrespect to the rest of the canon, concentrated more or less exclusively on the study and practice of the sūtra of their choice. In the case of Far Eastern Buddhism, this was one of the factors responsible for the development of the various doctrinal and practical schools.

Yet the real nature of the difference between the Mahāyāna and the Hīnayāna sūtras is not disclosed by any of the traditional appellations. To put the matter as briefly as possible, the former are more universal. The Hīnayāna sūtras, too, are universal in the sense that their message is addressed to humanity at large – in the traditional phrase, 'to gods and men' – and not merely to the members of a particular class or community. Yet at the same time, quite apart from any limitations imposed by the nature of the Hīnayāna spiritual ideal, the Āgama/Nikāya dialogues and discourses have as their venue a definite location in space and time. They occur embodied in a specific historic moment which, while serving to reveal, may equally well conceal, their fundamental significance. Even as the Buddha himself, far from appearing on the stage of history in his true spiritual glory, instead

> Looks through the horizontal misty air
> Shorn of his beams[74]

in the guise of a shabbily dressed *parivrājaka*, so the Hīnayāna sūtras are not only replete with allusions to contemporary events, customs, conditions, and personalities but perforce employ the contemporary religious and philosophical idiom, with all the possibilities for misunderstanding that this entails.

The Mahāyāna sūtras, on the other hand, are emancipated from the historical context. Besides proclaiming a universal spiritual ideal, that of the Bodhisattva, they frequently have for their background a radiant and flower-adorned cosmos transcending the universe of space and time. Their language is not that of ordinary life but a sonorous and hieratic speech saturated with colour and loaded with imagery. Spiritual truths are conveyed, not through the medium of words alone, but symbolically by means of gorgeous phantasmagoria. Sometimes there are tremendous silences lasting for ages. In other words, whereas the Hīnayāna sūtras are preached by the Buddha's *nirmāṇakāya* or 'Created Body', those of the Mahāyāna are revealed, either directly or indirectly, by his *sambhogakāya* or 'Body of Glory'. The audience therefore consists not only of monks, nuns, laymen, and laywomen but of a multitude of Bodhisattvas and other exalted spiritual beings. Moreover, emancipated as they often are from the immediate historical context, and revealed in a supra-spatial and supra-temporal spiritual plane, the Mahāyāna sūtras are not really to be thought of as having been delivered, once and for all, on a particular occasion, in a particular spot, to a particular audience. Though each sūtra begins with the traditional formula 'Thus have I heard', followed by specific details of the place and the congregation, they in fact represent the eternal outpourings of the Absolute, the Buddha's unceasing communication to the members of his spiritual family of the inexhaustible content of his transcendental experience. They are the sacred word which, uttered everlastingly on the heights of existence, reverberates throughout limitless space and unending time. As such they are accessible, not only indirectly by way of the canonical texts bearing their names, but directly to all who, during the lifetime of the Buddha's *nirmāṇakāya* or at any other time, are capable of ascending in meditation to the plane on which the Body of Glory eternally reveals them to the Bodhisattvas.

Besides being different from those of the Hīnayāna, the Mahāyāna sūtras are much more difficult to describe. In fact, the difficulty is due to the difference. The contents of a work of symbolic religious art, which is what many of the Mahāyāna sūtras are, cannot really be summarized in the way that those of a quasi-scientific treatise can. A description of a work of art must, to do justice to it, be itself a work of art, as in the case of the celebrated word picture of the *Mona Lisa* beginning, 'She is older than the rocks among which she sits ...'. Only a sūtra can adequately summarize a sūtra, as the *Hṛdaya* or *Heart Sūtra* does for the *Prajñā-pāramitā* corpus.

Even supposing this difficulty to be overcome by a modern Walter Pater or Bodhisattva Avalokiteśvara, others remain that are insuperable. To begin with, though tradition speaks of a council presided over by Mañjuśrī at which the Mahāyāna sūtras were recited, there is actually no definitive collection or fixed canon of these works. The Buddhists of Nepal venerate a series of texts known as the nine Dharmas, which is probably short for the nine *Dharma-paryāyas*; but whether this catalogue reflects traditions of ancient Indian or modern Nepalese origin, or when or in accordance with what principle, if any, it was compiled, we have no means of telling. The nine Dharmas, also termed vaipulya sūtras, are: *Aṣṭasāhasrikā Prajñā-pāramitā, Saddharma-puṇḍarīka, Lalita-vistara, Laṅkāvatāra, Suvarṇa-prabhāsa, Gaṇḍavyūha, Guhyasamāja, Samādhirāja* and *Daśabhumīśvara*. Of these the third is a biography of the Buddha and the seventh not a sūtra at all but a *tantra*.

The Tibetan and the various Chinese Tripiṭakas are not regular canons, in the sense of bodies of texts which some competent authority, after careful scrutiny, has pronounced authentic, so much as collected editions of whatever translations of sūtras happened to be available at the time of their compilation. Not a few sūtras have, of course, entirely perished, surviving neither in the original nor in translation. Śāntideva's famous anthology the *Śikṣā-samuccaya* or 'Compendium of Instruction', a handbook for Bodhisattvas, refers by name to, and *inter alia* quotes from, numerous texts which were evidently regarded as canonical in seventh-century India but which are not known from any other source. Many sūtras have come down to us only in translation. Even so, what remains constitutes, in Eliot's words, 'the largest body of sacred writings extant anywhere in the world'.[75]

This fact alone makes a description of the Mahāyāna sūtras a much more onerous undertaking than that of their comparatively manageable Hīnayāna counterparts. Moreover, quite a number of Mahāyāna sūtras seem to have existed in various recensions, and in some cases we possess, besides one or more recensions of the original text, various translations which appear to have been made from recensions different from the ones now extant. Description is made still more difficult by the fact that some sūtras are divided into chapters and others not, as well as by the fact that one and the same sūtra may be so divided in one recension but not in another, or divided differently in different translations. The same sūtra may also circulate under different titles, or quite different sūtras all be known by a single title.

All this, though exasperating to the scholar and confusing to the general reader, is quite in accordance with the overall attitude of the Mahāyāna. As contrasted with more literalist traditions beside which it grew up, and upon which it eventually supervened, it sought to give expression to the spirit rather than merely to conserve the letter of the Buddha's teaching. In fact, though in the course of its subsequent career it sporadically developed a quasi-literalism of its own, so far as the initial historical impulse is concerned it was essentially a movement that, without actually repudiating any of the existing doctrinal categories and disciplinary forms, realized the importance of conserving the essence of the Dharma as a living spiritual force. For this reason it was impossible for it ever to identify the Dharma with any particular set of words and phrases, however sacrosanct, so that the movement tended to adopt towards the textual integrity of the scriptures it produced an attitude of comparative indifference if not of downright negligence. When the meaning was all-important, what did it matter if the wording was altered a little here and there? Indeed, if a new reading gave a better sense than the old, or brought out the significance of the Buddha's teaching more clearly, it was obviously the correct one. Mahāyāna sūtras therefore tend to be even more fluid in form than those of the Hīnayāna had been in the early stages of their composition.

Amongst other resultant inconveniences, this makes them extremely hard to date. Like the Āgamas/Nikāyas they passed through two successive, indeed continuous, stages of transmission, one oral and one literary, and like them underwent, during both stages, a process of accretion. Whether these accretions are regarded as human additions, or as supplementary revelations from the *sambhogakāya*, depends on the point of view adopted.

In the majority of cases it is not known when the sūtras were committed to writing. Some might even have been written down outside India, for instance in Central Asia. This fact need not, of course, militate against their basic authenticity. According to Theravāda tradition, the Pāli canon was committed to writing in Sri Lanka half a millennium after the *parinirvāṇa*. With the exception of a few outstanding works, such as the *Saddharma-puṇḍarīka* and the *Aṣṭasāhasrikā Prajñāpāramitā*, which as literary documents are contemporaneous with the Pāli canon, the Mahāyāna sūtras were committed to writing at a later date, or rather at various later dates. In many cases an upper limit is provided by the Chinese translations, which were always carefully dated. For example, if the Chinese version of a sūtra bears a date corresponding, say, to the year 450CE, we may reasonably infer that the original work must have been in circulation as a literary document for at least a century prior to that time. For how many centuries before that it might have been preserved and handed down we have no means of knowing. But in any case, it is impossible to argue, as some have done, that having been committed to writing at a later date than the contents of the Theravāda Tipiṭaka, the Mahāyāna sūtras are less authentic or even entirely spurious. Even to counter with the plea that as literary documents the Pāli canon and this or that Mahāyāna sūtra are contemporaneous only begs the question. It is better to face the issue squarely and to point out that if a text can be transmitted orally for five centuries it can be transmitted orally for ten. So far as this particular argument is concerned, the canonical literature, whether Hīnayāna or Mahāyāna, stands or falls together. No argument can be brought against the veracity of the Mahāyāna sūtras without simultaneously impugning that of their Hīnayāna counterparts.

This need not prevent us from admitting, at the same time, that in the case of the vaipulya sūtras the process of literary accretion generally lasted much longer. Reference must once again be made to the Chinese translations. If the sūtra translated in 450CE was translated again in 650CE, and if the later version contains a chapter not found in the earlier one, we are justified in concluding that this chapter was probably added during the interval between the two translations. Hence it is clear that the composition of a Mahāyāna sūtra as a literary document might have taken as many as five or six centuries. This too makes dating difficult, especially as the checks from Chinese sources, being partial and incomplete, serve like flashes of lightning on a dark night only to reveal to us how much we cannot see. Taking what appear to be their nuclear chapters as the basis of computation, it is, of course, possible to divide the Mahāyāna sūtras into two groups, an earlier and a later, but in the present state of our knowledge ordering of these texts in approximate chronological sequence is entirely out of the question.

How, then, are we to deal with the Mahāyāna sūtras? An outline of the Mahāyāna canon, such as was given in the case of the Dialogues and Anthologies, is impossible, for no such canon exists. Chronological treatment is precluded, as we have just seen, by the fact that for various reasons the Mahāyāna sūtras are hard to date. The problem is not a new one. Indeed, in ancient times it was rendered more acute still by the belief that these sūtras were all preached in their present form during the earthly lifetime of the Buddha.

The Chinese T'ien-t'ai School, basing itself on Indian traditions, elaborated a doctrine of the Five Periods and Eight Doctrines according to which all the Buddha's discourses, whether Hīnayāna or Mahāyāna, could be distributed into five successive chronological periods, the *Avataṃsaka Sūtra* being preached during the first period, the Āgamas during the second, and so on. Such a classification, though of great interest and value, when taken literally is too artificial, and too much at variance with what we know of the literary history of these texts, to be able to serve our present purpose.

In the absence of an alternative, we shall evade rather than solve the problem by describing only some of the better-known texts, and by dealing with them in two main groups, an earlier and a later. Though within each group chronological sequence will be respected whenever known, it should be remembered that we are concerned with a question infinitely more complex than that of whether a play by Shakespeare is earlier or later than another by Marlowe. As the sūtras of the earlier period assumed their present literary form partly in protest, if not in actual reaction, against the narrowness of the Hīnayāna presentation of the teaching, they tend to be distinguished from those of the later period not only by a more frequent, but also by an unmistakably more urgent and personal, reference to the shortcomings of the disciples and Pratyeka-Buddhas, as the ideal followers of the Hīnayāna are termed. Individually and collectively, indeed, the most important and influential early sūtras give the impression of constituting in the first place a repudiation of the Hīnayāna attitude, and in the second a complete restatement of Buddhism in terms more consonant with the personal example of the Buddha and the spirit of his teaching.

Buddhism being comprised, above all, in the Three Jewels, which constitute its lifeblood, its very heart, and the most precious part of its heritage, the Mahāyāna restatement of Buddhism naturally began with an elucidation of the true meaning of the terms Buddha, Dharma, and Sangha. In the *Saddharma-puṇḍarīka* or 'White Lotus of the True Dharma' the Buddha reveals himself as not merely a human being, but as a cosmic principle, Reality itself. The *Prajñā-pāramitā* or 'Perfection of Wisdom' teaches the emptiness of the dharmas, which the Hīnayāna has regarded as ultimate entities, and by proclaiming the unconditioned identity of the conditioned and the unconditioned breaks down the dualistic basis of religious life. While the *Vimalakīrti-*

*nirdeśa* or 'Exposition of Vimalakīrti' presents the Bodhisattva ideal in its active form as wisdom, and teaches the possibility of its full realization by the layman, the *Sukhāvatī-vyūha* or 'Array of the Happy Land' sūtras, both the Larger and the Smaller, present it, as it were, passively as simple faith in the saving power of the Buddha's Original Vow.

Of course there are overlappings. So closely are the Jewels interconnected, and so much are they the facets of a single iridescent gem, rather than three separate stones, that it is indeed impossible to treat any one of them without reference to the other two. Yet the distribution of relative emphasis as between the sūtras mentioned is, in the case of the early sūtras, sufficiently pronounced to justify our classification.

We shall, therefore, deal first with the *Saddharma-puṇḍarīka*, the *Prajñā-pāramitā*, and the *Vimalakīrti-nirdeśa*, etc. (chapters 9–11), and then with the rest of the Mahāyāna sūtras. It would have conduced to greater symmetry of arrangement if we could have dealt with the late sūtras (chapters 13–15), in the same way as the early sūtras, but though the *Laṅkāvatāra* might be regarded as elucidating the true meaning of the term Dharma, and the *Gaṇḍavyūha* and the *Daśabhūmika* the true meaning of the term Sangha, there was no sūtra in this group that could be regarded as elucidating the true meaning of the term Buddha in the way that the *Saddharma-puṇḍarīka* does. We shall therefore deal with the late sūtras in approximately chronological order.

In any case it should be borne in mind that both the earlier and the late sūtras are being treated not only on a different principle from the Dialogues and Anthologies but on a vastly different scale. The latter is a limitation imposed by the length and number of the works to be reviewed. Treated on the scale on which we have already treated the contents of the Āgamas/Nikāyas, the Mahāyāna sūtras would occupy not merely one chapter, but the whole of this volume. An exception will be made in favour of the *Saddharma-puṇḍarīka* which, being not only intrinsically of the highest importance, but also a means of transition to the Mahāyāna, will be dealt with in greater length than any of the works which follow. Such a course is all the more admissible inasmuch as this scripture illustrates particularly well the characteristics of a vaipulya sūtra.

# 9

# THE SADDHARMA-PUṆḌARĪKA

## The White Lotus of the True Dharma

So far as literary form is concerned, as distinct from doctrinal substance, the *Saddharma-puṇḍarīka* or 'White Lotus of the True Dharma' is contemporaneous, as we have seen, with the Pāli Tipiṭaka. That is to say, it belongs to the first century CE. So much, at least, is generally acknowledged even by the most rigorous of scholars, though sometimes not without the reservation that only the nucleus of the work is as old as this. Winternitz, for example, remarks, 'We shall most probably be right in placing the nucleus of the work as far back as the first century AD, as it is quoted by Nāgārjuna, who probably lived towards the end of the second century AD.'[76] With the exception of chapters 21–26 of the extant Sanskrit text, however, which are patently extraneous, the sūtra is so much a literary unity that it is difficult to pick out any one chapter or group of chapters as constituting its original nucleus. Even so, this is not to assert that even the main body of the sūtra is of one uniform chronological texture throughout. Although – apart from amplifications, elaborations, and minor interpolations – it was not produced by a process of gradual accretion, the character of the work as a literary composition is such as still to admit of differences of age between one portion and another. The differences occur, however, not with regard to the main body of the sūtra taken as a whole but within its individual constituent chapters.

Each of these chapters consists of two kinds of material, one alternating with the other: *gāthaṣ* or verses, and prose. While the language of the former is what is variously termed Mixed or Buddhist Hybrid Sanskrit, or sometimes the Gāthā Dialect, that of the latter is Pure

Sanskrit. The subject matter of the two is more or less identical. As in some other parts of the canon, whatever is said in verse is repeated, sometimes with variations, in the prose portions, so that in the case of the *Saddharma-puṇḍarīka* 'each section, prose and verse, would, if separated, make a fairly complete whole.'[77] For reasons into which we cannot enter here, most scholars believe that the verse portion is on the whole earlier than the prose and that the latter consisted originally of short connecting passages which, as the language of the *gāthās* became obsolete, were expanded so as to constitute a rough guide to the meaning of their more archaic verse counterparts. N. Dutt is apparently of a different opinion. He points out that 'the use of Mixed Sanskrit in the *gāthās* and Pure Sanskrit in the prose portions was the rule in the first or second century AC or earlier when the Mahāyāna texts were being composed for the first time. In the *gāthās*, emphasis was laid more on diction and melody than on grammar, provided the content was anyhow intelligible.'[78]

Whatever be the truth of the matter, it ought in any case to be borne in mind that the terms commonly used by scholars to describe the respective languages of the prose and verse portions of the *Saddharma-puṇḍarīka* are apt to be misleading. This is all the more necessary inasmuch as these terms are used with reference not only to this sūtra but in connection with other canonical works. By 'Pure' Sanskrit is meant that form of the language which conforms to the rules established by the grammarian Pāṇini. Thus neither the Vedas nor the Upaniṣads are written, or rather composed, in Pure Sanskrit. By Mixed Sanskrit, which because it is used in Buddhist works and represents a cross between the literary and the spoken language, is also called Buddhist Hybrid Sanskrit, is meant that form of the language which, instead of conforming to the 'classical' Pāṇinian model, kept close to the richer and grammatically less hidebound speech-forms of the vernacular. Despite the disapproval of modern purists, no pejorative connotation really attaches to the term Mixed Sanskrit. The difference between the two is not unlike that between Elizabethan English, with its greater exuberance, and the more 'correct' medium favoured by writers of Queen Anne's reign.

There appear to have existed two recensions of the *Saddharma-puṇḍarīka*, one consisting of twenty-seven chapters, literally 'turnings' (*parivarta*) of the wheel of the Dharma, and one of twenty-eight. Fortunately for our knowledge of this supremely important work, the former has survived complete in Nepal, whence various copies have been procured, ranging in age from the eleventh to the beginning of the eighteenth century CE. Fragments of much older manuscripts, dating from the fifth to the sixth century and representing both recensions, have also been recovered, in recent times, from Central Asia and eastern Turkestan, while from Gilgit in Kashmir has come an equally ancient copy of more than three-quarters of the work that agrees with the Nepalese manuscripts.

Another manuscript, discovered at Turfan, contains an Uighur-Turkish translation of the *Samantamukha-parivarta*, corresponding to chapter 24 of the complete Sanskrit text, to the divisions of which all our references will be made. This difference in the number of chapters is due, not to the presence in one recension of an additional chapter not found in the other, but simply to the fact that the latter part of chapter 11 in the Nepalese or complete Sanskrit text has been reckoned as an independent chapter.

According to Nanjio, eight or nine translations of this sūtra were made into Chinese, the earliest, now lost, being executed by Dharmarakṣa in the year 265CE. Three translations are still available. The first, that of Dharmarakṣa, a multilingual Yüeh-chih who may or may not be identical with the first translator, was made in 286CE. The second, that of Kumārajīva, followed in 406CE. Both these versions consist of twenty-eight chapters and in both of them, more importantly, chapter 27 of the complete Nepalese Sanskrit text occurs not at the end of the work but about three-fifths of the way through as chapter 23, in the case of Dharmarakṣa's version, and as chapter 24, in the case of Kumārajīva's, the discrepancy being due to the fact that whereas the former places the *Samantamukha-parivarta* immediately before this 'concluding' chapter the latter places it immediately after. What inferences can be drawn from these differences it is difficult to say. Chapter 27 of the Nepalese Sanskrit text undoubtedly forms the natural conclusion of the sūtra, but whether Kumārajīva, realizing that chapters 21–26 (of this text) were an interpolation, relegated them to the end of his version, or whether he found them already so relegated in the Kucha script text from which he is said to have worked, we do not know. The sequence of chapters found in Dharmarakṣa's version, however, may well indicate that the *Samantamukha-parivarta* came to be associated with the *Saddharma-puṇḍarīka* at an earlier date than the remaining five interpolated chapters. The third Chinese translation still extant is that produced in 601CE, by Jñānagupta and Dharmagupta, two monks reputed to be of Indian origin. In number and sequence of chapters this version agrees with the Sanskrit text, as well as with the Tibetan translation.

Of the three versions Kumārajīva's is undoubtedly the most popular. The *Saddharma-puṇḍarīka* is not only a religious classic, but a masterpiece of symbolic spiritual literature, and his rendering, with the help of Chinese poets and scholars during one of the most creative periods of Chinese art and letters, though hardly a literal translation does ample justice to these qualities. It therefore occupies, throughout the Far East, a position analogous to that of the Authorized Version of the Bible in Anglo-Saxon lands.

Scholars have remarked on the comparative paucity of explicit doctrinal instruction in the *Saddharma-puṇḍarīka*. While concurring with their observation, we cannot agree that this constitutes a defect, as they would seem to imply. Corresponding to the distinction between the intellect and the emotions, between science and poetry, there are two great modes for the communication of spiritual truths, and therefore two principal types of religious literature. One mode is conceptual, addressing itself to the understanding by means of abstractions; the other is existential, appealing to the emotions and the will through concrete actions and sensuous images. While the first excogitates systems of religious philosophy and theologies, the second gives birth to magic, myths, and legends. To one, as its natural literary expression, appertains the treatise and the tractate, the polemic, and the discursive, descriptive treatment of religious ideals; to the other the religious drama, the story, and the song. As representatives of the first stand such works as Aristotle's *Metaphysics*, Śaṅkara's commentary on the *Brahma-sūtras*, and St Thomas Aquinas's *Summa Theologica*. The second is exemplified by pre-Euripidean Greek tragedy, the Gospel parables, the stories of Chuang-tzu and St Francis's *Canticle of the Sun*. Broadly speaking, the latter belong to the historically earlier and more creative stages of religious development, the former to the later.

Within the limits of the Buddhist canon, the sciential type of religious literature is represented by the treatises of the Abhidharma Piṭaka and by the *Prajñā-pāramitā* corpus, and the imaginative by the Birth-Stories and the Glorious Deeds, as well as by a class of Mahāyāna sūtras of which the *Saddharma-puṇḍarīka* is the first example. It is, therefore, a mistake to search for, and yet a greater one to bemoan the absence of, a content which the nature of this sūtra as a work of symbolic spiritual literature precludes it from possessing. This is not to say that conceptual elements are altogether lacking. Many of the more important Hīnayāna and Mahāyāna doctrinal categories occur in one place or another; but their position is a subordinate one, and while contributing to the composition of the sūtra, they do not in any way determine its basic structure.

The *Saddharma-puṇḍarīka* constitutes, in fact, a remarkable, perhaps a unique, synthesis of all the principal imaginative elements. In form it is dramatic; its significance resides not only in what is said, but in what is done. For example, instead of merely stating that the more conceited among the śrāvakas were unable to accept the Mahāyāna teaching, it actually shows them, as though on a stage, rising from their seats and quitting the assembly when the Buddha announces that they have something more to learn (chapter 2). Similarly, we are not just given a discourse on the universality of the Mahāyāna, and how the highest spiritual attainment is open to all irrespective of sex, but allowed to see for ourselves the Nāga princess transforming herself, in the twinkling of an eye, into a male Bodhisattva, departing for a distant universe called, significantly, 'The Pure' (*vimalā nāma lokadhātu*), and becoming a Buddha there (chapter 11).

Soothill – from whose incomplete but poetic version from Kumārajīva most of our quotations will be taken – is therefore right in his general estimation of the sūtra:

> From the first chapter we find The Lotus Sūtra to be unique in the world of religious literature. A magnificent apocalyptic, it presents a spiritual drama of the highest order, with the universe as its stage, eternity as its period, and Buddhas, gods, men, devils, as the dramatis personae. From the most distant worlds and from past aeons, the eternal Buddhas throng the stage to hear the mighty Buddha proclaim his ancient and eternal Truth. Bodhisattvas flock to his feet; gods from the heavens, men from all quarters of the earth, the tortured from the deepest hells, the demons themselves crowd to hear the tones of the Glorious One.[79]

Obviously such a drama as this is not naturalistic but symbolic.

The *Saddharma-puṇḍarīka* has for one of its principal contents another of the grand imaginative elements, namely myth and legend.

Instead of depicting the petty vicissitudes of human life, much of it describes the sublime activities of colossal and mysterious beings, Buddhas and Bodhisattvas, in world systems unthinkably remote from our own in both space and time. Dramatic unity is preserved by the device of a Jātaka-like identification of one or another of these beings, or one of their disciples, with Mañjuśrī, or Maitreya, or one of the other actors in the drama, including its great protagonist, Śākyamuni himself. Such descriptions do not merely illustrate the universality of the Mahāyāna and its teaching in a general way. For when Śākyamuni takes his seat in the sky, with Prabhūtaratna, on a single lion throne, the incident is clearly symbolical, showing that the two Buddhas, the former belonging to the present and the latter to the infinitely remote past, are in essence one, and that in the Mind of Supreme Enlightenment distinctions of time and place are transcended (chapter 11).

Closely connected with the myths and legends are the phantasmagoria. Just as the former, though understood literally by Mahāyānists in the past, are essentially neither history nor geography, so the latter are not really magic. Śākyamuni projects from between his eyebrows a ray of light which reveals all the worlds in the eastern quarter (chapter 1). Or, to take a more striking, perhaps even grotesque, example, he and the vast concourse of Buddhas foregathered from other worlds protrude their tongues until they reach up to the Brahmā world, thus illuminating all directions of space (chapter 21). Except in appearance, these are not exhibitions of supernormal power like the Double Miracle (*yamaka-ṛddhi*) at Śrāvastī, when the Master walked up and down in the air emitting simultaneously from his body streams of water and flames of fire. They are visual symbols, and like the myths and legends their real import is spiritual. The ray issuing from between the Buddha's eyebrows is the light of Truth, which does not annihilate the world of concrete particulars but, on the contrary, transfigures it and reveals its true meaning and significance. In the same way the protrusion of the organ of speech symbolizes the Absolute's unlimited power of communication with sentient beings.

Yet despite this predominance of the existential mode, action no more excludes utterance in the *Saddharma-puṇḍarīka* than it does in other forms of dramatic composition. Truth is not only exhibited but also explained. Even here, however, the sūtra remains true to its essential nature. Though conceptual statement is not absent, the favourite medium for the explicit communication of its central teaching is the parable.

The parables of the *Saddharma-puṇḍarīka* are unsurpassed in the entire range of Buddhist literature, and, together with the grandiose conception of the whole work, they stamp this sūtra ineffaceably with the hallmark of literary genius. All the more important of them are summarized below. Especially with reference to the Buddha's Enlightenment, or to his knowledge, the sūtra moreover attempts to convey the meaning of infinity not mathematically but by means of concrete images. We are not told how many aeons have passed since a certain Buddha attained *parinirvāṇa*, but asked to imagine the earth-element of a whole galactic system ground into ink and then someone going in an eastern direction and letting fall one drop every time he had traversed a thousand such systems: the time which has passed since that Buddha's *parinirvāṇa* would still immeasurably exceed the time needed to exhaust the ink (chapter 7). Here this mode of expression, too, is in keeping with the fundamentally non-conceptual character of the sūtra.

As in the case of a number of other sūtras, both Hīnayāna and Mahāyāna, the venue of the great revelation is the Gṛdhrakūṭa or 'Vulture's Peak' overlooking Rājagṛha. In the *Saddharma-puṇḍarīka*, however, the earth is spiritualized, and the Peak represents, not a geographical expression, but the summit of existence. This is indicated by the fact that around the Buddha are gathered not only 12,000 Arhants but 80,000 Bodhisattvas, besides tens of thousands of gods and other non-human beings with their followers. To this vast assembly he preaches the vaipulya sutrānta known as the *Mahā-nirdeśa* or 'Great Exposition'. Flowers fall from the heavens and the universe shakes. He then enters into deep meditation, whereupon there issues from between his eyebrows a ray of light which illumines, upward to their highest heavens and downwards to their lowest hells, innumerable world-systems in the infinitude of space, revealing in each one of them a Buddha teaching the Dharma to his disciples, and Bodhisattvas sacrificing life and limbs for the sake of Supreme Enlightenment. Voicing the curiosity of the whole congregation, Maitreya enquires of Mañjuśrī the meaning of this sublime spectacle. The latter, who has witnessed such wonders before, under previous Buddhas, replies that the emission of the ray has always preceded the promulgation of the

*Saddharma-puṇḍarīka Sūtra*, which he believes the present Exalted one to be about to preach (chapter 1).

Emerging from his meditation, the Buddha proceeds to justify the transition between the more elementary teaching to which he had hitherto confined himself and the higher one now to be disclosed. Addressing Śāriputra, and through him the whole assembly, he declares that truth in its plenitude can be understood only by the Tathāgatas. Others must have faith in the word of the Buddha and approach it gradually, step by step, through a series of progressive stages. For this reason it had been necessary for him to preach, by way of introduction, first the lower, preparatory ideals of the Arhant and the Pratyeka-Buddha. Had he all at once revealed to his disciples the highest truth, telling them outright that they too were one day to attain Supreme Enlightenment, they would never have believed him. Even now, despite the entreaties of Śāriputra, he is doubtful whether the congregation is ready for his ultimate revelation. For some, who refuse to accept it, it may even be an occasion of spiritual disaster. As though in confirmation of his words, 5,000 Hīnayāna disciples, recoiling in dismay from the threatened supersession of their cherished ideals and achievements, withdraw from the assembly. To the faithful that remain, Bodhisattvas and disciples (*śrāvakas*) both, the Buddha reveals the final truth.

The three different *yānas* or vehicles which he has appeared to preach, representing the Arhant, the Pratyeka-Buddha, and the Bodhisattva ideals, are only temporary expedients made necessary by the diversity of temperament among the disciples, as well as by their varying degrees of spiritual development. In reality there is but One Vehicle (*ekayāna*), the Great Vehicle (*mahāyāna*), wherein the Buddha himself abides and by means of which he delivers sentient beings, leading them from the provisional to the final truth, from partial to complete Enlightenment. Were he to act otherwise he would be guilty of spiritual selfishness. Supreme Buddhahood alone is for all the ultimate goal. Whoever practise the *pāramitās*, 'engage in devotional observances' – offering even a single flower in worship – have, as it were, already become Buddhas. The one thing needful is faith (*śraddhā*), not in the sense of belief in unverifiable propositions, but in that of the existential response of one's total being when confronted by the image of the highest spiritual perfection (chapter 2).

This response the Buddha's words elicit from Śāriputra, who, overjoyed that he is to become a Fully Enlightened One, regrets having hitherto devoted himself to the realization of an inferior ideal. The Buddha tells him that he and the other disciples took the Bodhisattva vow under him aeons ago, but that temporarily forgetful of the fact he had, in his present existence, wrongly imagined the Hīnayānic Nirvāṇa to be the highest possible achievement. In the inconceivably distant future, he predicts, Śāriputra will become a Tathāgata called Padmaprabhāsa or 'Lotus Radiance', his Buddha-field (*-kṣetra*) will be known as the Vimala, 'Dustless' or 'Passionless', and his aeon (*kalpa*) as the Mahāratnaprati-maṇḍita or 'Great Jewel-Adorned'. He will train and mature countless Bodhisattvas.

Though Śāriputra had accepted the new dispensation with such alacrity, other members of the congregation are still tormented by doubts. Was the previous teaching actually false? Have they gained nothing at all by following it so devotedly over such a long period? Has the Buddha not deceived them? In order to reassure and finally convince these disciples the Buddha tells the first of his tremendous parables, that of the Burning House. At great length, with splendour of language and abundance of picturesque detail, he describes how a prominent elder, possessed of inexhaustible riches, lived with his numerous progeny in an old, dilapidated, vermin-infested mansion. One day fire breaks out. The children, absorbed in play, do not notice what has happened; but their father, who is outside, realizes that they are in imminent danger of destruction and calls to them to come out. Since they ignore his appeals, and go on playing, he resolves to have recourse to a stratagem. Knowing that his boys were inordinately fond of playthings of various kinds, he again calls out to them, this time promising to some goat-carts, to others deer-carts, and to yet others bullock-carts. On hearing these words they all come rushing and tumbling out of the burning house. Having brought them to safety, the elder bestows upon them, in response to their demands, not the three different kinds of cart actually promised, but bullock-carts only, all of the most splendid workmanship imaginable. For he feels that possessed as he is of inexhaustible riches it would be unbecoming for him to bestow upon his own offspring inferior things. The burning house is conditioned existence; the children, sentient beings; the wise elder, the Buddha. By the three kinds of vehicle are typified the Arhant, the Pratyeka-Buddha, and the Bodhisattva ideals. The bullock-carts in which, after their escape from the house, the children all equally ride, is the Buddhayāna or Mahāyāna. In promising one thing and giving another the elder was not guilty of falsehood, for he had from the beginning determined to save his children by means of an expedient. No more, therefore, is the Buddha himself guilty of falsehood in first preaching the Three Vehicles to attract all sentient beings and afterwards saving them by means of the One Vehicle only (chapter 3).

This parable is not without effect. Four of the leading elders, Subhūti, Mahākātyāyana, Mahākāśyapa, and Mahāmaudgalyāyana, though at first amazed by the Buddha's prediction of Śāriputra to Supreme Enlightenment, now realize that even for Arhants like themselves who, owing to age and decrepitude, have so far remained content with the Hīnayānic Nirvāṇa, it is not too late to transfer their allegiance to the higher Bodhisattva ideal and aspire after Buddhahood. Elated by the glorious prospect, they give expression to their joy, which Mahākāśyapa, with the Buddha's permission, explains in the form of a parable. A young man has left home and for many years wandered from place to place abroad, becoming all the while poorer and more wretched. His father, after searching for him in vain, settles in a certain city and, engaging in business, amasses immense riches. Eventually, by accident, the son reaches that very place and happens to see his father seated in his mansion surrounded by all the paraphernalia of wealth, but cannot recognize him. The rich man, however, at once recognizes his son, and dispatches his attendants to call him. The poor wretch, afraid of being arrested, falls down senseless with fear. Realizing that years of poverty have debased his son's mind, the rich man decides not to announce their relationship all at once. Instead, he sends first an attendant to set him at liberty, and afterwards two shabbily dressed men to hire him as a scavenger. When he has been employed for some time the father, disguising himself, contrives to approach him periodically, admonishing him to work well, promising to increase his wages, and eventually declaring that he will henceforth regard him as his own son. As a result of this treatment, mutual confidence develops between the two, and the son gradually learns to go in and out of his adoptive father's mansion as he pleases. One day the rich man falls ill, and knowing he will soon die, commits the management of his entire property, and all his affairs, to the son, who is now equal to the responsibility. Finally, on his deathbed, he publicly relates the whole story, declaring that the supposed manager is in reality his son and the natural heir to his immense riches. The son, on hearing these words, is filled with joy at such an unexpected stroke of good fortune.

As Mahākāśyapa proceeds to explain, the rich man is the Buddha, while the poor son represents himself and the other disciples who, after removing the dirt of the passions, have been content to receive Nirvāṇa as it were for their day's wages. The announcement that the real relation between the two was that of father and son is like the Buddha's declaration that the Arhants are not hirelings of the Dharma but his own true sons, that is to say Bodhisattvas, and heirs to the infinite riches of Supreme Enlightenment. Like the poor man, they too are astounded and rejoice (chapter 4).

Praising the four elders for their discernment, the Buddha explains that the qualities of the Tathāgata are beyond calculation. Knowing as he does both the Absolute Truth and the inmost hearts of sentient beings, he leads them into the way of Supreme Enlightenment by tactfully adapting his teachings to their individual dispositions and capacities. This procedure is illustrated by two parables. A dense raincloud arises, its moisture universally nourishing the plants, shrubs, and trees; but though nourished by the same rain, and springing from a common soil, all these grow according to their own species, and bring forth different kinds of flowers and fruits. In the same way the Buddha preaches one universal Dharma, but sentient beings are benefited by it in accordance with their different capacities. Again, as the sun shines on all alike, making no distinction of great or small, high or low, so the Buddha diffuses over all beings impartially the Light of Truth.

At this point Mahākāśyapa raises various questions, which the Buddha answers with the help of two more parables. According to the first of these the differences of nomenclature between the three *yānas* is comparable to that between, for example, a curd-jar, a butter-jar, and so on, which derive their respective designations from their contents, the jars themselves being the same. Even so, though the Buddhayāna is one only, three *yānas* are spoken of by the Tathāgatas by reason of the difference of mental endowment among sentient beings. In the second parable, a blind man, after having his eyesight restored by a skilful physician, is urged to acquire, by means of meditation, the still more powerful supernormal vision of the Saint. Just as ordinary eyesight occupies an intermediate place between blindness and yogic vision, so the Nirvāṇa of the Arhants constitutes a respite on the way from a state of spiritual ignorance to the final and complete illumination of a Buddha. Ultimately there is one Nirvāṇa for the followers of all three *yānas*, not three separate Nirvāṇas (chapter 5). Mahākāśyapa and his brother elders being now satisfied by these explanations, Śākyamuni predicts that they too, after worshipping countless Buddhas and erecting stupas over their remains, will attain to Supreme Enlightenment. The names by which they will then be known, together with those of the Buddha-fields over which they will preside and the aeons in which they will flourish, are also particularized (chapter 6).

Interest now shifts from the future to the past. Addressing the whole body of his disciples, the Buddha speaks of Mahābhijñājñānābhibhū, a Tathāgata who had flourished incalculable aeons earlier and whose career in certain respects parallels his own. While the rest of this Buddha's followers had remained content with the Hīnayāna doctrine, his sixteen *śrāmaṇera* sons, born before his retirement from the world, had aspired to Supreme Enlightenment, and for their benefit he had preached the *Saddharma-puṇḍarīka*. All of them had subsequently been crowned with the highest spiritual achievement, the youngest being none other than the speaker, Śākyamuni, himself. The countless beings to whom the sixteen, as *śrāmaṇeras*, had given instruction, were now reborn as human beings and had become Hīnayāna bhikshus. Similarly those who, at the time of his *parinirvāṇa*, were still unable to accept the Mahāyāna, would be reborn in other world-systems where, under his guidance, they would continue their training and be led, eventually, into the way of Supreme Enlightenment.

His seeming entry into *parinirvāṇa* was only a device for training monks of lower aims. In reality there could be only one *parinirvāṇa* and one *yāna*, not a second or a third. The Tathāgata preached the Hīnayāna Nirvāṇa for the sake of those who were bent on the enjoyment of trifling things and deeply attached to human desires. This is illustrated by a parable. A guide is conducting a large party of travellers through a dense forest, along a dangerous and difficult road, to Ratnadvīpa, 'The Place of Jewels', their destination. On the way the travellers become exhausted, and tell the guide they want to turn back. The latter, out of pity, thereupon conjures up a magic city and invites them to rest and refresh themselves therein. Only when they have regained their strength does he cause the city to disappear and urge them to complete their journey. The magical city is the Hīnayānic Nirvāṇa conjured up, as it were, by the Buddha out of compassion for those who might otherwise have turned back, discouraged, before reaching Supreme Enlightenment. It is a temporary, provisional state, for the true Nirvāṇa is Buddhahood itself.

> The Buddhas, the onward Leaders,
> Call the resting-place Nirvana,
> But, perceiving their people rested,
> They lead on to Buddha-Wisdom.[80]
> (chapter 7)

The effects of Śākyamuni's exhortations now begin to be felt among the congregation at large, and more and more disciples come forward to confess their shortcomings and announce their acceptance of the new teaching. Pūrṇa Maitrāyaṇīputra, whom the Buddha extols as the foremost of his preachers, is predicted to Supreme Enlightenment, likewise five hundred other distinguished Arhants. As Mahākāśyapa had done, they give expression to their feelings by means of a parable which, being shorter than most of the others, may be quoted in full:

> World-honoured One! It is as if some man goes to an intimate friend's house, gets drunk, and falls asleep. Meanwhile his friend, having to go forth on official duty, ties a priceless jewel within his garment as a present, and departs. The man, being drunk and asleep, knows nothing of it. On arising he travels onward till he reaches some other country, where for food and clothing he expends much labour and effort, and undergoes exceedingly great hardship, and is content even if he can obtain but little. Later, his friend happens to meet him and speaks thus: 'Tut! Sir, how is it you have come to this for the sake of food and clothing? Wishing you to be in comfort and able to satisfy all your five senses, I formerly in such a year and month and on such a day tied a priceless jewel within your garment. Now as of old it is present there and you in ignorance are slaving and worrying to keep yourself alive. How very stupid! Go you now and exchange that jewel for

what you need and do whatever you will, free from all poverty and shortage.'[81]

The jewel represents the aspiration after Supreme Enlightenment which, though taught them by the Buddha in a previous existence, the Arhants had temporarily forgotten (chapter 8).

Further predictions follow. Ānanda, Rāhula, and 2,000 other disciples are in turn assured of the highest spiritual perfection. The apparent favouritism shown to Ānanda, whose prediction is couched in particularly glowing terms, is explained as the consequence of his Original Vow that, till the time of his own Supreme Enlightenment, he would be the guardian of the Dharma of future Buddhas (chapter 9).

The Hīnayāna disciples having been persuaded to accept the higher spiritual ideal, Śākyamuni impresses upon all the Bodhisattvas present the supreme importance of the *Saddharma-puṇḍarīka* and the necessity for its preservation. Addressing the Bodhisattva Bhaiṣajyarāja or 'King of Healing', he declares that those sentient beings, of the various types and classes represented in the assembly, who hear but a single verse or word of this sūtra, or by so much as a single thought delight in it, are all assured of Supreme Enlightenment. Moreover, the written text is not only to be read, recited, copied, and expounded, but ceremonially worshipped with all manner of precious things. Thereby incalculable spiritual benefits will accrue. On the other hand, while all other blasphemy, even of the Buddha, is comparatively trivial, the sin of abusing this sūtra, or defaming its devotees, is extremely grave. Such, indeed, is its transcendent virtue, that beings having even the remotest connection with it are blessed. Those who worship it become themselves worthy of worship.

In particular should the preacher of this sūtra be honoured – even with flowers, perfumes, and jewels. The preacher himself, however, must be endowed with qualities commensurate with those of the discourse. He should 'enter into the abode of the Tathāgata, be clad with the Robe of the Tathāgata, and sit on the sacred Seat of the Tathāgata.... The abode of the Tathāgata is love (*maitrī*) towards all sentient beings. The Robe of the Tathāgata is great patient forbearance (*mahākṣanti*). The sacred Seat of the Tathāgata is the Voidness of all the elements of existence (*sarvadharma-śūnyatā*).'[82] Besides cherishing and protecting such a preacher, Śākyamuni promises, he will from time to time appear before him in a pure and shining spiritual form (chapter 10).

This assurance having been given, we come to the most impressively dramatic scene of the whole marvellous pageant. Suddenly there springs up from the earth, and towers into the sky, a stupa of stupendous size and unbelievable magnificence. Made of the seven precious things, and most superbly adorned, its light, fragrance, and music fill the entire earth. From the midst of the stupa there comes a mighty voice praising Śākyamuni for his preaching of the *Saddharma-puṇḍarīka* and bearing witness to the truth of all that he has said. In response to the enquiry of Mahāpratibhāna or 'Great Eloquence', a Bodhisattva, Śākyamuni explains that the stupa contains the entire body of an ancient Buddha called Prabhūtaratna, or 'Abundant Treasures', who, ages ago, had made a vow that, after his *parinirvāṇa*, his stupa would spring forth wherever the *Saddharma-puṇḍarīka* was being expounded, so that he would bear testimony to the truth of its teaching.

The assembly is naturally desirous of beholding the actual body of the Tathāgata, miraculously preserved within the stupa. But according to another vow made by Prabhūtaratna, if a Buddha in whose presence his stupa has sprung forth is desirous of showing him to his disciples, that Buddha must first of all cause all the Buddhas who have emanated from him, and who are preaching the Dharma throughout the universe, to return and assemble in one place. To fulfil this condition, Śākyamuni emanates a ray which illuminates innumerable pure Buddha-fields in the ten directions of space, revealing the Buddhas there. Knowing the significance of the summons, each of them informs the host of his Bodhisattvas that they must go to the Sahā-world and worship Śākyamuni Buddha and the stupa of the Tathāgata 'Abundant Treasures'. Thereupon the Sahā-world is instantly purified for their reception. The earth, transformed into the blue radiance of lapis lazuli, becomes adorned with jewel trees, and marked off in squares with golden cords. Gods and men, other than those of the congregation, are translated elsewhere; villages, towns, mountains, rivers, and forests disappear. The earth smokes with incense, and its ground is strewn with heavenly flowers.

To a world so purified come 500 Buddhas, each attended by a great Bodhisattva, and take their seats on 500 magnificent lion thrones beneath as many jewel trees. All the available space in the world-system is thus already exhausted, and the Buddhas who have emanated from Śākyamuni Buddha have hardly begun to arrive. In the same way that he has already purified and transformed the Sahā-world, the latter therefore purifies for the reception of the incoming multitudes untold millions of worlds in the eight directions of space. Only when all these Buddhas have arrived, taken their seats beneath the innumerable jewel trees, and worshipped him each with a double handful of jewel-flowers does Śākyamuni, understanding the desire of the congregation, ascend into the sky and with a sound like thunder open the door of the stupa.

Seated in his entire body, within, as though meditating, they see the Buddha Prabhūtaratna, who, lifting up his voice, again commends Śākyamuni. Awestruck, the congregation praises the unprecedented marvel, and scatters over the two Buddhas heaps of celestial jewel-flowers. Prabhūtaratna invites Śākyamuni to share his throne. Seeing the two Buddhas seated side by side in the stupa, far above their heads, the congregation desires to be raised to the same level. Whereupon, by his supernormal power, Śākyamuni receives the whole assembly into the sky, at the same time demanding, in a loud voice: 'Who is able to declare the *Saddharma-puṇḍarīka Sūtra* in this Sahā-world? Now indeed is the time. The Tathāgata not long hence must enter Nirvāṇa. The Buddha desires to bequeath this *Saddarma-puṇḍarīka Sūtra*, so that it may endure for ever.'[83]

Before anyone can reply there occurs the episode, or rather the group of episodes, that constitutes chapter 12 of Kumārajīva's Chinese version. In the extant Sanskrit text this forms the latter half of the previous chapter. Interrupting to some extent the continuity of the 'action', it may well be an interpolation; though in spirit and style it fully accords with the text as so far delivered. The Buddha recounts how, in one of his previous existences, he had as a king sacrificed possessions, body, and life itself for the sake of the Dharma. Eventually, after abdicating in favour of his son and making a public proclamation offering himself as a servant to whomsoever would teach him a Great Vehicle, he had received the *Saddharma-puṇḍarīka* from a hermit. This hermit was none other than Devadatta who also, the Buddha now predicts, in the far distant future will become a Tathāgata. Numerous advantages, moreover, will accrue from the hearing of this 'Devadatta Chapter' of the sūtra.

At this point occurs an interruption. Emerging from the nadir, a Bodhisattva named Prajñākūṭa, or 'Wisdom-Heap', solicits the return of Prabhūtaratna to his own world-system. At Śākyamuni's request, however, the latter stays to have a talk with Mañjuśrī, who arrives on a thousand-petalled lotus from the Nāga Palace in the depths of the ocean, where he had converted innumerable beings. In the course of conversation it transpires that his most gifted pupil is the eight-year-old daughter of the Nāga king, who has, so the great Bodhisattva declares, the power of speedily attaining Buddhahood. Prajñākūṭa doubts this; but the princess appears in person before them, and extols the Buddha in verse. Śāriputra is still more sceptical, doubting not only that she should be able to attain Buddhahood speedily, but that a woman should be capable of such an achievement at all. However, the princess transforms herself into a male Bodhisattva who, going instantly to a distant world-system, attains Supreme Enlightenment there and preaches the Dharma.

Both these episodes illustrate the universality of the Mahāyāna, from the benefits of which even evil-doers like Devadatta are not excluded, and within whose embrace superficial differences such as those of age and sex have no significance (chapter 11).

No sooner are they over than a response to Śākyamuni's demand for persons able to declare the sūtra is forthcoming. Bhaiṣajyarāja and another Bodhisattva, appropriately called Mahāpratibhāna, or 'Great Eloquence', declare their readiness to preserve and propagate it throughout the world-system after his *parinirvāṇa*. Even in the evil age to come, they promise, when beings would be difficult to convert, they will patiently propagate this sūtra, pay it every kind of homage, and be unsparing of body and life. All the Arhants who have been predicted to Buddhahood pledge themselves to do likewise. Seeing Mahāprajāpati Gautami and Yaśodharā standing disconsolate, as no prediction has been made concerning them, Śākyamuni not only assures his foster-mother and former wife that they were included in his previous prediction of the entire assembly to Buddhahood but now gives them each an individual prediction, whereupon, amidst universal rejoicings, they undertake to preserve and propagate the sūtra throughout all world-systems except the Sahā-world, which has already been covered by the preceding vows.

Finally, having appealed in vain for an absolute directive from the Buddha, the Irreversible Bodhisattvas announce their determination to disseminate it throughout the world-systems in all the directions of space. These various promises given, the assembly in unison begs the Buddha to have no anxiety about the future of the sūtra, assuring him that despite abuse, calumny, and persecution, it will proclaim it in the dreadful dark age to come (chapter 12). Mañjuśrī points out that this is a tremendous responsibility. The Buddha, agreeing with him, declares that in order to accomplish their mission the Bodhisattvas will have to be endowed with four qualities (*dharmas*). They must (1) be perfect in their conduct (*ācāra*), (2) confine themselves to their proper sphere of activity, avoiding unsuitable company, and dwelling inwardly in the true nature of Reality, (3) maintain a happy, peaceful state of mind (*sukhasthita*), unaffected by zeal or envy, and (4) cultivate feelings of love (*maitrī*) towards all sentient beings. These are explained in detail, the exposition constituting a fine description not only of the ideal preacher of the sūtra, but also, in effect, of the perfect monk as conceived by the Mahāyāna. Endowed with such qualities, the Buddha tells the assembly, a Bodhisattva will be able to gain a hearing from all classes of people, from kings and ministers to ordinary householders. He impresses upon the minds of his auditors the unique value of the sūtra committed to their charge by means of the following parable.

Desirous of extending his domains, a great 'wheel-rolling' (*cakravarti*) king goes to war. His soldiers fight heroically, so that, well pleased with their conduct, the king bestows upon them, according to their desert, all manner of things by way of reward, from houses and lands, including whole cities, to gorgeous apparel, slaves, conveyances, and treasures of gold, silver, and gems. Only the crown-jewel on his head he gives to none. Even so the Tathāgata, pleased with the conduct of his disciples in the holy war against Māra, graces them with spiritual gifts such as the meditations, the emancipations, and the powers, together with the whole wealth of the Dharma. In addition, he gives them the city of Nirvāṇa. Yet he does not yet preach to them the *Saddharma-puṇḍarīka Sūtra*. However, just as the king, seeing the valour of his troops, eventually bestows upon them even the priceless crown-jewel itself, so the Tathāgata, beholding the exploits of his spiritual warriors, at last reveals to them this supreme sūtra (chapter 13).

The great Bodhisattvas, numerous as the sands of the Ganges, who have come with their Buddhas from the other world-systems, now offer their services to Śākyamuni in his Buddha-field. Telling them that their help is not required, the latter declares that he has in his Sahā-world innumerable Bodhisattvas who will be able, after his *parinirvāṇa*, to protect and keep, read and recite, and preach abroad the sūtra. At this the universe trembles and quakes, and from the space below the earth there issues a great host of Irreversible Bodhisattvas all accompanied by their retinues. Advancing one by one, they salute in turn all the Buddhas, beginning with Śākyamuni and Prabhūtaratna, and then glorify them in various hymns. So numerous are the Bodhisattvas that these proceedings occupy fifty minor *kalpas*, during which time the whole assembly remains silent; but through the supernormal power of Śākyamuni the period seems but half a day. An exchange of civilities follows between Śākyamuni and the four leaders of the vast host.

Maitreya and the disciples, who all this while have been amazed at the sudden apparition of all these unknown Bodhisattvas, ask whence they have sprung and how Śākyamuni can claim them for his own. The disciples of the other Buddhas present put each to their own Buddha the same question. Approving their enquiries, and urging them to be resolute, Śākyamuni tells Maitreya:

> Ajita! Know thou!
> These Great Bodhisattvas,
> Who, from past numberless kalpas,
> Have observed the Buddha wisdom,
> All of these are my converts,
> Whose minds I have set on the Great Way.
> These Bodhisattvas are my sons
> Who dwell in this Buddha-world.
> Ever practising the Dhuta deeds,
> Joyfully devoted to quiet places,
> Shunning the clamour of crowds,
> With no pleasure in many words.
> All these sons of mine,
> Learning and keeping the Law of my Way,
> Are always zealous day and night,
> For the sake of seeking Buddhahood;
> They dwell below the Saha-world,
> In the region of space beneath it.
> Firm in their powers of will and memory,
> Ever diligent in seeking wisdom,
> They preach every kind of mystic law,

Their minds devoid of any fear.
I, near the city of Gaya,
Sitting beneath the Bodhi-tree,
Accomplished Perfect Enlightenment;
And rolling the supreme Law-wheel,
I then taught and converted them
And caused them to seek the One Way.
Now they all abide in the never-relapsing state,
And every one will become a Buddha.[84]

This declaration serves only to increase the perplexity of Maitreya and the disciples. How is it possible, they wonder, that the Master should have instructed so great a host in so short a time? They remind him that only fifty years have passed since his own Enlightenment beneath the bodhi tree, yet he is claiming to have converted and trained an incalculable host of Bodhisattvas belonging, it would seem, to past ages and other world-systems. It is as though a young man of twenty-five should claim centenarians as his sons, and the latter acknowledge him as their father (chapter 14).

In reply to these questions Śākyamuni now makes his grand revelation. The scene is therefore the climax of the entire spiritual drama of the *Saddharma-puṇḍarīka*, up to which the preceding scenes have led, and the truths of which their teachings have to some extent foreshadowed. Herein Śākyamuni reveals himself as being, *sub specie aeternitatis*, the Eternal Buddha; or rather, the Eternal Buddha reveals himself as Śākyamuni and all the other Buddhas, who are not independent entities but the various guises under which he, the Supreme Reality, appears at different places and in different ages.

All the worlds of gods, men and asuras declare: 'Now has Śākyamuni-Buddha, coming forth from the palace of the Śākya-clan, and seated at the place of enlightenment, not far from the city of Gaya, attained to Perfect Enlightenment.' But, good sons, since I veritably became Buddha, there have passed infinite, boundless, hundreds, thousands, myriads, kotis, nayutas of Kalpas. [That is to say, he is eternally enlightened.][85] From that time forward I have constantly been preaching and teaching in this Sahā-world, and also leading and benefiting the living in other places in hundreds, thousands, myriads, kotis, nayutas of numberless domains.[86]

He it was who, according to the dispositions of beings, had created Dīpaṅkara and other Buddhas, and made them, as an expedient, deliver discourses and attain *parinirvāṇa*. Appearing as Śākyamuni, he tells beings of his birth in the world and of how, retiring from the household life as a youth, he had attained *sambodhi*. Had he announced that he had become a Buddha millions of years ago it would not have produced a favourable effect on people's minds. Nevertheless he was not guilty of falsehood, because a Tathāgata viewed the universe as devoid of origination and cessation, without rebirth or *parinirvāṇa*, neither existent nor non-existent, neither real or unreal, neither the same nor different. His viewpoint being completely different from that of an ordinary person it does not constitute a lie when, in order to teach the Dharma to beings of different conduct, aspirations, and ideas, he has recourse to various expedients. In reality the life of a Tathāgata is unlimited; he never dies. Were he to remain constantly among men, however, familiarity would breed contempt, and beings would become arrogant and lazy. In order to increase their longing for his presence, he tactfully tells them that the appearance of a Tathāgata in the world is a rare occurrence and manifests the phenomenon of entering into *parinirvāṇa*. This is illustrated by a parable.

An eminent physician who has been away for a long time returns home to find his sons suffering from the effects of poisoning. Happy to see their father again, they ask him to cure them. While some of the sons take the medicines he prescribes and are restored to health, others, who are deeply affected by the poison, refuse to do so. In order to bring the latter to their senses the physician therefore retires to a distant country and sends them word of his death. The shock produces the desired effect. Realizing that they are now orphans with no one to help them, the sons take the medicines their father had left behind and are cured. Hearing of their recovery, the physician later on returns and shows himself to them still alive. Being actuated by a desire to benefit others, neither the Buddha nor the physician can be accused of falsehood (chapter 15).

The effect of this revelation on the congregation is profound. Vast hosts, innumerable as the sands of the Ganges, attain various spiritual insights and powers. All the while flowers, incense, and jewels, together with other precious things, fall in showers on the assembly; celestial canopies are raised on high, and countless Bodhisattvas sing the praises of the Buddhas. Śākyamuni then tells Maitreya that the merit of developing faith in the Eternal Life of the Tathāgata, as just revealed, incalculably surpasses that of cultivating the first five *pāramitās* throughout infinite ages. Besides exceeding in value all formal religious observances, whether erecting stupas, temples, or monasteries, such faith in fact renders them superfluous. Possessing such faith, one will see the Buddha on the Spiritual Vulture's Peak surrounded by the celestial host ever preaching this Dharma. One will see, too, the realm in which one lives resplendent with palaces and jewels. By the preservation and propagation of the sūtra, in conjunction with the practice of the first five *pāramitās*, infinite merit will be gained and one will speedily reach Perfect Knowledge. He adds:

> If any one reads and recites, receives and keeps this Sūtra, preaches it to other people, or himself copies it, or causes others to copy it; moreover, is able to erect stupas and build monasteries, and to serve and extol the śrāvaka-monks, and also with hundreds, thousands, myriads, kotis of ways of extolling, extols the merits of the Bodhisattvas; also if he to other people, with various reasonings, according to its meaning, expounds this Law-Flower Sūtra; again, if he is able to keep the commandments in purity, amicably to dwell with the gentle, to endure insult without anger, to be firm in will and thought, ever to value meditation, to attain to profound concentration, zealously and boldly to support the good, to be clever and wise in ably answering difficult questionings;… those people have proceeded towards the Wisdom-terrace, and are near to Perfect Enlightenment, sitting under the tree of enlightenment.[87]

So great is the value of the sūtra that one who preaches it is to be venerated as the Buddha himself, and a stupa erected wherever he expounds as much as a phrase of the sacred text (chapter 16). A person who expresses appreciation of even a single *gāthā* heaps up incalculable merit, far surpassing that of providing the six classes of beings in four hundred millions of *kotis* of numberless worlds with all the necessaries of life and then, by the gift of the Dharma, leading them to the realization of the Eight Emancipations (*vimokṣa*) of the Hīnayāna (chapter 17).

When the merits of a hearer are so vast, how much greater will be those of a preacher of this sūtra! He or she will attain to an extraordinary development of the powers of the six sense-organs, including the mind. Eye and ear, for instance, will become sensitive to the point of universal clairvoyance and clairaudience, while the preacher's mental powers will become such as to enable him 'on hearing a single verse or sentence, to penetrate its infinite and boundless meanings. Moreover, having discerned those meanings, he will be able to discourse on that single sentence or verse for a month, for four months, even a year.'[88] Whatever such a person preaches will be the Dharma of former Buddhas (chapter 18).

Addressing Samantabhadra, another of the great Bodhisattvas, Śākyamuni declares that it is impossible to recount the demerits of one who discards or disparages the sūtra. This warning introduces the episode of Sadāparibhūta, a Bodhisattva monk who, at an unthinkably remote past epoch, had lived in a former Buddha-field under the dispensation of a Buddha known as Bhīṣmajarjiteśvararāja or 'King of Majestic Voice', the first of a series of 20,000 *kotis* of Tathāgatas of that name. He was in the habit of approaching every monk or nun, male or female lay devotee, and telling them, 'I am not here to give you any direction (*nāhaṃ yuṣmākaṃ paribhavāmi*). You are free to do anything you like. But I would advise you to take up the Bodhisattva career so that, ultimately, you may become Perfect Buddhas.' Some of those whom he addressed in this way became highly incensed, and not only abused him but fell upon him with sticks and stones. Far from bearing his assailants any ill will, however, he patiently endured their persecutions, and while escaping to a distance continued to cry out, 'I am not here to give you any direction. You are all to become Buddhas.' For this reason he was nicknamed Sadāparibhūta or 'Never Direct'. At the time of his death this Bodhisattva heard a voice from the sky proclaiming the *Saddharma-puṇḍarīka Sūtra* and descanting upon the merit of preserving and preaching it. He therefore delayed his departure from the world in order to devote himself to its propagation. Eventually, after he had developed supernormal powers, his erstwhile persecutors all became his disciples. This Bodhisattva, the Buddha now tells Samantabhadra, was none other than himself in a previous existence, and the persecutors who became disciples are at present monks, nuns, and Bodhisattvas (chapter 19).

At this juncture the vast body of Bodhisattvas who sprang out of the earth, headed by the chief of their four leaders, Viśiṣṭacaritra or 'Distinguished Character', and the other Bodhisattvas and remaining members of the congregation under the leadership of Mañjuśrī, all declare that, in whatsoever worlds the Buddha, in any of his transformations, may exist and cease to exist, they will preach this sūtra. The unanimity of the declaration moves Śākyamuni to an exhibition of his supernormal power. In the presence of the great assembly, he protrudes 'his broad and far-stretched tongue, till it reaches upward to the Brahmā world, every pore radiating the light of infinite, numberless colours, shining everywhere throughout each direction of the universe.'[89]

Prabhūtaratna and the other Buddhas all do likewise. While they are thus revealing their supernormal powers, hundreds of thousands of years pass. After this they retract their tongues, cough simultaneously, and snap their fingers in unison. These two sounds penetrate into every region of the Buddha-fields, causing them to shake in every direction. Through the supernormal power of the Buddha, all the living beings thereof, while remaining in their own fields, 'see infinite, boundless, hundreds, thousands, myriads, kotis of Buddhas, seated on Lion-thrones under the jewel-trees; and see Śākyamuni-Buddha, together with the Tathāgata Abundant-Treasures, seated on Lion-thrones in the midst of the stupas; and also see infinite, boundless, hundreds, thousands, myriads, kotis of Great Bodhisattvas, and the four groups of disciples who reverently surround Śākyamuni-Buddha.'[90] The latter is joyfully hailed by the gods, who from every quarter strew flowers, incense, garlands, and jewels, which, massing like clouds, transform themselves into a jewelled canopy covering the sky above the Buddhas. Upon this the worlds of all the universes are fused without obstruction as one Buddha-field.

Taking advantage of the occasion, Śākyamuni points out that even if, by means of the supernormal powers just exhibited, he were to proclaim throughout infinite ages the merits of this sūtra, he would be unable to exhaust them. Reminding the assembly yet again of the importance of preserving and propagating it, he insists that wherever the sacred volume is kept, stupas must be erected and offerings made. Such places are thrones of Enlightenment. On these spots the Buddhas attain the Supreme Enlightenment, revolve the wheel of the Dharma, and enter *parinirvāṇa* (chapter 20).

In the Sanskrit text as now extant there ensues a series of episodes, devoted to the cult of various Bodhisattvas, such as Bhaiṣajyarāja, who offer spells (*dhāraṇīs*) for the protection of the sūtra, Gadgadaśvara, and Avalokiteśvara (chapters 21–6). As these interrupt the continuity of the action, and are no doubt interpolations, they are described in chapter 11, below. The Great Drama concludes with Śākyamuni Buddha's final commission to his disciples before entering *parinirvāṇa*. Rising from his lion throne in the sky, where he has been seated with Prabhūtaratna, he thrice places his right hand in blessing on the heads of the countless Irreversible Bodhisattvas and solemnly entrusts to them the preservation and promulgation of the sūtra. This done, he requests all the Buddhas present to return to their own domains, saying: 'Buddhas! Peace be upon you. Let the Stupa of the Buddha Abundant-Treasures be restored as before.'[91] As these words are pronounced, the innumerable emanated Buddhas from every direction, who are seated on lion thrones under the jewel trees, as well as the Buddha Abundant Treasures, the host of infinite, numberless Bodhisattvas, Viśiṣṭacaritra and others, also the four groups of śrāvakas, Śāriputra, and the rest, as well as the worlds, gods, men, asuras, and so on, hearing the words of the Buddha, all rejoice greatly.

Though the ramifications of its symbolism might well be the study of a lifetime, the *leitmotiv* of this tremendous apocalyptic drama emerges from the welter of scenes and exuberance of language with sufficient force and clarity. To give a conceptualized abstract of its teaching is therefore superfluous. This does not mean, however, that there are no misunderstandings to be avoided. Largely on account of chapter 15, entitled *Tathāgata-ayuṣpramāṇa* or 'The Tathāgata's Infinite Life', modern writers, both Buddhist and non-Buddhist, have accused the Mahāyāna of deifying the founder of Buddhism and thus introducing into his religion a theistic element incompatible with the decidedly non-theistic character of what is supposed to have been the primitive evangelium. Based as it is on a misunderstanding, the accusation cannot be sustained. Theism involves the conception of an eternal, omnipotent creator, but since no Buddhist text, of any school, attributes to the Buddha the creation of the universe, it is impossible to speak of him as God without radically modifying the traditional meaning of this term.[92]

Far from deifying the Buddha, in the sense of formally investing him with theistic attributes, what the *Saddharma-puṇḍarīka* really does is to reveal another, a transcendental dimension of the Buddha's human greatness, thus enabling us to see him, and with him the totality of existence, not according to the flesh but *sub specie aeternitatis*. In terms of the *trikāya* doctrine, some acquaintance with which is indispensable to an understanding of the Mahāyāna, it enables us to see not merely his *nirmāṇakāya* but his *sambhogakāya* and *dharmakāya* as well. The latter are, however, not so much independent or, as it were, superadded, bodies, but the former in its *ultimate depth*, for which reason the Buddha of the *Saddharma-puṇḍarīka*, however transcendent in his glory, is not any new, supra-historical figure, of the type of which there were many to hand when the sūtra was composed, but still Śākyamuni the mendicant Indian teacher. Though expressed with help of mathematical symbols, his infinite life therefore represents not the indefinite prolongation, in time, of a particular enlightened personality, but the fact that Enlightenment, being the full realization of ultimate Reality, transcends time altogether. Hence the Buddha, as the possessor of this Infinite Life, is not to be identified with the eternal God of popular theism. In the same way his various exhibitions of supernormal power, such as the protrusion of the tongue and the shaking of the universe, are not evidence of omnipotence, nor even magic feats, as they might be in a Hīnayāna sūtra, but concrete symbols of spiritual truths.

The minor details of the parables, also, are not to be applied too literally nor pressed too far. The fact that, in the Parable of the Burning House, the Buddha is spoken of as the father and sentient beings as his sons means simply that his compassion for those involved in the Saṃsāra is analogous to the love of a father for his children. It certainly does not imply that according to the *Saddharma-puṇḍarīka* he is actually the creator of mankind.

These misunderstandings having been corrected, all that need be remarked, by way of conclusion, is that in a sense the subject matter of the sūtra is the sūtra itself. Like a world, it revolves on its own axis. The dramatic 'situation' out of which the whole action develops is the Buddha's proclamation that he is about to reveal a truth transcending all his previous teachings, in other words, that he is going to preach the *Saddharma-puṇḍarīka*. Again, the revelation of his Infinite Life, forming the climax of the entire work, follows, by way of elucidation, upon his declaration that, having sufficient Bodhisattvas of his own to protect and propagate the sūtra after his *parinirvāṇa*, he has no need of the services of those hailing from other Buddha-fields.

Finally, the ideal Buddhist is depicted as one who is ardently devoted to the sūtra. In terms of the Three Jewels, the Buddha is the revealer of the *Saddharma-puṇḍarīka*, the Dharma is the spiritual life and dramatic action of which it consists, and the Sangha the community of those who, participating in that life and action, have pledged themselves to the preservation of the sacred text and promulgation of its teaching. Thus, the *Saddharma-puṇḍarīka* represents a synthesis, at the Mahāyāna level, of the most precious part of the Buddhist heritage, with the first of the Three Jewels predominating. Indeed, certain more glowingly eulogistic passages of the text would seem to suggest that the words *Saddharma-puṇḍarīka* connote much more than just the title of a sūtra, however great, being in truth the appellation of a 'figured flame' that not only blends but as a unity transcends the Three Jewels, and is itself the supreme object of devotion and transcendental knowledge, the mysterious, all-comprehending ultimate Reality.

# 10

# THE PRAJÑĀ-PĀRAMITĀ SŪTRAS

## The Perfection of Wisdom Sūtras

The *Prajñā-pāramitā* or 'Perfection of Wisdom', which represents the Dharma-Jewel, is not so much a sūtra as a family of sūtras or even a dynasty. Like most distinguished families, its origins are obscure, and like most Indian families, it consists of numerous members, the history of whom extends over a considerable period. Edward Conze, who devoted the greater part of his life to studying, translating, and explaining these documents, collates from Sanskrit, Chinese, Tibetan, and Khotanese sources, a list of forty Prajñā-pāramitā texts, not all of them sūtras or canonical, the composition of which began about 100BCE, and continued steadily until the time of the virtual disappearance of Buddhism from India in the thirteenth century CE.

This immense period he divides into four phases, the first three of which, lasting for two centuries each, saw respectively the elaboration of a basic text, the expansion of that text, and the restatement of the doctrine in short sūtras and in versified summaries. The fourth and longest phase, occupying the remainder of the period, witnessed on the one hand the incorporation of Tantric elements, and on the other, the composition of commentaries. Even after eliminating from the above list most of the quasi-canonical works of the last phase, we are still left, according to Hikata's estimate, with a total of no fewer than twenty-seven indisputable Prajñā-pāramitā sūtras at present extant.

Eight of these have survived complete in the original Sanskrit, another is partly extant in Sanskrit, and one occurs partly in Sanskrit and partly in Khotanese. Most of them, as also the remaining seventeen, exist in Chinese or Tibetan or both. The biggest single block of translation is Hsüan-tsang's 'Great Prajñā-pāramitā' in six hundred Chinese fascicules, on which he was engaged between 659 and 663CE, and which consists of 'sixteen meetings in six places'. This great work is really a rendering not of one text but of sixteen different sūtras. Apart from the *Heart Sūtra*, which he had translated in 649, and one text already known in China which he did not translate, the Prajñā-pāramitā sūtras not included in this collection are assumed to have made their appearance after his departure from India about the middle of the seventh century. Many of these were translated at a later date by other hands.

The classification, mutual relations, and relative priority of the numerous members of this great 'family', together constituting not only the biggest but probably the most valuable group of Mahāyāna sūtras, has been the subject of considerable investigation. Conze speaks of ordinary Prajñā-pāramitā sūtras, Special texts, and Tantric texts. The traditional classification is simply in terms of length. Taking the *śloka* or verse of thirty-two syllables as the unit of measurement, there are 'large' sūtras consisting of 18,000, 25,000, and 100,000 'lines', all of which made their appearance during the second of Conze's four phases of development, and 'small' ones consisting of anything from a few hundred lines or less, up to 8,000 lines, that appeared during the first and during the third phase.

Mutual relations are highly complex. Sūtras expand or contract, or select from one another, in a most bewildering manner. Sometimes one text includes another, or part of another, or a recast of it. To add to the confusion, several sūtras exist, or at least existed, in various recensions, and different translations might have been based on different ones. In some cases the original text of a sūtra survives in a recension different from any of those from which the extant translations seem to have been made. Moreover, as might have been expected, all the large and some of the small sūtras were composed over a long period by the familiar process of interpolation and accretion. This makes the dating of these texts, and therewith the ascertainment of their relative priority, a matter of some difficulty.

Fortunately the identity of the progenitor of this illustrious family, or the founder of the Prajñā-pāramitā dynasty, in other words of the basic text or *Urtext* that was elaborated during the first phase, and out of which, during the succeeding phases, all the other texts were at various removes developed, is not much in doubt. With only one possible rival, to be mentioned below, the oldest Prajñā-pāramitā text is the *Aṣṭasāhasrikā* or Perfection of Wisdom 'in 8,000 lines', the nucleus of which probably dates back to at least 100BCE. Regarding its place of origin, the text itself represents the Buddha as prophesying: 'These sūtras associated with the six perfections will, after the passing away of the Tathāgata, appear in the South. From the South they will spread to the East, and from there to the North'.[93] Modern scholarship on the whole tends to confirm this account.

The Mahāsaṅghikas, who had two important settlements in the Andhra country, between the Godavari and the Kiṣtna, near Amarāvatī, are known to have been the matrix of the Mahāyāna as a historical development, and it is more than likely that the Prajñā-pāramitā literature originated amongst them. Apart from the fact that the *Kathā-vatthu* attributes to the 'Andhakas' doctrines akin to those of the Mahāyāna, the teaching of the Mahāsaṅghikas coincided with that of the Prajñā-pāramitā in several important particulars. Moreover, one of their offshoots, the Prajñaptivādins, are credited from early times with the transmission of a teaching on Wisdom. A strong tradition also connects the Prajñā-pāramitā with the name of Nāgārjuna, who likewise came from the south of India, and who seems to have been associated, during the latter part of his career, with the great monastic centre at Nāgārjunikoṇḍa, not far from Amarāvatī. Other factors too are indicative of the southern origin of the Prajñā-pāramitā; but as Conze points out, the evidence is merely circumstantial, and by no means conclusive.[94]

Nāgārjuna's association with this literature is not, however, dependent on its connection with the South. According to an ancient and widespread belief, the great sage recovered the Prajñā-pāramitā from the depths of the ocean, where since the days of the Buddha the Nāgas had preserved it. Buddhist art depicts him as seated on a raft, while a Nāga maiden, emerging from the waves, presents him with a volume generally identified with the Large Prajñā-pāramitā 'in 100,000 lines'.[95] The identity of the Nāgas has been the subject of much debate. For some they are a primitive tribe with a serpent totem. We have elsewhere suggested that they may represent a community of human Adepts.[96] It is also possible, of course, that tradition for once is to be taken quite literally, and that the Prajñā-pāramitā teachings actually were preserved on a plane that does not coincide with any geographical locale by a race of spiritually gifted non-human beings.

The *Saṃyutta Nikāya* contains a remarkable prophecy which is of special interest in this connection.

> Once upon a time [the Buddha tells the monks], the Dasārahas had a kettledrum called Summoner. As it began to split, the Dasārahas fixed in ever another peg, until the time came when the Summoner's original drumhead had vanished and only the framework of pegs remained. Even so, monks, will the monks come to be in the future. Those discourses spoken by the [Tathāgata], deep, deep in meaning, [transcendental], dealing with emptiness [*suññatā*] – to these they will not listen....
>
> But, monks, those discourses which are made by poets, which are poetry, which are a manifold of words and phrases, alien, the utterance of disciples – to these they will listen.... Thus it is that the discourses spoken by the [Tathāgata], deep, deep in meaning, [transcendental,] dealing with emptiness, will come to vanish.[97]

In the Pāli canon the principal locus of the *suññatā* teaching is the *Suññatā-vagga* of the *Majjhima Nikāya*, the first two discourses of which, the Lesser and the Greater 'Discourses on Emptiness', deal with this topic. Neither goes very deep. Moreover, for a subject about which the Buddha, according to the above prophecy, manifests such concern, the two medium-length discourses clearly seem hardly enough. We can only conclude that so far as the Theravāda tradition is concerned the discourses referred to did, as anticipated, vanish. The Prajñā-pāramitā sūtras, on the other hand, fit the Buddha's characterization perfectly. They are deep in meaning, they are transcendental, and they most certainly deal with Emptiness. In fact, they deal with little else. In addition, they are all written entirely in prose. Rather than postulating two sets of discourses on *śūnyatā*, thus raising the question of how the second set came into existence, it is reasonable to infer that the 'discourses spoken by the Tathāgata deep, deep in meaning, transcendental, dealing with Emptiness' were none other than the Prajñā-pāramitā sūtras, or, at any rate, the oral exemplars of these texts.

After the *parinirvāṇa*, in the unfavourable atmosphere of coenobitical monasticism, with its double emphasis on the formal and the analytical aspects of the teaching, they virtually disappeared, being preserved by an obscure group outside what was, during that period, the main stream of historical development. It was with this group that Nāgārjuna came into contact. Realizing their importance, he not only published the Prajñā-pāramitā sūtras, thus shifting the entire religion back on to its original spiritual foundations, but systematized their teaching in a series of highly influential *śāstras* of his own composition. Whether the Nāgas from whom he obtained the sūtras were a primitive tribe, a community of Adepts, or a race of non-human beings, does not materially affect our argument.

It is also futile to object that the theory of an oral transmission lasting 400 years, after which the Prajñā-pāramitā began to be published more than a thousand miles away from the Middle Country,[98] puts too severe a strain on our credulity. The Theravāda Pāli canon was transmitted orally for a similar period and written down at a place even more remote from its original home. In neither case can the basic authenticity of the traditions so preserved be doubted. As insisted earlier on, the Buddhist scriptures stand or fall together. Those who refuse to accept the Perfection of Wisdom sūtras as Buddhavacana have, in any case, to explain the authorship of these unique works.

An impartial comparison with the Pāli Sutta Piṭaka, or its Sanskrit equivalents, shows that in sublimity of conception, and grandeur of thought, the Prajñā-pāramitā sūtras transcend the whole body of Hīnayāna sūtras as much as the awe-inspiring icy crags of Everest and Kanchenjunga overtop the foothills of the Himalayan Range. The only possible exception is the *Aṭṭhaka-vagga* which, though much slighter in both form and content, belongs to the same general order of ideas. If the Buddha did not preach the Prajñā-pāramitā, whoever did must therefore have been a spiritual genius of the first magnitude, greater than even the Buddha. The Hīnayānists accused Nāgārjuna of composing the texts himself. But far from claiming a superior degree of insight, and founding a new religion, Nāgārjuna not only continued to venerate the Buddha as Teacher, but devoted all his energies to the consolidation of his Doctrine. Consequently it is difficult to resist the conclusion that the Prajñā-pāramitā, embodying the Dharma in its profoundest form, in essence at least derives from the personal teaching of the Master.

The composition of the *Aṣṭasāhasrikā* extended over a period of about two centuries, from 100BCE to 100CE. As now extant, the Sanskrit text is divided into thirty-two chapters, not all of which coincide with a change of topic. This division may be later than the earliest Chinese translation, made by Lokakṣema in 179–180CE, which besides possessing only thirty chapters frequently gives different chapter headings. Among the most obvious accretions upon the basic original text are chapters 29–32, containing the edifying story of how the Bodhisattva Sadāprarudita or 'Ever Weeping' sought for the 'Perfection of Wisdom', and a set of four additions in which occurs the name of the Buddha Akṣobhya. Although the remainder of the text, in its turn, must have grown gradually, in form and content it is sufficiently homogeneous to defy attempts at detecting further stratifications. The first two chapters, which, according to Conze, contain its essential doctrines, nevertheless probably constitute the original nucleus of the sūtra. As the work is devoid of both literary form and logical connection, and jumps from one topic to another in a most disconcerting manner, we shall, therefore, take advantage of this circumstance and present first an account of the contents of these two chapters, and then a rapid survey of the rest. Before that can be done, however, the remaining translations of the *Aṣṭasāhasrikā* must be noted. Most of them are in Chinese.

Lokakṣema's version was followed by five others, one of which, executed by Dharmapriya about 382CE, was incomplete. Complete translations were made by Chih-ch'ien about 225CE, Kumārajīva in 408CE, Hsüan-tsang about 660CE, and Dānapāla in 985CE. There are also translations in Tibetan and Mongolian. Conze has produced an English version.

The Bodhisattva aims not merely at liberation but at Supreme Enlightenment, and chapter 1 is therefore entitled *Sarvākārajñatācaryā* or 'Practice of the Knowledge of All the Modes', by which is meant the Tathāgata's clear cognition of all dharmas in all their aspects. As in the case of the *Saddharma-puṇḍarīka*, the venue of the discourse is Rājagṛha, on the Vulture's Peak. But this time there is a difference. There are no lavish descriptions, and the Buddha is surrounded, not by hosts of Bodhisattvas and various orders of non-human beings, but simply by 1,250 monks, all of them, with the exception of Ānanda, Arhants. Miracles are absent. In fact, the sūtra opens as soberly as any Hīnayāna discourse. Modern scholarship of course detects in this circumstance evidence of superior antiquity, but it may just as well be that, teaching as it does the unconditioned identity of the conditioned and the unconditioned, the sūtra feels no need for introducing any special effects. As Zen, applying the same principle, was afterwards to insist, ordinary life is itself miraculous.

Like the Hīnayāna sūtras again, and unlike the *Saddharma-puṇḍarīka*, the work is couched in dialogue form, the interlocutors in this chapter being the Buddha, Subhūti, and Śāriputra. Pūrṇa Maitrāyaṇīputra also participates, but soon retires discomfited. Śāriputra represents the Hīnayāna in general and the Abhidharma in particular. He is a rationalist rather than a mystic, and despite his praises of the Prajñā-pāramitā often clearly fails to understand it, for, of course, it cannot be 'understood' at all. Subhūti, who does not figure prominently in the Hīnayāna scriptures, is here the chief exponent of the 'Perfection of Wisdom', ranking even above Bodhisattvas like Maitreya.

The discussion opens with the Buddha calling upon Subhūti to make it clear 'to the Bodhisattvas, the great beings, starting from perfect wisdom, how the Bodhisattvas, the great beings, go forth into perfect wisdom'.[99] In response to Śāriputra's unspoken doubt whether Subhūti will do so of himself, through the operation and force of his own power of revealing wisdom, or through the Buddha's might, the latter says:

> Whatever ... the Lord's Disciples teach, all that is to be known as the Tathāgata's work. For in the dharma demonstrated by the Tathāgata they train themselves, they realize its true nature, they hold it in mind. Thereafter nothing that they teach contradicts the true nature of dharma. It is just an outpouring of the Tathāgata's demonstration of dharma.[100]

This is, in effect, the basic Mahāyānic argument in support of the spiritual, as distinct from the textual, authenticity of these scriptures. What Subhūti is really saying is that whatever issues from the experience of Enlightenment must be regarded as canonical, a position that does not greatly differ from the one adopted by the Buddha in his advice to the Mahāpajāpati Gotami as recorded in the Pāli canon.[101]

Having disposed of any possible objections to his teaching as being that of a mere disciple, not the Master's own, Subhūti proceeds:

> I do not, O Lord, see that dharma 'Bodhisattva', nor a dharma called 'perfect wisdom'. Since I neither find, nor apprehend, nor see a dharma 'Bodhisattva', nor a 'perfect wisdom', what

> Bodhisattva shall I instruct and admonish in what perfect wisdom? And yet, O Lord, if, when this is pointed out, a Bodhisattva's heart does not become cowed, nor stolid, does not despair nor despond, if he does not turn away or become dejected, does not tremble, is not frightened or terrified, it is just this Bodhisattva, this great being who should be instructed in perfect wisdom. It is precisely this that should be recognized as the perfect wisdom of that Bodhisattva, as his instruction in perfect wisdom. When he thus stands firm, that is his instruction and admonition. Moreover, when a Bodhisattva courses in perfect wisdom and develops it, he should so train himself that he does not pride himself on that thought of enlightenment (with which he has begun his career). That thought is no thought, since in its essential nature thought is transparently luminous.[102]

The rest of the chapter consists of an exploration by Subhūti of some of the implications of these recondite propositions, the exploration being conducted largely by way of corrections of Śāriputra's misunderstandings and replies to his objections. From time to time the Buddha, who is understood to be all the time speaking through Subhūti, interposes and makes a personal contribution to the proceedings. The elusiveness of Perfect Wisdom is repeatedly stressed. She cannot be appropriated, as she does not possess the mark of being Perfect Wisdom. In fact the marked does not possess the own-being of being marked. Moreover, all dharmas being unborn are unapproachable and unappropriable and a Bodhisattva does not, therefore, settle down in any of them. Such terms as 'Buddha', 'Bodhisattva', and 'Perfect Wisdom' are, in fact, all mere words. What they denote is something uncreated.

Subhūti's exposition, as he penetrates deeper and deeper into the meaning of Perfect Wisdom, is not systematic in the formal sense, with one topic following upon another in strict logical sequence. In Henry Miller's phrase it is 'a serpentine movement through incalculable dimensions'. Definitions are given, *inter alia*, of four key terms, 'Bodhisattva', 'Mahāsattva', 'armed with the great armour', and 'Mahāyāna'. As the Lord himself makes clear, by the word 'Bodhisattva' nothing real is meant, because a Bodhisattva trains himself in non-attachment to all dharmas. He awakes in non-attachment to Full

Enlightenment in the sense that he understands all dharmas. The Prajñā-pāramitā definition of 'Mahāsattva' is given by Subhūti. First, however, the Buddha and Śāriputra give the more usual explanations of the word.

A Bodhisattva is called 'a great being' in the sense that he will cause a great mass and collection of beings to attain the Highest, and in the sense that he will demonstrate Dharma so that the great errors should be forsaken – such erroneous views as the assumption of a self, a being, a living soul, a person, of becoming, of not-becoming, of annihilation, of eternity, of individuality, etc. Subhūti then says:

> A Bodhisattva is called a 'great being', if he remains unattached to, and uninvolved in, the thought of enlightenment, the thought of all-knowledge, the thought without outflows, the unequalled thought, the thought which equals the unequalled, unshared by any of the Disciples or Pratyekabuddhas. Because that thought of all-knowledge is (itself) without outflows, and unincluded (in the empirical world). All in respect of that thought of all-knowledge, which is without outflows and unincluded, he remains unattached and uninvolved. In that sense does a Bodhisattva come to be styled a 'great being'.[103]

According to the Buddha, a Bodhisattva is called 'armed with the great armour' when he thinks that he should lead countless beings to Nirvāṇa and that yet there are none to lead to Nirvāṇa, or who should be led to it. Dharmas are illusory. It is as if a magician were to conjure up a great crowd of people, and then make them vanish again. No one would have been killed by anyone, or made to vanish. Even this does not satisfy Subhūti, who declares that, in the ultimate sense, the Bodhisattva is not armed with an armour at all. The Lord agrees. Replying to an objection by Pūrṇa Maitrāyaṇīputra, who has already interposed once, Subhūti says:

> The form of an illusory man is neither bound nor freed. Because in reality it is not there at all, because it is isolated, because it is unproduced. This is the great armour, the great non-armour of a Bodhisattva, a great being, who is armed with the great armour, who has set out in the great vehicle, who has mounted on the great vehicle.[104]

Perhaps the most interesting definitions are those of the 'Great Vehicle' or Mahāyāna. The Lord's is particularly beautiful.

> 'Great vehicle', that is a synonym of immeasurableness. 'Immeasurable' means infinitude. By means of the perfections has a Bodhisattva set out in it. From the triple world it will go forth. It has set out to where there is no objective support. It will be a Bodhisattva, a great being who will go forth, – but he will not go forth to anywhere. Nor has anyone set out in it. It will not stand anywhere, but it will stand on all-knowledge, by way of taking its stand nowhere. (And finally,) by means of this great vehicle no one goes forth, no one has gone forth, no one will go forth. Because neither of these dharmas, – he who would go forth, and that by which he would go forth, – exist, nor can they be got at. Since all dharmas do not exist, what dharma could go forth by what dharma? It is thus, Subhūti, that a Bodhisattva, a great being, is armed with the great armour, and has mounted on the great vehicle.[105]

Despite the profundity of this statement it is Subhūti who manages to have the last word on the subject.

> The Lord speaks of the 'great vehicle'. Surpassing the world with its Gods, men and Asuras that vehicle will go forth. For it is the same as space, and exceedingly great. As in space, so in this vehicle there is room for immeasurable and incalculable beings. So is this the great vehicle of the Bodhisattvas, the great beings. One cannot see its coming, or going, and its abiding does not exist. Thus one cannot get at the beginning of this great vehicle, nor at its end, nor at its middle. But it is self-identical everywhere. Therefore one speaks of a 'great vehicle'.[106]

From these definitions it is clear that the Mahāyāna is primarily a profound metaphysical principle, and the application of that principle in spiritual life. Only later, as a corrective to certain one-sided developments within the Buddhist fold, did it emerge on the historical plane and assume, by degrees, the characteristics of a distinct religious and philosophical movement.

In chapter 2 the discussion is mainly between Subhūti and Śakra, the king of the gods, who arrives accompanied by thousands of greater and lesser divinities. On their behalf he enquires of Subhūti how a Bodhisattva should stand in Perfect Wisdom, how train in it, and how devote himself to it. After exhorting not only the gods, but even the Arhants, to aspire after Supreme Enlightenment, and pointing out that they should all be grateful to the Buddha, not ungrateful, Subhūti tells them that the Bodhisattva should stand in Perfect Wisdom through standing in Emptiness. This means that he should not take his stand on the aggregates, sense-fields, or elements, nor indeed on any of the other doctrinal categories from the four foundations of mindfulness right up to Supreme Buddhahood.

In the ultimate sense these categories have only a nominal existence; they do not denote realities. So-called objective facts, including the various classes of Holy Persons, from Stream-Entrant to Buddha, are like a magical illusion or a dream. Even Nirvāṇa is unreal. Like the mind-made flowers which, in order to pay homage to the exposition, Śakra now conjures up and scatters over Subhūti, things do not in the ultimate sense either appear or disappear. A Bodhisattva should therefore train himself by way of a no-training, for Buddhahood is not an entity standing, as it were, 'out there' ready for him to grasp. He has nothing to increase or decrease, nothing to appropriate or let go, nothing to produce or make disappear. In this way he trains in All-knowledge. Objective facts are in their true nature infinite and boundless, and so too is the Perfection of Wisdom. Gods and men hereupon thrice shout in triumph, hailing the Dharmahood of the Dharma, after which they recognize Subhūti as a potential Tathāgata. This the Buddha confirms with a reference to his own prediction to Supreme Enlightenment by Dīpaṅkara.

From this point onwards the Lord takes an increasingly active part in the discussion, though Subhūti remains prominent until practically the end of the sūtra. In addition to Śāriputra and Śakra, who continue to participate, Maitreya and Ānanda and a few figures of minor importance make occasional contributions to the proceedings. Chapters 2–5 detail the various advantages accruing from the practice of the Perfection of Wisdom, worldly benefits being especially emphasized. Much is also made of the fact that infinitely greater merit is derived from paying homage to the Perfection of Wisdom than from worshipping the Buddha's relics, which suggests that the cult of the stupa as advocated in the *Mahāvastu* and elsewhere had already attained great popularity. Yet although, compared with the first two, these chapters seem to represent a descent into straightforward popular religion, the Buddha in fact is taking, as it were, a step backward before launching into the profundities of chapter 6, which deals with the metaphysical problem of dedicating all merit to the full Enlightenment of all beings.

Practically speaking, this is one of the most important parts of the sūtra. Taking 'rejoicing in merits' (*puṇyānumodana*) by way of example, it teaches how wholesome roots, which otherwise would lead to either the lower spiritual attainments of the Arhant and Pratyeka-Buddha or rebirth in heaven, can be transmuted into Supreme Enlightenment through being conjoined with Emptiness. It gives, in other words, the technique for making the transition from the Hīnayāna to the Mahāyāna.

Chapters 7–10 touch on a variety of topics, such as the attributes of Perfect Wisdom, its predominance over the other *pāramitās*, the reasons why some believe in it and others do not, its depth and purity, its relation to attachment and non-attachment, to reality and illusion, its effects on the believer, its being the second great turning of the wheel of the Dharma in Jambudvīpa, its modes and qualities, the qualifications of a Bodhisattva who gets it, obstacles to its study, and a prophecy about its diffusion. Chapter 11, dealing with the deeds of Māra, is again of practical interest. In detail, and with considerable insight, it describes the various psychological and other obstructions which may arise in connection with the study of the Perfection of Wisdom. Chapter 12 describes how the Buddha knows the world and minds of sentient beings, and chapter 13 enumerates the five attributes of Tathāgatahood and applies them to all dharmas. In chapter 14 are disclosed the past deeds of Bodhisattvas who fail in Perfect Wisdom, after which chapter 15 lists the ways in which Bodhisattvas help beings and indicates how Perfect Wisdom is understood by them. Chapter 16 opens with Subhūti's rhapsody on the Suchness of the Tathāgata, which, being signalized by an earthquake, probably marks the culmination of the sūtra. The rest of the chapter is devoted to Perfect Wisdom and skill in means, Enlightenment and Emptiness, and similar topics.

Chapter 17 is a lengthy disquisition on the attributes, tokens, and signs of irreversibility, special attention being given to Māra's attempts to mislead the Bodhisattva on account of his real or supposed attainment of this stage. Chapters 18–27 again range over a wide variety of topics, such as Emptiness, conditioned co-production, the five places which inspire fear, the importance of good friends, the meaning of Emptiness, the value of Perfect Wisdom, the conditions which lay one open to the influence of Māra, the marks of perfect training, the nature of illusion, the praise of the life of a Bodhisattva, and the prediction to Buddhahood of many thousands of monks. In the course of chapter 28 the Buddha entrusts and transmits the Perfection of Wisdom, as 'laid out in letters', to Ānanda, and with this act, which forms a fitting conclusion to the discourse, the sūtra no doubt once ended.

The only challenge to the *Aṣṭasāhasrikā*'s right to be considered the oldest Prajñā-pāramitā text comes from the *Ratnaguṇa-saṃcaya-gāthā*, or 'Verses on the Accumulation of the Precious Qualities of the Perfection of Wisdom'. This is a metrical work in thirty-three chapters, the first twenty-eight of which summarize, or at least correspond to, large blocks of chapters 1–28 of the *Aṣṭasāhasrikā*. Though the presence of many Prakritisms undoubtedly indicates extreme antiquity, the nature of its relation to the sūtra is not known. It might originally have constituted the verse portion of the sūtra, from which it was subsequently separated, or have been its original form, or again it might have been composed afterwards simply by way of summary. In any case, the original text has been lost, and all that we possess is Haribhadra's revision, which to some extent brings the text in line with the chapter divisions of the *Aṣṭasāhasrikā*, as they existed in the eighth century CE. It is a notable feature of the work that, unlike the sūtra, it expounds the teaching largely in the form of chains of similes.

During the second phase in the development of the Prajñā-pāramitā literature, which lasted from about 100 to 300CE, the *Urtext* 'in 8,000 lines' was expanded into a 'Large Prajñā-pāramitā'. Tradition speaks of detailed versions, intermediate and abridged, consisting respectively of 1,000,000,000, 10,000,000, and 100,000 *ślokas*, the first being preserved in the abode of the king of the Gandharvas, the second in the realm of the king of the gods, and the third, in its entirety, in the region of the Nāgas.[107]

As known to history, the Large Prajñā-pāramitā consists of three texts of comparatively modest dimensions. They are the *Śatasāhasrikā* or Perfection of Wisdom 'in 100,000 lines', said to be an incomplete version of the text belonging to the Nāgas, the *Pañcaviṃśati-sāhasrikā* or Perfection of Wisdom 'in 25,000 lines', and the *Aṣṭadaśa-sāhasrikā* or Perfection of Wisdom 'in 18,000 lines'. As Conze has shown, these three texts are really one and the same book, and differ in the extent to which the repetitions are copied out.[108] If one takes, for instance, he says, the statement that 'X is emptiness and the very emptiness is X', then the version in 100,000 lines applies this principle to about 200 items, beginning with form, and ending with the dharmas, or attributes, which are characteristics of a Buddha. The two other versions are so much shorter because they enumerate fewer items, sometimes only the first and the last. Conze estimates that four-fifths of the *Śatasāhasrikā*, or at least 85,000 of its 100,000 lines, consists of the repetition of doctrinal formulas, which sometimes continue for hundreds of pages together.

The sūtra falls into three somewhat unequal parts. Part 1, consisting of thirteen chapters, is an expansion of chapter 1 of the *Aṣṭasāhasrikā* to which have been added seven items of new matter, beginning with the cosmic miracles which here precede the teaching. Part 2, consisting of thirty-seven chapters, follows the *Aṣṭasāhasrikā* chapters 2–28 fairly closely, usually expanding the text, but often, especially in the later portions, abbreviating it instead. New matter appears only at the very beginning. Part 3 is an independent treatise. It is throughout concerned with 'the obvious conflict which exists between an ontology which proclaims the emptiness of everything, and the practical needs of the struggle for enlightenment'.[109] It also gives a number of useful definitions, e.g. of the three kinds of omniscience, of the Buddha, of Enlightenment, of Perfect Wisdom, of *prapañca* or 'manifoldness', of the major and minor marks of a Buddha's body, and so on.

The *Pañcaviṃśati* or version 'in 25,000 lines' existed in a variety of recensions, all of which appear to have corresponded more or less closely to the text of its more voluminous counterpart. This version was a favourite with the commentators. On it Nāgārjuna composed his *Mahā-prajñā-pāramitopadeśa Śāstra*, a gigantic work of encyclopedic content, the Sanskrit original of which is lost but which survives in the Chinese translation made by Kumārajīva in 405CE.[110] Large portions of the Sanskrit text of the sūtra itself have been found at Gilgit, while fragments are preserved on Indikutasaya copper plaques in Sinhalese script of the eighth or ninth century. Apart from the various recensions there also exists a recast version of the *Pañcaviṃśati* belonging perhaps to the fifth century, which superimposes upon the text of the other large Prajñā-pāramitās the framework of the

*Abhisamayālaṅkāra*.[111] The Sanskrit original of this version is extant in manuscripts of Nepalese provenance.

The *Aṣṭadaśa* or Perfection of Wisdom 'in 18,000 lines', consisting of eighty-seven chapters, is said to have been popular in Central Asia. Portions of the Sanskrit text of this sūtra, also, have been found at Gilgit. All three texts of the Large Prajñā-pāramitā were translated, at different periods, into Chinese, into Tibetan, and into Mongolian.

A *Daśasāhasrikā* or Perfection of Wisdom 'in 10,000 lines' is also sometimes classed with the larger sūtras. Its special feature is that the definitions of the terms, which are scattered through the three main versions of the Large Prajñā-pāramitā, have here all been gathered together into the first two chapters, in 57 groups. As the remaining 31 chapters are described as a somewhat erratic contraction of that work the *Daśasāhasrikā* really belongs more to the next phase of development.

The Large Prajñā-pāramitā being of prodigious size and chaotic in arrangement, this third phase, lasting from 300 to 500CE, was not unnaturally one of condensation. This was effected in two ways: by the composition of versified summaries and by the publication of short philosophical sūtras. The summaries, which attempt to arrange systematically all the topics dealt with in the Large Prajñā-pāramitā, stand in much the same relation to that work as the Abhidharma does to the Hīnayāna sūtras. They constitute, in fact, a sort of neo-Abhidharma of the Mahāyāna, though, of course, this term is never actually applied to them.

Among the summaries the most outstanding is the *Abhisamayālaṅkāra* or 'Memorial Verses on the Reunion (with the Absolute)', a work of the fourth century ascribed to Maitreya or Maitreyanātha. Conze describes it as follows:

> A brilliant versified Table of Contents, which in 273 memorial verses and in nine chapters of unequal length, sums up the contents of the *Pañcaviṃśatisāhasrikā Sūtra*, brings out the logical sequence of its arguments, and at the same time assigns to each section of the text a place on the stages of spiritual progress which Buddhist tradition had mapped out, thus everywhere showing the practical way by which one can become a Buddha.[112]

Though it is extremely useful, and has wielded enormous influence, this work does not concern us here, as the summaries are not sūtras but *śāstras*, and therefore excluded from the canonical literature. The Maitreya or Maitreyanātha who composed the *Abhisamayālaṅkāra* is, however, traditionally identified with the Bodhisattva of that name. This poses a question which will be discussed in Chapter 18 below.

Among the shorter sūtras, the finest are the two earliest, both appearing before 400CE, the *Vajracchedikā* and the *Hṛdaya*. The *Vajracchedikā* or 'Diamond Cutter' sūtra (vajra is really the mythical 'thunderbolt', and denotes something of irresistible strength) is also known as the Perfection of Wisdom 'in 300 lines'. A short text in two parts and thirty-two chapters, it is in the form of a dialogue between the Buddha and Subhūti. The Sanskrit original does not, however, give any chapter division, and the one adopted by Max Müller and other scholars dates back to c. 530CE when in China it was introduced into Kumārajīva's translation. It is not really of much help. Unlike the summaries, the *Diamond Sūtra* (as it is popularly known) does not attempt to give a systematic survey of the Prajñā-pāramitā teachings. Instead, it confines itself to a few central topics, which it inculcates by addressing the intuition rather than the logical intelligence. The result is not one that is calculated to endear the work to scholars.

While Part 1, which ends at the beginning of chapter 13, is fairly coherent, the same cannot be said of Part 2. Even Asaṅga, Vasubandhu, and Kamalaśīla, all of whom commented on it, failed to unravel its complications. According to Conze this part may well be no more than 'a chance medley of stray sayings', or the palm leaves of the original manuscript may at some time have been displaced.[113] Were this so, it would be difficult to account for the sūtra's immense prestige and popularity, as well as impossible to explain the undeniable force of its spiritual impact.

Fortunately, Han-shan, an enlightened Ch'an Master of the Ming dynasty, has written a commentary which offers a satisfactory solution of the problem along traditional lines.[114] According to him, the full title *Diamond Prajñā-pāramitā Sūtra* (as it reads in Kumārajīva's version) indicates that the teaching of the sūtra aims at revealing the Buddha's Diamond Mind, so as to cut off people's doubts and awaken their faith. This Diamond Mind is the Absolute Mind of Supreme Enlightenment. What the Buddha does, in the course of his dialogue with Subhūti, is simply remove the latter's doubts as they arise one by one in his mind as he listens to the Buddha's discourse. The apparent disorder of the sūtra is due to the fact that it generally reports only one side of the discussion: for Ānanda, by whom the sūtra was transmitted, recorded the Buddha's replies, but not Subhūti's unspoken doubts, which he was of course unable to perceive. When these doubts are discovered and made explicit the whole sūtra will become perfectly intelligible.

Following Vasubandhu, who had listed twenty-seven, Han-shan gives thirty-five such doubts. They concern, (1) the true nature of the Buddha, (2) the Dharma, which has been expounded in an apparently contradictory manner, and (3) the student himself, who may well wonder if he is qualified to understand and practise this sublime teaching. Part 1 of the sūtra, here consisting of chapters 1–16, is held to deal with seventeen coarse doubts, and Part 2, consisting of chapters 17–32, with eighteen subtle ones. It was thus a continuous string of the disciple's wrong conceptions, from the coarsest to the finest, which the Buddha broke up successively in his teaching of *prajñā*. 'When all one's doubts and repentance [for them] are wiped out for ever, one will abide in the Wisdom of Reality.'[115]

A more positive statement is found in the following passage, which occurs twice, once at the beginning of Part 1 and once at the beginning of Part 2, and the propounding of which, first at a lower and then at a higher level of significance, is according to Han-shan the occasion for the arising of the various gross and subtle doubts that the Buddha proceeds to break up. Subhūti has enquired how those who have set out in the Bodhisattva-vehicle should stand, how progress, how exert their thought. The Buddha replies:

> Here, Subhūti, someone who has set out in the vehicle of a Bodhisattva should produce a thought in this manner: 'As many beings as there are in the universe of beings, comprehended under the term "beings" – either egg-born, or born from a womb, or moisture-born, or miraculously born; with or without form; with perception, without perception, or with neither perception nor non-perception – as far as any conceivable universe of beings is conceived: all these should by me be led to Nirvāṇa, into that Realm of Nirvāṇa which leaves nothing behind. And yet, although innumerable beings have thus been led to Nirvāṇa, no being at all has been led to Nirvāṇa.' And why? If in a Bodhisattva the perception of a 'being' should take place, he could not be called a 'Bodhi-

being'. And why? He is not to be called a Bodhi-being, in whom the perception of a self or a being would take place, or the perception of a living soul or a person.[116]

These paradoxical words epitomize the fundamental teaching not of this sūtra only but of the entire Prajñā-pāramitā literature. Herein the sublimest religious ideal, that of absolute altruism, is conjoined with the realization of the profoundest metaphysical truth, that of *anātma* or no-self. The Bodhisattva of the Mahāyāna represents not the mere juxtaposition but the living spiritual unity of these two basic themes of Buddhism. Moreover, while from the practical standpoint (which, despite its appearance of rarefied metaphysics, the sūtra at bottom adopts) this is its principal application of the doctrine of *anātma*, it is by no means the only one. The consequences of seeing all things as void of self are worked out for various other universes of discourse. In this way, although the word 'empty' is not even once mentioned, the sūtra also 'places' the doctrine of *śūnyatā* in an ontological, a psychological, a logical, and a soteriological context.

Ontologically, the selflessness of everything means that there is no *dharma*. The ultimate elements into which the Abhidharma had so painstakingly analysed the whole psychophysical universe do not exist in themselves, nor does the doctrine which contains that analysis. In the absolute sense all the categories of Buddhist thought are unreal. Even 'Buddha' and 'Bodhisattva' are merely names. Psychologically, the disciple is urged to develop a thought which is not fixed, or attached, or established anywhere; which does not settle down anywhere taking the data of experience for the 'signs' (*nirmita*) of an actually existent entity whether 'beings' or 'Nirvāṇa'. Logically, the sūtra teaches that each of the great categories of Buddhist thought is identical with its opposite. For example, a mass of merit is so-called because it is a no-mass. Symbolically, A = not-A. Soteriologically, the Buddha and his Enlightenment are strictly transcendental.

If the publication of the short sūtras was intended to make the message of the Prajñā-pāramitā more widely accessible, then the *Diamond Sūtra*, at least, may be said to have performed that function to perfection. Its popularity throughout the whole Far Eastern and Central Asian Buddhist world is attested in numerous ways. The original Sanskrit text of the sūtra has survived complete in three different forms: in a manuscript from Japan, a blockprint from China, and a bilingual

Tibetan blockprint from Beijing. Extensive fragments have also been recovered from eastern Turkestan, where an incomplete version in old Khotanese was also found, and from Gilgit in Kashmir. Six Chinese translations are extant, beginning with Kumārajīva's (402CE), and proceeding through those of Bodhiruci (509CE), Paramārtha (562CE), Dharmagupta (605CE), and Hsüan-tsang (648CE), to that of I-tsing (703CE). They were not all made from the same recension; Kumārajīva's, indeed, was not made direct from the Sanskrit text at all. In addition there are various Tibetan, Mongolian, and Manchu translations, as well as one in Sogdian which has not survived complete. The hundred or so commentaries in Sanskrit, Tibetan, and Chinese, though of no concern to us here are nevertheless further evidence of the overwhelming popularity of the sūtra. In the West it has begun to attract a corresponding degree of attention. Editions of the Sanskrit text, and renderings into English, French, and German, have already appeared. In English alone there are at least eight complete translations, besides incomplete ones. Versions have also appeared in modern Japanese and in Thai. It would seem that the *Diamond Sūtra* is destined to exert no less influence in the future than it did in the past, and over an even vaster field.

The *Hṛdaya* or 'Heart' *Sūtra*, often bound up in one volume with the *Diamond Sūtra*, is the only Prajñā-pāramitā text that rivals it in popularity. Indeed, so closely are the two allied, both intrinsically and extrinsically, that it is really quite improper to speak in terms of rivalry at all. Though an extremely concentrated work, consisting of only a single leaf in most editions, it exists in two recensions, a long and a short one. These agree in the body of the sūtra, but the longer recension has, both at the beginning and the end, an account of the circumstances of its preaching. Like Strindberg's *The Stronger*, the sūtra is really a dialogue in which, although only one of them actually speaks, the two participants constitute, as it were, two poles between which is generated the energy that determines the dialectical movement of the exposition.

The participants are the Bodhisattva Avalokiteśvara, who does not figure prominently elsewhere in the Prajñā-pāramitā literature, and Śāriputra. It is the former who speaks. Addressing the great disciple by name, he reveals to him the content of his transcendental spiritual experience as he courses in the profound Perfection of Wisdom. In so doing, however, he employs the language of the Abhidharma, for this is the language Śāriputra understands. Thus the *Heart Sūtra* may be described as a debate between the Mahāyāna and the Hīnayāna wherein, in order to reveal the spiritual truths realized by the one, the doctrinal categories already established by the other are negated.

Specifically, as Conze has shown, the sūtra is a restatement of the four Noble Truths in the light of the dominant idea of Emptiness.[117] As in the case of several other very short sūtras, by far the greater portion of the material has been taken from the Large Prajñā-pāramitā. Nevertheless, the parts have been welded together into a convincing artistic unity, and the dialectical stages through which Avalokiteśvara conducts Śāriputra follow one upon another as inevitably, and as beautifully, as the movements of a Beethoven quartet. As if the message of the Prajñā-pāramitā were not already sufficiently condensed, the body of the sūtra proper concludes with a short *mantra* constituting as it were its veritable quintessence: *gate gate pāragate pārasaṃgate bodhi svāhā*. By the proper intonation of these words one's heart is opened to the influence of Perfect Wisdom.

The *Heart Sūtra* being as popular as the *Diamond Sūtra*, its literary backwash is no less impressive. The Sanskrit text of both recensions has been found in palm-leaf form in Japan, the shorter one having been brought there in 609CE and the longer in 850CE. In the course of six centuries seven Chinese translations of the sūtra were produced, by Kumārajīva – or one of his disciples – (c. 400CE), Hsüan-tsang (649CE), Dharmacandra (741CE), Prajñā (790CE), Prajñācakra (861CE), Fa-cheng (856CE), and Dānapāla (c. 1000CE). It was translated into Tibetan by Vimalamitra. There are also Mongolian and Manchu versions. Commentaries and expositions abound. Its popularity in the West is attested by a dozen English translations, besides six in French and one in German.

Three other short philosophical sūtras, though comparatively neglected, are hardly inferior to the *Diamond Sūtra* and the *Heart Sūtra* and must be accorded honourable mention. These are the Perfection of Wisdom 'in 500 lines', 'in 2,500 lines', and 'in 700 lines'. The first, extant only in Tibetan and Mongolian translation, is a simple and straightforward account of the ontology of the Prajñā-pāramitā. In the presence of 'a large congregation of monks and a great number of Bodhisattvas' the Buddha explains to Subhūti, whom he addresses throughout, how, with regard to the five *skandhas*, the Bodhisattva should comprehend and forsake the five poisons, develop the four boundless states, exert himself in the six *pāramitās*, tend the good friends, worship the Tathāgata, know the emptiness, the signless, and the wishless concentrations, and fully know the three characteristics of conditioned existence and the quiet calm of Nirvāṇa.

The Perfection of Wisdom 'in 2,500 lines', generally known as *Suvikrāntivikrāmī-paripṛcchā* or 'Question of Suvikrāntivikrāmin', which survives in the original Sanskrit, as well as in Chinese, Tibetan, and Mongolian, enjoys the distinction of being 'easily the most advanced Prajñā-pāramitā text' that we possess.[118] It is pitched on a high spiritual and metaphysical level and fairly bristles with references to the Abhidharma.

The third and last work, the Perfection of Wisdom 'in 700 lines', sometimes known as the Perfection of Wisdom 'as taught by Mañjuśrī', that Bodhisattva being after the Buddha the chief interlocutor of the sūtra, has come down to us in Sanskrit, Chinese (three translations), Tibetan, and Mongolian. Though like the *Diamond Sūtra* it endeavours to bring out the startling and paradoxical nature of the teaching, and again and again returns to the identity of seemingly contradictory opposites, it exhibits several distinctive features. Repetitions are rare. The 'hidden meaning' (*saṃdhā*), mentioned once in the *Vajracchedikā*, but never in the Large Prajñā-pāramitā sūtras, here plays an important part. Moreover, in dealing with the contradictory opposites the sūtra goes so far as to identify Enlightenment and the five deadly sins. While the first of these developments shows affinities with the Yogācāra, the second points in the direction of the *tantras*.

The last and longest phase in the development of the Prajñā-pāramitā literature, which extended from 600 to 1200CE, was one of further contraction and growing Tantric influence. To it belong about a dozen very short philosophical sūtras, six of them named after the Bodhisattva to whom the teaching is principally addressed. In the manner of the *Hṛdaya*, most of these works conclude with, or contain, a magical formula with which the limit of condensation is reached and which concentrate into a few words, or even into a single syllable, the 'thrice-repurèd' essence of Perfect Wisdom.

One sūtra, the *Svalpākṣarā* or Perfection of Wisdom 'in a few syllables', the text of which exists in Sanskrit, Chinese, Tibetan, and Mongolian, was evidently designed as a sort of Tantric counterpart to the *Hṛdaya*. The interlocutors are the Buddha and Avalokiteśvara. Unlike the *Heart Sūtra*, which is addressed to the spiritual elite, this version of the Perfection of Wisdom teachings is meant for those of meagre endowments and modest aspirations. According to Avalokiteśvara, who solicits the Lord to preach, it is 'of great merit: When they merely hear it, all beings will extinguish the obstacles (arising from their past) deeds, and they will definitely end up in enlightenment; and the Mantras of the beings who labour zealously at the evocation of Mantras will succeed without fail.'[119] One short *mantra* and a long *dhāraṇī*, which comprise the 'few syllables' of the title, are subsequently given.

Other works of this phase are shorter still, consisting of magical formulas only, with no discursive matter other than a short introduction and conclusion. Texts of this class are usually known as *dhāraṇīs*, a term which thus covers not only the magical formula itself but the type of short canonical text wherein such a formula (or formulas) constitutes the principal, if not the sole, content.

Longer than the dozen sūtras already mentioned, and rather different in style, is the *Adhyardhaśatikā* or Perfection of Wisdom 'in 150 lines', which survives in Sanskrit, Chinese (six translations), Tibetan, Mongolian, and (though imperfectly) in Khotanese. Quoted though it is by Candrakīrti and Haribhadra as an authoritative Prajñā-pāramitā text, this work is as much a *tantra* as a sūtra and therefore belongs equally to the next section. It comprises fifteen chapters. In the first fourteen (each of which is really a small litany) a 'mythical' Buddha – and in the first ten chapters a great Bodhisattva also – expounds not only the Prajñā-pāramitā teachings but a distinctively Tantric method (*naya*) for their realization. These methods all belong to the Outer Tantra. The terminology of the work is largely esoteric and the message of each chapter is summed up in *bījas* or magically powerful germ-syllables, literally 'seeds', such as *aṃ* and *bhyo*.

Tantric influence also resulted in the production of a number of ritual texts, including liturgies and evocations, devoted to the iconography of the Prajñā-pāramitā, conceived as a 'goddess', for purposes mainly of ritual worship and meditative visualization. One at least of these texts is called a sūtra, but for the evocations, at least, *sādhana* is the more usual term. In these texts the Holy Prajñā-pāramitā, the Blessed Lady, appears in a great variety of forms, red, white, blue, yellow, or green in colour, with either two or four arms, and supporting different emblems. An early non-canonical source describes her as sitting cross-legged on a white lotus. The body is golden yellow, grave and majestic, with a precious necklace and a crown, from which silken bands hang down on both sides. Her left hand, near her heart, carries the book. Her right hand, near her breasts, makes the gesture of argumentation.[120] It is amidst solemn and gorgeous visions of this type that the canonical Prajñā-pāramitā literature, after more than a millennium of development, at last comes to an end.

# 11

# THE VIMALAKĪRTI AND SUKHĀVATĪ SŪTRAS

## The Exposition of Vimalakīrti and the Happy Land Sūtras

The Mahāyāna's elucidation of the true meaning of the term Sangha, or spiritual community, is contained principally in the *Vimalakīrti-nirdeśa* or 'Exposition of Vimalakīrti', probably the most important sūtra of its class. As the earliest Chinese translation of this work was made in 222–229 CE (according to some sources an even earlier translation was made in 188 CE), and as it is in any case cited in his *Mahā-prajñā-pāramitā Śāstra* by Nāgārjuna, who flourished not later than the middle of the second century CE, this is undoubtedly one of the oldest Mahāyāna scriptures, belonging to the same period, approximately, as the *Saddharma-puṇḍarīka* and the *Aṣṭasāhasrikā*.

According to its own account, the sūtra originated in Vaiśālī. In view of the fact that it not only upholds the Bodhisattva ideal, but glorifies as its supreme exemplar one who is formally a layman, this circumstance is of special significance. Vaiśālī, conspicuous during the Master's lifetime for devotion to him and to his teaching, was the venue, a century after the *parinirvāṇa*, of the so-called Second Council, in connection with which there occurred the serious disagreement within the monastic community which, in the course of two or three decades, led to the first great schism in the Sangha, that between the Sthavīravādins and the Mahāsaṅghikas. It is well known that the latter were opposed to an exclusively monastic interpretation of the Dharma-Vinaya, and stood for a common spiritual ideal – that of the Bodhisattva – for all sections of the Buddhist community. Whether or not the actual exponent of the teachings here attributed to him, Vimalakīrti might therefore well have been a historical personage who, either before or after the schism, occupied a prominent place in the Mahāsaṅghika movement and who, on account of his extraordinary spiritual attainments, lived on in the imagination of the Mahāyāna.

Unfortunately, except for a few passages quoted in Śāntideva's famous compendium the *Śikṣā-samuccaya* and in Kamalaśīla's *Bhāvanā-krama*, the Sanskrit text of the sūtra is no longer available. The Chinese translations also suffered heavy casualties. Out of the nine or ten that were made, only six are now extant. Among these are the translations of Kumārajīva (406CE) and Hsüan-tsang (650CE), Kumārajīva's version being the one most widely read and studied. There are also two Tibetan translations, while fragments of a version in Khotanese are among the texts recovered from the sands of eastern Turkestan. From the fact that the former is said generally to agree with the Chinese versions it may be concluded that, unlike so many other Mahāyāna sūtras, in the case of the *Vimalakīrti* there are no problems connected with the existence of a multiplicity of different recensions of the text. Numerous commentaries on the sūtra were composed by Chinese and Japanese scholars. In modern times, six complete English translations have appeared, as well as one French and one German translation.

By what seems a case of correspondence rather than coincidence, in much the same way that the Sangha is, so to speak, the offspring of the Buddha and the Dharma, the *Vimalakīrti* represents, if not a joint product of the *Saddharma-puṇḍarīka* and the Prajñā-pāramitā, at least the result of a confluence of the same great streams of influence which had found, in these two sūtras, a separate and independent expression. While the spiritual and doctrinal content of the *Vimalakīrti* is ultimately identical with that of the Perfection of Wisdom corpus, so far as literary form is concerned it resembles the *Saddharma-puṇḍarīka*. Although not conceived on the same colossal scale as the latter, the main body of the work nevertheless possesses both artistic unity and dramatic interest. Moreover, the narrative and dramatic, the discursive and symbolic, elements are nicely blended, so that the prevailing impression is one of balance, proportion, and harmony. The sūtra comprises fourteen short chapters and, so far as one can judge from the translations, it was written mainly in prose.[121] There are no repetitions, and no recapitulations in one medium of what has already been delivered at length in another. As already noticed, the scene of the discourse is Vaiśālī, the immediate venue being the park or garden which Āmrapāli, the celebrated courtesan, had donated to the Buddha.

Chapter 1, entitled 'The Purification of the Buddha-field' (*Buddha-kṣetra*), opens with the usual description of the congregation. Attending upon the Buddha in Āmrapāli's park are 8,000 great monks and 32,000 Bodhisattvas. After the qualities and attributes of the latter have been detailed in the usual grandiloquent terms, the fifty-two most prominent Bodhisattvas, ending with Maitreya and Mañjuśrī, are enumerated by name. In Hsüan-tsang's version, Ajita, usually identified with Maitreya, occurs separately. Mention is also made of 10,000 Brahmā gods, thousands of deities and non-human beings of various classes, and many monks and nuns and male and female lay devotees.

Surrounded by this innumerable host of beings, the Buddha was preaching the Dharma. He sat on a jewel-adorned lion throne, and, towering above the assembly, seemed like Sumeru, the king of mountains, appearing in the midst of the great ocean. At that time Ratnakūṭa[122] or 'Jewel-Heap', the son of a wealthy merchant of Vaiśālī, came with five hundred companions to worship the Blessed One. Each of them offered a canopy adorned with the seven precious things. By the supernormal power of the Buddha, these were all transformed into one great canopy which, covering the whole chiliocosm, was seen clearly to reflect all the features of the worlds. Amazed at the phenomenon, the assembly worshipped the Lord, while Ratnakūṭa burst forth into a hymn of praise. This done, Ratnakūṭa informed the Buddha that his five hundred companions all cherished the Will to Supreme Enlightenment and wished to hear from him about the purity of the Buddha-land. Would the Buddha preach the way to the Pure Land, which the Bodhisattvas ought to walk?

Acceding to his request, the Buddha declared that beings of all kinds constitute the Buddha-land of the Bodhisattvas, for it is for their sake, and in accordance with their needs, that such a realm comes into being. Just as a palace can be built on the ground, but not way up in the sky, so a Bodhisattva establishes his Buddha-land for the purification of beings where beings actually exist, not somewhere out in empty space. Furthermore, he tells the young merchant, the sincere mind is the Pure Land of the Bodhisattva; when he shall have arrived at Supreme Enlightenment, beings who never flatter will be reborn therein. The same formula is repeated for the firm mind and the

Mahāyāna-mind. Similarly, all those who practise the six *pāramitās*, the four boundless states, and the four elements of conversion, will, after their attainment of Enlightenment, be reborn in his Pure Land. In this way a number of standard doctrinal categories are enumerated.

Finally, the Buddha declares, 'O Ratnakūṭa, if a Bodhisattva wishes to obtain a Pure Land, he should purify his mind. When his mind is pure, his Buddha-land will be pure.'[123] Śāriputra, who is among the bhikshus present, doubts this. How is it, he wonders, that this Buddha-land of ours should be so impure, seeing that the Buddha established it out of his pure mind when he was a Bodhisattva? Reading the disciple's thoughts, the Buddha explains that, just as the sun and moon remain bright whether the blind perceive their brightness or not, so his Buddha-land is ever pure, only Śāriputra is unable to see its purity. Śankhacūḍa, or 'Conch Crest', a Brahmin king, then rebukes Śāriputra, and the two have an argument as to whether or not the present Buddha-world is really pure. Thereupon, as though to settle the dispute, the Buddha, exercising his supernormal power, reveals the whole chiliocosm in all its flawless purity and jewel-adorned splendour to the assembly, all of whom find themselves seated on jewelled lotuses. Śāriputra is at last convinced. The seeming impurity of his realm, the Buddha explains, is only a device to save beings of inferior capacities. If one's mind is pure, he will behold the world adorned with splendour. Ratnakūṭa and his companions attain a high stage of spiritual progress, the Buddha withdraws his supernormal power, and, after the world has resumed its everyday appearance, even followers of the Hīnayāna (here called the Śrāvakayāna) are benefited. Here chapter 1 ends and, so far as the rest of the sūtra is concerned, Ratnakūṭa disappears from the scene.

It is, indeed, possible that this chapter originally formed an independent sūtra. Continuity of narration between it and the remainder of the *Vimalakīrti*, the main body of which is fairly well unified, is lacking, the sole connecting link being the fact that Vimalakīrti, like Ratnakūṭa, lived at Vaiśālī. Nevertheless, apart from their similarity of tone and spirit, there is a real, though not very obvious, connection between the two parts. Or rather, there is a connection between the Pure Land idea, constituting the subject matter of this chapter, and the glorification of the lay Bodhisattva in the main body of the work. The nature of this connection will be made clear below, after the

*Vimalakīrti* has been dealt with, when we come to the 'Happy Land' group of sūtras.

Chapter 2, entitled 'Inconceivable Skilful Means' (*upāya-māga*), at once introduces us to Vimalakīrti, or 'Pure Repute', the wealthy householder of Vaiśālī. In view of the misunderstandings to which the conception of lay Bodhisattvaship is open, it should be pointed out that Vimalakīrti is not an ordinary layman who is, at the same time, a Bodhisattva, but a Bodhisattva appearing in the guise of a layman – quite a different thing. After describing him as having done homage to the countless Buddhas of the past, planted deep the roots of merit, and attained to the patient acceptance of the non-origination of all dharmas, and so on, as well as loyal to the Mahāyāna, following the conduct of a Buddha, and great in mind as the ocean, the sūtra in fact explicitly states that he dwelt in Vaiśālī only as a skilful means, out of a desire to save sentient beings. As we shall see, this conception of the Bodhisattva's skilful means (*upāya-kauśalya*), not only gives its name to the present chapter, but dominates the thought and action of the entire work.

If the Prajñā-pāramitā sūtras show us *prajñā* or Perfect Wisdom, in the *Vimalakīrti* we see that Wisdom in its soteriological functioning. Thus the latter is not only 'profound' in principle but 'ample' in practice. That Vimalakīrti is a layman only in name is clear from the way in which the description continues.

> Though but a white-robed *upāsaka*, yet observing the pure monastic discipline; though living at home, yet never desirous of anything; though possessing a wife and children, always exercising pure virtues; though surrounded by his family, holding aloof from worldly pleasures; though using the jewelled ornaments of the world, yet adorned with spiritual splendour; though eating and drinking, yet enjoying the flavour of the rapture of meditation; though frequenting the gambling house, yet leading the gamblers into the right path; though coming in contact with heresy, yet never letting his true faith be impaired; though having a profound knowledge of worldly learning, yet ever finding pleasure in things of the spirit as taught by Buddha....[124]

By countless such expedients as these, the passage at length concludes, Vimalakīrti, the wealthy householder, benefited all sentient beings.

One day, through the same skilful means, he brought upon himself a sickness. Many prominent persons came to see him. Taking his sickness as the occasion, he preached to them a discourse of the transiency, impotence, untrustworthiness, unreality, impurity, and danger of the physical body which, for its starkness and vehemence, would have done credit to the most body-hating Hīnayāna ascetic. Abhorring such a body, he told his visitors, they should desire the body of a Buddha, that is to say the *dharmakāya*, which is born of infinite pure virtues (*puṇya*) and knowledge (*jñāna*). As the result of this exhortation, countless thousands of people came to cherish the Will to Enlightenment. The episode is of great significance. Vimalakīrti preached the Mahāyāna only *after* preaching the Hīnayāna. This is because, the latter being the foundation of the former, any attempt to develop Mahāyāna Wisdom and Compassion without first having had recourse to Hīnayāna renunciation and purification is doomed to failure.

In chapter 3, the Buddha, coming to know of Vimalakīrti's sickness, asks Śāriputra to go and enquire after his health. But the great disciple protests his unworthiness for such a mission. Once, he tells the Lord, he was sitting quietly under a tree in the forest, meditating. Vimalakīrti came to him and declared that to sit quietly meant to withdraw both body and mind from the triple world, not to rise from the meditation of cessation (of all thought-processes); and yet to exercise all the modes of daily life, as well as not to relinquish the qualities of Enlightenment and yet to display the activities of common people – together with much else to the same effect. Śāriputra was astounded. Consequently he was not worthy, he felt, to go and enquire about Vimalakīrti's health. The Buddha then asks, in turn, Mahāmaudgalyāyana, Mahākāśyapa, Subhūti, Pūrṇa Maitrāyaṇīputra, Mahākātyāyana, Aniruddha, Upāli, Rāhula, Ānanda, and the rest of the five hundred great disciples. But one and all they refuse, each having had in the past some encounter with Vimalakīrti, which they relate, and on account of which they consider themselves unworthy to visit him.

Including Śāriputra's, ten of these stories are given in the text. Each one centres upon that branch of the Dharma in which the disciple in question was, according to tradition, particularly proficient. The formidably ascetic Mahākāśyapa, for example, while begging alms in a poor village, was rebuked for showing compassion to the poor but not to the rich, and treated to a discourse on universal sameness. Pūrṇa Maitrāyaṇīputra, preaching to novices under a tree, was warned to examine people's minds before instructing them. Bad food should not be put in a jewelled bowl; in the same way the Hīnayāna should not be preached to those who, in a previous life, had followed the Mahāyāna, but temporarily forgotten it. Upāli, the expert in monastic discipline, was expounding the Vinaya to two monks who had broken the precepts. Vimalakīrti, however, taught them that mind in its absolute essence is free from both purity and impurity, which are only false assumptions. The Vinaya is truly observed by one who knows that all dharmas are unreal.

Thus in this chapter, entitled 'The Reluctance of the Disciples', the limitations of the Hīnayāna are exposed and corrected in the light of higher teachings. Śāriputra and the rest having proved unequal to the task, in chapter 4, entitled 'The Reluctance of the Bodhisattvas', the Buddha asks their Mahāyāna counterparts to visit Vimalakīrti. But the Bodhisattvas are no less unwilling than the disciples. They too, it transpires, have been worsted in encounters with the wily old sage. All recount their experiences, only those of the Bodhisattva Maitreya, the young man Prabhavyūha, Bodhisattva Vasuṃdhara, and Sudatta, the son of a wealthy merchant, being actually included in the text.

Maitreya, whom the Buddha had assured of Supreme Enlightenment after one more birth, was taught the relativity of time and impossibility, in the absolute sense, of any such attainment. 'In reality, there is none cherishing the Will to Supreme Enlightenment, nor is there anyone who regresses therefrom. O Maitreya, thou shouldst strive to make those gods (i.e. of the Tuṣita *devaloka*, where the future Buddha now resides) abandon the false idea that there is Bodhi by itself.'[125]

Vasuṃdhara's experience is particularly interesting. Māra, the Evil One, appearing in the guise of Indra, king of the gods, offered to bestow upon him 12,000 heavenly nymphs. Being a monk, he refused them. Vimalakīrti thereupon appeared, exposed Māra in his true colours, and demanded the nymphs for himself. Māra having been forced to hand them over, Vimalakīrti not only induced them to cherish the Will to Supreme Enlightenment but instructed them in the pleasures of the Dharma, as opposed to the pleasures of the senses, with such effect that, eventually, they were reluctant to return with their erstwhile master to his heavenly palaces. Vimalakīrti, however, sent them back, though not without first teaching them the doctrine of the Inextinguishable Light:

> By the Inextinguishable Light is meant this – just as from one light we can produce a hundred or even a thousand other lights, brightening up the darkness, yet the original light is not thereby exhausted: thus, sisters, a Bodhisattva can teach a hundred or even a thousand beings to cherish the Will to Supreme Enlightenment, yet his own Will to Supreme Enlightenment is not at all extinguished.... Though ye be in the palace of the Evil One, yet possessing this Inextinguishable Light ye can make the innumerable Gods and heavenly nymphs cherish the Will to Supreme Enlightenment.[126]

This chapter serves to expose the limitations of a literalistic understanding of the Mahāyāna itself.

Chapter 5 is entitled 'The Consolation of the Invalid'. In compliance with the Buddha's request the great Bodhisattva Mañjuśrī, though fully aware of the difficulty of the undertaking, agrees to visit Vimalakīrti. Accompanied by an immense concourse of Bodhisattvas, śrāvakas, and gods, all of whom are eager to hear the discussion, he accordingly enters the city of Vaiśālī. Apprised of their coming, Vimalakīrti, by his supernormal power, empties his chamber of everything except a bed, on which he lays himself down. After a brisk exchange of Prajñā-pāramitā subtleties, from which it is evident that the great Bodhisattva is not to be so easily caught out, Mañjuśrī comes to the point and tells Vimalakīrti that the Buddha has sent him to ask after his health and enquires the nature of his sickness. In a passage which is as famous as any from a Mahāyāna sūtra, Vimalakīrti replies:

> From ignorance we hold attachment, and my sickness is thus caused. Since all beings are sick, I am sick. If they are no more sick then my sickness would cease. And why? A Bodhisattva enters (a life of) birth and death for the sake of all beings; where there are birth and death, there is always sickness. If all beings were free from sickness, then there would be no more sickness with a Bodhisattva. Just as when the only son of a wealthy merchant becomes sick, then his parents (from their anxiety) become sick also, and when he is restored to health,

> then they also recover their health; even so, a Bodhisattva loves all beings as parents love an only son. As long as all beings are sick he is sick; when they recover their health, he also recovers his health. Again thou hast enquired about the cause of my sickness. The sickness of a Bodhisattva is caused only by his Great Compassion.[127]

Next, Mañjuśrī enquires why Vimalakīrti's chamber is empty. This leads to a discussion of *śūnyatā*. Further questions follow. What is the form of Vimalakīrti's sickness? How should a Bodhisattva console another Bodhisattva who is unwell? How should a sick Bodhisattva conquer his mind? In reply to the last question Vimalakīrti delivers a long and important discourse which occupies the greater part of the chapter. The main point of the discourse is that the life of a Bodhisattva consists in the perfect unity of wisdom and skilful means.

Chapters 6–8 are taken up with further discussions, and a lot more exposition, though in the latter part of chapter 6, entitled 'The Inconceivable Emancipation', an element of symbolic phantasmagoria is introduced. Śāriputra having worried about the absence of seats, and been sharply rebuked, Vimalakīrti by his supernormal power not only produces 32,000 lion thrones each 84,000 *yojanas* in height but enlarges his chamber so as to accommodate them all. Only the more advanced Bodhisattvas are able to mount these thrones, not the novice Bodhisattvas and the disciples. Vimalakīrti therefore advises the latter to worship the Tathāgata Sumerupradīparāja, from whose Buddha-field the thrones had been sent, after which they are able to take their seats. Thereupon Vimalakīrti delivers a discourse on the Inconceivable Emancipation (*acintya-vimokṣa*), by means of which, so he tells Śāriputra and the rest of the assembly, a Bodhisattva can enclose Mount Sumeru in a mustard seed, lengthen seven days to an aeon and reduce an aeon to seven days, and manifest himself as a Buddha or in whatever other form he chooses.

Chapter 7, 'The Goddess', which opens with an explanation of how the Bodhisattva, though regarding all beings as unreal, yet practises compassion, is occupied mainly with Śāriputra's encounter with a heavenly nymph. This episode is a longer and more interesting counterpart of the conclusion of *Saddharma-puṇḍarīka* chapter 11. Here, however, Śāriputra is more roughly handled, for the nymph, who is an enlightened being, not only lectures him on the highest truths of the Mahāyāna but, by her supernormal powers, transforms him into a female shape and herself into the likeness of Śāriputra in order to demonstrate that, in the ultimate sense, the distinction of masculine and feminine is unreal.

In chapter 8, 'The Family of the Tathāgata', Vimalakīrti tells Mañjuśrī that the Bodhisattva understands the Buddha's Way by walking in no-way, after which he proceeds to explain, in the same paradoxical manner, how he so walks. This is followed by a long and exceptionally fine verse passage in which Vimalakīrti, questioned as to where his household is, replies that Wisdom is the Bodhisattva's mother, Skilful Means his father, Enjoyment of the Doctrine his wife, Sympathy and Mercy his daughters, Goodwill and Sincerity his sons, Emptiness and Quietude his house, the Crowd of Passions his disciples, the Wings of Enlightenment his companions, the Perfections his 'good friends', and so on.[128] He then describes the various expedients by means of which the Bodhisattva helps sentient beings.

With chapter 9, entitled 'Entering the Dharma-Door of Non-Duality', we come to what is, from the dramatic point of view, the climax of the sūtra. Vimalakīrti asks all the Bodhisattvas present to explain how a Bodhisattva enters the Dharma-Door of Non-Duality (*advaya-dharma*). Thirty-one of the replies which they give to this question are recorded in the text. Śrīśiras says: 'Purity and impurity make two. If you see the real nature of impurity, then there is no state of purity, and you conform to the state of purity. This is entering the Dharma-Door of non-duality.' Sādhumati says: 'Saṃsāra and Nirvāṇa make two. See the (true) nature of Saṃsāra, and then there is no Saṃsāra, no bondage, no liberation, no burning and no cessation.' In the same way self and no-self, knowledge and ignorance, form and the emptiness of form, together with various other pairs of doctrinal categories, are disposed of by the Bodhisattvas. This having been done, Mañjuśrī is asked for his opinion. He says: 'According to my idea, to have no word and no speech, no showing and no awareness about any of the dharmas, and to keep away from all questions and anwers, is to enter the Dharma-Door of non-duality.' It is now Vimalakīrti's turn to speak. But upon his own question being put to him by Mañjuśrī 'Vimalakīrti kept silent, without a word.'[129]

After this 'thunderous silence' nothing more, one would have thought, remained to be said, and the sūtra perhaps ought to have ended here. Apart from the conclusion, however, there are still four more chapters to come. These have little or no connection with the main line of dramatic action, and confine themselves to developing certain aspects of the teachings already delivered. The element of symbolic phantasmagoria is prominent. In chapter 10, 'The Food Brought by the Emanated Bodhisattva', the entire assembly is fed from a single bowl of perfume, and a bowlful remains. In the following chapter, chapter 11, dealing with 'The Instruction of the Exhaustible and the Inexhaustible', Vimalakīrti, Mañjuśrī, and the assembly go to pay homage to Śākyamuni Buddha, who explains to Ānanda the countless forms of Buddha-service and skilful means which the Bodhisattvas employ. Chapter 12, entitled 'Seeing Akṣobhya Buddha', may be an interpolation. Herein, for the benefit of the assembly, Vimalakīrti manifests Akṣobhya's Buddha-field, known as Abhirati, the Land of 'Exceeding Great Delight'. The last of these four chapters deals with 'Worship of the Dharma'.[130] Śākyamuni tells a story to illustrate that Dharma-worship is the supreme form of worship, and that it is with this that the Buddha should be revered.

Chapter 14, with which the sūtra concludes, is entitled 'The Final Commission'. The Buddha entrusts the sūtra to Maitreya. He then explains to him that Bodhisattvas are of two types, one fond of diverse phraseology and literary ornament, the other unafraid of profound teachings and able to penetrate deeply into true Suchness. While the former are new to the training, the latter have cultivated the path for a long time. The two ways in which those new to the training may fail to accept the profound teachings, and the two ways in which though accepting them, they may still injure themselves and be unable to acquiesce in the non-origination of all dharmas, are also made clear. Delighted by these explanations, Maitreya promises to protect and propagate the sūtra. Hereupon all the Bodhisattvas declare that, after the *parinirvāṇa*, they will proclaim the Doctrine of Supreme Enlightenment and introduce this scripture to all preachers of the Dharma. The gods known as the Four Great Kings undertake to protect whoever reads, recites, and explains it. Finally, the Buddha entrusts the sūtra to Ānanda, who asks by what name it should be known. He is told that it is called 'The Sūtra of Vimalakīrti's Exposition', also known as 'The Doctrine System of Inconceivable Emancipation'. Amidst the usual rejoicings the scene closes.

Before proceeding to a rapid survey of the 'Happy Land' sūtras we must examine the nature of their connection with the *Vimalakīrti*, or rather, with the Bodhisattva ideal understood as a restatement, or reinterpretation, of the third of the Three Jewels – that is to say, as an ideal for the layman as well as for the monk. Though monk and layman were originally on a footing of complete spiritual equality, with the growth of the coenobium Arhantship in the narrower, more individualistic, Hīnayāna sense came to be regarded as the prerogative of monks and nuns, and rebirth after death in a happy heavenly abode as the goal of the laity.

These developments, which had been invested with the authority of the Master and enshrined in the Buddhavacana, the Mahāyāna, as yet nascent and inchoate, could hardly reject out of hand; but it could, and did, transform them. Gradually, the old heavens were spiritualized, and peopled not with gods but with Buddhas and Bodhisattvas, while rebirth in them came to depend not only on almsgiving and ethics but also on the adoption of a definitely 'religious' attitude and the cultivation of distinctively religious virtues. The urge to self-transcendence is inalienable. What in fact happened was that, the laity as such having been denied the right to aim at Arhantship and relegated to the pursuit of an inferior ideal, heaven assumed for them in their eyes some of the characteristics of Nirvāṇa.

This development was facilitated by, or associated with, the conception of *Buddha-kṣetra* or Buddha-field, which came into prominence at about the same time. A Buddha's field of knowledge is co-extensive with the entire universe; but his field of influence, within which he exercises spiritual authority, and for the spiritual evolution of whose inhabitants he is personally responsible, is limited to a particular range of world-systems. These are known as his Buddha-field. Buddha-fields are of two kinds, impure and pure. An impure Buddha-field – of which our own Buddha-field, presided over by Śākyamuni Buddha, is an example – is identical with a range of natural world-systems inhabited by all the six classes of sentient beings, namely gods, men, anti-gods, animals, revenants, and tormented spirits. A pure Buddha-field, on the contrary, is not natural but ideal, standing outside the three planes of conditioned existence. Apart from the presiding Buddha and his Bodhisattvas, it is inhabited exclusively by gods and men.

In certain respects a Pure Land, as this kind of Buddha-field is generally called, resembles the Suddhāvāsa or 'Pure Abodes' of Hīnayāna cosmology, that is to say, the five highest heavens of the world of form (*rūpaloka*), where the *anāgāmins* or Non-Returners are born and attain Nirvāṇa; for in a Pure Land, as in these *devalokas*, conditions are more favourable to the attainment of Enlightenment than those on earth, and there is no regression to a lower state of existence. Otherwise, the Pure Land is entirely Mahāyānic. While the *anāgāmin* has the companionship only of those of the same degree of spiritual attainment as himself, and continues to rely on his own efforts, those who are born in a Pure Land are not only thrilled and dazzled by its supernatural beauty, but enjoy the beatific vision of its Buddha and his Bodhisattvas, and have the privilege of hearing the Mahāyāna Doctrine from their lips.

The connection between the 'Happy Land' sūtras, which describe the Pure Land of Buddha Amitābha, and the Bodhisattva ideal understood as a restatement of the third of the Three Jewels, is now obvious. Both were part of the laity's creative response to their exclusion from full participation in the spiritual life of Buddhism. Moreover, after existing for some time in a comparatively crude and unsublimated religious form, both were fully integrated into the profoundest Mahāyāna philosophy, that is to say, into the Perfection of Wisdom teachings.

The Sukhāvatī or 'Happy Land' group of sūtras comprises three works. Of these, two bear the same title, both being known as the *Sukhāvatī-vyūha* or 'Array of the Happy Land'. Though one is eight times as long as the other, and though there are important discrepancies of content between them, they are probably different recensions of one and the same text, the long recension being undoubtedly the earlier one. In practice, the two are treated as independent works. The third member of the group is the *Amitāyur-dhyāna Sūtra* or 'Meditation on Amitāyus', the Buddha of Eternal Life, who is, of course, identical with Amitābha, the Buddha of Boundless Light. Far Eastern Buddhists sometimes refer to these three works as the *Large Sūtra*, the *Small Sūtra*, and the *Meditation Sūtra*, and for the sake of convenience we shall adopt this nomenclature.

After being lost for centuries, the original Sanskrit texts of the *Large* and *Small Sūtras* are again available, both having come to light in Japan during the latter half of the nineteenth century. Out of twelve Chinese translations of the *Large Sūtra* said to have been made, five are still extant, the earliest having been done between 147 and 186CE. Thus the date of composition of the sūtra cannot be placed later than the first century CE. Internal evidence also points to its antiquity. The venue of the discourse is the Vulture's Peak at Rājagṛha. Here the Buddha dwelt with a large company of bhikshus, all Arhants. While the qualities of the Arhants are described at length, with the usual stock epithets, and thirty-four of them are mentioned by name, the Bodhisattvas are referred to in the briefest terms, as though as an afterthought, mention being made simply of 'many noble-minded Bodhisattvas, led by Maitreya'. In a late Mahāyāna sūtra the Bodhisattvas would have occupied a much more conspicuous place.

The body of the sūtra opens with a dialogue between the Buddha and Ānanda. Observing the Lord to be in a superconscious state, his face bright as a golden cloud, Ānanda asks him what he is seeing or thinking. The Buddha thereupon enumerates a line of eighty-one Tathāgatas, beginning with Dīpaṅkara. During the period of the last of these, known as Lokeśvararāja, a monk named Dharmākara resolved to become a Buddha. He therefore went to Lokeśvararāja and asked him to describe the perfections of a Buddha-field. Having heard the perfections of eighty-one hundred thousand *niyutas* of *kotis* of Buddha-fields, Dharmākara concentrated them all into one and resolved to establish a Buddha-field eighty-one times more excellent still. This resolution he expressed before Lokeśvararāja in a series of forty-eight *praṇidhānas* or vows (two of which are missing from the Sanskrit text). Each vow embodied a different aspect of Sukhāvatī, the Land of Bliss, as it appeared to the creative imagination of Dharmākara.

Thereafter, life after life, he followed the course of a Bodhisattva, the sūtra's account of his conduct constituting, in effect, a short but attractive description of the Mahāyāna spiritual ideal. All this the Buddha relates to Ānanda as a kind of vision of what happened ten *kalpas* ago. Ānanda then asks what has become of the Bodhisattva Dharmākara. The Buddha replies that he now lives and teaches the Dharma in the Western quarter, in the world called Sukhāvatī, the Happy Land. As his light (*abha*), which illuminates in all directions Buddha-fields innumerable, and his length of life (*ayu*), are both immeasurable (*amita*), he is called by the names Amitābha and Amitāyus. This leads to a long and detailed description of the *vyūha* of the 'Happy Land' which takes up half the sūtra and constitutes its main subject matter. *Vyūha*, also *viyūha*, is a difficult and significant Buddhist Hybrid Sanskrit word meaning (according to Edgerton) 'arrangement', and implying magnificence and splendour.[131]

Addressing Ānanda, the Buddha says that in Sukhāvatī there is neither hell nor animal birth, nor revenants, nor anti-gods. This blessed land is fragrant with various sweet-smelling scents. Jewel trees in many hundreds of thousands of colours grow there, also wonderful lotus-blossoms. There are no mountains, the country being level like the palm of the hand, with districts full of jewels and treasures. Delightful rivers yield sweet, pleasant water, and the sound they make, in flowing along, is the heart-ravishing sound of the various categories of the Doctrine. The beings who are born in Sukhāvatī are all endowed with the most excellent qualities, physical and mental, and enjoy all imaginable pleasures. There is no difference between gods and men, no question of night and day, and no darkness. From time to time heavenly perfumed water, heavenly flowers, and other precious things, rain down in abundance. Even a *kalpa*, the Buddha declares, would not suffice to exhaust all the causes of happiness in the Pure Land of Amitābha. Nonetheless, the sūtra does its best. Descriptions are refined, epithets multiplied, and numbers raised to ever higher powers until the imagination staggers.

One impression, however, remains predominant throughout: light and colour. This is no accident; much less still is it a merely literary question of 'superabundant diction' and 'gushing eloquence', as one at least of an older generation of orientalists thought. Recent work in experimental psychology enables us to have a truer understanding of the sūtra's predilection for jewels and flowers. 'Praeternatural light and colour', writes Aldous Huxley in the course of an interesting study, 'are common to all visionary experiences. And along with light and colour there goes, in every case, a recognition of heightened significance. The self-luminous objects which we see in the mind's antipodes possess a meaning, and this meaning is, in some sort, as intense as their colour.'[132] Such things as precious stones and flowers, besides gold, silver, and crystal, and even glass, are by reason of their affinity with the luminous hinterland of the mind not only themselves vision-inducing but the best medium for the description of visionary experience. For this reason they figure prominently in certain kinds of religious, especially mystical, literature. The *Large Sūtra* is a detailed record of a visionary experience of a highly developed type. The heightened significance of which Huxley speaks is represented by the sound of the waters, which murmur the categories of the Doctrine. What he calls the mind's antipodes correspond to the lower levels of *dhyāna*, the divine inhabitants of which, when these are conceived cosmologically as planes of existence, have names indicative of various degrees of light.

The remainder of the sūtra deals chiefly with the causes leading to rebirth in the Happy Land and the various conditions of its inhabitants. Whoever again and again thinks reverently of Amitābha, the Buddha tells Ānanda, whoever increases his stock of merits, whoever develops the Will to Enlightenment, whoever prays to be reborn in that world, to him Amitābha appears at the time of his death, and he is reborn in Sukhāvatī. Indeed, even those who only think of Amitābha are born there. Further descriptions of the glories of the Happy Land and the virtues of its inhabitants, both in prose and in verse, then follow. At last Ānanda expresses a wish to see Amitābha. No sooner has he spoken than the Buddha emits from the palm of his hand a ray of light which illumines the whole universe, so that not only Ānanda but every living being can see Amitābha and his retinue of Bodhisattvas in the Happy Land, while they in Sukhāvatī can see Śākyamuni and the whole of his Buddha-field. Turning to Ajita, or Maitreya, the latter points out that the beings in Sukhāvatī, who are not born of woman, appear there seated on lotus-blossoms if they have firmly believed in Amitābha, or reposing inside the calyx of the unopened flower if their faith has been not quite firm. He also discloses the number of Bodhisattvas who will be born into the Happy Land from each Buddha-field. Finally, after the merits of the sūtra have been extolled, and the effect of the preaching on the congregation described, various miracles take place and the whole assembly, enraptured, praises the utterance of the Buddha.

The *Small Sūtra* was translated three times into Chinese, first by Kumārajīva in 402CE, and subsequently by Guṇabhadra and Hsüan-tsang. According to its own testimony, it was preached at the Jeta Grove at Śrāvastī. This time, not only the leading Arhant disciples, but also some of the most prominent Bodhisattvas, are mentioned by name. Addressing Śāriputra, the Buddha without preamble proceeds to describe the glories of the Happy Land. Apart from the fact that Sukhāvatī is here represented as 'adorned with seven terraces', instead of as being perfectly flat, the description, though much shorter than that of the *Large Sūtra*, is substantially the same. The sole innovation is a doctrinal one. Whereas in the *Large Sūtra* it is taught that rebirth in the Happy Land is dependent partly on the accumulation of a stock of merits, in the *Small Sūtra* this is explicitly denied. Beings are not born in that Buddha-field, the Buddha tells Śāriputra, as a result of good works performed in this present life. The one thing needful is that, having heard the name of Amitābha (in this passage called Amitāyus), a son or daughter of good family should, with thoughts undisturbed, keep it in mind for one, two, three, four, five, six, or seven nights. It appears that, while taking for granted the transcendental topography of Sukhāvatī as already given in the *Large Sūtra*, it is the special function of the *Small Sūtra* to make this revelation. We have discussed elsewhere the true significance of such a teaching.[133] Suffice it here to say that it serves to mark the discontinuity of the conditioned and the unconditioned, and that it is, if at all a teaching of salvation by faith, then of faith understood, not in the sense of credulity, but as the emotional counterpart of Wisdom.

The *Meditation Sūtra* was translated into Chinese by Kālayaśas, who arrived in China from India in 424CE. The Sanskrit original has been lost.[134] Once again the venue of the teaching is the Vulture's Peak at Rājagṛha. This time mention is made simply of 'a large assembly of monks' and 'thirty-two thousand of Bodhisattvas, led by Mañjuśrī Kumārabhūta'. Unlike the two other members of the Happy Land group, the *Meditation Sūtra* is rooted, as regards the circumstances of its preaching, in the facts of history. Indeed, the Buddha's discourse grows out of a dramatic situation in a way that reminds us of the *Saddharma-puṇḍarīka* and the *Vimalakīrti*. The transition from drama to discourse is managed, perhaps, more naturally than in either of these.

Ajātaśatru, heir-apparent to the throne of Māgadha, has imprisoned his righteous old father king Bimbisāra and attempted to starve him to death. The king is saved by his faithful consort Vaidehi, who secretly provides him with nutriment. On hearing of this, Ajātaśatru becomes so enraged that he is ready to kill his mother, but is restrained, and shuts her up within the palace instead. Saddened and distressed by her son's unnatural conduct, Vaidehi prays to the Buddha, who by his supernormal power at once appears in splendour before her, attended by Mahāmaudgalyāyana and Ānanda. After lamenting that she had given birth to such a wicked son, the queen in her wretchedness begs the World-Honoured One to tell her in detail of all the places where sorrow and trouble are unknown, where she can go to be reborn. She is weary, she says, of this sinful world, which is full of evil-doers. In future may she not hear or see any wicked person! May the Buddha teach her to meditate on a world wherein all actions are pure!

In response to this entreaty, which voices the yearning of humanity itself, afflicted by the miseries of existence, the Buddha delivers the discourse which constitutes the main body of the sūtra. First, he emits a golden ray which, having encircled the universe, comes to rest on the crown of his head and transforms itself into a golden pillar wherein Vaidehi sees reflected all the Pure Lands of the universe. Out of these she chooses Sukhāvatī, the Pure Land of Amitābha, and asks the Buddha to teach her how to concentrate her mind so as to obtain a right vision of that country. Śākyamuni explains that those wishing to be born in the Happy Land have to cultivate a threefold goodness:

> Firstly, they should act filially towards their parents and support them; serve and respect their teachers and elders; be of compassionate [heart], abstain from doing any injury, and cultivate the ten virtuous actions. Secondly, they should take and observe the vow of seeking refuge with the Three Jewels, fulfil all moral precepts, and not lower their dignity or neglect any ceremonial observance. Thirdly, they should give their whole mind to the attainment of [Enlightenment], deeply believe in (the principle of) cause and effect, study and recite (the Sūtras of) the Mahāyāna doctrine, and persuade and encourage others who pursue the same course as themselves.[135]

These instructions are of a preparatory nature. Sixteen meditations follow. Vaidehi is asked to visualize successively the disc of the setting sun; water, ice, and a blue ground intersected with golden cords; the foregoing in detail; the jewel trees of Sukhāvatī; the lotus ponds; the divine jewelled music galleries; the jewelled lotus throne; the golden form of Buddha Amitāyus, flanked by Avalokiteśvara on the right and Mahāsthāmaprāpta on the left; his bodily signs and aura; the signs of Avalokiteśvara; the signs of Mahāsthāmaprāpta; and herself reborn in Sukhāvatī, seated on a lotus. These twelve meditations constitute a progressive series. The rest are really not meditations at all. While the first explains how one should concentrate on the image of Amitāyus, each of the other three describes three grades of persons who are born in the Happy Land, making nine grades in all, together with the size and colour of their respective lotuses, and the degree of splendour with which, upon their arrival there, they are welcomed.

The discourse concluding, Vaidehi and her five hundred maidens are blessed by an epiphany of Amitāyus and the two Bodhisattvas in Sukhāvatī, and the Buddha assures them that they all will be reborn in that place. Ānanda is told the name, or rather names, of the sūtra, the merits of which are briefly extolled, after which the Buddha, traversing the sky, returns to the Vulture's Peak.

The philosophy of the spiritual exercises prescribed by the sūtra is explained in connection with the sixth meditation:

> Every Buddha Tathāgata is one whose (spiritual) body is the *Dharmadhātu-kāya* [Sphere of Reality], so that he may enter into the mind of any beings. Consequently, when you have perceived Buddha, it is indeed that mind of yours that possesses those thirty-two signs of perfection and eighty minor marks of excellence [which you see in him]. In fine, it is your mind that becomes Buddha, nay, it is your mind that is indeed Buddha. The ocean of true and universal knowledge of all the Buddhas derives its source from one's own mind and thought. Therefore you should apply your thought with an undivided attention on that Buddha Tathāgata, Arhat, the Holy and Fully Enlightened One.[136]

In other words, what one meditates upon, that one becomes. Hence the surest method of being born in Sukhāvatī after death is to meditate on it here and now.

This does not greatly differ from the Buddha's teaching to Ratnakūṭa, that if a Bodhisattva wishes to obtain a Pure Land, he should purify his own mind. It is possible, indeed, starting with the *Large Sūtra*, to discern a process of progressive refinement of the Pure Land conception. In the *Large Sūtra*, the Happy Land retains some of the features of an exoteric heaven, and rebirth there is brought about by remembrance of the Buddha, by good works, and by prayer. The *Small Sūtra* transposes the Dharma from the intellectual-conceptual to the emotional-symbolic key. By teaching psychologically that one is born in Sukhāvatī through faith, here really the emotional counterpart of Wisdom, it suggests that ontologically Sukhāvatī is a colourful symbol for Nirvāṇa. The *Meditation Sūtra*, going a step further, teaches that the Happy Land is 'not far from here'[137] and can be attained through meditation. Going furthest of all, the Ratnakūṭa chapter of the *Vimalakīrti* declares that this world itself is the Pure Land, but that we perceive it as impure owing to the irregularities of our own minds.

Besides the Happy Land group of sūtras, there exist a number of other canonical texts that describe the Pure Lands of Buddhas other than Amitābha/Amitāyus. Such, for example, are the *Akṣobhya-vyūha*, devoted to the praises of Abhirati, the 'Land of Exceeding Great Delight'; the *Karuṇā-puṇḍarīk a* or 'White Lotus of Compassion', which gives an acccount of Padma or 'Lotus', the Buddha-field of the Buddha Padmottara; and the *Bhaiṣajyaguru Sūtra*, wherein Śākyamuni, addressing first Mañjuśrī and then Ānanda, relates how, as a Bodhisattva, the Buddha Vaiduryaprabha or 'Azure Radiance', making twelve great vows, established a Pure Land in the East, and how beings may be reborn there.

A Pure Land is also described in the *Śrīmālādevi-siṃhanāda* or 'Queen Śrīmālā's Asseveration' (literally 'Lion-Roar'), a work that continues and develops the 'feminist' tendencies of the *Saddharma-puṇḍarīka* and the *Vimalakīrti* and also forms, together with the *Saṅdhi-nirmocana* and *Mahā-parinirvāṇa*, one of the principal canonical sources of the obscure and difficult *tathāgatagarbha* theory. The chief character of the sūtra is a woman, Queen Śrīmālā, to whom the Buddha appears and predicts that, after 20,000 aeons, she will become a Buddha named 'Universal Radiance'. In her Buddha-field – which is not mentioned by name – there will be no evil destiny (i.e. no rebirth as an animal, revenant, anti-god, or infernal being), and sentient beings will stay on the path of the ten skilful actions. Moreover, 'Any sentient being born in that Buddha land will surpass the Paranirmitavaśavartin deities in pleasure; glory of shape and colour; splendour in the sense objects of form, sound, odor, smell, tangibles; and ecstasy of that sentient being in all enjoyment.'[138] Having received her prediction Śrīmālā makes ten great vows, the first five constituting Hīnayāna ethics, the second five, Mahāyāna ethics. She also preaches the One Vehicle (*ekayāna*), that is to say, the Mahāyāna, asserting that the vehicles (*yānas*) of the disciples and the Pratyeka-Buddhas are included in the Great Vehicle and that, therefore, 'Great Vehicle' is an expression for Buddha Vehicle. Thus the three vehicles are reckoned as one vehicle, and it is by realizing the 'one vehicle' that one attains Supreme Enlightenment. Later she expounds the theory of the *tathāgatagarbha* or 'matrix' or 'embryo' of the Tathāgata, according to which there exists in sentient beings an intrinsically pure element capable of developing into Buddahood – a theory that may be seen as a reification of the principle of potentiality.

All the different Pure Lands described in the Mahāyāna sūtras appear to have enjoyed, at first, more or less equal distinction. Especially in India, the faithful aspired, according to their individual inclinations, to be reborn in Sukhāvatī, or Abhirati, or Padma, or even with Maitreya in the Tuṣita heaven. In the Far East, however, in China, Japan, and Korea, the unexampled popularity of Amitābha and Sukhāvatī led not only to the comparative eclipse of the other Buddhas and their respective Pure Lands but to the growth of a great devotional movement the canonical basis of which was the Happy Land group of sūtras. It is for this reason, historical rather than religious, that the three members of this group have been accorded a more detailed treatment than the other works of the same type just mentioned. Accounts of the Buddha-fields of Bodhisattvas, also, are not unknown. The *Mañjuśrī-Buddhakṣetra-guṇa-vyūha* describes the 'array of excellences' of the domain established by the Bodhisattva Mañjuśrī.

Other sūtras, again, deal with the legendary exploits of individual Buddhas and Bodhisattvas in a more general way. Notice has already been taken of the fact that chapters 21–26 of the *Saddharma-puṇḍarīka*, corresponding to chapters 26, 22, 24, 25, 27, and 28 of Kumārajīva's Chinese version, are posterior to the main body of that work, having been annexed thereto at a later date on account, probably, of its immense prestige. Each chapter eulogizes a particular Bodhisattva. Chapter 22 (of the Sanskrit text), for example, relates how Bhaiṣajyaguru (subsequently promoted to Buddhahood in the *Bhaiṣajyaguru Sūtra*) in one of his previous lives had worshipped the Buddha by an act of self-immolation, while in another life he had burned his hands for incense. Chapter 23 is devoted to Gadgadaśvara. This Bodhisattva, Śākyamuni tells an enquiring disciple, appears in numerous forms to preach the *Saddharma-puṇḍarīka*. 'Sometimes he appears as Brahma, or appears as Sakra, or appears as Isvara, or Mahesvara, or as a deva-general, or as the deva-king Vaisravana, or as a Holy Wheel-rolling king, or as one of the ordinary kings, or as an elder, as a citizen, or a minister,... as a monk, a nun,... a youth or maiden,... a man, or a non-human being.'[139] According to the inclinations of the beings to be saved, he transforms himself into a Hīnayāna teacher, into a Bodhisattva, or into a Buddha. All this he is able to do through the powers obtained from *samādhi*.

Best known of all the seven chapters, however, is chapter 24, which celebrates the praises of the great Bodhisattva Avalokiteśvara, here also called Samantamukha, and which even now often circulates as an independent work. Asked why Avalokiteśvara is so called, the Buddha replies that it is because he delivers from fire, flood, shipwreck, and other calamities those who invoke his name. He, too, assumes different forms according to the needs of sentient beings. Towards the end of the chapter his compassionate regard for suffering humanity is hymned in verses of uncommon pathos and beauty:

> O you, whose eyes are clear, whose eyes are friendly,
> Whose eyes betray distinguished wisdom-knowledge;
> Whose eyes are pitiful, whose eyes are pure,
> O you, so lovable, with beautiful face, with beautiful eyes!
>
> Your lustre is spotless and immaculate,
> Your knowledge without darkness, your splendour like the
> sun,
> Radiant like the blaze of a fire not disturbed by the wind,
> Warming the world you shine splendidly.
>
> Eminent in your pity, friendly in your words,
> One great mass of fine virtues and friendly thoughts,
> You appease the fire of the defilements which burn beings,
> And you rain down the rain of the deathless Dharma.[140]

Chapter 26 is dedicated to Samantabhadra. This Bodhisattva having undertaken to protect the *Saddharma-puṇḍarīka*, the Buddha in turn promises that he will himself protect all those who remember and recite Samantabhadra's name. The merit of such remembrance and recitation, he declares, is equal to that of visualizing the Tathāgata.

Prominent among independent sūtras devoted to the Bodhisattva cult is the *Kāraṇḍa-vyūha*, which narrates the exploits of Avalokiteśvara. This work has survived complete in Sanskrit, there being two different versions, one metrical, the other in prose. Although the *Guṇa-kāraṇḍa-vyūha*, as the metrical version is called, is said to be an elaboration, and although its existence prior to the fourth century CE[141] has been thought improbable, the prose version, containing a large section in the style of the *tantras*, in its complete form may be of even later date. The Tibetan translation, based upon a recension of the prose version, is said to have originated in 616CE. The fundamental idea of the sūtra, the glorification of the wonderful being Avalokiteśvara, is the same in both versions. Avalokiteśvara here appears as the typical Bodhisattva of popular imagination, who refuses to attain Buddhahood until all beings have been delivered. His one and only task is 'to bring the doctrine of salvation to all beings, to help all sufferers, to save them from every distress, and to exercise infinite pity that does not even shrink from sin, and does not stop at the gates of hell.'[142] The work consists mainly of various legends illustrating these functions.

# 12

# THE RATNAKŪṬA AND SAMĀDHI SŪTRAS

## The Jewel-Heap Sūtras and the Samādhi Sūtras

Both the *Large Sukhāvatī-vyūha* and the *Akṣobhya-vyūha*, as well as the *Śrīmālādevi-siṃhanāda* and the *Mañjuśrī-Buddhakṣetra-guṇa-vyūha*, are works of the Ratnakūṭa or 'Jewel-heap' class, which in the Chinese Tripiṭaka comprises forty-eight or forty-nine and in the Tibetan Tripiṭaka forty-four or forty-five works. The scope of the *Mahāratnakūṭa Sūtra* – as the works of this class, collectively considered, are sometimes called – is considerable. In the words of Garma C.C. Chang, the general editor of a volume of selections from the collection/sūtra:

> We have found this work to contain a broad coverage of various subjects. The topics discussed range from the monastic precepts (Vinaya) to intuitive wisdom (*prajñā*), from good deportment to the manifestation of the Tathāgata's light, from illusion (*māyā*) and ingenuity (*upāya*) to the nature of consciousness and the Pure Land practice. It can perhaps be called a small encyclopedia of Mahāyāna Buddhism, which should be useful to general readers as well as to scholars.[143]

The time covered by the composition of the work is no less broad, individual sūtras seemingly having appeared over a period of several centuries. A number of sūtras illustrate the transition from the Hīnayāna to the Mahāyāna, while others, especially those containing *dhāraṇīs*, illustrate the transition from the Mahāyāna to the Vajrayāna or, in terms of the canonical literature, from the Mahāyāna sūtras to the *tantras*.

Since some of the Ratnakūṭa sūtras were translated into Chinese as early as the latter part of the second century CE, at least part of the collection is of great antiquity. Indeed, the original nucleus of the collection may well have been identical with one or another of the Bodhisattva Piṭakas with which some of our sources credit certain early schools. A 'Bodhisattva Piṭaka' is, in fact, referred to in one of the Ratnakūṭa sūtras, besides which the collection contains a work entitled the *Bodhisattva-piṭaka Sūtra*.

Whatever the Ratnakūṭa's connection with the Bodhisattva Piṭaka, undoubtedly one of the oldest members of the Jewel-heap class, if not the original *Ratnakūṭa Sūtra*, is the *Kāśyapa-parivarta*. This work, the text of which is represented by a single incomplete manuscript from the neighbourhood of Khotan, in Central Asia, is said to have been translated into Chinese for the first time (three other translations were subsequently made) as early as between 178 and 184CE. If it is really as old as this – and the archaic form of its language strongly suggests antiquity – it is one of the oldest Mahāyāna sūtras known. The work consists of a dialogue, almost a monologue, in which the Buddha expounds to his disciple Kāśyapa the qualities of a Bodhisattva and the doctrine of *śūnyatā*. The greater part of the exposition is not discursive but imaginative, consisting of about a hundred similes and brief parables, resembling the shorter ones of the *Saddharma-puṇḍarīka*. As in that work, moreover, whatever is said in prose is repeated, or retold, in verse. Some of the comparisons are not without charm. Speaking of the Bodhisattva, the Buddha says:

> It is just like the kalaviṅka bird.
> Even while it is still inside the egg,
> Though it has never seen body or form,
> Yet, being different from other birds,
> It emits fine, exquisite melodies
> So that men always take pleasure in it.
> Even so is the son of the Buddha
> When he first aspires to enlightenment
> And has not emerged from the passions' womb.[144]

The *Kāśyapa-parivarta* is also the original source of a famous simile in which the Bodhisattva is exalted above the Buddha. 'O Kāśyapa, just as the new moon is worshipped, and the full moon is not worshipped to the same degree, even so, Kāśyapa, a Bodhisattva should be honoured far more than a Tathāgata, by my followers. And why? Because the Tathāgatas arise from the Bodhisattvas.' Doctrinally the sūtra is most remarkable for its interpretation of *śūnyatā* in terms of the Middle Way, which apparently anticipates Nāgārjuna. Things are said to be, for example, neither eternal nor not eternal, neither one thing nor its opposite. According to Edgerton, 'There is an evident echo here from the First Sermon of the Buddha, but there these terms were only ethical in content, not ontological.'[145]

The qualities of the Bodhisattva and the doctrine of *śūnyatā* are the subject matter not only of the *Kāśyapa-parivarta* but also of a number of other Ratnakūṭa sūtras, some of which are devoted mainly to the exposition of one or the other of these topics. *Śūnyatā* being the 'object' of *prajñā* it is not surprising that those sūtras which are devoted mainly to the exposition of *śūnyatā* should have much in common with the sūtras of the *Prajñā-pāramitā* or 'Perfection of Wisdom' class. One such sūtra is, in fact, included in the Perfection of Wisdom corpus, as well as in the Ratnakūṭa collection. This is the *Saptaśatikā-prajñā-pāramitā Sūtra* or 'Perfection of Wisdom in 700 Lines', also known as the 'Perfection of Wisdom as Taught by Mañjuśrī', which has already been described in chapter 10. Other Ratnakūṭa sūtras devoted mainly to the exposition of *śūnyatā* include the *Vidyutprāpta-paripṛcchā* or 'Questions of (Bodhisattva) Lightning Attainment', the *Vimaladatta-paripṛcchā* or 'Questions of Pure Giving', the *Aśokadatta-vyākaraṇa* or 'Sorrowless Giving's Prediction (to Buddhahood)', and the *Susṭhitamati-paripṛcchā* or 'Questions of (the god) Well-Abiding Mind', also known as '(the Sūtra of) How to Kill with the Sword of Wisdom'.

In the first of these works, the *Vidyutprāpta-paripṛcchā*, the Buddha explains, at Lightning Attainment's request, the five great, inexhaustible stores (of wisdom), possessed of which a Bodhisattva is relieved from poverty for ever, achieves superior virtues, and quickly achieves Supreme Enlightenment with little effort. These five stores are the various kinds of method by means of which the Bodhisattva liberates the different classes of beings, such as the lustful, the angry, and the deluded, without being defiled by dualistic concepts. Regarding the way in which a Bodhisattva liberates the lustful, for example, the Buddha says:

> If a man considers a woman to be pure and becomes deeply infatuated with her, the Bodhisattva will transform himself into a woman of great beauty and elegance, adorned with

> jewels and necklaces, as desirable a celestial maiden as the man has ever seen before, and allow him to lavish on her his passionate love. When the man has indulged his passion to the utmost, the Bodhisattva will, using means commensurate with the man's capacity, pluck out the poisonous arrow of lust in him. Then, by his miraculous power, he will change back from the female form and appear before the man to expound the Dharma for him until he has penetrated the dharmadhātu. After that, he will disappear from sight.[146]

This passage provides a canonical basis for the well-known Japanese paintings in which Samantabhadra, the Bodhisattva of compassionate action, is depicted as a courtesan.

In the fourth work, the *Susthitamati-paripṛcchā* or 'Questions of (the god) Well-Abiding Mind', also known as '(the Sūtra of) How to Kill with the Sword of Wisdom', the Sword of Wisdom in question is that belonging to Mañjuśrī, the Bodhisattva of Wisdom. Through the power of his *samādhi* Mañjuśrī pervades the entire universe with a great light, as a result of which innumerable Bodhisattvas come from each of the innumerable Buddha-fields in each of the ten directions of space. When they are all gathered on Mount Gṛdhrakūṭa, and have been made visible to the assembly, Mañjuśrī asks the Buddha three questions. These questions concern the meaning of the term 'Bodhisattva', the nature of the Bodhisattva's initial generation of (the transcendental) Bodhicitta, and the nature of the realization of the non-arising of dharmas and how it can be achieved by a Bodhisattva, and the Buddha's replies to these questions constitute the central part of the sūtra. Both before and after putting his questions, Mañjuśrī engages in a kind of supplementary dialogue with Well-Abiding Mind, and there is also a three-cornered discussion between the Buddha, Mañjuśrī, and Mahākāśyapa, who represents the Arhants. The Sword of Wisdom makes its appearance only towards the end of the sūtra. In a highly dramatic episode, Mañjuśrī, inspired by the Buddha's miraculous power, rushes towards the Buddha sword in hand to kill him. This he does in order to get rid of the mental discrimination of five hundred Bodhisattvas who were obsessed with remorse on account of their past evil karma and could not achieve the realization of the profound Dharma. Suddenly calling on Mañjuśrī to stop, the Buddha declares that since from the beginning there is neither self nor others the best way to 'kill' him is to perceive in one's mind the existence of an ego. On hearing these words the five hundred Bodhisattvas realize that all the phenomena of existence are like a magical illusion, that there is no sentient being, no Buddha, no killing or killer and, therefore, no sinner and no sin. Having understood this, they immediately achieve the realization of the non-arising of dharmas and, overwhelmed with joy, ascend into the air to the height of seven palm trees and give expression to their realization in verse. It is significant that, 'when performing this great miraculous feat, the World-Honoured One, by the power of ingenuity, caused all the novice Bodhisattvas in the assembly who had few good roots, as well as the sentient beings who had not parted with discrimination and who were attached to forms, not to see Mañjuśrī wielding the sword, nor to hear the doctrine explained.'[147]

Both the second and third works, the *Vimaladatta-paripṛcchā* and the *Aśokadatta-vyākaraṇa*, are not only profound in content but attractive in form. In this respect they resemble the *Śrīmālādevi-siṃhanāda*, and even the *Vimalakīrti-nirdeśa*. Though quite short, each of them mirrors in its depths the entire spiritual universe of the Mahāyāna – just as even a tiny pond reflects the immensity of space and the multitudinousness of the stars. In the first of these two sūtras, the *Vimaladatta-paripṛcchā*, Princess Pure Giving, the eight-year-old daughter of King Prasenajit, engages eight great śrāvakas headed by Śāriputra and eight great Bodhisattvas headed by Mañjuśrī in discussion and reduces all of them except Mañjuśrī to silence. She also questions the Buddha about the Bodhisattva path and, when he has answered her questions, transforms herself from a girl into a sixteen-year-old boy and converts the five hundred brahmins who had sought, originally, to dissuade her from meeting the Arhants and Bodhisattvas on the grounds that the sight of monks was inauspicious. As the Buddha explains, Pure Giving is in reality a great Bodhisattva who has followed the Bodhisattva path for countless ages.

The heroine of the *Aśokadatta-vyākaraṇa* is Princess Sorrowless Giving (or Fearless Virtue, as she is called in some sources), the twelve-year-old daughter of King Ajātaśatru. She is sitting on a couch in the royal hall wearing jewel-studded golden slippers when numerous great śrāvakas, headed by Śāriputra, come to the palace for alms, and despite her father's remonstrances refuses to show them any respect. Instead, she compares the śrāvakas with the Bodhisattvas in a series of brilliant similes that give vivid and vigorous expression to the Mahāyāna's rejection of the ideals of the Hīnayāna, and besides defeating them in argument in much the same way that Pure Giving did, exhibits magical powers of a far higher order than Mahāmaudgalyāyana's. Eventually, she pays homage to them (they are, after all, monks) and offers them food, after which they all go to see the Buddha accompanied by Sorrowless Giving's parents and countless people of Rājagṛha. Śāriputra praises Sorrowless Giving, who also in reality is a great Bodhisattva, and after she has transformed her female body into a male one and ascended into the air the Buddha predicts him and his mother Queen Moonlight to Supreme Enlightenment, after which (the male) Sorrowless Giving changes into a dignified young monk.

Among the Ratnakūṭa sūtras dealing mainly with the qualities of the Bodhisattva are the *Surata-paripṛcchā* (also known as the *Surata Sūtra*), the *Sumatidārikā-paripṛcchā*, the *Upāli-paripṛcchā*, and the *Akṣayamati-paripṛcchā*. Between them these four works illustrate the process whereby the Hīnayāna Monastic Code was modified, or at least supplemented, in the interests of the Mahāyāna's greatly developed Bodhisattva ideal. At times, indeed, the Bodhisattva Vinaya, as it came to be called, seems to supersede, even to contradict, the Bhikshu Vinaya. Even when contradicting the Bhikshu Vinaya, however, to the extent that it is a Vinaya in the sense of a code at all, the Bodhisattva Vinaya remains under the influence of Hīnayāna formalism. It was for this reason, mainly, that we selected the *Vimalakīrti-nirdeśa* and the Happy Land sūtras to represent the Mahāyāna's elucidation of the true meaning of the term Sangha, rather than any of the four Ratnakūṭa sūtras mentioned, for it is in those glorious products of the spiritual imagination of the Mahāyāna that we see the Bodhisattva ideal in action, as it were, rather than a set of rules, or even a list of qualities.

The *Surata-paripṛcchā* or 'Questions of (the Bodhisattva) Surata' describes how the monk-Bodhisattva of that name resists the temptations of Śakra, the king of the gods, and succeeds in convincing King Prasenajit that despite his immense wealth he is, in fact, the poorest man in Śrāvastī. Then, on his making a solemn asseveration, the Buddha bursts from the ground surrounded by his usual assembly and at Surata's request teaches the Dharma. After declaring that there are three accumulations of merits which are immeasurable, i.e. to protect and uphold the true Dharma, to bring forth the Bodhicitta, and to persuade others to make unexcelled vows, the Buddha declares that there are thirty-two dharmas 'that good men and good women must practise industriously in order not to have met the Tathāgata in vain.' Though Surata is a Bodhisattva, and has already told Śakra that he seeks only the birthless and deathless (*dharma*)*kāya*, these thirty-two dharmas or precepts represent a blending of Hīnayāna and Mahāyāna spiritual ideals, with the Hīnayāna ideal in fact predominating.

In the *Sumatidarika-paripṛcchā* or 'Questions of the Girl Sumati', in which the Buddha enumerates another thirty-two dharmas, there is also a blending of Hīnayāna and Mahāyāna spiritual ideals. This time, however, it is the Mahāyāna ideal that predominates. There is also a brief exchange between Mañjuśrī and Sumati in which the great Bodhisattva tests the eight-year-old Sumati's understanding of *śūnyatā*.

In the *Upāli-paripṛcchā* or 'Questions of (the Arhant) Upāli' the Hīnayāna spiritual ideal has disappeared almost completely, and reference is made to the Bhikshu Vinaya only to show that it has been superseded. Various great Bodhisattvas having undertaken to protect the Dharma in the Last Era, the Buddha tells Śāriputra that Bodhisattvas should guard against breaches of discipline committed out of hatred and ignorance, rather than against those committed out of desire. Monk-Bodhisattvas should confess breaches of the Monastic Code to an assembly of pure monks, or alternatively they should confess to the Thirty-five Buddhas. They should contemplate the Thirty-five Buddhas single-mindedly, pay homage to all Tathāgatas, and repent with a pure mind. In this way they will repent their offences, and be free from worry and remorse. (There is, of course, no provision for this kind of confession and repentance in the Hīnayāna Monastic Code.)

Upāli, who according to Hīnayāna tradition recited the Vinaya Piṭaka at the First Council, asks what should be the *prāṭimokṣa* of śrāvakas and Pratyeka-Buddhas and what should be the *prāṭimokṣa* of Bodhisattvas. In reply the Buddha explains that there is a great difference between the precepts observed by śrāvakas and the precepts observed by Bodhisattvas. What is a precept for the former may be a great breach of discipline for the latter, and *vice versa*. While śrāvaka precepts must be observed strictly and literally, Bodhisattva precepts need not be. For Bodhisattvas, the main thing is to preserve the Bodhicitta. So long as the Bodhicitta is preserved, they are not said to break the precepts. For a Bodhisattva, breaking precepts out of desire is a minor offence, even if he does so for innumerable *kalpas*, whereas breaking precepts out of anger even once is a very serious offence. The reason for this is that 'A Bodhisattva who breaks precepts out of desire still holds sentient beings in his embrace, whereas a Bodhisattva who breaks precepts out of hatred forsakes sentient beings altogether.'[148] A Bodhisattva should not, in fact, be afraid of the passions which can help him hold sentient beings in his embrace. A Bodhisattva who is thoroughly conversant with the Vinaya will not be afraid when he transgresses out of desire, but only when he transgresses out of hatred.

At this point Mañjuśrī enquires why regulations are necessary at all, for are not all the phenomena of existence ultimately Vinaya, i.e. capable of being used as means to Enlightenment? The Buddha replies that all the phenomena of existence are indeed ultimately Vinaya, but since ordinary people do not realize this regulations are necessary in order that they may eventually attain Enlightenment. At the Buddha's request, Mañjuśrī then expounds the subtle meaning of the Ultimate Vinaya for Upāli's benefit, after which the Buddha himself further explains the teaching in a lengthy series of verses, and the sūtra comes to an end.

The *Akṣayamati-paripṛcchā* or 'Questions of (the Bodhisattva) Akṣayamati' does not even mention the Hīnayāna Bhikshu Vinaya. In reply to questions put by Akṣayamati or 'Infinite Intelligence', the Buddha describes, with the help of ten similes, the way in which the Bodhisattva is to cultivate the ten *pāramitās* or 'perfections', from generosity (*dāna*) to knowledge (*jñāna*), after which he explains the ten ways in which the Bodhisattva practises each *pāramitā* by regarding ten things as foremost. He also explains the thirty functions of the *pāramitās*, besides describing the visions in which the Bodhisattva will abide, the *pāramitās* he will perfect, the *samādhis* and *dhāraṇīs* he will attain, and the *dhāraṇīs* from which he will not be separated, at each of the ten stages (*bhūmis*) of the Bodhisattva path. Thus the work constitutes a comprehensive account of the Bodhisattva's qualities and a systematic survey of the Bodhisattva Vinaya. Though making no mention of the Bhikshu Vinaya, it therefore also constitutes a Mahāyāna counterpart to the Monastic Code in a way that the more radical and thoroughgoing *Upāli-paripṛcchā* never does.

Besides *śūnyatā* and the qualities of a Bodhisattva, there are various other topics to which works of the Ratnakūṭa class particularly devote themselves. Among these topics are magic, the nature of consciousness, and the Bodhisattva's skilful means (*upāya-kauśalya*).

Magic is the subject matter of the *Bhadramāyākāra-paripṛcchā* or 'Questions of Bhadra the Magician', though it also features in a number of other sūtras of this class (as it does in Mahāyāna sūtras of all classes), in some of which it indeed plays a prominent part. Thinking to demonstrate his superiority in magic (*māyā*), i.e. the conjuring up of illusory forms, Bhadra invites the Buddha for a meal, but his plan miscarries and very soon he is forced to recognize that the Buddha's magical powers are infinitely superior to his own. Having confessed his arrogance, he has a profound spiritual experience in which he sees nothing except the Buddha everywhere. The Buddha then explains the ten-times-four things that constitute the path of a Bodhisattva and predicts Bhadra's eventual attainment of Buddhahood. The Buddha's 'magic' is superior to Bhadra's because it is achieved through the realization that all the phenomena of existence are, in reality, just like a magically produced illusion, and like a magically produced illusion only appear to come into existence and pass out of it.

The nature of consciousness is dealt with in the *Bhadrapāla-śreṣṭhi-paripṛcchā* or 'Questions of the Merchant Wise Protector', wherein the Buddha argues that the existence of consciousness can be inferred from its functions, just as the existence of the wind can be inferred from the swaying of trees, or the existence of the puppeteer from the movements of his puppets. Though consciousness has no form, it can manifest all forms. It cannot be perceived by the ordinary mind any more than the substance of the sun can be perceived by ordinary people, even though they may experience its light and heat. This sūtra would appear to be one of the canonical sources of the Mind-Only doctrine of the Yogācāra School. Indeed, the Buddha's comparison of consciousness to a seed suggests the *ālaya-vijñāna* or 'store consciousness', also called the *mūla-vijñāna* or 'fundamental consciousness', which stores up or preserves memory, impressions, and karmic potency.

Skilful means forms the subject matter of the *Jñānottarabodhisattva-paripṛcchā* or 'Questions of the Bodhisattva Supreme Knowledge', a sūtra of the same radical and thoroughgoing type as the *Upāli-paripṛcchā*. In it the Buddha describes the various ways in which a Bodhisattva practises skilful means, among them being the six *pāramitās* or 'perfections', all of which are treated as manifestations of this all-important principle. Since the Dharma of a Bodhisattva is different from the Dharma of the śrāvakas and Pratyeka-Buddhas, a transgression is in his case not a transgression at all but a skilful means and it is therefore wrong for anyone to criticize him on this account. 'As long as good men and good women are not apart from the aspiration to all-knowing wisdom,' the Buddha tells Ānanda, 'they can amuse themselves with the five delightful sensuous pleasures when they encounter them.'[149] Once again, the main thing is to preserve the Bodhicitta. If the Bodhisattva does that he can even kill, as the Buddha himself once did in a previous existence. For actions of this kind, performed out of Great Compassion, there is no karmic retribution, and those incidents in the Buddha's own present lifetime which are usually understood to be instances of karmic retribution, such as his being wounded by Devadatta and slandered by Cinca, are themselves skilful means.

In fact all the events and activities of the Buddha's earthly career are skilful means, from his descent from the Tuṣita heaven to his *parinirvāṇa* or 'final passing away'. Being born with a knowledge of all arts and sciences he did not really study, as being free from desire he did not really marry and beget a son. Rāhula entered his mother's womb after descending from heaven, and was not the product of carnal copulation, having previously made a vow to be the son of a Bodhisattva who would attain Buddhahood in that lifetime. In this way the Bodhisattva's skilful means comes to imply a 'docetic' view of the human personality of the Buddha similar to that of the *Mahāvastu*. Since the original nucleus of the Ratnakūṭa collection seems to have been part of the canon of one of the offshoots of the Mahāsaṅghika School, as was the *Mahāvastu*, this is not surprising.

From the works already mentioned it will be clear that sūtras of the Ratnakūṭa class, regardless of the nature of their contents, are frequently of the *paripṛcchā* or 'question' – or better 'questioning' – type. Approximately half the sūtras of the entire collection, in fact, are *paripṛcchās*, though many of them have one or more alternative titles.

Prominent among the remaining works of this type belonging to the Ratnakūṭa collection is the *Rāṣṭrapāla-paripṛcchā* or 'Questions of Rāṣṭrapāla', also known as the *Rāṣṭrapāla Sūtra*. Like the *Kāśyapa-parivarta*, the *Urga-paripṛcchā*, and the *Large Sukhāvatī-vyūha*, this work is extant in Sanskrit, and was translated thrice into Chinese, as well as once into Tibetan. It consists of two parts. Part 1 opens with Rāṣṭrapāla's question, in which he asks the Buddha to describe the origin and nature of the Bodhisattva career. The answer is a relatively brief schematic statement of the various qualities which a true Bodhisattva should and should not possess, and the actions which he should or should not perform. These comprise twelve sets of four categories. There are four qualities possessed of which one may hope for Bodhisattvahood, four qualities wherefrom the Bodhisattva gains encouragement, four things that cause him joy, four things to which he must be indifferent, down to four types of persons he must not cultivate, four things that have evil results for him, and four bonds. All these positive and negative aspects of the Bodhisattva ideal were exemplified by Śākyamuni in countless previous existences. Reference is therefore made to fifty Jātakas or Birth-Stories, some of which appear to be exclusive to this sūtra. The Buddha then excoriates the bad monks who, he prophesies, will one day disgrace the Sangha.

> My monks will be without shame and without virtue, haughty, puffed up and wrathful ... intoxicating themselves with alcoholic drinks. While they bear the banner of the Buddha, they will only be serving the householders.... They themselves will have wives, sons and daughters like householders. 'You are not to indulge in sensual pleasures, in order that you may not be born again as animals, ghosts or beings of hell', thus they will preach to the householders, but they themselves will be uncontrolled.[150]

Part 2 opens with a similar condemnation of false Bodhisattvas. Most of it is devoted, however, to relating at length the story of Śākyamuni's former birth as Puṇyaraṣmi, already briefly alluded to in Part 1.

Prophecies of the decline of the Dharma, and the degeneration of both monk and lay people, also appear in a much longer and more important sūtra which, having grown by a process of accretion spanning, in all probability, as many as six or seven centuries, bridges the gap between the early and the late Mahāyāna sūtras in much the same way that the *Ratnakūṭa* or Jewel-heap collection does. This is the *Samādhirāja* or 'King of Meditations', originally known as the *Candrapradīpa Sūtra*.

So far as can be judged from the surviving Sanskrit texts of this work, and the Chinese and Tibetan translations, it passed in the course of its long literary history through three distinct phases of development. The first of these is represented by the earliest Chinese version, made in 148CE by An Shih-kao, but subsequently lost. Two incomplete fifth-century versions apart, the second phase is attested by Narendrayaśa's complete Chinese translation of a longer text, made in the sixth century, as well as by the Sanskrit text of the sūtra as preserved in a Gilgit manuscript assigned, on palaeographical grounds, to the sixth or seventh century CE. The original sūtra cannot have appeared later than the first century CE, and seems to have been composed entirely in verse. During this second phase of its development, however, it was enlarged by the insertion of a number of prose passages, some introductory to the older metrical portion of a chapter, while others are repetitions of what follows in verse. Additions were at the same time made to the metrical portion of the sūtra. Whereas the language of the prose passages is 'correct' Pāṇīnian Sanskrit, all the metrical portions, including the later additions, are composed in Buddhist Hybrid Sanskrit. The third phase was one of further expansion. It is represented by the Tibetan translation which Śailendrabodhi and Dharmatāśīla made in the ninth century CE of the longest text of all, as well as by various comparatively modern manuscripts of Nepalese origin. Each of the sūtra's different stages of development seems to have been associated with, or registered by, a corresponding change of title.

Originally it was known as the *Ārya-Candrapradīpa-samādhi Sūtra*, Candrapradīpa or Candraprabha being the name of the youth who figures throughout as the Buddha's principal interlocutor. This is the title given in the earliest Chinese translation, as well as the name by which Śāntideva, as late as the seventh century, uniformly cites the work. Candrakīrti, who flourished a century earlier, knows it as the *Samādhirāja Sūtra* or *Samādhirāja-bhaṭṭāraka*. Subsequent titles are of greater length. In the opening verses of the Gilgit manuscripts of the text, the sūtra is apostrophized as *Ārya-Candrapradīpasūtrarāja*, while the latest title, as recorded in the Tibetan translation, is *Ārya-sarvadharma-svabhāva-samatā-vipañcita-samādhirāja*.

In the more expanded form in which it is now extant, the text of the sūtra consists of thirty-nine chapters in mixed prose and verse. Subjected as they were to so long a process of accretion, one hardly expects to find in them much evidence of artistic plan or arrangement. The work is, in fact, entirely episodic. Unlike the *Saddharma-puṇḍarīka*, it does not even possess an artistically unified original nucleus upon which the subsequent accretions to the text accumulated. Yet the work is by no means devoid of literary merit. Although certain topics occur again and again, such is the variety of treatment, diversified with similes and symbolic phantasmagoria, so smooth the flow of versification, so sweet the language, that without our being aware of it monotony is lost in delight.

The sūtra opens on the Vulture's Peak at Rājagṛha, where the Buddha sits surrounded by a great concourse of bhikshus and by innumerable Bodhisattvas of whom Ajita, Mañjuśrī, and Bhadrapāla are mentioned as the chief. From here the scene shifts, in chapter 10, to Candraprabha's house within the city; and thence, in chapter 17, back to the Vulture's Peak. On each of these occasions Candraprabha puts various questions to the Buddha. First, he enquires how it is possible to attain the inconceivable truth and realize the true nature of conditioned things, and how one ought to perfect oneself in *śīla*, *dhyāna* and *prajñā*. Next, after lavish entertainment of the Buddha, he asks by what practices a Bodhisattva can realize the true nature of dharmas, be a performer of proper deeds, be able to recall his former births, possess a Sangha free from dissension, and so on. Finally, after their return to the Vulture's Peak, he wants to know what duties are to be performed for the attainment of the *sarvadharma-svabhāva-samatā-vipañcita-samādhi* or 'meditation productive of (the knowledge of) the sameness of the self-nature of all dharmas'. He also enquires about the meaning of *samādhi*.

Within this meagre dramatic framework the Buddha delivers the discourses and narrates the legends which make up the body of the sūtra and which, though beginning ostensibly as replies to Candraprabha's questions, in fact range over almost the entire field of Mahāyāna religion and ethics. The discourses are interspersed with a number of narratives. These are, for the most part, of the *jātaka* and *avadāna* type, for they relate how, in ancient times, the sūtra was preached by this or that former Buddha, and how its teachings were practised by various ancient worthies who are identified as the Buddha himself or Candraprabha in one of their previous existences. Owing to its episodic character, as well as to the fact that, although individual topics are handled with distinction, the connection between one topic and another is not always explicit, a systematic account of the contents of the sūtra is hard to give. A few only of the more salient topics will, therefore, be touched upon.

The philosophical basis of the sūtra is the Perfection of Wisdom teaching, though at the same time there are traces, in at least one passage, of the teaching which, in its more systematized form, came to be known as the Yogācāra or Vijñānavāda. Chapter 9, entitled *Gambhira-dharma-kṣānti*, or 'Patient Acceptance of the Profound Dharma', offers a fully-fledged exposition of the *śūnyatā* doctrine. Objects are, in reality, non-existent like a mirage, and one does not find anything which can, in the ultimate sense, be the cause of greed, hatred, and delusion. They are like floating clouds, like sea foam, like the reflection in a mirror or in water, like an echo, or like objects seen in a dream. All extreme assertions, such as that things exist, or do not exist, are to be avoided.

In general, however, the *Samādhirāja* is more 'positive' than the *Prajñā-pāramitā*, and less inclined to stress the emptiness of existence than the fact that being equally empty, and equally devoid of origination and decay, all dharmas, whether transcendental or mundane, remain in their self-nature eternally in a state of 'sameness'. The sameness of the self-nature of all dharmas (*sarvadharma-svabhāva-samatā*), as it is called, is to be realized in a state of *samacitta* or 'same-mindedness', which *samādhi* constitutes, as the various titles of the sūtra would indicate, the ultimate purport of the entire work. Similarly, while the Perfection of Wisdom scriptures inculcate, over and over again, *prajñā* as the sole means to the realization of Emptiness, even the other perfections being practically ignored, the *Samādhirāja*, though no less alive to the relative value of all spiritual 'attainments', wisely emphasizes that, at the same time, the traditional religious disciplines can by no means be neglected. Such exercises are termed *samādhi-parikarma*, or preparations for *samādhi*.

Special importance is attached to *kṣānti*, patience or forbearance, the third *pāramitā*. Originally a purely moral virtue, this was interpreted by the Mahāyāna metaphysically as unruffled acquiescence in the deeper truths taught by the Buddha. In the *Samādhirāja* the term possesses an ever richer connotation. According to chapter 7, entitled *Trikṣāntyavatāra*, or 'Entry into the Threefold Patience', three kinds of *kṣānti* are indispensable to perfection in the highest *samādhi*. By the first of them, one avoids quarrels, realizes the illusory nature of things, acquires knowledge of the scriptures, comprehending their esoteric and exoteric meanings, develops faith, and vows to attain to Supreme Enlightenment. By the second, one becomes steadfast like a mountain, develops mental concentration, acquires the five super-knowledges, and ultimately extends his thought beyond limitation. Finally, by the third *kṣānti* one visualizes the innumerable Buddhas preaching to sentient beings, comprehends their ways and manners, and remains unmoved by worldly acquisitions or fame. On the attainment of these three *kṣāntis*, a Bodhisattva is predicted to Buddhahood. He realizes that beings are in reality subject neither to origination nor to cessation, and is convinced that all dharmas are empty and abide eternally in the same state. At this stage he is endowed, not only with *kṣānti* but also with *maitrī* (love) and *karuṇā* (compassion).

*Samādhi* itself is dealt with in a number of places. Chapter 6, for example, entitled simply *Samādhi-parivarta* or 'Chapter on Samādhi', enumerates various preparatory exercises by means of which one is perfected in the highest meditation. Different lists are given in the prose and the verse portions. The former enumerates the exercises as:

(1) development of a compassionate heart;
(2) accumulation of merits;
(3) worship of the *dharmakāya* and not the *rūpakāya* of the Buddha.

In the last the list is as follows:

(a) worship of the Buddha with incense;
(b) practice of *kṣānti*;
(c) realization of the non-existence of selfhood (*nairātmya saṃjñā*);
(d) extirpation of greed, lust, etc.;
(e) development of firm faith in the Buddha;
(f) regard for fellow monks;
(g) practice of the constituents of Enlightenment (*bodhyaṅgas*), the foundations of mindfulness (*smṛtyupasthānas*), and superconscious states (*dhyānas*).

Chapter 18 enumerates various advantages of meditation. Other chapters discourse at length on *dāna* or giving and *śīla* or morality, the first and second perfections, and celebrate the benefits derived therefrom.

The ethical and spiritual fervour of the sūtra is, indeed, very pronounced, and the work contains, as Edgerton observes, 'some very fine didactic passages'.[151] Several passages eulogize the forest-dwelling monk, who lives alone practising austerities, and in chapter 15 the Buddha tells Maitreya that Candraprabha, having been a perfect *brahmacāri* or celibate under previous Buddhas, will remain such until his final attainment of Supreme Enlightenment.

The Buddhology of the sūtra is no less sublime. In various places, but especially in chapter 22, entitled *Tathāgatakāya* or 'Body of the Tathāgata', it is expressly denied that the Buddhas possess a *rūpakāya* in the sense of an ordinary gross material body. They possess only the *dharmakāya*, which is homogeneous and identical with Absolute Reality. This *dharmakāya* or 'body of truth', we are further told, may also be defined as the embodiment of the infinite merits acquired by the Buddhas. Immeasurable, imperturbable, and invisible to mortal sight, it is transcendent over pleasure and pain, the three poisons, and karmic results. It is pure and unoriginated. Although in conventional terminology it is spoken of as eternal, that terminology itself is non-existent. The *dharmakāya* is not to be characterized by words or signs, not even by the word *nirvāṇa*. It is the Ultimate, the Supreme; it does not admit of any speculation; its only possible designation is *śūnyatā*. While the Buddha does not possess a true material form, however, what is called his Created Body (*nirmitaḥ*) appears in various Buddha-fields for the happiness and welfare of sentient beings. There is no mention of the *trikāya* doctrine.

The negative side of the sūtra's ethical and spiritual fervour is represented by its denunciation of bad monks. In chapter 16 the Buddha tells Candraprabha that there would in future be monks who, though donning the yellow robes, would abuse the privileges of a monk, and who, though adhering to the notion of a really existent self and fearful of hearkening to the doctrine of *śūnyatā*, would nevertheless enjoy the respect of the people. Chapter 24 foretells even greater corruptions. Monks would hanker after gains and fame. They would be idle, indolent, and neglectful of the precepts. Others would be attached to the words of the scriptures, build stupas and monasteries, become addicted to women, and get entangled with householders. The householders themselves would be no better. Although having few possessions, they would be disinclined to part with them. Many of them would be beaten, imprisoned, and otherwise punished by the king. Their span of life would be short. In their professional work they would be negligent and unskilful. They would be adulterous, jealous, and criminal, and yet in spite of their unholy deeds they would claim that they would all become Buddhas in the long run (chapter 29). Despite the occurrence of such gloomy prophecies, which do not occupy a disproportionate amount of space in the work, the note struck by this sūtra is one of optimism, even exultation. As a combination of aesthetic and religious values, of devotion and philosophy, asceticism and literary style, meditation and active altruism, it is unique among the Mahāyāna scriptures.

The word *samādhi* occurs in the title, and is in a sense the subject, of another sūtra which, being in the present state of our knowledge difficult to classify either as early or as late, may well be mentioned immediately after the *Samādhirāja* and before the *Saṅdhi-nirmocana*, the *Laṅkāvatāra* and the *Avataṃsaka*. This is the *Śūrāṅgama-samādhi Sūtra* or 'Sūtra of the Heroic Advance'. Nine Chinese translations of this work are said once upon a time to have been in existence, all save that by Kumārajīva having perished. There is also a ninth-century Tibetan translation, as well as a few fragments in Khotanese. The original Sanskrit text survives only in quotations in Śāntideva's *Śikṣā-samuccaya* and in a single folio of a manuscript found in eastern Turkestan. In modern times Lamotte has produced a French translation based almost entirely on Kumārajīva's Chinese version. Though in respect of content and ideas the *Śūrāṅgama-samādhi* is closely linked to the *Vimalakīrti-nirdeśa*, as regards form and literary composition it is a much less unified and less effective work.

The scene of the sūtra is laid at Rājagṛha, on the Vulture's Peak, where the Buddha is seated in the midst of a great assembly consisting of 32,000 bhikshus, 72,000 great Bodhisattvas, and an immense number of other beings of all kinds. Dṛḍhamati, the last of the twenty-six great Bodhisattvas to be actually mentioned by name, wishes to ask a question. He wishes to ask it in order to protect the lineage of the Three Jewels and for various other good reasons. He wants to know, in effect (the question has a huge number of subordinate clauses), through what *samādhi* the Bodhisattva is able to manifest all sorts of wonderful qualities and activities throughout the entire range of conditioned existence, but without definitely entering into *parinirvāṇa*. The Buddha replies that it is through the *śūrāṅgama-samādhi* or 'concentration of the heroic advance'. It is through this *samādhi* that the Bodhisattvas are able to manifest *parinirvāṇa* without becoming definitely 'extinguished', and to function in the Saṃsāra in various ways without being misled by it.

Upon hearing this new teaching various gods have the idea of offering the Buddha a magnificent lion throne, with the result that eighty-four thousand times an unthinkably vast number of lion thrones appear before the Buddha simultaneously. On all these lion thrones the Buddha takes his seat, but each god sees the Buddha seated on his throne and not on any of the others. In order to demonstrate the power of the *śūrāṅgama-samādhi* the Buddha then reveals to the whole great assembly the eighty-four thousand times an unthinkably vast number of Buddhas seated on a corresponding number of lion thrones. This raises the question of which is the real Buddha, a question which the Buddha, i.e. each and all of the Buddhas, explains by saying that all the Buddhas are real, and they are real because they are not-born, non-existent, incomposite, without sameness or difference, and so on.

The Buddha then declares that the *śūrāṅgama-samādhi* can be obtained only by Bodhisattvas of the tenth stage (*bhūmi*), after which he proceeds to enumerate the one hundred aspects of the *samādhi,* which in fact includes all spiritual attainments whatsoever. 'Just as the springs, streams, rivers, tributaries and water courses flow into the great sea, so all that a Bodhisattava possesses in the way of *dhyāna* and *samāpatti* is to be found in the *śūrāṅgama-samādhi.*' In the same way, just as the king is accompanied everywhere by a heroic general and the entire fourfold army, as well as by his seven treasures, so the *śūrāṅgama-samādhi* is always accompanied by all *samādhis* and all the thirty-seven *bodhipakṣika-dharmas* or conditions favourable to Enlightenment.

The Buddha next describes to Dṛḍhamati how the Bodhisattva in the *śūrāṅgama-samādhi* practises the six *pāramitās* or perfections and how, in respect of each *pāramitā,* he is characterized by a special fruit. Since each one of these fruits possesses a number of different aspects, the Buddha's account of them is, in some cases, of considerable length. Most aspects of the respective fruits of the *pāramitās* are representative of spiritual experiences of a highly advanced nature, and they are accordingly often described in highly paradoxical terms, but some aspects relate to experiences of a more ordinary kind. One aspect of the fruit of the Bodhisattva's special practice of the *dhyāna-pāramitā* or 'perfection of meditation', for instance, is that if he appears in white raiment he does not have the heedlessness (*pramāda*) of a layman (*upāsaka*), and if he appears as a monk he does not have the arrogance (*manyanā*) of a monk.

So great a being, indeed, is the Bodhisattva in the *śūrāṅgama-samādhi* that those who see and hear him are all liberated. Such a Bodhisattva practises the six *pāramitās* uninterruptedly. He is, in fact, the veritable embodiment of the *pāramitās,* his body, speech, and mind being, as it were, saturated by them. As for the way in which the Bodhisattva should train himself in the *śūrāṅgama-samādhi*, it is like training oneself in archery, where one learns to aim at objects of increasing subtlety, from a heap of earth to the hundredth part of a hair. In the same way the Bodhisattva who wishes to train himself in the *śūrāṅgama-samādhi* passes through all the different stages of spiritual progress, from training himself in good intentions (*āśaya*) to the obtaining of the *śūrāṅgama-samādhi* itself when, although capable of doing the work of a Buddha, he refuses to abandon the practices of a Bodhisattva.

The work just described should not be confused with a *Śūrāṅgama Sūtra* known in Chinese as 'The Buddha's Great Crown Sūtra', which though traditionally regarded as having been translated from a Sanskrit original by Paramārtha in the eighth century, is now generally acknowledged to be a native Chinese production. An attractive literary composition, it teaches a form of 'Absolute Idealism', and lists twenty-five methods of controlling the mind by meditation on the six sense-objects, the six sense-organs, six consciousnesses and seven elements. Each of these methods is expounded, on the basis of his own experience, by an Arhant or great Bodhisattva.

At the Buddha's request, the Bodhisattva Mañjuśrī compares the twenty-five methods with a view to ascertaining which of them is best adapted to the needs of Ānanda, whose backslidings are the occasion for the preaching of this sūtra, as well as to the needs of the disciples of the future. He eventually comes to the conclusion that the best method is that of meditation on sound, taught by the Bodhisattva Avalokiteśvara. Concerning this meditation Avalokiteśvara has already said:

> Continuing my practice, I gradually advanced until all discrimination of the hearing nature of my self-hood and of the intrinsic Transcendental Hearing was discarded. As there ceased to be any grasping in my mind for the attainment of intrinsic hearing, the conception of Enlightenment and enlightened nature were all absent from my mind. When this state of perfect Emptiness of Mind was attained, all arbitrary conceptions of attaining to Emptiness of Mind and of enlightened nature, were discarded. As soon as all arbitrary conceptions of rising and disappearing of thoughts were

> completely discarded, the state of Nirvana was clearly realized.[152]

No complete translation of this second, purely Chinese *Śūrāṅgama Sūtra* exists in any Western language. Two incomplete English versions are available, one much more extensive than the other, but neither the translator of the shorter version, nor the editor and translator of the longer version, give the unsuspecting reader any inkling that what he is reading is anything other than a work of Indian origin.

Another sūtra of the *Samādhi* class now generally acknowledged to be a native Chinese production is the *Vajra-samādhi* or 'Diamond Meditation' Sūtra. Like the equally well-known 'Sūtra of Perfect Enlightenment', both the Chinese *Śūrāṅgama Sūtra* and the *Vajra-samādhi Sūtra* seem to have made their appearance – perhaps not surprisingly – within the Ch'an (= Dhyāna) or Meditation School.

# 13

# THE LAṄKĀVATĀRA SŪTRA

Passing from the earlier to the later Mahāyāna sūtras, one cannot fail to be struck by a shift of ontological emphasis. Generalization in so rich and varied a field is, of course, hazardous, but it may be safely asserted that whereas for one group of scriptures Reality is above all *śūnyatā*, the other generally prefers to speak of it in terms of Mind. Not that the difference is absolute, or that a particular emphasis is uniformly distributed among the members of either group. The *śūnyatā* doctrine is common to the *Saddharma-puṇḍarīka* and the *Aṣṭasāhasrikā*; but whereas in the first it is mentioned incidentally, in the second it constitutes the principal subject matter of the whole discourse. Similarly, the two emphases are not mutually exclusive. The *Aṣṭasāhasrikā* speaks of *citta* or thought as being in its essential original nature transparently luminous,[153] and the *Samādhirāja* of the Buddha's emancipated *vijñāna* as functioning only in the realm of consciousness, without reference to external objects, while conversely in the *Laṅkāvatāra* and the *Gaṇḍavyūha* there are repeated references to Reality as *nairātmya* and *śūnyatā*. Indeed it would appear that the two tendencies, one speaking of Reality in terms of Emptiness and one in terms of Mind, were both present in Buddhism from the beginning, though with the former much more conspicuous than the latter and, in fact, always predominating.

The difference is perhaps methodological rather than metaphysical. Seen from the standpoint of Wisdom, Reality appears as Emptiness; from that of Meditation, as Mind. Owing to the undisputed primacy of Wisdom in the Buddhist tradition, it was natural, indeed inevitable, that the significance of the concept of Reality as Emptiness should have been thoroughly explored before that of the concept of Reality as Mind. Indeed, had this procedure not been followed grave misunderstandings might have ensued. As it is, the later sūtras are full of warnings to the effect that psychologically oriented doctrinal concepts such as those of the *ālaya-vijñāna* or 'store consciousness' and the *Tathāgatagarbha* or 'matrix of the Tathāgata' should not be confused with the *paramātma* or supreme self of certain non-Buddhist schools of thought.[154] Despite unavoidable resemblances in terminology, the Absolute Mind of the later sūtras differs from that of the Advaita Vedanta, for example, in that it has been ontologically purified by passing through the fires of *śūnyatā*. Thus, so far as its fully developed metaphysical form is concerned, the concept of Absolute Mind is not so much an independent alternative formulation of Reality as one which grows out of the concept of Emptiness after the latter has been adequately established and continues to be not only dependent upon it but unintelligible without it.

From the *Saṅdhi-nirmocana*, which belongs to the first or second century CE, the line of 'idealist' sūtras descends through the *Laṅkāvatāra* to the sūtras of the Avataṃsaka group, including the *Gaṇḍavyūha* and the *Daśabhūmika*. The *Daśabhūmika* may, however, be older than some parts of the *Saṅdhi-nirmocana* which is, in fact, a highly composite work which the ancient Chinese translators themselves regarded as a collection of separate sūtras. While the idealist sūtras share a common metaphysical foundation, each of them at the same time possesses a distinctive religious and literary character of its own.

The *Saṅdhi-nirmocana*, literally the 'Untying of the Knots', a comparatively short work in ten chapters, elucidates, as its name suggests, the deeper, hidden meaning of statements made by the Buddha in certain earlier sūtras, particularly those of the 'Perfection of Wisdom' corpus. As translated into Chinese (there are five versions in that language, two of them partial, and one in Tibetan), the work contains the following noted stanza on the *ālaya-vijñāna* – here called the *ādāna-vijñāna*, meaning 'grasping' or 'receiving' consciousness – which according to Suzuki is quoted whenever there is an allusion to the philosophy of the Yogācāra:

> The Ādāna-vijñāna is deep and subtle,
> Where all the seeds are evolved like a stream;

I do not elucidate this for the ignorant,
For they are apt to imagine it an ego-substance.[155]

Except for the chapter on meat-eating, the *Laṅkāvatāra* is almost entirely psychological in content, though with the proviso that, within the context of the philosophical tradition represented by this sūtra, psychology and metaphysics are apt to coincide. It is devoid of symbolism, and its literary form may be said to be a no-form. The *Avataṃsaka*, on the other hand, besides being predominantly religious and devotional in character, is replete with dramatically organized symbolic elements of the richest and most concrete description. The *Daśabhūmika*, however, though its import is fundamentally ethical and spiritual, is preoccupied with doctrinal categories to such an extent as to give the work a decidedly scholastic cast. Out of these voluminous and varied works it is the *Laṅkāvatāra* which, as the principal canonical source of the Buddhist system of 'Absolute Idealism', has the first claim on our attention. The *Avataṃsaka*, important though it is for intrinsic value and historical influence alike, must be allowed to suffer comparative neglect, for its enormous bulk precludes all but a cursory account of its two main components, the *Gaṇḍavyūha* and the *Daśabhūmika*.

Besides the Sanskrit text of the *Ārya-saddharma-Laṅkāvatāra Mahāyāna Sūtra* or 'Holy Entry of the True Dharma into Lanka', which is the full title of the work, three out of the four Chinese translations known to have been made are still extant, as well as two translations in Tibetan. In determining the date and tracing the development of the sūtra the Chinese translations are, as usual, most helpful. The earliest of these, now lost, was the work of Dharmakṣema, a monk of central India who reached China in 412CE and was assassinated there in 433CE. As translated by him, the work was known simply as the *Laṅkā Sūtra*. The second translation was produced by Guṇabhadra in 433CE, the third by Bodhiruci in 513, and the fourth between 700 and 704, with Śikṣānanda as the chief translator. As now extant, the Sanskrit text comprises ten chapters. The first and last two of these do not appear in the earliest extant Chinese version, that of Guṇabhadra. From these facts it may be inferred that while the greater part of the text, comprising chapters 2–8, was compiled not later than the fourth century CE, the remainder, consisting of chapters 1, 9, and 10, must have been added at some time between 443 and 513.

Such a breakdown of the sūtra, however, by no means disposes of all the problems connected with its literary history. To begin with, the division into chapters is itself late. In Guṇabhadra's version there are no divisions at all, the text constituting one continuous block of material designated, as though by way of subtitle to the entire sūtra, *Sarvabuddha-pravacana-hṛdaya* or 'Essence of the Teaching of all the Buddhas'. Bodhiruci's version, on the other hand, divides the text into eighteen comparatively short sections, seven of which agree with later chapter divisions, the rest being, as it were, subdivisions of the remaining three. Śikṣānanda's version has the same chapter divisions as the Sanskrit text. Of the two Tibetan translations, only one appears to have been made direct from the Sanskrit, the other being a rendition of Guṇabhadra's Chinese version by Chos-grub, a Tibetan scholar of the ninth century. The former consists of seven chapters only, chapters 7, 9, and 10 of the existing Sanskrit text being unrepresented.

Whether more or less, with the exception of chapters 1, 9, and 10, which are later additions, and chapter 8, 'On Meat-Eating', none of these chapter divisions occurs in the text itself. This consists for the most part of an amorphous mass of self-contained paragraphs dealing with different, but not wholly unconnected, themes; and though all these paragraphs are permeated by a common spirit, and addressed to a single interlocutor, in no sense do they constitute a continuous discourse. D.T. Suzuki, the author of the pioneer English translation of the Sanskrit text of the sūtra, indeed goes so far as to state that 'the whole *Laṅkāvatāra* is just a collection of notes unsystematically strung together, and frankly speaking, it is a useless task to attempt to divide them into sections, or chapters (*parivarta*), under some specific titles.'[156]

How these notes came to be strung together in this way at all is a mystery. Certain discrepancies in the text itself seem to indicate that the constituent paragraphs of the sūtra were excerpts from an older and more extensive work that was subsequently lost. Thus the *Laṅkāvatāra* may be, in reality, not so much a sūtra as a series of extracts from a sūtra. Chapter 1, entitled *Rāvaṇādhyesaṇā* or 'Rāvaṇa's Request', which we know to have been a later addition, must have been composed after the nature and origin of the collection had been forgotten in order to give it a more conventionally canonical appearance. It describes how the Buddha and Rāvaṇa met at the Castle of Laṅkā, on the Peak of Mount Malaya, in the midst of the great ocean, and how the latter, after undergoing a profound spiritual revulsion (*parāvṛtti*) and realizing that the world was nothing but his own mind, was instructed by the Buddha in the significance of this experience. Though complete in itself, and written in a fluent style, this chapter belongs to the same general order of ideas as the rest of the sūtra. It may be regarded as a dramatic presentation of the same truths which, in the earliest chapters, had been taught in a more discursive and disconnected manner. Chapter 9, entitled *Dhāraṇī*, in which the Buddha imparts to Mahāmati various protective formulas, is the shortest in the entire work and, from the ideas which it incorporates, obviously reflects a phase of Tantric influence.

Chapter 10 is entitled *Sagāthaka* or 'With Verses'. It consists, in fact, entirely of verses, the total number of which is 884. More than 200 of these having occurred in the main body of the work, about 680 are original. Whether this chapter represents the primitive form of the entire sūtra, or whether the verses not occurring in chapters 2–8 were taken from the hypothetical earlier, larger work already referred to, or whether, again, they are simply later accretions upon the chapter itself – all these are matters of conjecture rather than of certain knowledge. Here, as elsewhere in the sūtra, disorder reigns supreme, besides which the verses themselves are of unequal value. Suzuki characterizes the chapter as 'a heap of rubbish and gems'.[157] Some of what appear to be the later verses deal, in the form of prophecies, with various historical events and personalities. There is a clear reference to Nāgārjuna, here called Nāgāhvaya (verses 165–166). Philosophically, the chapter is more developed than the rest of the sūtra, though it is not without what would appear to be deviations from doctrinal orthodoxy.

Out of the seven earlier chapters, only chapter 8, entitled *Maṃsabhakṣaṇa* or 'Meat-Eating', constitutes a unified literary composition. As its nature suggests, it contains a strong denunciation of carnivorous food habits. A Bodhisattva, the Buddha tells Mahāmati, should not eat meat. All sentient beings are undergoing a process of transmigration in the course of which they may pass from the animal to the human, or from the human to the animal state, so that to take flesh food is like devouring one's own relatives. Moreover, meat-eating is incompatible with the practice of the Great Compassion, which is the essence of Bodhisattvahood. It is an unaesthetic and unhygienic practice, a source of terror to animals and of displeasure to the gods, who are alike offended by the foul odour of the habitual meat-eater. Animal food is unclean, and a source of physical and mental pollution. A Bodhisattva should be a strict vegetarian. Those who say that the Buddha himself partook of flesh calumniate him.

This chapter is one of the principal canonical sources of the Mahāyāna emphasis on vegetarianism. On account of its subject matter and style, it has been suspected to be an interpolation; but as Winternitz points out, the question of whether or not meat-eating is permissible is already discussed in chapter 2, so that chapter 8 may well belong to the nucleus of the work.[158] In any case, when dealing with a Mahāyāna sūtra one can hardly argue from *a priori* assumptions of consistency.

As for the six remaining earlier chapters, only the beginning of chapter 2, where Mahāmati puts the Buddha 108 oddly assorted questions, has any literary pretensions. However, the Buddha's replies are merely repetitions of the questions, and after 108 doctrinal and other miscellaneous categories have been negated, and a short discussion on the *vijñānas* has taken place, the chapter collapses into the sūtra's characteristic amorphousness. Hence it is impossible to give a coherent account of the main body of the work by way of a résumé of its contents. We shall therefore first allow the sūtra to speak for itself by quoting a passage that may be regarded as summarizing, according to Suzuki, the principal thesis of the *Laṅkāvatāra*, after which we shall briefly enumerate some of the more important topics dealt with in the work as a whole. The passage in question occurs towards the beginning of chapter 2, wherein, after he has described various erroneous views of the *lokāyatas* or 'worldly philosophies', and warned Mahāmati that some of them may be attributed by the simple-minded to the Omniscient One himself, the Buddha proceeds:

> Again, Mahāmati, there are some Brahmans and Śramaṇas who recognizing that the external world which is of Mind itself is seen as such owing to the discrimination and false intellection practised since beginningless time, know that the world has no self-nature and has never been born, it is like a cloud, a ring produced by a firebrand, the castle of the Gandharvas, a vision, a mirage, the moon as reflected in the ocean, and a dream; that Mind in itself has nothing to do with discrimination and causation, discourses of imagination, and

terms of qualification (*lakshya-lakshaṇa*); in that body, property, and abode are objectifications of the Ālayavijñāna, which is in itself above (the dualism of) subject and object: that the state of imagelessness which is in compliance with the awakening of Mind itself, is not affected by such changes as arising, abiding, and destruction.

The Bodhisattva-Mahāsattvas, Mahāmati, will before long attain to the understanding that Nirvāṇa and Saṃsāra are one. Their conduct, Mahāmati, will be in accordance with the effortless exhibition of a great loving heart that ingeniously contrives means (of salvation), knowing that all beings have the nature of being like a vision or a reflection, and that (there is one thing which is) not bound by causation, being beyond the distinction of subject and object; (and further) seeing that there is nothing outside Mind, and in accordance with a position of unconditionality, they will by degrees pass through the various stages of Bodhisattvahood and will experience the various states of Samādhi, and will by virtue of their faith understand that the triple world is of Mind itself, and thus understanding will attain the Samādhi Māyopama. The Bodhisattvas entering into the state of imagelessness where they see into the truth of Mind-Only, arriving at the abode of the Pāramitās, and keeping themselves away from the thought of genesis, deed, and discipline, they will attain the Samādhi Vajravimbopama which is in compliance with the Tathāgatakāya and with the transformations of suchness. After achieving a revulsion in the abode (of the Vijñānas), Mahāmati, they will gradually realize the Tathāgatakāya, which is endowed with the powers, the psychic faculties, self-control, love, compassion, and means; which can enter into all the Buddha-lands and into the sanctuaries of the philosophers; and which is beyond the realm of Citta-mano-manovijñāna. Therefore, Mahāmati, these Bodhisattva-Mahāsattvas who wish, by following the Tathāgatakāya, to realize it, should exercise themselves, in compliance with the truth of Mind-Only, to desist from discriminating and reasoning erroneously on such notions as Skandhas, Dhātus, Āyatanas, thought,

> causation, deed, discipline, and rising, abiding, and destruction.
>
> Perceiving that the triple existence is by reason of the habit-energy of erroneous discrimination and false reasoning that has been going on since beginningless time, and also thinking of the state of Buddhahood which is imageless and unborn, (the Bodhisattva) will become thoroughly conversant with the noble truth of self-realization, will become a perfect master of his own mind, will conduct himself without effort, will be like a gem reflecting a variety of colours, will be able to assume the body of transformation, will be able to enter into the subtle minds of all beings, and, because of his firm belief in the truth of Mind-Only, will, by gradually ascending the stages, become established in Buddhahood. Therefore, Mahāmati, let the Bodhisattva-Mahāsattva be well disciplined in self-realization.[159]

Besides summarizing the principal thesis of the *Laṅkāvatāra*, this passage well illustrates the sūtra's richness and density of thought, as well as its occasional obscurity. Some of the deep truths adumbrated therein may become clearer from a consideration of what follows:

(1) Despite its apparatus of what might be mistaken, at first sight, for imperfectly systematized speculative philosophy, the emphasis of the sūtra throughout is on the necessity of a direct, personal experience of Reality. According to Suzuki 'the thesis of the sūtra must be regarded as centered upon the idea of an inner perception of the deepest truth, which goes beyond language and reasoning',[160] and further, 'the Laṅkāvatāra has come to see that the whole of the Buddhist life is not in merely seeing into the truth, but in living it, experiencing it, so that there will be no dualism in one's life of seeing and living: seeing must be living, and living seeing, with no hiatus between them except in language.'[161]

This experiential emphasis is not, of course, peculiar to the *Laṅkāvatāra*. So radically had it been exemplified in the life, and so rigorously upheld in the preaching, of the Buddha, that it could not but constitute, at all periods, both theoretically and practically, one of the most vivid and vital elements in Buddhism. Nevertheless, owing to the predominantly cognitive approach not only of the Abhidharma, but even of the Prajñā-pāramitā, literature, in the course of nearly a millennium of development first the Hīnayāna and then the Mahāyāna had in practice tended to attach greater importance to an intellectual understanding of the Doctrine than to actual application. It was the mission of the *Laṅkāvatāra* to restore the original emphasis. At the same time, neither tradition nor the contemporary philosophical situation could be ignored. We find, in this sūtra, as perhaps we find in no other Mahāyāna scripture, not only a 'perpetual upholding of the intuitive element in religion'[162] but a full awareness of, and complete mastery over, the accumulated riches of Buddhist thought and a delicate sensitivity to the various currents of philosophical opinion that were agitating the depths of Indian religious life at the time of its promulgation.

From being relatively naïve and dogmatic, the experiential emphasis of Buddhism has in the *Laṅkāvatāra* become more critical and mature. It is this ingredient, more than any other, which imparts to the sūtra its unique flavour, and renders its thought, if not its style, especially attractive and palatable to the more complex intelligence of the modern reader. As might have been expected, the cardinal emphasis of the *Laṅkāvatāra* is reflected in its choice of terminology. For example, instead of *bodhi* or *sambodhi*, the denotation of which is definitely cognitive, it speaks of *gocara* or *gatigocara*, meaning experience, and *pratyātma gocara*, or state of inner realization. Though the term is used once or twice by Mahāmati, the Buddha himself does not refer to the Bodhicitta. This is probably because the sūtra on the whole teaches not a gradual, but an abrupt realization of the truth, through a sudden revulsion, in the deepest seat of consciousness, from the false (in the sense of a wrong mental construction) to the real.

(2) Being a matter of direct experience, the truth is inexpressible. It is therefore said that from the night of his Enlightenment till the night of his *parinirvāṇa* the Tathāgata did not utter a single word.[163] Nevertheless, despite its keen awareness of the limitations of language, the *Laṅkāvatāra* also fully recognizes that even in spiritual affairs recourse to it as a medium of communication is unavoidable. In other Buddha-fields the Dharma may be transmitted by a look or a smile, or even telepathically; but so far as this world is concerned the Buddha must make use of the current coin of ordinary human speech.

At the same time a sharp distinction is drawn between words and meaning, in particular between the spirit and the letter of the sacred texts, any confusion of the one with the other being declared ruinous to the spiritual life and destructive to the whole tradition. The relation between the two is like that between the tip of the finger and the object to which it points. Just as one should look, not at the finger, but at the thing or person indicated, so instead of getting attached to the letter of the scriptures the disciple should direct his attention to their meaning, that is to say, to the Ultimate Reality to which they are pointers. Whereas meaning is alone with itself (*vivikta*) and is the cause of Nirvāṇa, words are bound up with discrimination and are the carrier of transmigration.[164] To be learned in the scriptures means to be conversant not so much with words as with meaning and significance.

Closely connected with this liberal outlook is the belief that the word of the Buddha conceals an esoteric sense which constitutes the real, as opposed to the superficial, meaning of a given text or doctrine. References to this esoteric sense or *saṃdhā*, as it is called, occur sporadically in the *Laṅkāvatāra*, as well as in other Mahāyāna sūtras, and its detection was later on elevated by the followers of the Yogācāra School almost into a science.

(3) The above facts have to be borne in mind when evaluating what might otherwise be termed the philosophy of the sūtra. This comprises, above all, the celebrated doctrine of Mind-Only (*citta-mātra*), for which the *Laṅkāvatāra* is our principal canonical authority, and on account of which, perhaps, it is most widely known. Far from being an abstract, purely rational construction, this doctrine is in fact a conceptual formulation of the essential content of the highest spiritual experience, this is to say, the experience of *sambodhi* or Enlightenment. As Suzuki pertinently observes, 'The main point we must never forget in the study of the *Laṅkāvatāra* is that it is not written as a philosophical treatise to establish a definite system of thought, but to discourse on a certain religious experience.'[165] Whatever philosophy or speculation it contains is therefore incidental, being either an introduction or an intellectual interpretation necessitated by the rational nature of humanity.

With this important qualification, the central doctrinal teaching of the sūtra is clearly a form of metaphysical idealism. Absolute Mind is the sole reality. All so-called objective things whatsoever, whether 'material' or 'mental', are like a mirage which, though perceived, is known to be unreal. Besides being the subject of lengthy disquisition, including a certain amount of rational demonstration and much analogical proof, this tremendous thesis is frequently enunciated in the form of aphorisms that, in their brevity and absoluteness, strike with the force of thunderbolts. The world is nothing but Mind (*cittamātraṃ lokam*). Nothing is to be seen outside the Mind (*cittabāhyādarśanam*). The triple world is Mind itself (*svacittamātraṃ traidhātukam*). Mind produces the triple world (*cittaṃhi traidhātuka-yoniḥ*). The triple existence is nothing but Mind (*tribhavacittamātram*). All is Mind (*cittaṃ hi sarvam*). When Mind evolves, all forms are manifested (*sarvarūpavabhāsam hi yadā cittaṃ pravartate*).

Notwithstanding the unequivocal nature of these statements, however, the word *citta* itself is by no means free from ambiguity. According to context, it may denote mind or thought in the ordinary sense, the *ālaya-vijñāna* or store consciousness in its absoluteness, or the whole system of conscious life (*citta-kalpa*). The term *citta-mātra* or Mind-Only therefore possesses a double meaning, one purely metaphysical, the other metaphysical with a psychological meaning superadded. This would seem to correspond to a certain doubleness of aspect under which Reality itself, as Mind-Only, may be considered, so that, instead of being treated as alternatives, the two meanings should, no doubt, be taken simultaneously.

(4) As we fail to see things as they really are there is evidently present within our mind some hindering or obscuring factor. According to the more ancient tradition the realization of bodhi was obstructed by *avidyā* (Pāli *avijjā*) or ignorance. In the less cognitive terminology of the *Laṅkāvatāra* it is said that we fail to experience the truth of Mind-Only because of the power of a mental psychological factor called *vāsanā*. This is one of the key terms of the sūtra. Deriving etymologically from the root *vas*, meaning 'to dwell' or 'to stay' as well as 'to perfume', it is used in the *Laṅkāvatāra* and other Mahāyāna sūtras in the two senses combined, that is, in the sense of 'a perfuming energy that leaves its essence permanently behind in the things it has perfumed.'[166] The Chinese translators generally render the term by *hsi-ch'i* or *hsün-hsi*, meaning 'habit-energy'. *Vāsanā* stands, therefore, for the impressions left by our thoughts, words, and deeds since beginningless time, which impressions, conserved in the *ālaya-vijñāna*, cause us to discriminate an external world and then to cling to it as something independent of our own mind. In the terms of popular psychology, *vāsanā* corresponds to memory in the widest sense.

(5) From a slightly different point of view, the *ālaya* is compared to the ocean and *vāsanā* to the wind blowing across its surface and

stirring up innumerable waves. These waves correspond to the *vijñānas* which, by their interaction with the *ālaya* and with one another, build up the appearance of an objective world. For this reason the *ālaya* is said to have two aspects: one pure, corresponding to the ocean unruffled by wind; the other impure, corresponding to the ocean with waves. The pure *ālaya* is identical with *citta*. Yet since the waves are as much water as the ocean itself, the term *citta* is also extended, as we have seen, to cover the whole system of the *vijñānas*. Including the *ālaya*, these are altogether eight in number, the remaining ones being the *manas*, also known as the *kliṣṭa-mano-vijñāna*, the 'afflicted' or 'defiled' mental consciousness, and the *vijñānas* associated with the six sense-organs including the mind.

Of these the most important, in a sense, is the *manas*, though this *vijñāna* is not to be too sharply distinguished from the ordinary *mano-vijñāna* or Mind Consciousness. With the latter, which is merely the organ for the perception of ideas, there is nothing wrong. Indeed it may even be described as ethically neutral. When, however, under the influence of *vāsanā* it becomes 'afflicted' or 'defiled' (*kliṣṭa*) by false discrimination (*vikalpa*), on the one hand imagining the *ālaya* to be its ego and on the other interpreting sense-data in terms of an external world, it not only becomes the locus of desire (*tṛṣṇā*) and ignorance (*avidyā*) but, performing under their influence various wholesome and unwholesome *karmas*, it brings itself into subjection to the process of repeated birth and death. It is then known as the *kliṣṭa-mano-vijñāna*. Liberation is obtained simply by reversing the whole process. For this reason the *Laṅkāvatāra* speaks of the crucial experience of the spiritual life as a *parāvṛtti*, literally a revulsion or turning-round, in the deepest seat of consciousness.

(6) That such a revulsion can take place at all is due to the fact that the pure *ālaya*, or Mind-Only, is all the time immanent in the whole system of impure, discriminating consciousness. As thus present it is known by the symbolical and religious, rather than abstract and philosophical, title of the *tathāgatagarbha*, 'womb' or 'matrix' of Buddhahood. Indeed it may be said that, in the *Laṅkāvatāra*, *citta* (in one of its senses), *ālaya*, and *garbha* tend to stand respectively for the metaphysical, the psychological, and the religious aspects of the same fundamental Reality. The *garbha* receives its designation from the fact that, as the child is produced from the womb, so the realization of

Buddhahood issues, as it were, from this element present equally in the minds of all beings.

Like the *ālaya*, therefore, the *garbha* possesses two aspects, one impure, inasmuch as it is involved in and obscured by ignorance and desire, the other pure, inasmuch as it is in reality no more affected by these wrappings than a golden image by the filthy habiliments by which it is concealed. Like its psychological counterpart, moreover, the *garbha* may be mistaken by the ignorant for a soul (*ātman*). But since it, too, is void of all selfhood, being *śūnyatā* by nature, and therefore incapable of constituting any such entity, the confusion is as ill-founded in this case as it was in that. In terms of semantics, the *garbha* may be regarded as the reification of the fundamental postulate of Buddhism that Buddhahood is within the reach of every human being who is prepared to fulfil the conditions of its realization.

(7) Besides being immanent the Tathāgata is also transcendent. The *Laṅkāvatāra* is, in fact, especially rich in unsystematized Buddhological elements. As with most of the great Mahāyāna sūtras, the basis of its teaching on this subject is the recognition of a distinction between the Absolute Buddha and the relative Buddha, between the transcendental principle of Buddhahood as it is in itself, free from all duality, and that same principle as it appears to, or is perceived by, sentient beings. In the unstandardized terminology of the sūtra the first of these is referred to not only as the *dharmakāya*, which was afterward to become the standard designation, but also as the Tathāgata-kāya, the Dharma- or Dharmatā-Buddha, the Mūla-Tathāgata, and the Tathāgata-jñāna-Buddha.

The second, or relative Buddha, comprises two distinct personalities, one known as the Dharmatā-niśyanda-Buddha or, for short, the Niśyanda-Buddha, the other as the Nirmāṇa-Buddha. The Dharmatā-niśyanda-Buddha, from the root *śyand*, literally 'flowing down', 'flowing out', is the transcendental personality which, out of compassion for sentient beings, or as the result of the *purva-praṇidhāna* or 'previous vow', flows out, as it were, from the innermost heart of the *dharmakāya*. In the *Laṅkāvatāra* this Buddha, or type of Buddha, is described as resplendent and as dwelling in the Akaniṣṭha heaven.

The Nirmāṇa-Buddha is not so sharply distinguished from the Niśyanda-Buddha as the latter is from the Dharmatā-Buddha, and the nature of the difference between them is somewhat obscure. Coming from the root *mā*, 'to measure', 'to form', 'to display', with the prefix *nir*, meaning 'out of', it is generally understood as a 'transformed' or '(magically) created' Buddha, and here represents a Buddha not poised as it were midway between the Absolute and humanity in some remote heaven but 'coming in direct contact with the world of suffering beings and listening to their fears and anxieties'.[167] Like the moon reflected in many different pools of water, the Buddha assumes, in response to the needs of sentient beings, innumerable forms. These forms are the Nirmāṇa-Buddhas, the term being properly plural rather than singular. In an important passage the Lord declares, 'I come within the range of hearing of ignorant people, in this world of patience, under many names, amounting to a hundred times three *asaṃkhyeyas*, and they address me by these names not knowing that they are all other names of the Tathāgata.'[168]

The text then enumerates, by way of example, a number of philosophical and religious terms and proper names, both Buddhist and non-Buddhist. Care should be taken to distinguish the teaching contained in this passage, which is a fine example of Mahāyāna catholicity, with the superficial syncretism propounded in recent times, with more enthusiasm than knowledge, by certain neo-Vedantic agencies. Mention is also made in the *Laṅkāvatāra* of a Vipāka- or 'Result'-Buddha. This is not a fourth type of Buddha, for, according to Suzuki; 'The nature of a Vipāka-Buddha is that of a Nishyanda-Buddha when this is understood in the sense of a result flowing from an antecedent cause, that is, as one of the five effects (*pañca-phala*), and not in the sense of something secondary which issues out of a more primary substance.'[169]

The Dharmatā-, Niśyanda-, and Nirmāṇa-Buddhas correspond to, without being the semantically exact equivalents of, the *dharmakāya, sambhogakāya*, and *nirmāṇakāya* of the systematized *trikāya* doctrine. Yet despite its use of the word *dharmakāya*, which serves only to distinguish the eternal from the temporal aspect of Buddhahood, the *Laṅkāvatāra* differentiates the various Buddha-personalities in terms of Buddha, not in terms of *kāya*, so that it teaches not a Triple Body, that is to say one Buddha with three *kāyas*, but rather a Buddha Trinity. With the possible exception of certain verses in the *Sagātha* chapter, foreshadowing later developments, the Buddhology of the sūtra, therefore, though rich, is from the philosophical point of view not fully unified, and occupies an intermediate position between the more primitive and the most advanced Mahāyāna conceptions.

(8) As if by way of exception to the general lack of order, certain teachings are presented in the time-honoured form of numbered lists of doctrinal categories. One of the best known of these, which systematizes the psychology of the sūtra in terms of the eight *vijñānas*, has already been noticed. Some of the most important lists are of an epistemological nature. Such are the five dharmas, the three *svabhāva-lakṣaṇas*, and the two *satyas*. The interest and significance of these categories, which together with the eight *vijñānas* and the two *nairātmyas* have been regarded, historically speaking, as constituting the principal subject matter of the sūtra, is not merely theoretical. Even as other teachings elucidate the basic spiritual experience from the psychological, the metaphysical, or the soteriological point of view, so these attempt to evaluate it in terms of theory of knowledge.

The five dharmas or categories are name (*nāma*), appearance (*nimitta*), discrimination (*vikalpa*), 'right' knowledge (*samyag-jñāna*), and suchness (*tathatā*). In the following passage the Buddha explains the significance of these terms:

> Appearance is that which is seen as having such characteristics as form, shape, distinctive features, images, colours, etc.... Out of this appearance ideas are formed such as a jar, etc. by which one can say, this is such and such, and no other; this is 'name'. When names are thus pronounced, appearances are determined and there is 'discrimination', saying this is mind and this is what belongs to it. That these names and appearances are after all unobtainable because when intellection is put away the aspect of mutuality (in which all things are determined) ceases to be perceived and imagined – this is called the 'suchness' of things. And this suchness may be characterized as truth, reality, exact knowledge, limit, source, self-substance, the unattainable.... When, in agreement with this, (the truth) is rightly understood as neither negative nor affirmative, discrimination ceases to rise, and there is a state conformable to self-realization by means of noble wisdom;... that is 'right knowledge'.[170]

Like those of the Abhidharma, these five categories purport to exhaust between them the entire universe of religious discourse.

The three *svabhāva-lakṣaṇas* are the *parikalpita*, the contrived or imagined, the *paratantra* or dependent, and the *pariniṣpanna* or perfect. Though *svabhāva* means 'self-nature' or 'self-substance' and *lakṣaṇa* 'characteristic mark', or what distinguishes one thing from another, in this context the term is epistemological rather than ontological, and connotes the three different degrees of reality. By *parikalpita* is meant a purely subjective construction on the basis of data objectively given. Such knowledge is wholly false. It is like the illusory snake which, on a dark night, a man perceives in a piece of rope. *Paratantra* or relative knowledge is that which, though not absolutely true, is not wholly false either, but true enough for practical purposes. It corresponds to the perception of the piece of rope as a piece of rope, twisted out of fibres, and useful for tethering a cow or letting down a bucket into a well. *Pariniṣpanna* or perfect knowledge is full and complete cognition of the non-dual Reality. It is analogous to a scientific knowledge of the chemical composition of the rope. (This does not, of course, mean that scientific knowledge and 'perfect knowledge' are themselves really comparable. They are alike only in respect of the position they occupy in relation to the subordinate degrees of knowledge within their special contexts.) Thus the three svabhāvas and the five dharmas clearly represent alternative classifications of the same body of material. *Parikalpita* corresponds to *nāma* and *nimitta*, *paratantra* to *vikalpa*, and *pariniṣpanna* to *samyag-jñāna* and *tathatā*.

The two kinds of truth (*satya*), a formula which unlike the previous lists is the common property of all the Mahāyāna schools, is even more succinct. Herein one grand distinction is made between *saṃvṛti-satya* or relative truth on the one hand, in which both *parikalpita* and *paratantra* are included, and *paramārtha-satya*, ultimate or absolute truth on the other, corresponding to *pariniṣpanna*.

(9) Apart from the teachings which, being more or less peculiar to the sūtra, constitute the *Laṅkāvatāra*'s special contribution to Buddhism, the *Laṅkāvatāra* is a repository of nearly all the principal tenets of the Mahāyāna. The nature of the work precludes, of course, continuous and systematic treatment; but it discourses, usually with originality and often with profundity, on an astonishing variety of subsidiary topics including, for example, the three aspects of Noble Wisdom (*ārya-jñāna*), instantaneous and gradual purification of the *āsravas*, the three classes of the *icchantikas* or persons incapable of attaining Buddhahood, the four kinds of *dhyāna*, the nature of *māyā* or magical illusion, the four Holy Persons, the four kinds of Nirvāṇa, the One Vehicle (*ekayāna*) and the Triple Vehicle (*triyāna*), Buddha-

nature, the nine transformations (*pariṇāma*), momentariness, and causation. Though some topics lend themselves more easily than others to interpretation in terms of the pervading idealism, there runs through all of them, like a golden thread through a string of alternately opaque and transparent beads, the sūtra's recurrent theme of a personal experience of the truth of Mind-Only by means of a sudden revulsion in the deepest seat of consciousness.

# 14

# THE AVATAṂSAKA SŪTRA

## The Flower-Ornament Sūtra

The *Avataṃsaka* or 'Flower-Ornament' *Sūtra*, also known as the *Buddhāvataṃsaka*, has been eulogized by Suzuki in the most enthusiastic terms.

> It is really the consummation of Buddhist thought, Buddhist sentiment, and Buddhist experience. To my mind, no religious literature in the world can ever approach the grandeur of conception, the depths of feeling, and the gigantic scale of composition, as attained by this sūtra. It is the eternal fountain of life from which no religious mind will turn back athirst or only partially satisfied.... Here not only deeply speculative minds find satisfaction, but humble spirits and heavily-oppressed hearts, too, will have their burdens lightened.[171]

Like the Prajñā-pāramitā and the Ratnakūṭa, however, the *Avataṃsaka* is not so much a sūtra as a family of sūtras.

The origin of the group, as well as the number and identity of the works of which it is composed, is something of a mystery. A large collection of works so designated exists in both Chinese and Tibetan, constituting the third of the seven great divisions of the Tibetan Tripiṭaka, and therein comprising, according to one analysis, forty-five subdivisions, some of which appear as separate treatises in the corresponding division of the Chinese Tripiṭaka.[172] According to Eliot, the principal works of the Avataṃsaka class in Chinese are two translations of the *Avataṃsaka Sūtra*, eleven other items being duplicate renderings of portions of this work.[173] Suzuki enumerates three

Chinese translations of the *Avataṃsaka*, in sixty, eighty, and forty fascicules respectively, the first having been made by Buddhabhadra in 418–420CE, the second by Śikṣānanda in 695–699CE, and the third by Prajñā in 796–797CE.[174] Individual sections of the work had been translated even earlier, however, and might originally have formed independent sūtras.

According to Chinese sources, there were six different *Avataṃsaka Sūtras*, the longest of which contained 100,000 verses and the shortest 36,000. It was the latter work which was translated by Buddhabhadra and his colleagues. Śikṣānanda's translation, in 45,000 verses, has as its fifteenth chapter the *Daśabhūmika Sūtra*. Prajñā's translation, which is the shortest of the three, is in fact the final chapter of the two earlier works, being chapter 34 of the first and chapter 39 of the second. This chapter, entitled 'Entering into the Dharmadhātu', comprises about one-fourth of the known works. It corresponds to the *Gaṇḍavyūha* or 'World-Array' *Sūtra* preserved in Nepal and is, therefore, together with the *Daśabhūmika*, the only portion of the Avataṃsaka division of the Chinese and Tibetan Tripiṭakas which is attested by a Sanskrit original. As Śāntideva's *Śikṣā-samuccaya*, which is as late as the seventh century, quotes only from the *Gaṇḍavyūha*, and never from the *Avataṃsaka*, it is, indeed, possible that, apart from the early duplicate renderings, and the material paralleled in Tibetan, the Chinese Avataṃsaka division incorporates much that is of indigenous origin and apocryphal. For practical purposes, therefore, the Avataṃsaka group reduces itself to the *Gaṇḍavyūha* and the *Daśabhūmika*.

The *Gaṇḍavyūha* resembles the *Saddharma-puṇḍarīka* in being a work of symbolic imagination rather than of conceptual thought, though again it differs from it in being, as regards literary form, not so much dramatic as narrative. Commenting on the change of scene that is noticeable when we come to this work from the *Laṅkāvatāra* and other Mahāyāna sūtras, Suzuki says: 'We find here nothing cold, nothing grey or earth-coloured, and nothing humanly mean; for everything one touches in the *Gaṇḍavyūha* shines out in an unsurpassable manner. We are no more in this world of limitation, obscurity, and adumbration; we are miraculously lifted up among the heavenly galaxies. The ethereal world is luminosity itself.'[175] He further remarks on the active sense of grand inscrutable mystery (*acintya*), beyond the power of thinking and description, which runs through the text as its one dominant feeling.

As a narrative, the sūtra is based on one of the legends of the *Divyāvadāna*, and describes the wanderings of a noble youth called Sudhana who, on the advice of the Bodhisattva Mañjuśrī, travels all over India seeking from one 'good friend' (*kalyāṇa mitra*) after another the highest knowledge essential for Enlightenment. For this reason the work has been aptly termed the 'Pilgrim's Progress' of Buddhism. Since Sudhana's ultimate object in making the pilgrimage is to identify himself with Samantabhadra, the *Gaṇḍavyūha* is in a deeper sense the history of the inner-religious consciousness of that Bodhisattva, whose wisdom-eye (*jñāna-cakṣus*), life of devotion (*caryā*), and original vows (*praṇidhāna*) make up its contents. It also exemplifies the important role which the 'good friends' or spiritual advisers play in the spiritual life.

The sūtra opens at Śrāvastī, where the Buddha is dwelling in the Jetavana surrounded by five hundred Bodhisattvas headed by Samantabhadra and Mañjuśrī. The assembly is waiting for the Buddha to preach. However, he enters into a certain *samādhi*, whereupon the Jetavana suddenly expands to the farthest limits of the universe, or what amounts to the same thing, the universe dissolves into the Jetavana, while innumerable Bodhisattvas from the ten quarters come and worship the Buddha, composing verses of praise. The Buddha then projects from between his eyebrows a ray of light which, falling upon Bodhisattvas and all the ten quarters of the world, causes them to be filled with a compassionate desire to benefit all beings. Such a transformation of the Jetavana is possible, we are told, because of the inconceivable (*acintya*) power of the Buddha, who can transform his one body and make it pervade the entire universe, make all the Buddhas and all the Buddha-lands with their splendours enter into his own body, manifest all the images of the *dharmadhātu* within one single particle of dust, reveal all the Buddhas of the past with their successive doings within a single pore of his skin, illuminate the entire universe with each one of the rays which emanate from his body, evolve clouds of transformation from a single pore of his skin and make them fill up all the Buddha-lands, and reveal in a single pore of his skin the whole history of all the worlds in the ten quarters from their first appearance until their final destruction.

Both the opening phantasmagoria, and the subsequent elucidation, are attempts to express what Suzuki calls the fundamental insight of the sūtra,[176] the insight, namely, into the truth of the perfect mutual interpenetration of all the seemingly separate and discrete objects of the universe, one entering into all and all into each without obstruction. The *Laṅkāvatāra* had established Absolute Mind as the sole reality of all phenomena. The *Gaṇḍavyūha*, going a step further, exhibits Absolute Mind not as annihilating the world of concrete particulars but as reflecting them in itself and as being, in its turn, reflected in every object in the universe down to the minutest particle of dust. This is not unlike Tennyson's feeling that complete knowledge of the 'flower in the crannied wall' would enable him to 'know what God and what man is', or Blake's vision of:

> ... a world in a grain of sand,
> And a heaven in a wild flower,
> ... infinity in the palm of your hand,
> And eternity in an hour.

But the *Gaṇḍavyūha* does not stop here. Every object reflects every other object, and is simultaneously reflected in it. Time and space as we know them disappear. Past and future are both revealed in the present moment of illumination which, instead of standing still with all its contents, moves continually on. Birds and flowers and mountains, instead of excluding one another, are seen to be mutually interfused, though without any loss of their respective individualities. In order to illustrate such a state of existence, the sūtra depicts everything as transparent and luminous, for 'luminosity is the only possible earthly representation that conveys the idea of universal interpenetration'.[177]

What emerges with the abolition of space and time, therefore, is a world of imagelessness or shadowlessness (*anābhāsa*) consisting of an infinity of luminous and beautiful objects in a state of perfect mutual intersolution. As distinguished from the *lokadhātu* or world of finite particulars, this glorious spiritual world is known as the *dharmadhātu*, entry into which constitutes the subject matter of the sūtra. At the same time, though not identical with the *lokadhātu*, the *dharmadhātu* is not absolutely different from it either. Here too there is mutual interpenetration. Towards the end of the sūtra, the *dharmadhātu* is represented symbolically under the figure of Vairocana's Tower.

The miraculous transformation of the Jetavana having taken place in the manner described, the Bodhisattva Mañjuśrī comes out into the human world and preaches the Mahāyāna doctrine to numerous people. While residing in the city of Dhanyakara he sees in the midst of the assembly a handsome youth of noble family called Sudhana who is listening to the discourse with the desire of learning, leading, and perfecting the life of a Bodhisattva. Knowing his aspiration, Mañjuśrī advises him of the necessity of finding a good friend (*kalyāṇa mitra*) to help him in his quest, and accordingly directs him to the Malaya Mountain, in a distant part of India, where he will find the bhikshu Sāgaramegha. This bhikshu will instruct him.

Sudhana therefore sets out on the first stage of his long pilgrimage and meets Sāgaramegha who, after praising the young man's resolution and describing the qualities necessary to the development of the Will to Enlightenment, directs him to go for further instruction to another good friend. This friend instructs him and sends him on to yet another. In this way Sudhana calls on fifty-three *kalyāṇa mitras* or spiritual advisers, all of whom instruct him in some aspect of the Bodhisattva ideal, either by delivering a discourse or, in many cases, by narrating the story of their own life and spiritual experiences in a manner reminiscent of the Avadānas.

The broad and liberal attitude of the Mahāyāna is exemplified by the fact that among these *kalyāṇa mitras* there are great differences of social class and ecclesiastical status. As enumerated by a modern student of the sūtra, they comprise five Bodhisattvas, five monks, one nun, eight householders, a physician, a perfume seller, a sailor, two kings, two laymen, four laywomen, three of whom were ladies and one a heavenly maiden, several children, a number of deities, a mendicant, a hermit, and two brahmins.[178]

Representative of the type of instruction imparted is the following extract from the reply, given by the Goddess of the Night, Sarvajagadrakṣapraṇidhāna-vīryaprabhā or 'Heroic Splendour of the Resolve to Guard All the World', to Sudhana's question as to how long she had been in possession of her specific Bodhisattva-knowledge:

> O son of a noble family, in the Bodhisattva's realm of knowledge there is no place for speculations about the aeons; therein will not be experienced or known either long duration of Saṃsāra or short duration of Saṃsāra; nor will there be experienced or known either depravity of aeons or purity of acons, or smallness of aeons or greatness of aeons, or multitude of aeons or diversity of aeons, or manifoldness of

> aeons or diversifyingness of aeons, or variety of aeons. For what reason is that so? Because, O son of a noble family, the Bodhisattva's realm of knowledge is pure in its very nature, is free from all the trammels of ideation, is beyond all the mountains of veiling obstructions. (This knowledge) rises in the (pure) intention (of the Bodhisattva) and sheds its radiance on all the beings who will in time be led to (spiritual) maturity (by different means) according to their (different) dispositions.
>
> In the same way, O son of a noble family, as in the disc of the sun the distinction of day and night cannot be found, nor does it reside there; but when the sun has set night is known and experienced, and when the sun has risen day is known and experienced – so also, O son of a noble family, in the Bodhisattva's realm of knowledge (which is like unto the disc of the sun and) which knows not of ratiocination, one cannot find any thought-constructions as to the aeons, nor can one find there any ideas about lives in this world, or about any paths (that one might walk). On the contrary, it is due to the fact that it takes time until all the beings have attained to (spiritual) maturity (i.e. Buddhahood), that in the ratiocinationless realm of knowledge which has risen from the pure intentions of the Bodhisattvas, ideas and calculations as to lives in the aeons, and as to the world in general, are found.[179]

Elsewhere, as might have been expected, the importance of spiritual friends is explicitly insisted upon. After telling Sudhana about their spiritual realizations, the boy Śrīsambhava and the girl Śrīmati pronounce a long eulogy on the subject, emphasizing that the *kalyāṇa mitras* must be sought for without weariness, and describing in detail the various ways in which they help the Bodhisattva. One paragraph reads:

> O Son of a noble family, kept back by friends in the good life the Bodhisattvas do not fall into the pits of woeful existences; surrounded by friends in the good life the Bodhisattvas do not turn away from the Great Career (*Mahāyāna*); exhorted by friends in the good life the Bodhisattvas do not forsake the teachings of the Bodhisattvas; guarded by friends in the good

> life the Bodhisattvas do not come under the power of bad friends; protected by friends in the good life the Bodhisattvas do not lose the essential qualities of Bodhisattvas; directed by friends in the good life the Bodhisattvas go beyond the world of ordinary men; taught by friends in the good life the Bodhisattvas do not lower themselves to the level of Śrāvakas and Pratyeka-buddhas; shielded by friends in the good life the Bodhisattvas have risen above the world; tended by friends in the good life the Bodhisattvas are not defiled by worldly things; guarded by friends in the good life the Bodhisattvas are irreproachable as to their behaviour in all walks of life; uplifted by friends in the good life the Bodhisattvas do not leave (unfinished) whatever (task) they have begun; taught and guarded by friends in the good life the Bodhisattvas cannot be attacked by the defilements of selfish actions; having gained their strength from friends in the good life the Bodhisattvas are invincible by all the armies of Māra; relying on friends in the good life the Bodhisattvas increase in the (seven) characteristics of Enlightenment.[180]

The last of the fifty-three teachers to be visited by Sudhana is the Bodhisattva Maitreya, who lives in a tower known as the Vairocana-vyūha-alaṅkāra-garbha or 'Repository of a Brilliantly Shining Array of Ornaments'. This structure, as Sudhana wonderingly reflects as he stands before it, is the *vihāra* or dwelling place not only of Maitreya, but of all those who understand the meaning of emptiness (*śūnyatā*), signlessness (*animitta*), and wishlessness (*apraṇihita*); who understand that all things are beyond discrimination, that the *dharmadhātu* is devoid of separateness, that a world of beings is not attainable, that all things are unborn – and so on through a long list of attributes. In other words, it is the abode of all the most highly advanced followers of the Mahāyāna, that is to say, of the Bodhisattvas.

The deeper, more esoteric significance of the idea of dwelling place, abode, or sphere of activity, in Buddhism is the subject of a brilliant piece of exposition by Suzuki, according to whom Bodhisattvahood, the Desire for Enlightenment or All-Knowledge (*bodhicittotpāda*), and the Bodhisattva's Abode (*vihāra*), are the three important notions which, in the *Gaṇḍavyūha*, distinguish the Buddhist life, especially after the attainment of an insight into the truth of Zen.[181] When the monastery where the master resides (as Maitreya resides in his tower) acquires a subjective sense, as it does in Buddhist literature, 'it is a general characteristic psychic or spiritual attitude a person assumes towards all stimuli'. Strictly speaking, though, it is not a mere attitude or tendency of mind, but 'something more fundamental constituting the very ground of one's being, that is to say, a field where a person in the profoundest sense lives and moves and has his reason of existence. This field is essentially determined by the depth and clarity of one's spiritual intuitions.'[182]

Maitreya and the other Bodhisattvas of the *Gaṇḍavyūha* live immersed in the light of the highest truth of interpenetration. Vairocana's Tower therefore stands for nothing less than the *dharmadhātu*. That this is so becomes clear as soon as Sudhana enters its magnificent portals. Before allowing him to do so, however, Maitreya congratulates the young pilgrim on having aroused the Desire for Enlightenment, enjoying various advantages such as having been born as a human being, residing in a world of sentient beings, living at a time when a Tathāgata has appeared, and having met Mañjuśrī, as well as being well provided with stocks of merit, well supported by works of purity, well cleansed in understanding, great in intuitive wisdom, well protected by all the Buddhas, and well guarded by the good friends, after which he pours forth, on the subject of the Bodhicitta, a stream of metaphors of astounding length and variety.[183] The flood of eloquence having subsided, Sudhana begs for admittance. Maitreya snaps his fingers, whereupon the doors fly open of their own accord to admit the youth and just as mysteriously close behind him. Sudhana finds himself standing inside Vairocana's Tower.

With the description that now ensues we reach the climax of the sūtra. As this refers, of course, not to any architectural monument, however imposing, but to the *dharmadhātu*, it is pitched in the loftiest strain of Mahāyāna eloquence.

To Sudhana's wondering gaze, the interior of the tower reveals itself as being as wide as the sky. Besides being all paved with precious stones, it contains countless palaces, porches, windows, and other features, besides a corresponding quantity of flowers, wreaths, incense burners, golden flakes, gem thrones, and tapestries. There are also innumerable figures wrought of gold and of jewels. Countless beautiful birds sing melodiously, while throughout the infinity of the tower are disposed infinitudes of lotuses in full bloom, rows of trees, and great *maṇi*-gems emitting rays of light. Moreover, within the tower there are hundreds of thousands of towers, each one as exquisitely adorned as the main tower and as wide as the sky, and each one, while preserving its individual existence, at the same time offering no obstruction to all the rest.

Thus in the state of mutual interpenetration there is this perfect harmony and perfect order. Sudhana sees himself within all the towers collectively, as well as within each single tower, and his joy knows no bounds. He is freed from individualistic notions, and revels in an emancipation transcending all limitations. Upheld by the sustaining power (*adhiṣṭhāna*) of Maitreya, he finds himself in each of the towers simultaneously, and witnesses in each one a marvellous panorama of the events of that Bodhisattva's career.

He sees Maitreya and other Bodhisattvas entering into *samādhi* and emitting from the pores of their skin multitudes of transformation-bodies of various kinds. He also hears all the teachings of the Buddha melodiously issuing from every single pore of the skin of all the Bodhisattvas. He beholds all the Buddhas, together with their respective assemblies, and is the spectator of their different activities. In one particularly high, spacious, and exquisitely decorated tower, of incomparable beauty, he sees at one glance the entire tri-chiliocosm, containing hundreds of *kotis* of Tuṣita heavens, and in each one of these worlds he sees Maitreya's descent to earth, his nativity, and all the subsequent events of his final existence. He hears bells, musical instruments, and voices, all of which proclaim the heroic deeds of the Bodhisattvas with a ravishingly beautiful sound. He sees in mirrors the incalculable assemblies of Buddhas, Bodhisattvas, śrāvakas, and Pratyeka-Buddhas, as well as pure worlds, impure worlds, and worlds of many different sizes, shapes, and types of inhabitants. In all these worlds Bodhisattvas innumerable exert themselves in various ways for the benefit of sentient beings. He sees, moreover, pillars emitting multi-coloured radiance, golden figures of young maidens offering all manner of precious things in worship to the Buddhas – pearl necklaces, banners, nets, streamers, and canopies – lotus-ponds planted with lotuses of various kinds, each lotus consisting of innumerable flowers, and each flower containing a human or a divine being in an attitude of devotion, together with numerous other marvels. All this, and much more besides, is described in such lavish detail, and with so brilliant a glow of light and colour, that no summary of the passage can hope to do justice to its more than apocalyptic splendours.

Finally, Sudhana sees Maitreya seated on a lion throne preaching the Dharma, then as practising the *pāramitās* for incalculable aeons, and again as himself befriended throughout his past lives by good friends adorned with multitudes of virtues. These good friends welcome the young pilgrim to the tower and trust that, beholding the wonders of Bodhisattvahood, he may not feel fatigued.

The sūtra now explains how it is that Sudhana could be accorded such a privilege, after which Maitreya, suspending his sustaining power and entering into the tower, snaps his fingers and explains to Sudhana the significance of what he has seen. In the course of their discussion he says,

> O son of a good family, the wonderful arraying of things thou hast seen comes from nowhere, passes away nowhere, stays nowhere accumulated, and it is there just because the Bodhisattva is to learn of his inconceivable Māyā-knowledge, because of the all-sustaining and all-ruling power of the Bodhisattva's vows and knowledge.'[184]

The same is true of the Bodhisattva himself. Questioned by Sudhana as to whence he has come, Maitreya replies in a strain of typical Prajñā-pāramitā paradox:

> The Bodhisattva comes as neither coming nor going; the Bodhisattva comes as neither moving nor staying, as neither dead nor born, as neither staying nor passing away, as neither departing nor rising, as neither hoping nor getting attached, as neither doing nor reaping the reward, as neither being born nor gone to annihilation, as neither eternal nor bound for death.

> And yet, O son of a good family, it is in this way that the Bodhisattva comes: he comes where an all-embracing love abides, because he desires to discipline all beings; he comes where there is a great compassionate heart, because he desires to protect all beings against sufferings; he comes where there are deeds of morality, because he desires to be born wherever he can be agreeable; he comes wherever there are great vows to fulfil because of the power of the original vows; he comes

> out of the miraculous powers because wherever he is sought after he manifests himself to please people; he comes where there is effortlessness because he is never away from the footsteps of all the Buddhas; he comes where there is neither giving nor taking because in his movements mental and physical there is no trace of striving; he comes out of the skilful means born of transcendental knowledge because he is ever in conformity with the mentalities of all beings; he comes where transformations are manifested because all that appears is like a reflection, like a transformed body.

Yet at the same time, in the *Gaṇḍavyūha*'s world of interpenetration, the transcendental does not exclude the mundane. Maitreya therefore continues:

> This being the case, O son of a good family, yet thou askest whence I come. As to that, I am here from my native country, Maladi. My object is to teach the Dharma to a young man called Gopālaka and all the other people living in my district each according to his or her fitness. It is also to get their parents, relatives, Brahmans, and others into the way of the Mahāyāna.[185]

The Bodhisattva Maitreya is simultaneously an ineffable spiritual being and a recognizable historical figure. *Dharmadhātu* and *lokadhātu* are identical. This world of defilement is itself the Pure Land.

Eventually, Maitreya directs Sudhana to go back to Mañjuśrī and enquire of him about the principle by which he could be initiated into the spiritual life of Samantabhadra. This life, or *caryā*, as it is technically called, finds expression in the Ten Vows of that Bodhisattva, with which, after Sudhana's return, the remainder of the sūtra is chiefly occupied. In substance they are:
(1) to worship the Buddhas;
(2) to praise the Tathāgatas;
(3) to make offerings to all the Buddhas;
(4) to confess past sins;
(5) to rejoice in the virtues and happiness of others;
(6) to request the Buddhas to preach the Dharma;
(7) to request the Buddhas not to enter into Nirvāṇa;
(8) to study the Dharma in order to teach it;

(9) to benefit all beings;
(10) to transfer one's stock of merits to others.

These vows having been made, Samantabhadra brings the *Gaṇḍavyūha* to a fitting conclusion by reciting the *Bhadracari-praṇidhāna-rāja* or 'King of Vows Concerning the Good Life', or series of sixty-two melodious Dodhaka verses which, in the words of Winternitz, 'ranks among the most beautiful expressions of Buddhist piety, and has been used for purposes of worship in all countries of Mahāyāna Buddhism ever since the fourth century AD.'[186]

The idea that from the time of his initial aspiration to that of his final consecration to Buddhahood, the Bodhisattva passes through a series of ten successive stages of spiritual development (*bhūmi*), forms an integral part of the Mahāyāna conception of his career. References to these stages occur in the *Lalita-vistara*, as well as in the Perfection of Wisdom 'in 25,000 lines', chapter 17, where Subhūti describes the preparations for each stage.[187] The most complete and systematic account, however, is found in the *Daśabhūmika* or *Daśabhūmiśvara Sūtra*, which, though regarded as a portion of the *Avataṃsaka*, just as frequently circulates as an independent work.

The Sanskrit text of this sūtra is still extant, and there are Tibetan and Chinese translations. Among the latter, the earliest is that made by Dharmarakṣa in 297CE, which enables us to fix an upper limit for the composition of this work, at least in its original form. Subsequent versions were made by Kumārajīva (406CE), Bodhiruci (500–516CE), and Śīladharma (789CE), the last two being now lost. To what extent the translations agree among themselves, or with the Sanskrit original as now extant, is uncertain. According to one modern authority, the *Daśabhūmiśvara* is the title of a recension augmented by Prakrit verses.[188] Unlike the *Gaṇḍavyūha*, which is composed in mixed prose and verse, the *Daśabhūmika* is entirely in prose, containing an admixture of Sanskrit verses only in chapter 1.

The scene of the sūtra is laid, not on earth, but in the paradise of Indra, where Śākyamuni is temporarily sojourning, and the speaker is the Bodhisattva Vajragarbha or 'Diamond Matrix', who plunges into deep meditation in a vast assembly of gods, Buddhas, and Bodhisattvas, and is then invited by Śākyamuni to explain the ten *bhūmis*, while rays of light emanate in all directions from all the Buddhas present. Since an account of the *bhūmis*, and their correlations with the ten *pāramitās* and other doctrinal categories, is readily available elsewhere,[189] a further enumeration of the series is not required. Instead, we quote from the description of how, by means of his patient acceptance of the non-origination of all dharmas (*anutpattika-dharma-kṣānti*), the Bodhisattva passes from the seventh to the eighth stage and attains a life of effortless spontaneity, a short passage not unrepresentative of the style and spirit of the sūtra. Having expounded the nature of the patient acceptance, Vajragarbha says:

> O son of the Buddha, as soon as the Bodhisattva attains this acceptance, he enters upon the eighth stage called immovable (*acalā*). This is the inner abode of Bodhisattvahood, which is difficult to comprehend, which goes beyond discrimination, separated from all forms, all ideas, and all attachments; which transcends calculation and limitation, as it lies outside (the knowledge of) the Śrāvakas and Pratyekabuddhas and above all disturbances and ever in possession of tranquillity.
>
> As a Bhikshu, furnished with supernatural faculties and freedom of mind and gradually entering into the Samādhi of Cessation, has all his mental disturbances quieted and is free from discrimination, so the Bodhisattva now abides in the stage of immovability, that is, detached from all works of effort (*ābhaga*); he has attained effortlessness, has put an end to strivings mental, verbal, and physical, and is beyond discrimination as he has put away all forms of vexation; he is now established in the Dharma itself which he enjoys as the fruit of his past work.
>
> It is like a man who, in a dream finding himself in a great river, attempts to go to the other side; he musters all his energy and strives hard with every possible means. And because of this effort and contrivance, he wakes from the dream, and being thus awakened all his strivings are set at rest. In like manner the Bodhisattva sees all beings drowning themselves in the four streams, and in his attempt to save them, exerts himself vigorously, unflinchingly, and because of his vigorous and unflinching exertion he attains the stage of immovability. Once in this stage, all his strivings are dropped, he is relieved of all activity that issues from the notion of duality or from an attachment to appearance.[190]

# 15

# THE NIRVĀṆA AND SUVARṆA-PRABHĀSA SŪTRAS

## The Nirvāṇa Sūtras and the Sūtra of Golden Light

Next to the Buddha's attainment of Enlightenment, the most important episode in his career was the *parinirvāṇa* or 'final passing away'. It is therefore natural that a number of sūtras should be associated with this episode, when in view of the solemnity of the occasion the Buddha might be expected to remind his disciples of the teachings to which he attached special importance or even to reveal completely new teachings. Thus thirteen works of the Nirvāṇa class of Mahāyāna sūtras are contained in the Chinese Tripiṭaka, though some of these are in fact Hīnayāna rather than Mahāyāna sūtras. 'The Sūtra of the Doctrine (or Teaching) Bequeathed by the Buddha', for instance, translated by Kumārajīva between 402 and 412CE, is a short work in which the Buddha, on the eve of his *parinirvāṇa*, admonishes his monk disciples with regard to such things as the observance of the monastic code, control of the senses, moderation in food and drink, the practice of patience and energy, and the development of concentration and wisdom. The emphasis throughout is thoroughly ascetic and, in a sense, spiritually individualistic. Only towards the end of the sūtra is there any hint of distinctively Mahāyāna teaching, when the Buddha speaks of what one English version of the work renders as 'the eternal reality of the Dharma-kāya of the Tathāgata'.[191]

The eternal reality of the *dharmakāya* is one of the principal themes of a work which is definitely a Mahāyāna sūtra and probably the most important work of the Nirvāṇa class. This is the *Mahā-parinirvāṇa Sūtra* in thirteen chapters translated by Dharmakṣema between 416 and 423CE. A revision of this work which, from the circumstance of its having been made at Nanking, is known as the Southern Edition of the *Mahā-parinirvāṇa Sūtra*, also exists, as well as two incomplete translations, one made during the Tang dynasty (618–907CE) while the other was the joint work of Fa-Hian and Buddhabhadra. The single sūtra which makes up the sixth or Nirvāṇa class of the Tibetan Tripiṭaka appears to correspond to this Chinese work. The original Sanskrit text is lost, though fragments have been found in the sands of Central Asia, as well as in a temple in Japan. Besides the fact of its translation by Dharmakṣema in the fifth century, the antiquity of the sūtra is attested by the *Nirvāṇa-śāstra* of Vasubandhu, translated by Dharmabodhi of the Northern or Eastern Wei dynasty (386–550CE), though the extent to which the text translated by Dharmakṣema agrees with that expounded by Vasubandhu is unknown. In modern times a complete English translation has appeared in three volumes, the product of the devoted labours of Kosho Yamamoto. This translation has been made from the Southern Edition of Dharmakṣema's version, comprising thirty-six Chinese volumes and twenty-five chapters. The work is thus one of the most extensive of all the Mahāyāna sūtras, being at least ten times the length of any of its Hīnayāna counterparts, whether Pāli or Sanskrit.

Length is not necessarily commensurate with variety of content, however – even in the case of a Mahāyāna sūtra. In the course of the *Mahā-parinirvāṇa Sūtra*'s one thousand pages (in the English translation) very little happens. There are no dramatic episodes comparable to the apparition of the stupa in the 'White Lotus of the True Dharma Sūtra' or Vimalakīrti's 'thunderous silence' in 'The Exposition of Vimalakīrti', and very little in the way of symbolic phantasmagoria to arouse interest and stimulate the imagination.

Though the assembly consists of representatives of all classes of sentient beings, from Bodhisattvas to bee-kings, the actual *dramatis personae* of the work are very limited, the principal interlocutors being the Bodhisattva Kāśyapa, the lay devotee Cunda, and the great Bodhisattva Mañjuśrī, together with the Bodhisattvas 'Highly Virtuous King' and 'Lion's Roar'. Only towards the very end of the work do any other characters appear. Historical facts are touched on in the lightest and most casual manner. The *mise-en-scène* once described, we hear little more of them beyond a reference to the 'last meal' offered by Cunda and the absence of Ānanda and Kāśyapa, and, towards the end of the work, to King Ajātaśatru's visit and the six sectarian teachers. The *parinirvāṇa* itself is not described, since the sūtra comes to an end before this great event occurs. For some half dozen chapters at a time, indeed, both history and geography fade into the background or disappear altogether, the greater part of the sūtra being entirely taken up by lengthy disquisitions of a doctrinal nature. These disquisitions are in prose, with occasional short passages in verse. Parables abound, though few if any of them are as memorable as those of the 'White Lotus of the True Dharma Sūtra'.

As a literary composition, the *Mahā-parinirvāṇa* is in fact distinctly inferior not only to the 'White Lotus' but to the 'Exposition of Vimalakīrti'. Not that this really matters. The strength of the sūtra lies in its disquisitions, in which the transcendentalist and universalist ideas that are the common property of practically the whole Mahāyāna movement are developed in a way that involves not only doctrinal innovation but a terminological departure from strict orthodoxy. A short résumé of the work will help to make this clear.

As in the case of the Hīnayāna sūtras which are its counterparts, and possibly its prototypes, the scene of the *Mahā-parinirvāna Sūtra* is laid in Kuśinagara, in the land of the Mallas, where the Buddha is lying between the twin sāl trees. He is surrounded by 'eighty billion hundred thousand great bhikshus' – the vastly inflated numbers serving to suggest the cosmic significance of the occasion. It is early morning. In a voice that fills the entire world, and reaches up to the highest heaven, the Buddha announces his impending *parinirvāṇa,* at the same time sending out from his mouth rays of five different colours – blue, yellow, white, crystal, and agate. These rays light up the entire three thousand great-thousandfold world system, taking away the sins of the beings in all six realms of existence. Dismayed at the prospect of losing the Buddha, people weep and wail, and eventually agree to go to the land of the Mallas and beg him to stay in the world for one more *kalpa*.

In this way there pour into Kuśinagara, in endless procession, host upon countless host of human and non-human beings, all bearing vast quantities of offerings of every conceivable kind. There are millions of monks and nuns, all of whom are either Arhants or great Bodhisattvas, millions of male and female lay devotees, millions of ministers and wealthy merchants, kings and queens and ladies of the harem, gods and goddesses of various kinds, from the highest to the lowest, pretas and witches, birds, animals, Vedic sages, and bee-kings. Even Māra the Evil One is there. From Jambudvīpa the only ones not present are Ānanda, Mahākāśyapa, and King Ajātaśatru, besides various poisonous snakes and noxious insects.

Despite the repeated entreaties of the assembly, the Buddha persists in his determination to enter *parinirvāṇa* that very night, and refuses to accept the offerings. He even refuses to accept the offerings brought by the countless Bodhisattvas coming from each of the innumerable Buddha-lands of the ten directions of space. Instead, there issues from the Buddha's face a five-coloured light which, having traversed the entire congregation, returns to the Buddha and is reabsorbed through his mouth. It is now clear to everyone that the Buddha really is about to enter *parinirvāṇa*, and the first chapter of the sūtra ends amid general consternation.

In chapter 2 the lay devotee Cunda, who is accompanied by fifteen companions, tearfully requests the Buddha to accept their final offerings; whereupon the Buddha assures him that the meal offered him before his attainment of Enlightenment and the meal offered him before his entry into *parinirvāṇa* are of equal merit. This part of the episode is common to both the *Mahā-parinirvāṇa Sūtra* and the corresponding Hīnayāna sūtras, such as the *Mahā-parinibbāṇa-sutta* of the Pāli canon. What is not common is the dialogue that now follows.

Cunda refuses to believe that the two meals can be of equal merit, objecting that whereas one is made to an ordinary material body the other is made to the adamantine *dharmakāya*, which is infinite and eternal. In reply the Buddha explains that his pre-Enlightenment body is none other than the *dharmakāya*, and that his attainment of Enlightenment is only apparent. Like the *parinirvāṇa* itself, it is a skilful means. In reality the Buddha has not had a material body for countless *kalpas*. He is the eternal, adamantine *dharmakāya*, and appears to accept food simply for the benefit of the śrāvakas, i.e. the followers of the Hīnayāna. As an exchange of 'Perfection of Wisdom'-type profundities then makes clear, the Buddha is by nature unconditioned and not to be equated with any conditioned thing. The point is illustrated by various parables. But even though Cunda knows that the Buddha does not really enter into *parinirvāṇa*, he still cannot bear the thought of losing him.

Despite the fact that both Mañjuśrī and the Buddha urge him to make his final offerings, he gives vehement expression to his grief. This grief is shared by the rest of the assembly, and in chapter 3 they all renew their entreaties to the Buddha to remain in the world. In the course of a lengthy reply the Buddha praises the bhikshus for their understanding of the true nature of conditioned existence. But it is not enough, he tells them, to see conditioned existence as painful, impermanent, void of self, and foul. They must also see the unconditioned, or the *dharmakāya*, in terms of the positive counterparts of these four characteristics, i.e. see it in terms of bliss, permanence, *self*, and pure beauty.

This is the *Mahā-parinirvāṇa Sūtra*'s famous teaching of the four positive aspects of Nirvāṇa, which although hinted at in earlier sūtras here receives its definitive expression. In contrast to conditioned existence, which was characterized as painful (*duḥkha*), impermanent (*anitya*), void of self (*anātma*) and foul (*aśubha*), both the Hīnayāna and the Mahāyāna traditions had from the beginning described Nirvāṇa, the Unconditioned Element, in terms of bliss, permanence, and pure beauty. But they had never described it in terms of the self (*ātma*) or the great self (*mahātma*), for conditioned and unconditioned dharmas were alike *anātma*.[192] In the *Mahā-parinirvāṇa Sūtra*, however, the Buddha is represented as himself now introducing just this 'heresy', so repugnant to the entire trend of his teaching, and as describing Nirvāṇa not only as bliss, permanence, and pure beauty but as the self (*ātma*) or great self (*mahātma*). This great self, besides being equated with Nirvāṇa, is also declared identical with the Tathāgata as well as with the Buddha-nature inherent in all beings.

In reality the novelty is linguistic rather than doctrinal. The prefix *mahā-* or 'great' stands for *śūnyatā*, so that the *mahātma* or great self is not the empirical self, or the self of Vedantic philosophy, but a self that has been thoroughly purified and transformed by the realization of *śūnyatā* and which is, therefore, neither an entity nor a non-entity. Indeed, it is explicity stated that in the Buddha's teaching the self is nothing but Buddha-nature, and that the meaning of no-self is equivalent to that of the great self or the Tathāgata.

The *Mahā-parinirvāṇa Sūtra*'s startling reversal of a standard Buddhist terminology is, no doubt, of the nature of a therapeutic shock, administered by the Buddha as a last reminder to his disciples that, as the *Laṅkāvatāra* repeatedly insists, words are but signs, and should not be mistaken for realities or adhered to as ends in themselves.

To the bhikshus who are the immediate recipients of the new revelation, it certainly comes as a shock to be told that they must see the *dharmakāya* in terms of self, as well as in terms of bliss, permanence, and pure beauty, and they ask the Buddha to explain the contradiction between his former teaching and what he is telling them now.

This the Buddha does with the help of an ingenious parable. An ignorant physician having treated all diseases alike with milk preparations of various kinds, and in this way done more harm than good, a wise physician persuades the king to banish the ignorant physician and prohibit treatment with milk preparations on pain of death. The wise physician then prepares various medicines and with them cures all the diseases in the land. One day the king himself falls ill, and the wise physician prescribes a certain milk preparation! Naturally the king is astonished, but the wise physician explains that what he had said before was not absolutely and literally true. In certain cases, and administered under certain special conditions, milk can in fact be beneficial. Milk is poison, and milk is ambrosia. Moreover, any resemblance between *his* milk preparation and the milk preparation with which the ignorant physician had treated people was purely accidental – just as worm holes may look like writing but are not really such.

Having reassured the bhikshus in this way, in chapter 4 the Buddha asks them if they have any doubts regarding the precepts of morality, whereupon a Bodhisattva called Kāśyapa, speaking in verse, puts to him a whole series of questions, the first of which is, 'How do we obtain long life, the adamantine and invincible body?' Replying in prose, the Buddha explains that a Bodhisattva obtains such a body, which is in fact the infinite and eternal *dharmakāya*, by looking upon living beings as upon an only son and by dwelling in the great friendliness, the great compassion, the great sympathetic joy, and the great equanimity. Besides this, he encourages them to practise the five precepts and the ten principles of ethics and even descends into hell for their sake.

Kāśyapa is doubtful whether the Buddha himself always looks upon living beings as upon an only son. Did he not cause a boy who was remiss in the observance of the precepts to be ground into dust with a vajra by a deity called Guhyapāda? The Buddha admits that he did – but the boy was only a 'transformed existence', specially created for the occasion by the Buddha's supernormal power, as were Guhyapāda and the vajra. He had appeared to act with such severity simply in order to inculcate the importance of observing the precepts and to demonstrate the workings of the law of karma. In reality he looks upon all living beings as upon an only son, just as he does in the case of Rāhula, and it is for this reason that he enjoys the eternal life of the *dharmakāya*. Friendliness is not incompatible with *seeming* violence, or even with a moderate degree of actual violence, as when bhikshus who are observers of the precepts expel from the monastic community those who do not observe them.

This topic is enlarged upon in chapter 5. Lay devotees, including kings, who protect precept-observing bhikshus with sword and stick are not guilty of any offence. Indeed, they are to be reckoned as upholders of the precepts. But they must not actually take life. In both chapter 4 and chapter 5 the upshot of the discussion is that the Buddha has always looked upon all beings as upon an only son. For this reason he is indeed possessed of the adamantine and indestructible *dharmakāya* and, as chapter 5 in particular points out, his entry into *parinirvāṇa* must be only apparent. Chapter 6 is extremely short. In it the Buddha tells Kāśyapa that the sūtra is to be upheld under the name of *Mahā-parinirvāṇa*, and it may well be that in its oldest form the work actually ended here.

In any case, though there are still a few surprises in store for the disciples, the distinctive message of the *Mahā-parinirvāṇa Sūtra* has been given. Besides proclaiming his own identity with the *dharmakāya*, the Buddha has declared that the *dharmakāya* itself, as the unconditioned, is endowed with the positive characteristics of bliss, permanence, *self*, and pure beauty. Our résumé of the remaining nine-tenths of the work will therefore be on a much reduced scale. Indeed, from now on the miscellaneous nature of the work permits not so much a résumé of its contents as a few samplings.

Having told Kāśyapa under what name the sūtra is to be upheld, in chapter 7 the Buddha explains to him the four ways in which a Bodhisattva discriminates and expounds it. The explanation involves, *inter alia*, a thoroughly 'docetic' interpretation of the events of his earthly life, a declaration that in order to guide living beings he manifests himself in innumerable different forms, and a vigorous denunciation of meat-eating. 'One who takes flesh,' he says, 'kills the seed of great compassion.'[193] He also points out that he does not lay down rules for the monks in advance, but only as they become guilty of wrongdoing.

Chapter 8 is concerned with the four reliances (*pratiśaraṇa*). These are explained both in terms of four kinds of beings and in terms of four kinds of mental attitude. In the latter case they consist in reliance on meaning (*ārtha*) and not on expression (*vyañjana*), on true awareness (*jñāna*) and not on discriminative consciousness (*vijñāna*), on truth (*dharma*) and not on the person (*pudgala*) who teaches it, and on sūtras of definitive meaning (*nītārtha*) and not on sūtras of interpretable meaning (*neyārtha*). These four reliances are of great importance for Mahāyāna Buddhism, being mentioned in a number of Mahāyāna sūtras, though not always in the present order.

In chapter 9 the Buddha tells Kāśyapa how to distinguish between the teaching of Māra the Evil One and the teaching of the Buddha. For instance, to say that the Buddha permitted the bhikshus to own property, cultivate the soil, and engage in trade, is the teaching of Māra. Conversely, to say that he did not permit the bhikshus to do any of these things is the teaching of the Buddha.

Chapters 10 and 11 are both very short, and both deal with a well-known doctrinal formula. Chapter 10 deals with the four Noble Truths and chapter 11 with the four perversities (*viparyāsa*). In each case the topic is explained in the light of the sūtra's own special teaching.

Chapter 12 is devoted to the Buddha-nature (*tathāgatagarbha*), a topic hardly less characteristic of the *Mahā-parinirvāṇa* than are the related topics of the Buddha's identity with the *dharmakāya* and the *dharmakāya*'s possession of the positive attribute of self. Self is, in fact, identical with the *tathāgatagarbha*. As the Buddha tells Kāśyapa at the beginning of the chapter, 'self' means '*tathāgatagarbha*'. Every being has the Buddha-nature. This is self.'[194] Men cannot see the Buddha-nature because it is obscured by innumerable delusions – a point that is illustrated by various parables. The Buddha Nature is identical with the Three Jewels, or rather, it is identical with the Buddha, to whom both the Dharma and the Sangha can be reduced. (The Buddha, of course, is not only in possession of the Buddha-nature but has actually realized it.) The Buddha-nature is beyond the notions of existence and non-existence. It is quite different from the 'self' of the non-Buddhist teachers, and it is extremely subtle. So subtle is it, indeed, that even Bodhisattvas of the tenth stage (*bhūmi*) have great difficulty in perceiving it – a point that is illustrated by more parables.

Chapter 13 explains the Dharma in terms of the significance of the different letters of the Siddham alphabet. Chapter 14 deals with the mutual dependence of the four perversities and their opposites, while chapter 15, returning to the topic of the *dharmakāya*, compares the Buddha to the moon, which only appears to wax and wane.

In chapter 16 the principal theme is the greatness of the sūtra itself. Just as the light of the sun and moon surpasses all other lights, the Buddha tells Kāśyapa, so the light of the *Mahā-parinirvāṇa Sūtra* surpasses the light of all other sūtras and *samādhis*. Permeated by this light, all beings give rise to the Bodhicitta or Will to Enlightenment – all, that is, except the *icchantikas*, i.e. those who have annihilated their 'skilful roots'.[195] Besides making the interesting point that 'if one does not know the Buddha-nature one cannot be called a man', the Buddha also declares that since the disciples (*śrāvakas*), Pratyeka-Buddhas, and Bodhisattvas all possess the same Buddha-nature, so that there is no difference between them, the three vehicles are in reality One Vehicle (*ekayāna*) – as the 'White Lotus of the True Dharma' and 'Queen Śrīmālā's Asseveration' also teach.

Except for a brief intervention by Mañjuśrī towards the end of chapter 16, from chapter 4 onwards the Buddha's sole interlocutor has been Kāśyapa. In the course of chapter 17, however, the lay devotee Cunda again appears. As the Buddha bathes him in multi-coloured light, he and his kindred make the final offerings, which the Buddha accepts amidst an impressive display of transcendental phantasmagoria. Then, having consoled the assembly in verse, the Buddha assures the monks and the nuns, and the male and female lay devotees, that all those who 'aspire to the highest vow of the Tathāgata' will be worthy of the offerings of the faithful. This statement leads to questions by Kāśyapa, Cunda, and Mañjuśrī, and the Buddha explains that even an *icchantika* can repent and that some of his earlier, 'Hīnayāna', teachings are not to be taken literally.

Several stanzas from the *Udānavarga/Dhammapada* are cited in this connection. The *Mahā-parinirvāṇa Sūtra* is, in fact, remarkable for the extent to which it refers to other canonical texts, among them the *Śūrāṅgama-samādhi* and the *Prajñā-pāramitā*. It is for this reason, perhaps, that it was regarded by some Chinese Buddhists not only as containing the Buddha's final revelation to mankind but also as recapitulating the whole of his previous teaching.

Be that as it may, having answered the questions put by Kāśyapa and the others, and having again refused to postpone his attainment of *parinirvāṇa*, the Buddha entrusts the sūtra to Mañjuśrī, who in turn is to entrust the True Dharma to Ānanda and Mahākāśyapa. Saying that he has a pain in his back, the Buddha lies down, 'like any child who is ill in bed'. This development leads to further questions from

Kāśyapa who, in chapter 18, asks for an explanation of the Buddha's action. It is impossible that he should be really ill, and equally impossible that, even in his present reclining posture, he should not continue to give the disciples the benefit of his teaching. Unless he teaches, his great compassion is useless, and Buddhahood itself only a name.

In response to this impassioned appeal, the Buddha resumes his normal upright, cross-legged posture. As he does so, his face shines like burnished gold and the universe is filled with a light surpassing that of a hundred thousand suns. From each pore of his skin issues a magnificent, thousand-petalled golden lotus, and from each lotus-flower light of various colours radiates into the lower realms. Each light declares 'All beings possess the Buddha-nature.' Moreover, on each lotus sits a Buddha who teaches the Dharma and manifests all kinds of wonders. The entire assembly then rejoices and praises the Buddha, who after exhorting Kāśyapa, and declaring that he in reality no more teaches or does anything else than the Void (*śūnyatā*) does, describes the three types of people who cannot be cured of illness and the five types of people who can. The latter are the Stream-Entrant, the Once-Returner, the Non-Returner, the Arhant, and the Pratyeka-Buddha. After eighty, sixty, forty, twenty, and ten *kalpas* respectively all five will attain the Supreme Enlightenment of a Perfect Buddha.

The remainder of the *Mahā-parinirvāṇa Sūtra* consists of six long chapters and one very short chapter which together amount to more than two-thirds of the entire work. These chapters deal, for the most part, with standard Buddhist teachings, i.e. with teachings common to both the Hīnayāna and the Mahāyāna, as well as with the sūtra's own more distinctive doctrine.

At the beginning of chapter 19 the Buddha tells Kāśyapa that the Bodhisattva should meditate exclusively on the five kinds of action, that is to say, on holy action, pure action, divine action, the action of the child, and the action of illness. The first of these, holy action, is the subject matter of chapter 19 itself, and consists in meditation on the four Noble Truths, which are explained at some length. Mention is also made of the twenty-five *samādhis* by means of which the Bodhisattva succeeds in overcoming the twenty-five spheres of existence.

The second kind of action, or pure action, is the subject matter of chapter 20. Still addressing Kāśyapa, the Buddha speaks first of the seven and then of the four kinds of pure action, the latter being identical with the four Sublime Abidings (*brahma-vihāras*). Though only friendliness (*maitrī*), the first Sublime Abiding, is actually explained, it is explained at considerable length and eulogized in the most glowing terms. Friendliness is the Buddha himself. It is the Mahāyāna. It is the path to Enlightenment. It is Great Brahmā. It is the Buddha-nature in all beings. It is the Dharma. It is the Sangha. Friendliness is, in fact, able to work 'miracles' and is the basis for the attainment of all spiritual qualities. Topics such as the four Analytical Knowledges (*pratisaṃvids*) and the ten epithets of the Buddha are also explained.

The scene then changes from Kuśinagara to Rājagṛha, where King Ajātaśatru of Māgadha is stricken with remorse for having murdered his father the ex-king Bimbisāra. His six ministers urge him to visit one or other of the six non-Buddhist teachers, but at the suggestion of Jīvaka the physician he eventually decides to visit the Buddha. (The episode parallels the *exordium* of the *Sāmaññaphala-sutta* of the *Dīgha Nikāya*.) On his arrival at Kuśinagara Ajātaśatru confesses his sins to the Buddha and prays that all beings may aspire to Enlightenment.

For an explanation of the third kind of action, or divine action, the Buddha refers Kāśyapa to the *Gaṇḍavyūha Sūtra*. The fourth kind of action, the action of the child, is dealt with in chapter 21, which is extremely short. Here the 'transcendental innocence' of the Buddha is described, in a way that is unusual for Buddhism, as analogous to the natural innocence of the child. The fifth and last kind of action, the action of illness, receives no mention.

In chapter 22, in which the interlocutors are Bodhisattva 'Highly Virtuous King' and Mañjuśrī, the Buddha describes the ten qualities that result from the practice of the *Mahā-parinirvāṇa Sūtra*, each of the ten being possessed of further qualities of its own. Within the framework provided by these subdivisions a huge number of topics are touched upon, among them the universality of the Buddha-nature and the 'non-fixedness' of the *icchantika*.

Chapter 23, in which the sole interlocutor is Bodhisattva 'Lion's Roar', is of a more consistently 'philosophical' nature than any other chapter. In it the Buddha is concerned mainly with the metaphysical implications of the principle of the middle way, especially in relation to the concept of the Buddha-nature. He also gives a résumé of the principal events of his life, including his various encounters with the six non-Buddhist teachers.

Chaper 24 is of a rather 'scholastic' nature. Kāśyapa, who is again the sole interlocutor, asks the Buddha for clarification on various finer points of doctrine, and in most cases the Buddha replies at some length. Among the topics to which Kāśyapa's queries relate are the *icchantika*, Buddha-nature, Stream Entry, meditation, and karma. At the beginning of chapter 25 the Buddha creates a furore among the non-Buddhists present by telling Kauṇḍinya that outside his teaching there is no true *brāhmaṇa* or *śramaṇa*, and the greater part of the chapter is taken up by his discussion with their most prominent representatives – all of whom are eventually converted.

The Buddha then relates the personal history of Ānanda, his personal attendant of twenty years' standing, whom he eulogizes in the highest terms. Ānanda is at that moment at some distance from Kuśinagara, however, surrounded by thousands of billions of Māras, and Mañjuśrī is dispatched to rescue him with the help of a *dhāraṇī*. After Ānanda's arrival the Buddha instructs Subhadra, the last of his personal disciples, and delivers his final exhortation to the assembly. As a result of this great exposition of the Dharma millions of Bodhisattvas attain higher stages of the transcendental path, beings innumerable as the sands of the Ganges develop the Will to Enlightenment, billions of women become men, and Subhadra gains Arhantship.

With the *Suvarṇa-prabhāsa Sūtra* or 'Sūtra of Golden Light', also known as the *Suvarṇa-prabhāsottama*, we pass from the later to the latest Mahāyāna sūtras. The widespread popularity of this medley of philosophy and devotion, legends and spells, is evinced not only by the survival of the Sanskrit text, complete in Nepal and fragmentarily in Central Asia, but by the existence of Uighur and Khotanese translations, besides the usual versions in Chinese and Tibetan.

Three Chinese versions have come down to us, the first having been made by Dharmakṣema between 414 and 433CE, the second by Paramārtha and his pupils between 552 and 557CE, and the last by I-tsing in 703CE. The fact that I-tsing's version is 'remarkably more extensive'[196] than Dharmakṣema's suggests that, while the compilation of the *Suvarṇa-prabhāsa* must have been completed by the end of the fourth century CE, the process of expansion and evolution of the work went on for at least another 300 years.

There survive three main Tibetan versions. The first corresponds exactly to the extant Sanskrit text, and it is possible that this is the version made by Mūlaśoka and Jñānakumāra in the first half of the eighth century. The second version was the work of Jinamitra, Silendrabodhi, and Ye-ses-sde, and belongs to the first half of the ninth century, while the third is simply a translation of I-tsing's version. In more recent times translations have been made into Mongolian, Japanese, German, and English, the doyen of modern *Suvarṇaprabhāsa* studies being the late Johannes Nobel.

As now extant, the Sanskrit text of the sūtra is divided into nineteen chapters, most of which are either wholly or partly in verse. The first chapter is of an introductory nature. We find ourselves with the Buddha on the Vulture's Peak, not far from the city of Rājagṛha. Ānanda questions the Buddha, who replies by praising 'the excellent Suvarṇabhāsa, king of *Sūtras*, very profound on hearing and profound on examination.'[197] In chapter 2 we are introduced to a Bodhisattva called Ruciraketu, 'Beautiful Comet', who lives in Rājagṛha and who wonders why it is that the Buddha, despite all the merits he has accumulated, should have a short life of only eighty years. As though in answer to his question, four Buddhas appear before him, and he comes to understand that the Buddha's length of life is in reality immeasurable. In chapter 3 the same Bodhisattva has a dream in which he sees a man with the form of a brahmin beating a golden drum. As the man beats the golden drum, which shines everywhere with golden light just like the sun, there comes forth from it a series of beautiful confessional verses. These verses constitute the original nucleus of the sūtra, around which the work was gradually built up, as Nobel has demonstrated.

> May the Buddhas watch over me with minds attentive [says the golden drum: in part, in words that are still used for liturgical purposes]. May they forgive my sin with minds given over to compassion. On account of the evil done by me previously even in hundreds of aeons, I have a troubled mind oppressed with wretchedness, trouble and fear. With an unhappy mind I continually fear evil acts. Wherever I go there is no enjoyment for me anywhere. All the Buddhas are compassionate. They remove the fears of all beings. May they forgive my sin and may they deliver me from fear. May the Tathāgatas take away for me the defilement of impurities (and) acts. And may the Buddhas bathe me with the surging waters of compassion.[198]

In chapter 4, entitled 'Abundance of Lotuses', the Buddha speaks of a king who had once praised the Buddhas of the past, present, and future. Though we are not explicitly told so, this king is apparently the Bodhisattva Ruciraketu in a previous existence. Chapter 5 is entitled 'On Emptiness', and deals with the subject of *śūnyatā* with such brevity as to be obscure. (The subject is expounded more clearly in chapter 10 of the Mongolian version of the sūtra, which has no counterpart in the extant Sanskrit text.)[199]

Chapter 6 is the longest chapter in the sūtra, accounting for one-fifth of its total length. In it the Four Great Kings, or guardians of the four quarters of the world, promise to protect the sūtra, and, in particular, the monks who proclaim it and the kings who promote it. In the next two chapters, and in chapter 10, three goddesses make a similar promise. They are Sarasvatī the goddess of learning, Śrī the goddess of wealth, and Dṛḍhā the earth goddess. Chapter 9 deals with 'the Maintenance of the Names of Buddhas and Bodhisattvas'. Here various Buddhas and Bodhisattvas are enumerated and saluted, among them being several who play a prominent part in other Mahāyāna sūtras.

In chapter 11 Saṃjñāya, the general of a class of deities known as *yakṣas*, also promises to protect the sūtra. Chapter 12 is entitled 'On Instructions Concerning Divine Kings' and deals with the ethical, even the spiritual, basis of kingship. In chapter 13 the Buddha – apparently it is he who is speaking – describes how in a previous life as a king called Susaṃbhava he invited a monk called Ratnoccaya to expound the 'Sūtra of Golden Light' and how he made offerings to the sūtra. Chapter 14 is entitled 'On the Refuge of the Yakṣas'. Here the Buddha addresses Śrī the goddess of wealth and explains how those who wish to worship the Buddhas of the past, future, and present should listen to the 'Sūtra of Golden Light'. He also enumerates a long list of deities who will protect the sūtra.

Chapter 15 is a chapter of prophecy and prediction. 10,000 'sons of gods' enter the presence of the Buddha in order to hear the Dharma and the Buddha predicts that, in the infinitely remote future, they will all attain to Buddhahood through their faith in the 'Sūtra of Golden Light'. Chapter 16 is entitled 'On Healing Illness'. It describes how Jalavāhana, the merchant's son, learned the medical art from his father and then travelled all over India curing people. This chapter contains information about ancient Indian ideas concerning the origin and treatment of disease, particular attention being paid to the influence on health of food and drink, and the seasons of the year.

Chapters 17 and 18 are versions of Jātaka stories. In the first of them Jalavāhana saves 10,000 fish from dying of drought. These fish are eventually reborn as gods and, out of gratitude, shower Jalavāhana with 40,000 pearl necklaces. In this chapter there is also a statement of the law of conditioned co-production (*pratītya-samutpāda*), or dependent origination. In the second Jātaka the Buddha, in a previous existence, sacrifices his own life to save a starving tigress and her cubs. This is, of course, one of the best known of all Jātaka stories, and it is here told at some length.

Chapter 19 is entitled 'On the Praise of All the Tathāgatas'. Innumerable Bodhisattvas sing the praises of the Buddha Suvarṇaratnākaracchatrakūṭa, whose praises are also sung by the Bodhisattva Ruciraketu and by the noble goddess Bodhisattvasamuccayā. Amid general rejoicings the sūtra then concludes.

Though such a summary is far from doing justice to the sūtra, particularly to its spirit of fervent devotion and its at times great literary beauty, it does perhaps do justice to its highly composite, not to say miscellaneous, character. Someone going through it for the first time could not be blamed for thinking it a sort of ragbag, albeit a ragbag that contained wonderful scraps of jewelled brocade. Despite its miscellaneous character, however, the sūtra manages to hang together and does, in fact, possess a spiritual unity of its own.

Broadly speaking, the nineteen chapters can be classified into three groups containing (1) the 'Chapter of Confession' which, as we have seen, is the original nucleus of the sūtra, (2) all those chapters in which gods and goddesses come forward and promise to protect the sūtra, and (3) all the remaining chapters. Most of the chapters comprising the third group can be regarded as representing an attempt, on the part of the sūtra, to draw into its own orbit all the principal Mahāyāna teachings, or all the different kinds of Buddhist scriptures. Thus chapter 2 deals with 'The Measure of Life of the Tathāgata', which is a major theme of both 'The White Lotus of the True Dharma' and the *Mahā-parinirvāṇa Sūtra*, while chapter 5 is concerned with *śūnyatā*, a subject treated at length in the 'Perfection of Wisdom' sūtras. Other chapters contain Jātakas, Avadānas, and Vyākaraṇas. What is really distinctive of the sūtra, and its special teaching, is contained in the first and second groups of chapters, which between them represent the purification – and transformation – of oneself and of the world.

Despite the miscellaneous character of the *Suvarṇa-prabhāsa*, the fact that in chapter 5 the *śūnyatā* doctrine is expounded suggests that the work as a whole is affiliated to the earlier rather than to the later line of Mahāyāna sūtras, and that it upholds Reality as Voidness rather than as Absolute Mind. Like its great sister line, however, the line to which the *Suvarṇa-prabhāsa* belongs has connections with the future no less than with the past. Not only does much of the sūtra consist of a glorification of the *Suvarṇa-prabhāsa* itself, the merit of reading which is repeatedly extolled, but the work is also praised as a *dhāraṇī* or protective magical formula. Moreover, in chapter 7 the goddess Sarasvatī teaches what are, in fact, Tantric rituals, and female deities are introduced in three other chapters. The appearance of these features warns us that with the *Suvarṇa-prabhāsa* we have reached one of the borderlands of Buddhist literature, where it is difficult to distinguish sūtras that are classified as *tantras* from *tantras* that are sometimes regarded as sūtras.

Having briefly noticed this work, we now pass, therefore, to a fresh canonical expression of the spirit of Buddhism.

# 16

# THE TANTRAS

Although a few *tantras* are included in the Chinese canon, it is only the Tibetan Tripiṭaka that contains a separate division devoted to this class of works. The Narthang edition of the Kangyur or 'Translation of the Word (of the Buddha)', which is the basic Tibetan collection of the canonical literature, contains twenty-two volumes of *tantras*, as compared with thirteen volumes of Vinaya works, twenty of Perfection of Wisdom texts, and forty-four of other Mahāyāna sūtras.

But the total number of *tantras* is, in fact, far greater than that contained in these volumes. Among the Nyingmapas of Tibet there circulate numerous *tantras* which, though regarded as non-canonical by some authorities, are such only in the sense of not having found a place in any of the great 'complete' editions of the Kangyur. Thus they are 'uncollected' rather than uncanonical within the strict meaning of the term. Numerous individual *tantras* are also found in the *vihāras* of the Kathmandu Valley, where they have survived in Mixed Sanskrit, including the original text of some of those that are available in Chinese and Tibetan translation. Among these is the celebrated *Guhyasamāja* or 'Esoteric Integration', reckoned as one of the nine Dharmas or authoritative works of Nepalese Buddhism. *Tantras* of which only the names are known are legion.

Presenting as they thus do such an immense wealth of material, most of it not only unexplored but inaccessible, these works constitute for the student of Buddhism a problem even more baffling than the Mahāyāna sūtras. The problem is, moreover, aggravated in various ways. To an even greater extent than sūtras like the *Laṅkāvatāra*, the *tantras* strike the rational mind as heterogeneous in content and unsystematic in arrangement. For this reason they do not lend themselves to summarization, so that the problem cannot be disposed of in this way.

They are also more or less unintelligible without the traditional commentary. This is not only because the latter may describe in greater detail rituals and yogic exercises, for example, to which the text contains only an allusion as to matters well known, or because it 'translates' the cryptic and frequently symbolic language of the text into its equivalent in the abstract conceptual idiom of standard Mahāyāna philosophy, whether Madhyamaka or Yogācāra. The commentary is important mainly because it helps to complete the framework of metaphysical and spiritual reference within which alone it is possible for the Tantric methods of practice to function as means to the perfect integration of Wisdom and Compassion, instead of remaining, as some at least of them would, mere unassimilated curiosities of anthropological research.

Yet so much are the *tantras* essentially manuals of actual practice, rather than disquisitions on the nature of the spiritual experiences to which the practices conduce that, even after they have been correctly 'placed' within a context of this kind, the problem of how to give a generalized account of their contents remains unsolved.

More important still, the *tantras* deal with methods of spiritual renovation which can be taken up only after receiving the appropriate *abhiṣeka* or 'consecration' from a competent master in the spiritual succession. From the traditional point of view this is the determining factor, which militates decisively against any profane survey of this literature, and converts – for the practising Buddhist – what would otherwise have been at best a task of extreme difficulty into an impossibility.

In the *Hevajra Tantra*, which by an irony of history is now available in English translation, the Lord says of the text of this work, as well as of the iconic representation of its central Buddha-figure, 'If someone unworthy should see either book or painting, one will fail to gain perfection either in this world or the next. To one of our tradition it may be shown at any time. Then on a journey the book should be hidden in the hair or under the arm.'[200] By 'the unworthy' is meant, of course, those who have not received the appropriate *abhiṣeka*.

Despite the fact that the Kangyur contains a number of *tantras*, which are thus physically accessible to any literate person, the prohibitions that circumvallate these works are on the whole still scrupulously respected by Tibetan Buddhists. No one would think of attempting to study or practise them, much less still write about them, except under the conditions imposed by tradition. What Conze has to say about certain Western productions, though severe, is therefore quite apposite, and tells with equal effect against popular and scientific works.

> In this field certainly those who know do not say and those who say do not know. There are two, and only two alternatives. Either the author of a book of this kind has *not* been initiated into a Tantra; then what he says is not first-hand knowledge. Or he has been initiated. Then, if he were to divulge the secrets to all and sundry just to make a little profit or to increase his reputation, he has broken the trust placed in him and is morally so depraved as not to be worth listening to.[201]

Nevertheless, one must beware of lapsing into obscurantism. Even in Tibet, information about the Tantric methods of spiritual practice is widely current; though here, again, it must not be forgotten that almost all Tibetan Buddhists have received at least one *abhiṣeka*, and that, in consequence, such information possesses, for them, a significance quite different from what it might have when disseminated through secular agencies in a profane milieu for the gratification of vulgar curiosity.

Though an account of the *tantras* such as we have already given of the Mahāyāna sūtras is precluded on both *a priori* and *a posteriori* grounds, we shall not, therefore, be guilty of any impropriety in rounding off our survey of the canonical literature with the indispensable minimum of exoteric facts about these works.

Etymologically, the derivation of the word *tantra* is analogous to that of sūtra. Just as the latter means a thread, the former (probably from the root *tan*, 'to spread') means anything elaborated or woven. Both, therefore, connote a work which, having been 'threaded' or 'woven' together, treats of a particular subject in a more or less detailed and comprehensive manner. Strictly speaking, *tantra* is not only not a Buddhist term but not even a purely religious one. It occurs as part of the title of individual works dealing with subjects ranging from logic to medicine, and from philosophy to mathematics. However, as designating a special class of religious texts, as well as individual works belonging to that class, it is traditionally limited to the type of works now under consideration.

The *tantras* also resemble the sūtras in being cast, as literary compositions, in dialogue-cum-discourse form with the Lord as principal interlocutor either in the person of the historic Śākyamuni, as in the *Guhyasamāja Tantra*, or in that of one of his innumerable 'mythological' hypostases, such as Mahā-vairocana or Hevajra. For this reason they are revered as Buddhavacana, and form part of the canonical literature.

Vajrayāna tradition, while assigning them to the terrestrial lifetime of Śākyamuni, does, however, regard them as having been promulgated on an exalted spiritual plane of existence inaccessible to ordinary followers of the Hīnayāna and the Mahāyāna. In the same spirit, but more systematically, the canonical works associated with each of the three *yānas* are sometimes correlated with the three *kāyas* of the Buddha,[202] the Hīnayāna and the Mahāyāna sūtras having been preached by the *nirmāṇakāya* and the *sambhogakāya* respectively, and the *tantras* directly by the *dharmakāya*.

On the whole the *tantras* are later than the sūtras. This is in accordance with the tendency, noted in an earlier chapter, for the order in which the canonical works appear as literary documents to correspond to that of their spiritual progression. Thus while the *Guhyasamāja* is generally assigned to the fifth or sixth century CE, the *Kālacakra* or 'Wheel of Time', which contains references to Mecca and Islam, can hardly be dated earlier than the tenth century. Almost all the remaining *tantras* fall somewhere in between, with the *Hevajra*, for example, appearing in its present form towards the end of the eighth century.[203] The literary history of the *tantras* spans, therefore, a period of about half a millennium, overlapping that of the Mahāyāna sūtras by two or three centuries.

The actual publication of each *tantra* is associated with the name of one spiritual master or more who, having specialized in the practice of its teachings, could sponsor its appearance in literary form among a circle of initiated disciples. These masters are known collectively as the eighty-four *siddhas* or 'perfected ones'. From the time of the Buddha to that of the *siddhas* the *tantras* were, of course, transmitted esoterically, though this is much more than a matter of simple oral transmission as in the case of the rest of the canonical literature. For the first few 'generations' the teaching was communicated telepathically, on an exalted spiritual plane, from one Buddha or Bodhisattva to another. Descending to earth, it was transmitted from one human teacher to another firstly by means of signs and then, starting from a particular *siddha*, 'from heart to ear'. Except in the case of those *tantras* which have been lost or destroyed, or the teachers of which have died without being able to achieve an effective transmission, the third type of lineage extends down to the present day.

# 17

# COLLECTED EDITIONS

Brief though it has necessarily been, the survey given in the preceding chapters may suffice to illustrate the vast extent and endless variety of the canonical literature. Far from being confined like the Bible to a single volume of short works, 66 in the Protestant and 78 in the Roman Catholic version, or limited like the Koran to a solitary book of 114 chapters, it comprises a whole library of works. The reason for this astounding profusion is self-evident. It resides not only in the unsurpassed spiritual vitality of Buddhism, due to which it could create one world of sacred literature after another, but in the very nature of the religion which, as it refused to identify the Buddhavacana with any one of its linguistic or literary vehicles, naturally encouraged the multiplication of as many alternative versions of the teaching as there were types of sentient beings to be delivered.

Minus the casualties suffered in the course of centuries of transmission, and apart from independent texts found in Nepal or recovered from the sands of Central Asia, the thousands of works thus produced have come down to us in three great collections, each of which constitutes, within its own sphere of influence, the scriptural foundation for the general study and practice of the Dharma. These collections are the Pāli Tipiṭaka, the Chinese San Tsang, and the Tibetan Kangyur.

*As a collection*, the Pāli Tipiṭaka is the oldest. It represents a Middle Indic version of the Buddha's teaching as preserved and elaborated by one of the early Hīnayāna schools, transmitted by oral means from India to Sri Lanka, and finally written down in the latter country according to one of the two different recensions then current at the time. From the circumstances of its literary origin it is sometimes referred to as the Sinhalese canon and sometimes as the Southern canon.

Like its lost Sanskrit counterpart, it comprises the 'three baskets' of Vinaya or monastic law, Suttas or dialogues, and the Abhidhamma or 'further teaching', each of which is a portmanteau term indicating not so much a particular set of constituent works as a certain type of contents.

In the case of the Pāli Tipiṭaka, the Vinaya Piṭaka consists of five books, respectively entitled: (1) *Pārājika* or 'Defeat', (2) *Pācittiyam* or 'Expiation', (3) *Mahā-vagga* or 'Great Section', (4) *Cūḷa-vagga* or 'Small Section' and (5) *Parivāra-pāṭha* or 'Accessory Reading'. Of these, (1) and (2) together constitute the *Sutta-vibhaṅga* or 'Analysis of the Rule', and (3) and (4) the *Khandakas* or 'Chapters'. The fifth book, which is a supplement and index, was composed in Sri Lanka.

The Sutta Piṭaka is made up of five separate collections or Nikāyas. These are: (1) *Dīgha Nikāya* or 'Long Collection' and (2) *Majjhima Nikāya* or 'Middle Length Collection', being the Dialogues proper; together with (3) *Saṃyutta Nikāya* or 'Grouped Collection', (4) *Aṅguttara Nikāya* or 'One Up Collection', and (5) *Khuddaka Nikāya* or 'Little Collection', which between them comprise the Anthologies, the 'Glorious Deeds', and the Birth Stories. Each Nikāya is subdivided in one way or another, the last being made up of fifteen independent works, among them the *Sutta-Nipāta* and the *Dhammapada*.

The Abhidhamma Piṭaka contains the seven scholastic treatises beginning with the *Dhamma-saṅgaṇi* or 'Enumeration of Elements'.

This great collection of texts is regarded as authoritative not only in Sri Lanka but throughout the Buddhist countries of South-East Asia, that is to say, in Burma, Thailand, Cambodia, and Laos also, all of which received from Sri Lanka, either directly or indirectly, both the Theravāda form of Buddhism and the Pāli scriptures.

In this part of the Buddhist world, indeed, it is traditionally believed that, having been rehearsed by successive conventions of monks from the time of Aśoka down to the present day, the Pāli Tipiṭaka is the only complete and authentic version of the Buddha's teaching. For Theravādin Buddhists it therefore constitutes a canon in the strict sense, that is to say, a body of sacred literature the authenticity of which has been attested by the highest ecclesiastical authority and which is held to possess, even verbally, absolute and exclusive validity.

Editions of the text of the entire forty-five-volume Tipiṭaka in the indigenous script have been brought out in Burma, Thailand, and Cambodia, while India has contributed an edition in Devanagari characters. In 1871 King Mindon-min of Burma had the complete text engraved on 729 marble slabs. The differences between these editions are negligible. The Royal Thai Tipiṭaka admits only seven out of fifteen works of the *Khuddaka Nikāya* regarded as canonical in Sri Lanka, whereas the Burmese editions contain fifteen, including the *Milindapanhā*, which is not even ostensible Buddhavacana. Otherwise the discrepancies are mostly verbal. Thanks to the Pali Text Society, a critical edition of the whole of the Tipiṭaka is now available in roman script.

The Chinese San Tsang, literally 'three storehouses', that is to say, Tripiṭaka, is a collection not of original texts but of translations. Beginning in the first century CE with the *Sūtra of Forty-Two Sections*, the work of translation was carried on for more than twelve centuries, in the course of which period several hundred Chinese and Indian scholars produced, from Sanskrit, but also from Pāli, Tibetan, and other sources, renderings of thousands of works regarded in India as canonical. These renderings were not only circulated independently but from time to time collected. Between 518CE and 1737CE twelve such collections were published, all by imperial authority, and several in more than one edition. While the first seven existed in manuscript only, the remaining five were printed, the first of the printed collections being brought out in 971CE by order of the Emperor T'ai Tsu, founder of the Tang dynasty. Only the last three of the twelve collections actually made survive, all the earlier ones having been lost, though their contents are known. These were published in 1368–98CE and 1403–24CE during the Ming dynasty, and the third in 1735–37CE under the Qing, and are substantially the same.

Associated with the collections are the catalogues. Forty-four of these useful works are said to have existed, but only thirteen are extant. The oldest of the thirteen, dated about 520CE, was called *Collection of the Records of the Translations of the Tripiṭaka*. Besides listing whatever translations were available at the time of their compilation, they present historical, biographical, and bibliographical information, and give notice of translations that have been lost.

According to Nanjio's analysis of a seventeenth-century Japanese edition of the second Ming collection, the Chinese Tripiṭaka consists of

1662 works classified in four great divisions: (1) Ching or Sūtra, (2) Lü or Vinaya, (3) Lun or Abhidharma, and (4) Tsa-tsan or Miscellaneous.

The first division is by far the largest, for it amounts to nearly two-thirds of the whole collection, and comprises no fewer than 1081 works subdivided into (a) Mahāyāna sūtras, 541, (b) Hīnayāna sūtras, 240, (c) Mahāyāna and Hīnayāna sūtras, 300 in number, admitted into the Tripiṭaka under the Sung and Yuan dynasties, 960–1368CE. The Mahāyāna sūtras fall again into seven groups; (i) Pan-jo (Po-jo) or Prajñāpāramitā, (ii) Pao-chi or Ratnakūṭa, (iii) Ta-chi or Mahā-sannipāta, (iv) Hua-yen or Avataṃsaka, (v) Nieh Pan or Parinirvāṇa, (vi) sūtras in more than one translation but included in any of the five previous groups, and (vii) other sūtras existing in only one translation. The Hīnayāna sūtras comprise only three groups: (i) A-han or Āgama, corresponding to the Pāli Nikāyas, (ii) sūtras in single translations, and (iii) sūtras admitted into the Tripiṭaka from 960 to 1368CE.

The second division is the smallest. It contains 73 Vinaya texts, 24 of which belong to the Mahāyāna and 49 to the Hīnayāna. Among the latter are five recensions of the whole Monastic Code.

The third division consists of 151 Abhidharma works subdivided, like those of the Sūtra division, into (a) Mahāyāna, 93, (b) Hīnayāna, 22, and (c) works of both schools, 22 in number, admitted into the Tripiṭaka from 960–368CE. Not all of these are strictly canonical. The Mahāyāna texts are, for the most part, philosophical treatises by Nāgārjuna, Aśvaghoṣa, Vasubandhu, and others. Prominent among the Hīnayāna texts are the *Jñāna-prasthāna* with its six accessory treatises or *pādas*, its commentary the *Mahā-vibhāṣā-śāstra* and the *Abhidharmakoṣa*.

The fourth and last division of the San Tsang consists of 340 miscellaneous works, 146 translated from Sanskrit and 194 composed in Chinese. While the first subdivision contains a mixture of canonical and non-canonical material, including four translations of the *Dharmapada*, the second is wholly non-canonical.

Having been compiled on no higher authority than that of the reigning emperor, the Chinese Tripiṭaka is a literary and bibliographical collection rather than an ecclesiastical canon. In Eliot's words, 'It does not provide an authorized version for the edification of the faithful, but it presents for the use of the learned all translations of Indian works belonging to a particular class which possess a certain age and authority.'[204] Nevertheless, consisting as it does of canonical works, and having been invested with the glamour of the imperial imprimatur, as a canon it is certainly esteemed not only throughout China but in all those countries which, like Japan, Korea, and Vietnam, received the gift of the Dharma from the 'Middle Flowery Kingdom'.[205] If in practice the recognition is less effective than that accorded the Pāli Tipiṭaka within its own field of influence, this is, no doubt, due to the tendency, strong in Chinese Buddhism, for each school to select from the riches of the Imperial Tripiṭaka a particular work or group of works as constituting the culmination of the Buddha's teaching and to make it the theoretical foundation and practical working basis of the religious life.

Editions of the Ming collection have been published, not only in China but in Japan and Korea. The most recent edition, considerably augmented, is the *Taishō Shinshū-Daizōkyō*, published in Japan from 1924–9. It comprises 2,184 works in 55 volumes of about a thousand pages each.

The Tibetan Kangyur or 'translated word (of the Buddha)' consists of canonical works translated into Tibetan between the seventh and the eleventh centuries CE. Most of these translations were made direct from the original Sanskrit, and at first circulated independently. In the fourteenth century a complete manuscript collection was formed and deposited in the temple of the monastery at Narthang, whence numerous copies were transmitted to different parts of Tibet. One copy was written with ink made from the dust of precious stones.[206] Translations coming to light after the formation of the collection were subsequently incorporated.

The first printed edition of the Kangyur appeared not in Tibet but in Beijing, being completed in 1411CE during the reign of the Ming Emperor Yun-lo. Further editions were published under the Emperors K'ang Hsi and Ch'ien Lung of the Qing dynasty. The earliest Tibetan printed edition was brought out at Narthang in 1731, while others from Lhasa, Derge, Labrang, Kumbum, and Co-ne, as well as from Punakha in Bhutan, followed in rapid succession. All these editions consist of either 100 or 108 massive xylograph volumes, with those of the lower number predominating.

In the editions sponsored by the numerically stronger Gelug School the whole collection is classified into six great divisions. These are: (1) Dulwa or 'Monastic Discipline' (Vinaya), 13 volumes; (2) Sher-chin or 'Perfection of Wisdom' (Prajñā-pāramitā), 21 volumes; (3), (4), and (5)

Phel-chen or 'Wreath' (Avataṃsaka), Kon-tsig or 'Jewel-Heap' (Ratnakūṭa), and Do or miscellaneous sūtras, in all 44 (or 46) volumes; and (6) Gyu or Tantra, 22 (or 20) volumes. In some editions (5) is split up to form a separate division entitled Yang-de or Nirvāṇa. As the Kangyur represents the Tripiṭaka, these six or seven divisions are sometimes distributed among the 'three baskets'. When this is done, the Dulwa is the Vinaya Piṭaka, the Sher-chin the Abhidharma Piṭaka, and all the other works whether sūtras or *tantras* are classed together as the Sūtra Piṭaka.

Although the text of the Kangyur was never formally approved at a general meeting of the Tibetan Sangha, this great collection was compiled by some of the most distinguished scholars of the day, while its printed editions were brought out, so far as Tibet was concerned, at famous monastic establishments under the auspices of the highest ecclesiastical authorities. Hence although like the Chinese San Tsang a collection of translations, it nevertheless constitutes, at the same time, a canon like the Pāli Tipiṭaka. As a canon in the full sense of the term it is indeed revered, not only in Tibet itself, but in Mongolia, part of China, and the countries of the Himalayan borderlands. Wrapped in rich brocade, and enclosed in carved and painted wooden covers, its volumes occupy an honoured place on every shrine, being kept either above or beside the image of the Buddha, but never on a lower level.

# 18

# CONTINUING REVELATION

One of the most important groups of Mahāyāna sūtras teaches us that Perfect Wisdom is elusive, in the sense that it is not something which can be picked out and laid hold of with the confidence that now one has really 'got' it. This elusiveness is characteristic of the Dharma as a whole. It was the great mistake of the Abhidharma – at least of some Abhidharmikas – to think that any card-index system of doctrinal categories, however exhaustive and however well organized, could give adequate expression to the spirit of the Buddha's teaching. At a much lower level of significance and to a lesser extent, elusiveness also characterizes the whole body of sacred writings wherein the Dharma finds literary expression.

Revelations on higher planes of existence apart, no collection of such writings, however large and however comprehensive, can be held to include even every word spoken by the Buddha in the course of forty-five years of indefatigable earthly ministry. No collection, therefore, is final in the sense of settling, once and for all time, the exact text of the complete Buddhavacana to the preclusion of any subsequent addition.

As the Chinese San Tsang in particular illustrates, the Tripiṭaka is a living and growing thing. Whereas the closed canons of most other religions are like pools, receiving after their original formation no addition to their contents, the canonical literature of Buddhism is like a river which, in its passage to the ocean, receives fresh accessions from rain and melted snow and flows on with an ever increasing volume of water. Appropriating a term already in use, one may therefore speak of there being in Buddhism a progressive revelation of sacred literature from the inexhaustible reservoir of the Dharma. This revelation, while it indeed culminates in the Tripiṭaka, does not come to an end there, but finds further expression in various other works continuous with and akin to those generally regarded as canonical.

Among the more obvious sources of accession are archaeological research and the oral tradition. Previous chapters have already testified to the fact that, in the course of centuries of transmission, the canonical literature sustained frequent casualties. Especially heavy losses were inflicted on the Sanskrit texts, many of which survived, as we have already learned, either in Chinese or Tibetan translation or not at all. So far, the sands of Central Asia and the cave-grottoes of Tun-huang, together with the vihāras of Nepal and the temples of Japan, have for the most part yielded up either the Sanskrit originals of texts previously known only from translations, or different recensions of texts which had happened to survive independently. However, the possibility that, in the future, texts that had hitherto been known only by name will come to light cannot be ruled out. On account of the general nature of Buddhism, in particular its attitude to the written records of the Buddha's teaching, any such discovery would be less disconcerting to the Buddhist world than the appearance of the Dead Sea Scrolls was to the Christian world. Far from spreading embarrassment and dismay, in the Mahāyāna countries at least a 'new' sūtra would be hailed with joy, eagerly studied, and incorporated forthwith in the Tripiṭaka. If rendered necessary by the sūtra's content, doctrinal adjustments would no doubt be made.

The importance of the oral tradition has been demonstrated already. From the Monastic Code to the *tantra*, the canonical literature represents a series of deposits, or crystallizations, from teachings handed down by word of mouth from master to disciple in unbroken lineal succession since the days of the Buddha. There is no more reason to assume that this vast reservoir dried up on the appearance of the *Kālacakra Tantra* than that it was exhausted with the compilation of the *Kathā-vatthu* or the *Suvarṇa-prabhāsa*. Only a few years ago, it is said, a wandering religious mendicant appeared at Benares and recited, from memory, the text of a hitherto unknown sūtra.[207] Whether it was a Hīnayāna or a Mahāyāna sūtra we are not informed. In China, Japan, and Tibet, but especially in Tibet, many of the more advanced Vajrayāna teachings are still transmitted exclusively by oral means.

Such of them as go back to the Buddha himself would constitute, when written down, an accession to the canonical literature.

A third source of accession, traditionally important but less obvious to the modern mind, is by means of direct revelation from higher planes of existence. References in earlier chapters have already familiarized us with the *trikāya* doctrine. According to this Yogācāra systematization of Mahāyāna Buddhology, the Enlightened One possesses three 'bodies' (*kāya*) or personalities, the *nirmāṇakāya*, the *sambhogakāya*, and the *dharmakāya*. Though spoken of in the plural, these are not separate entities, but the one non-dual Buddha-nature as it manifests on earth to human beings and earth-bound deities, in the form of Śākyamuni, as it appears in the highest heavens to advanced Bodhisattvas, as the Eternal Buddha, and as it is in reality.[208] Each of these *kāyas* preaches the Dharma in an appropriate manner on its own plane. Whereas the discourses of the *nirmāṇakāya* or 'created body' are limited in number and confined to the comparatively short period of forty-five years, those of the *sambhogakāya* or 'body of glory' constitute an uninterrupted stream of supernal eloquence of infinite duration. The mysterious 'preachings' of the *dharmakāya* transcend all limitations whatsoever.

Inasmuch as the discourses of Śākyamuni terminated with his *parinirvāṇa*, twenty-five centuries ago, they are accessible only indirectly, firstly from the oral and secondly from the literary tradition. Moreover, after the disappearance of the original source no real addition to their number could be made possible. In the case of the discourses preached by the *sambhogakāya*, however, the position is quite different: their number is infinite, and their source eternal. They are, therefore, accessible not only indirectly, in the form of the Mahāyāna sūtras, but directly as well, for even in the absence of the *nirmāṇakāya* it is possible to ascend, in meditation, to a stage of *samādhi* corresponding to the plane on which their transcendental prototypes are everlastingly promulgated. There, from the lips of the Eternal Buddha, appearing in one or another of his innumerable guises, the yogin receives teachings which may, in certain cases, surpass anything he had ever heard on earth. When committed to writing, such revelations would constitute another accession to the canonical literature.

Some of the Mahāyāna sūtras seem actually to have originated in this manner, rather than from the utterances of the historical Śākyamuni on the terrestrial plane. This applies not only to works that, whatever the circumstances of their origin might have been, are undoubtedly of Indian provenance, but also, more particularly, to a number of sūtras that are sometimes regarded as Chinese forgeries and which, it must be admitted, tradition itself tricks out with an array of names and dates and presents as translations from the Sanskrit. Such are the 'Sūtra of Complete Enlightenment', said to have been translated by Buddhatrāta of Kabul about 650CE, and the *Śūrāṅgama Sūtra*, also known as the 'Buddha's Great Crown Sūtra', said to have been translated by Paramārtha in 717–9CE, both of which are included in the Chinese Tripiṭaka. While these two works are of exceptional merit, and no doubt in principle canonical, such is hardly the case with all productions of this type. Even ruling out the possibility of deliberate forgery, some of them might have originated, not from a higher plane of existence, but more or less subjectively, by way of ordinary mediumistic inspiration. Sūtras like the one revealed to the Empress Jen-Hsiao on New Year's Day, 1398CE, must, therefore, be treated with reserve.

Revelations may be received not only from the Buddhas but the Bodhisattvas. According to tradition, the Five Books of Maitreya, beginning with the *Abhisamayālaṅkāra*, which modern scholarship attributes either to Asaṅga or to a historical teacher called Maitreya-nātha, were revealed to Asaṅga by the Bodhisattva Maitreya in the Tuṣita heaven. Other advanced practitioners of meditation had similar experiences. The autobiography of Master Han-shan gives a vivid description of how, in a dream, he visited the palace of Maitreya and heard him say, 'That which discriminates is consciousness; that which does not discriminate is Wisdom. From relying on consciousness, defilements come; from relying on Wisdom, purity comes. From the defilements arise life-and-death. (If one realizes the purity) there are no Buddhas.'[209] Since Han-shan was an enlightened Ch'an master, and his experience therefore genuine, these words are Buddhavacana, or at least Bodhisattva-vacana, and as such to be included in the canonical literature.

Whether the fourth and last source of accession is truly such or not depends on the degree of liberality with which we define our terms. Broadly understood, the Buddhavacana or canonical literature consists not merely of the teachings of the historical Śākyamuni but of any reflection of the transcendental state of Supreme Enlightenment in terms of human speech. In principle it therefore includes the utterances of his enlightened disciples from the earliest times down to the present day.

The Pāli Tipiṭaka does, indeed, contain a number of *suttas* which, though preached by Sāriputta or Dhammadinnā, for example, are canonical inasmuch as the Master had subsequently approved them, while both the Theravāda and the Sarvāstivāda Abhidharma Piṭakas consist of, or at least contain, works admittedly composed by Arhant *ācāryas* living several generations after the Buddha. The Mahāyāna carried this tendency to its logical conclusion. Besides accepting as Buddhavacana sūtras which had been preached, either wholly or in part, not by the Buddha personally but by disciples upheld by his *adhiṣṭhāna* or 'sustaining power,' it conceded canonical or quasi-canonical status to the sayings and writings of enlightened masters living many hundreds of years after the Buddha and, in some cases, in lands other than India.

Material of this sort was included either in the Tripiṭaka or in various subsidiary collections. Attention has already been drawn the fact that, in China, the works of the Indian *ācāryas* such as Nāgārjuna, Aśvaghoṣa, and Asaṅga are to be found in the Mahāyāna subdivision of the Lun-Tsang or Abhidharma Piṭaka. Similarly, the writings of the patriarchs of the various Chinese schools, such as those of Chih-I, founder of the T'ien T'ai School, in three volumes, are included in the fourth great division of the Tsa-tsan Tsang or Saṃyukta Piṭaka under the heading of Chinese Miscellaneous Works. Also included is the 'Dharma Treasure of the Platform Sūtra of the Sixth Patriarch (of the Ch'an School),' better known as 'The Sūtra of Hui-neng (Wei Lang)'. This short but profound and immensely influential series of discourses, together with the Patriarch's answers to various questions, is celebrated as 'the only sūtra spoken by a native of China,' the use of the appellation sūtra, otherwise reserved for the discourses of the Buddha, indicating that Hui-neng was popularly regarded as an Enlightened One.

In Tibet a different procedure was followed. No work of any *ācārya*, however important, was thought fit to be included in the Kangyur along with the Buddhavacana proper. Instead, a separate collection was formed, known as the Tangyur or 'translation of treatises.' As arranged by Bu-ston in the fourteenth century it consists of 225 volumes and is divided into three parts. The first part, of one volume only, gives sixty-four hymns, the second 2,664 commentaries on *tantras*, in eighty-six volumes, while the third, which is less homogeneous, contains commentaries on the Prajñā-pāramitā, the *śāstras* or treatises of the Madhyamaka School, commentaries on various sūtras, the *śāstras* of the Yogācārins, and scientific works belonging to the Hīnayāna – in all ninety-four volumes – followed by thirty volumes of treatises on logic, grammar, medicine, *et cetera* and thirteen of indigenous Tibetan works on technical subjects. Though distinct from the Kangyur, and less authoritative, the Tangyur enjoys equal honours, its volumes also being wrapped in brocade and decently enshrined.

The works of *ācārya* Padmasambhava are a special case. While a few are found in the Tangyur, the majority of them go to make up the contents of an independent collection, compiled in the time of the Thirteenth Dalai Lama, known as the *Rinchen Termo* or 'Precious Treasury of Unearthed Literature.' According to Nyingmapa tradition, after being hidden by the Great Guru in various remote parts of Tibet and the adjacent Himalayan regions, these *termas* or 'unearthed works' were from time to time discovered by certain spiritually gifted persons known as *tertons* or 'treasure-revealers', the most prominent of whom were in fact manifestations of Padmasambhava himself.

Western critics, of course, dismiss these works as forgeries pure and simple. Their views have been controverted by Lama Govinda:

> Such critics underestimate the religious sincerity and the deep respect for the sanctity of spiritual tradition which is engrained in every Tibetan, layman and lama alike. To add to or omit from the Sacred Scriptures a single word or letter has ever been looked upon by Tibetans as a heinous sin, which even the most impious would fear to commit.
>
> Furthermore, these same critics underestimate the difficulties of forging and issuing such scriptures, for the forging would require a technical and critical knowledge of history and linguistics such as was not only unknown in Tibet, but such as would have required a master-mind for its execution. Had a genius of that sort existed in Tibet, he would have had no need to resort to the subterfuge of forgery, for he could have stood on his own feet, as did many scholarly geniuses who wrote and taught in their own name. Nor is it likely that men who could create and propagate such profound thoughts and lofty ideals as the *Termas* contain would stoop so low as to deceive

> their fellow men. And when we consider that the literature in question is not a matter of a few isolated treatises but of about a hundred big volumes (according to tradition 108 volumes), running into tens of thousands of folios, then the theory of wilful deception becomes not only improbable, but absurd.[210]

Of the *termas* known in the Western world as the *Tibetan Book of the Dead*, Jung has written, 'For years, ever since it was first published, the *Bardo Thödol* has been my constant companion, and to it I owe not only many stimulating ideas and discoveries, but also many fundamental insights.'[211]

As the Nyingmapas honour Padmasambhava as the Second Buddha the *termas* are, for them, part of the canonical literature, the Kangyur and Tangyur being held to comprise the 'remote tradition' and the *Rinchen Termo* the 'near tradition'. Another type of collection, in principle also canonical inasmuch as its author is believed to have reached Buddhahood, is the *Gur-bum* or 'Hundred Thousand Songs' of Milarepa.

In Japan there is the *Dai Nippon Bukkyō Zencho* or 'Complete Works of Japanese Buddhism', in 160 volumes, which brings together the writings of more than thirty generations of saints and sages.

# AFTERWORD

With the brief mention of the Chinese, Tibetan, and Japanese products of 'continuous revelation' with which we ended the last chapter our survey of the canonical literature of Buddhism is complete, and we must now conclude this work with a few observations of a more general nature.

Even though the Buddhavacana or living word of the Buddha has not been dealt with in the way it deserves, the student who has gone through the previous eighteen chapters will again and again have been struck, in the most forcible manner, by the vast extent and endless variety of Buddhist canonical literature, as well as by the inexhaustible wealth of insight, imagination, and inspiration it contains. This literature was produced, by way of a series of deposits from oral traditions going back to Gautama the Buddha himself, mainly during the first millennium of the Buddhist era, and even though much was lost due to the ravages of time, the hostility of the brahmins, or hereditary Hindu priesthood, and the iconoclastic fury of the Muslim invaders of India, who, besides smashing images and murdering monks, committed whole libraries of Buddhist sacred books to the flames, enough has survived whether in the original or in Chinese and Tibetan translation – to show that the historical phenomenon known as Buddhism represents one of the greatest outpourings of spiritual energy the world has ever seen.

Without the testimony of the canonical literature, or what remains of it, we should have known very little about that outpouring, and very little about the supremely enlightened being whose life and work for humanity – indeed, for 'gods and men' – was its immediate source. Archaeological evidence is very scanty, and such references to the Buddha and his teaching as occur in post-Vedic Hindu literature are not only short and far apart but tendentious and misleading in the extreme. Even now, when lineal descendants of some of the major historical forms of Buddhism are still extant in the East, it is the Buddhavacana itself that is our most reliable guide to the true nature of Buddhism – a guide far more reliable than a great deal of contemporary Eastern Buddhist practice and observance. Indeed, without going so far as to set the authority of scripture against the authority of tradition in the way that some Protestant Christian sects do, it must be insisted that Buddhist practice and observance is to be judged by whether it is in accordance with the Buddhist scriptures rather than the Buddhist scriptures invoked to justify practices and observances which, though clearly at variance with the basic principles of the Dharma, have come to be regarded as traditional by this or that section of the Buddhist community.

As will be obvious from the very nature of the survey attempted in these pages, by the canonical literature of Buddhism is meant the *whole* of that literature. This was in fact made clear at the beginning of the first chapter, when the canonical literature was described as 'the written records of the Buddhavacana or living word of the Buddha, or what purports to be such, whether original or translated, or what is traditionally regarded as such by the Buddhist community or any section thereof.' Just as a knowledge of Buddhism worthy of the name must be solidly based on the Buddhist tradition in its entirety, and not simply on an acquaintance with the teachings of this or that individual school or group of schools, so a knowledge of the canonical literature of Buddhism worthy of the name must be solidly based on the Āgamas/Nikāyas as well as on the Mahāyāna sūtras, on the Birth Stories and Glorious Deeds as well as on the Abhidharma, and not simply on an acquaintance with this or that text or group of texts, however important a place these may occupy in the history of Buddhism.

This is not to say that the serious student will need to read every single one of the vast number of independent works that make up the canonical literature – or even all the works mentioned in *The Eternal Legacy*. Such an undertaking is in any case beyond the capacity of all save the full-time specialist, whether that specialist be a monk in his cell or a profane scholar in his study. But the serious student will certainly need to have a good general idea of the contents of the canonical literature as a whole, as well as a closer and more detailed acquaintance with a representative selection of key texts, which should include the majority of those dwelt upon at any length in the preceding pages, e.g. the Long Discourses, the *Sutta-Nipāta*, the *Udāna*, the *Saddharma-puṇḍarīka*, the Perfection of Wisdom 'in 8,000 lines', the *Sukhāvatī-vyūha sūtras*, and so on.

A comprehensive view of the canonical literature will be naturally accompanied by a comprehensive view of Buddhism itself and *vice versa*, for Buddhadharma and Buddhavacana are interconnected. Indeed, they may be said to be inseparable, for even those schools which claim to be the repositories of 'a special transmission outside the scriptures' do not, in practice, neglect to study the scriptures, so that their claim is perhaps best understood as representing a recognition of the importance of transmitting the spirit as well as the letter of the sacred texts.

Yet although the term 'canonical literature' denotes the whole of that literatue, and although a knowledge of that literature – and indeed of Buddhism itself – must be based on a knowledge of all the canonical texts, until quite recently the canonical literature was not available in its entirety in any one language. The three biggest and most important 'collected editions' were, of course, the Pāli Tipiṭaka, the Chinese San Tsang, and the Tibetan Kangyur, all of which were described in Chapter 17. Of these great collections the second and third are very much more comprehensive than the first, mainly because they include not only the Hīnayāna but also the Mahāyāna sūtras, and the form of Buddhism that is based on them, i.e. Chinese Buddhism and Tibetan Buddhism or Lamaism respectively, is more comprehensive and catholic than the form of Buddhism that is based only on the Pāli Tipiṭaka, i.e. South-East Asian Buddhism or the Buddhism of Sri Lanka, Burma, Thailand, Cambodia, and Laos.

In recent times, however, the entire canonical literature, as represented mainly by the three great collections and the nine Dharmas, has become available, or is in process of becoming available, in at least two languages: Japanese and English. In the case of Japanese the extant canonical literature is available practically *in toto*, but the fact that Japanese is hardly spoken outside Japan means that its usefulness is strictly limited. The situation is somewhat different in the case of

English. A much smaller proportion of the canonical literature is available in English than in Japanese (though it is a proportion that is constantly increasing), but because English is an international language whatever canonical texts are translated into English immediately become accessible to a greater number of people than it would be possible for them to reach in any other way. This has important consequences in a number of different areas, and for Buddhists and non-Buddhists alike.

The fact that the entire canonical literature of Buddhism is in process of becoming available in English means that the most important literary products of more than 2,000 years of Buddhist spiritual life and experience are gradually being fed into the mainstream of Western thought and culture and are beginning to make their influence felt in such diverse fields as those of philosophy, religion, science, literature, the fine arts, economics, and sport. It also means that English-speaking Eastern Buddhists, especially those in South-East Asia, have been made aware that Buddhist canonical literature is not limited to the Pāli Tipiṭaka and that their own form of Buddhism represents only one part of the total Buddhist tradition, since, in the well-known words of Edward Conze, 'the doctrine of the Buddha, conceived in its full breadth, width, majesty and grandeur, comprises all those teachings which ... work out methods leading to the extinction of individuality by eliminating the belief in it.'[212]

So far as English-speaking Western Buddhists are concerned, the fact that it is the whole of the canonical literature – in Sanskrit, Pāli, Chinese, Tibetan, and Khotanese – that is being made available in English means that it will be impossible, in the long run, for Western Buddhism to be limited to any one form of Eastern Buddhism. Whether they are English-speaking or not, it is inevitable that those Westerners who are drawn to Buddhism should derive inspiration and spiritual guidance from the whole of the canonical literature of Buddhism, for eventually this literature will be available in its entirety not only in English but in all the major Western languages, just as at the time of the Revival of Learning the whole surviving corpus of Greek classical literature eventually became available not only in Latin but also in all the leading European vernaculars.

But even though Western Buddhism derives inspiration and spiritual guidance from the whole of the canonical literature of Buddhism it will not necessarily derive it equally from every part of that literature. As in the case of Eastern Buddhism, where entire schools have sometimes grown up round a single sūtra or group of sūtras, Western Buddhism will probably derive more inspiration and spiritual guidance from some canonical texts than from others. Indeed, it is quite possible that from some canonical texts it will derive no inspiration or spiritual guidance at all, even though these texts may have been highly popular among Eastern Buddhists for many centuries and may have exercised a decisive influence upon their spiritual life. Conversely, it is conceivable that Western Buddhism may derive a great deal of inspiration and spiritual guidance from canonical texts which in the East have suffered comparative neglect.

At present it is difficult, if not impossible, to say which canonical texts will play a more, and which a less, important role in the future of Western Buddhism. All that can be said – and the fact is perhaps not without significance – is that the three canonical texts which have so far been most popular with Western Buddhists, as well as with Westerners sympathetic to Buddhism, are probably the *Dhammapada*, the *Diamond Sūtra*, and the *Bardo Thödol* or 'Tibetan Book of the Dead'.

Whichever texts play an important role in the future of Western Buddhism, they will play that role for one reason and for one reason only. Whether Mahāyāna sūtras or books of the Fundamental Abhidharma, Birth Stories and Glorious Deeds or 'taken out' texts, they will play it because they are able to satisfy the spiritual needs of individual Western Buddhists; and of course the greater the number of Western Buddhists whose spiritual needs are satisfied by a particular canonical text, the more important will be the role played by that text in the development of Western Buddhism.

In principle, all canonical texts are able to satisfy the spiritual needs of all Buddhists, whether Eastern or Western, but in practice some texts appeal more strongly to Buddhists of one kind of temperament, or one kind of spiritual aspiration, than they do to those of another. This is the main reason for the vast extent of the canonical literature, which may be regarded as one and the same Dharma in varying degrees of expansion and contraction, concentration, and dilution, rather than as a collection of separate teachings. The canonical literature is like the pharmacopoeia. All the different drugs and medicinal preparations which are listed in the pharmacopoeia have one and the same object, the restoration of the sick person to health, but some drugs and medicinal preparations are suited to the cure of one kind of disease and some to the cure of another. The sick person does not have to swallow the entire contents of the pharmacopoeia. In the same way, it is not necessary for the individual Western Buddhist, any more than for the individual Eastern Buddhist, to study and put into practice the entire contents of the Buddhist canonical literature. What he has to do is to find out which canonical text, or which collection or selection of texts, is best suited to his individual spiritual needs, and then devote himself to the concentrated study and intensive practice of the teachings contained in those texts – of course without any diminution of his reverence for the canonical literature as a whole.

In other words the criterion for determining whether this or that canonical text will play an important role in the future of Western Buddhism is not theoretical but practical. No prediction can therefore be made as to the exact nature of the form Western Buddhism will take, since despite the widespread popularity of the *Dhammapada*, the *Diamond Sūtra*, and the *Bardo Thödol*, as yet too few Western Buddhists have come into contact with too few canonical texts for any definite general tendency to be discernible. We can be reasonably certain, however, that at least some of the canonical texts which have played a major role in the development of Eastern Buddhism – such as the 'White Lotus Sūtra' and the Perfection of Wisdom 'in 8,000 lines' – will play a similar role in the development of Western Buddhism too. In any case, it should not be forgotten that eventually the whole of the canonical literature will be available in all the major Western languages, beginning with English. This in itself will have a profound effect on the future of Western Buddhism, since it will mean that the possibilities of inspiration and spiritual guidance will be far greater for Western Buddhists than they ever were for Eastern Buddhists, who often had access only to a comparatively limited range of canonical texts. Within a framework of overall unity Western Buddhism could, therefore, be characterized by unprecedented richness and diversity.

But although the criterion for determining whether this or that canonical text will play an important role in the future of Western Buddhism is not theoretical but practical, the criterion is not an easy one to apply. Though the canonical literature is like a pharmacopoeia, in that some texts are better suited to the spiritual needs of individual Buddhists than others, just as some medicines are better suited to the cure of certain diseases than others, there is at least one respect in which the canonical literature is not like a pharmacopoeia at all.

Whereas the pharmacopoeia lists not only the drugs and medicinal preparations themselves but also tests for their identity, purity, and strength, and lists formulas for making the preparations, in the case of the canonical literature such precision is not possible and no corresponding information about 'tests' and 'formulas' is, therefore, available.

Though it is to be expected that teachings that have met the spiritual needs of Eastern Buddhists will, in a general way, be able to meet the spiritual needs of Western Buddhists too, the question of the specific manner in which Buddhism is to be practised in the secularized and industrialized societies of the modern West is one that can be solved only in the actual lives of individual Western Buddhists. It is not one that can be solved, in advance, by profane authorities on 'comparative religion', by Eastern Buddhist teachers with little or no understanding of the psychology and cultural background of their Western students, or by armchair Buddhists whose contribution to the Buddhist movement is limited to the occasional book review.

If they are really to solve the problem of the specific manner in which Buddhism is to be practised in the modern world, Western Buddhists will have to do two things. They will have to study the canonical literature as Buddhavacana, that is to say, as the expression or reflection of the transcendental state of Supreme Enlightenment in the medium of human speech, and they will have to relate that study to the living of their own spiritual lives or, in other words, to their personal efforts to attain higher levels of being and consciousness and, eventually, the same transcendental state as that which is the ultimate source of the canonical literature itself. But whether the canonical literature is studied as Buddhavacana or not, it is hardly possible for one to study that literature, even to a limited degree, without first obtaining a general idea of its extent and variety. Whether one is a Western Buddhist, a student of Religion or of Literature, or simply one who wishes to make himself acquainted with all that is best in the cultural and religious heritage of mankind, one will first need to obtain an overview of the whole field which one is about to enter. In short one will need an introduction to the canonical literature of Buddhism, and it is such an introduction that *The Eternal Legacy* seeks to provide.

It should not be forgotten, however, that the purpose of an introduction is simply to introduce. The reading of *The Eternal Legacy* cannot, therefore, be regarded as a substitute for the actual study of the canonical texts themselves, and the work will have failed in its purpose if it does not inspire the reader to become more closely acquainted with at least some of the outstanding spiritual classics described in the foregoing pages. In the absence of personal contact with the Buddha, either in his historical or his archetypal form, a knowledge of the canonical literature is indispensable to an understanding of Buddhism as well as to its actual practice.

Unfortunately, those seeking to understand Buddhism only too often turn, or are directed, not to the canonical literature of Buddhism but to works which have very little connection with that literature – if indeed they have any connection with it at all. In the past this was unavoidable, since the treasures of the Buddha's teaching were either locked up in unknown ancient languages or available, if they were available at all, only in the form of translations that in many cases were both unattractive and unreliable. But now all this has changed. During the last forty or fifty years, especially, the flow of translations from Sanskrit, Pāli, Chinese, and Tibetan – even from Khotanese and Sogdian – has been increasing steadily, some important canonical texts being translated not once but several times.

Though the door of the Cave of Treasures may not have been flung wide open, it at least now stands ajar, and it is possible for us to obtain a glimpse of the untold wealth that sparkles within. It is even possible for us – as in the present work – to run a few diamonds and rubies through our fingers and, in this way, begin to appreciate at their true value the inexhaustible riches which the Buddha, in his infinite wisdom and boundless compassion, has bequeathed 'as an eternal legacy' to the entire human race.

# BIBLIOGRAPHY

## GENERAL BIBLIOGRAPHY

### ANTHOLOGIES OF CANONICAL TEXTS

Ambedkar, B.R. (ed.), *The Buddha and His Dhamma* (Bombay 1957).

Beyer, Stephan (ed. & trans.), *The Buddhist Experience: Sources and Interpretations* (Belmont, California 1974).

Burtt, E.A. (ed.), *The Teachings of the Compassionate Buddha* (New York 1955).

Conze, Edward, *Buddhist Scriptures* (Harmondsworth 1959).

Conze, Edward (ed.), *Buddhist Texts through the Ages* (London 1954).

Goddard, Dwight (ed.), *A Buddhist Bible* (London 1956).

Humphreys, Christmas (ed.), *The Wisdom of Buddhism* (London 1960).

Jennings, J.G. (ed. & trans.), *The Vedantic Buddhism of the Buddha* (London 1947).

Ling, Trevor (arranged & ed.), *The Buddha's Philosophy of Man: Early Indian Buddhist Dialogues* (London 1981).

Maurice, David (U Ohn Ghine), *The Lion's Roar: An Anthology of the Buddha's Teachings Selected from the Pāli Canon* (London 1962).

Parrinder, Geoffrey (comp.), *The Wisdom of the Early Buddhists* (London 1977).

Robinson, R. (ed. & trans.), *Chinese Buddhist Verse* (London 1954).

Thomas, E. J., *Buddhist Scriptures: A Selection Translated from the Pāli with Introduction* (London 1913).

Thomas, E. J. (ed. & trans.), *Early Buddhist Scriptures* (London 1935).

Thomas, E. J., *The Quest for Enlightenment: A Selection of the Buddhist Scriptures Translated from the Sanskrit* (London 1950).

Warren, Henry Clark (ed. & trans.), *Buddhism in Translations* (Harvard 1896).

Woodward, F. L. (ed. & trans.), *Some Sayings of the Buddha* (Adyar, Madras 1925).

## BOOKS ON BUDDHISM

Conze, Edward, *Buddhism: Its Essence and Development* (Birmingham 2001).

Conze, Edward, *Buddhist Thought in India* (London 1954).

Conze, Edward, *A Short History of Buddhism* (Bombay 1960).

de Silva, C.L.A., *The Four Essential Doctrines of Buddhism* (Colombo 1948).

Dutt, N., *Aspects of Mahāyāna Buddhism in Its Relation to Hīnayāna* (London 1930).

Dutt, Sukumar, *The Buddha and Five Centuries After* (London 1957).

Dutt, Sukumar, *Early Buddhist Monachism* (London 1924).

Evola, J., *The Doctrine of Awakening* (London 1951).

Glasenapp, Helmuth von, *Buddhism: A Non-Theistic Religion* (London 1970).

Govinda, Lama Anagarika, *The Psychological Attitude of Early Buddhist Philosophy* (London 1961).

Guenther, Herbert V., *Buddhist Philosophy in Theory and Practice* (Boulder 1971).

Jayatilleke, K.N., *The Message of the Buddha* (London 1975).

Joshi, Lal Mani, *Discerning the Buddha* (New Delhi 1983).

Joshi, Lal Mani, *Studies in the Buddhistic Culture of India* (Delhi 1967).

Morgan, K.W. (ed.), *The Path of the Buddha* (New York 1956).

Murti, T.R.V., *The Central Philosophy of Buddhism* (London 1955).

Rhys Davids, C.A.F., *A Manual of Buddhism for Advanced Students* (London 1932).

Rhys Davids, C.A.F., *Outlines of Buddhism: An Historical Sketch* (London 1938).

Sangharakshita, *Human Enlightenment* (Birmingham 1993).

Sangharakshita, *A Survey of Buddhism* (Birmingham 2001).

Sangharakshita, *The Three Jewels* (Birmingham 1998).

Sogen, Y., *Systems of Buddhistic Thought* (Calcutta 1912).

Stcherbatsky, T., *The Central Conception of Buddhism and the Meaning of the Word 'Dharma'* (Calcutta 1961).
Suzuki, D.T., *On Indian Mahāyāna Buddhism* (New York, Evanston, and London 1968).
Takakusu, J., *The Essentials of Buddhist Philosophy* (Hawaii 1947).
Warder, A.K., *Indian Buddhism* (Delhi 1980).
Wayman, A., *The Buddhist Tantras* (London 1974).

## CHAPTER BIBLIOGRAPHIES

### CHAPTER 1. BUDDHISM AND LANGUAGE

Edgerton, Franklin, *Buddhist Hybrid Sanskrit Language and Literature* (Banaras 1954).
Rhys Davids, C.A.F., *Sakya or Buddhist Origins* (London 1928).
Rhys Davids, C.A.F., *To Become or Not to Become (That is the Question!): Episodes in the History of an Indian Word* (London 1937).
Sangharakshita, *The Essence of Zen* (Birmingham 1997).

### CHAPTER 2. THE ORAL TRADITION

Pande, Govind Chandra, *Studies in the Origins of Buddhism* (Allahabad 1957).
Rhys Davids, C.A.F., *Gotama the Man* (London 1928).
Rhys Davids, C.A.F., *What was the Original Gospel in 'Buddhism'?* (London 1938).

### CHAPTER 3. THE MONASTIC CODE

Banerjee, Anukul Chandra, *Sarvāstivāda Literature* (Calcutta 1957), chapter 4.
Horner, I.B., (trans.), *The Book of the Discipline (Vinaya Piṭaka)*, 6 vols. (London 1938–1966).
Law, Bimala Churn, *A History of Pāli Literature* (Calcutta 1933), vol.1, pp.42–80.
Ñāṇamoli Thera (trans.), *The Pāṭimokkha: 227 Fundamental Rules of a Bhikkhu* (Bangkok 1966).
Prebish, Charles S., *Buddhist Monastic Discipline: The Sanskrit Prāṭimokṣa Sūtras of the Mahāsāṃghikas and Mūlasarvāstivādins* (Pennsylvania and London 1975).
Rhys Davids, T.W., and Oldenberg, Hermann (trans.), *Vinaya Texts*, 3 vols. (Oxford 1882).

### CHAPTER 4. THE DIALOGUES

Bennett, A.A.G., (trans.), *Long Discourses of the Buddha (Dīgha Nikāya 1–16)*, (Bombay n.d.).

Bhikkhu Bodhi (trans.), *The Discourse on the All-Embracing Net of Views: The Brahmajāla Sutta and its Commentarial Exegesis* (Kandy 1978).

Chau, Bhikṣu Thich Minh, *The Chinese Madhyama Āgama and the Pāli Majjhima Nikāya (A Comparative Study)* (Saigon n.d.).

Horner, I.B. (trans.), *The Collection of the Middle Length Sayings (Majjhima Nikāya)*, 3 vols (London 1954, 1957, 1959).

Law, Bimala Churn, *A History of Pāli Literature* (Calcutta 1932), vol.1, pp.80–157.

Norman, K.R., *Pāli Literature: Including the Canonical Literature in Prakrit and Sanskrit of all the Hīnayāna Schools of Buddhism* (Wiesbaden 1983), pp.32–49.

Rhys Davids, T.W. (trans.), *Buddhist Suttas* (Oxford 1881).

Rhys Davids, T.W. (trans.), *Dialogues of the Buddha*, Part 1: (London 1899). Parts 2 and 3: trans. from Pāli of *Dīgha Nikāya* by T.W. and C.A.F. Rhys Davids (London 1910, 1921).

### CHAPTER 5. THE ANTHOLOGIES

Beal, Samuel (trans.), *Dhammapada: with accompanying narratives* (London 1878).

Bhagwat, N.K. (trans.), *The Dhammapada* (Bombay 1935).

Blofeld, John (Chu Ch'an) (trans.), *The Sūtra of 42 Sections* (London 1977).

Buddhadatta, Mahāthera A.P. (ed. & trans.), *Dhammapadaṃ: An Anthology of the Sayings of the Buddha* (Colombo n.d.).

Chalmers, Lord, (ed.), *Buddha's Teachings: Being the Sutta-Nipāta or Discourse Collection*, Harvard Oriental Series, vol.37 (Cambridge MA 1932).

Dharmatrāta (comp.), *The Tibetan Dhammapada* (trans. from Tibetan) (New Delhi 1983).

Geham, H.S. (trans.), *The Minor Anthologies of the Pāli Canon*, vol.4: Vimānavatthu: 'Stories of the Mansions', Petavatthu: 'Stories of the Departed', (London 1974).

Hare, E.M. (trans.), *The Book of the Gradual Sayings (Aṅguttara Nikāya)* or More Numbered Suttas, vols. 3, 4 (London 1934, 1935).

Hare, E.M. (trans.), *Woven Cadences of the Early Buddhists (Sutta-Nipāta)* (London, second ed. 1947).
Horner, I.B. (trans.), *The Minor Anthologies of the Pāli Canon*, vol.3: Buddhavaṃsa: 'Chronicle of Buddhas', Cariyāpiṭaka: 'Basket of Conduct', (London 1975).
Jayasundere, A.D. (trans.), *The Book of the Numerical Sayings (Aṅguttara Nikāya)*, Part 2 (Adya, Madras 1925).
Law, Bimala Churn, *A History of Pāli Literature* (Calcutta 1932), pp.157–267.
Moore, Justin Hartley (trans.), *Sayings of the Buddha: The Itivuttaka* (Columbia, New York 1908).
Norman, K.R. (trans.), *Elders' Verses* (Theragāthā) (London 1969).
Norman, K.R. (trans.), *Elders' Verses* (Therigāthā) (London 1970).
Norman, K.R., *Pāli Literature: Including the Canonical Literature in Prakrit and Sanskrit of All the Hīnayāna Schools of Buddhism* (Wiesbaden 1983), pp.49–70, 72–77.
Radhakrishnan, S., (trans.), *The Dhammapada* (Oxford 1950).
Rhys Davids, C.A.F. (trans.), *The Book of the Kindred Sayings (Saṃyutta Nikāya)* or Grouped Suttas, parts 1 and 2 (London 1917).
Rhys Davids, C.A.F. (trans.), *The Minor Anthologies of the Pāli Canon*, vol.1: Dhammapada and Khuddakapāṭha (London 1931).
Rhys Davids, C.A.F., *Poems of Cloister and Jungle* (London 1941).
Rhys Davids, C.A.F. (trans.), *Psalms of the Brethren* (Theragāthā) (London 1913).
Rhys Davids, C.A.F. (trans.), *Psalms of the Sisters* (Therigāthā) (London 1909).
Woodward, F.L. (trans.), *The Book of the Gradual Sayings (Aṅguttara Nikāya)* or More Numbered Suttas, vols. 1, 2 and 5 (London 1932, 1933, 1936).
Woodward, F.L. (trans.), *The Book of the Kindred Sayings (Saṃyutta Nikāya)* or Grouped Suttas, parts 3, 4, and 5 (London 1924, 1927, 1930).
Woodward F.L. (trans.), *The Minor Anthologies of the Pāli Canon*, vol.2: Udāna: 'Verses of Uplift', Itivuttaka: 'As it Was Said', (London 1935).

### CHAPTER 6. THE JĀTAKAS AND AVADĀNAS

Cone, Margaret, and Gombrich, Richard F. (trans.), *The Perfect Generosity of Prince Vessantara: A Buddhist Epic* (Oxford 1977).

Cowell, E.B. (ed.), *The Jātakas or Stories of the Buddha's Former Births*, 6 vols. (Cambridge 1895).
Francis, H.T. and Thomas, E.J. (trans.), *Jātaka Tales* (Cambridge 1916).
Horner, I.B. (trans.), *Cariyāpiṭaka: Basket of Conduct* (included in the Minor Anthologies of the Pāli Canon, vol.3) (London 1975).
Horner, I.B. (trans.), *Ten Jātaka Stories: each illustrating one of the ten Pāramitās*, with Pāli text (London 1957).
Jones, J.J. (trans.), *The Mahāvastu*, 3 vols. (London 1949, 1952, 1956).
Bimala Churn Law, *A History of Pāli Literature* (Calcutta 1932), pp.267–277.
Norman, K.R., *Pāli Literature: Including the Canonical Literature in Prakrit and Sanskrit of all the Hīnayāna Schools of Buddhism* (Wiesbaden 1983), pp.77–84, 89–95.
Rahula, Bhikkhu Telwatte (trans.), *A Critical Study of the Mahāvastu* (Delhi 1978).
Wickramsinghe, Martin, *The Buddhist Jātaka Stories and the Russian Novel* (Colombo 1956).

### CHAPTER 7. THE FUNDAMENTAL ABHIDHARMA

Aung, S.Z., and Rhys Davids, C.A.F. (trans.), *Points of Controversy (Kathā-vatthu)* (London 1915).
Banerjee, Anukul Chandra, *Sarvāstivāda Literature* (Calcutta 1957), ch.5.
Kashyap, Jagdish, *The Abhidhamma Philosophy*, vol.2 (Benares 1943).
Law, Bimala Charan (trans.), *A Designation of Human Types* (Puggala-paññati) (London 1922).
Law, Bimala Churn, *A History of Pāli Literature* (Calcutta 1932), vol.1, pp.303–342.
Malalasekara, G.P. (ed.), 'Abhidharma Literature', *Encyclopaedia of Buddhism* (Colombo 1961), fascicule A–Aca, pp.64–72.
Nārada, U (trans.), *Conditional Relations (Paṭṭhāna)*, 2 vols. (London 1969, 1981).
Nārada, U (trans.), *Discourse on Elements (Dhātu-kathi)* (1962).
Norman, K.R., *Pāli Literature: Including the Canonical Literature in Prakrit and Sanskrit of all the Hīnayāna Schools of Buddhism* (Wiesbaden 1983), pp.96–107.
Nyanatiloka Mahāthera, *Guide Through the Abhidhamma Piṭaka* (third edn. Kandy 1971).
Rhys Davids, C.A.F. (trans.), *Buddhist Psychological Ethics (Dhamma-saṅgaṇī)* (London 1900).

Thittila, U (trans.), *The Book of Analysis (Vibhaṅga)* (London 1969).

**CHAPTER 8. TRANSITION TO THE MAHĀYĀNA SŪTRAS**

Hadani, Ryōtai, *An Introduction to Mahāyāna Sūtras*, trans. Kōshō Yamamoto (Uke City 1971).

Nariman, J.K., *A Literary History of Sanskrit Buddhism* (Bombay 1919).

**CHAPTER 9. THE SADDHARMA-PUṆḌARĪKA**

Hurvitz, Leon (trans. from the Chinese of Kumārajīva), *Scripture of the Lotus Blossom of the Fine Dharma* (New York 1976).

Katō, Bunnō; Tamura, Yoshirō; and Miyasaka, Kōjirō (trans.), *The Threefold Lotus Sūtra: Innumerable Meanings, The Lotus Flower of the Wonderful Law, and Meditation on the Bodhisattva Universal Virtue*, with revisions by W.E. Soothill, Wilhelm Schiffer, and Pier P. Del Campana (New York and Tokyo 1975).

Kern, H. (trans.), *Saddharma-Puṇḍarīka or the Lotus of the True Law* (Oxford 1884).

Soothill, W.E. (trans.), *The Lotus of the Wonderful Law* (Oxford 1930).

Sangharakshita, *The Drama of Cosmic Enlightenment: Parables, Myths, and Symbols of the White Lotus Sūtra* (Birmingham 1993).

**CHAPTER 10. THE PRAJÑĀ-PĀRAMITĀ SŪTRAS**

Conze, Edward (trans.), *Buddhist Wisdom Books: Containing The Diamond Sūtra and the Heart Sūtra* (London 1970).

Conze, Edward (trans.), *The Large Sūtra on Perfect Wisdom with the divisions of the Abhisamayālaṅkāra* (Berkeley, Los Angeles, London 1975).

Conze, Edward (trans.), *The Perfection of Wisdom in Eight Thousand Lines & Its Verse Summary* (Bolinas 1973).

Conze, Edward, *The Prajñāpāramitā Literature* (Tokyo 1978).

Conze, Edward (trans.), *The Short Prajñāpāramitā Texts* (London 1973).

Gemmell, William (trans.), *The Diamond Sūtra (Chin-Kang-Ching) or Prajñā-Pāramitā* (London 1912).

Müller, F.M. (trans.), 'The Vagrakkhedikā', 'The Larger Pragñā-pāramitā-hridaya Sūtra', and 'The Smaller Pragñā-pāramitā-hridaya Sūtra', in *Buddhist Mahāyāna Texts* (Oxford 1894), Part 2, pp.109–154.

Price, A.F. (trans.), *The Diamond Sūtra or the Jewel of Transcendental Wisdom* (London 1955).
Suzuki, D.T. *Essays in Zen Buddhism (Third Series)* (London 1970), chs. 5, 6, 7.

CHAPTER 11. THE VIMALAKĪRTI AND SUKHĀVATĪ SŪTRAS

Birnbaum, Raoul, *The Healing Buddha* (London 1980).
Chang, Garma C.C., general ed., *A Treasury of Mahāyāna Sūtras*, trans. Buddhist Association of the United States (Pennsylvania and London 1983).
Fujimoto, Ryukyo, *An Outline of the Triple Sūtra of Shin Buddhism*, vol.1, 'The Sūtra on the Eternal Buddha' (Kyoto 1955).
Lamotte, Étienne (trans.), *L'Enseignement de Vimalakīrti* (Vimalakīrtinirdeśa), (Louvain 1962).
Lamotte, Étienne (trans.), *The Teaching of Vimalakīrti (Vimalakīrtinirdeśa)*, rend. Sarah Boin (London 1976).
Liebenthal, Walter (trans.), *The Sūtra of the Lord of Healing (Bhaishajyagurū Vaiduryaprabha Tathāgata)* (Peiping 1936).
Lu K'uan Yü (Charles Luk) (trans.), *The Vimalakīrti Nirdeśa Sūtra (Wei Mo Chieh So Shuo Ching)* (Berkeley and London 1972).
Müller, F. Max (trans.), 'The Larger Sukhāvatī-vyūha' and 'The Smaller Sukhāvatī-vyūha'; J. Takakusu (trans.), 'The Amitāyur-dhyāna-sūtra', in *Buddhist Mahāyāna Texts* (Oxford 1894), part 2, pp.1–103, 161–201.
Thurman, Robert A.F. (trans.), *The Holy Teaching of Vimalakīrti* (Pennsylvania and London 1976).
Wayman, Alex, and Wayman, Hideko (trans.), *The Lion's Roar of Queen Śrīmālā: A Buddhist Scripture on the Tathāgatagarbha Theory* (New York and London 1974).
Yamada, Isshi (ed.), *Karuṇāpuṇḍarīka*, 2 vols. (London 1968).

CHAPTER 12. THE RATNAKŪṬA AND SAMĀDHI SŪTRAS

Chang, Garma C.C., general ed., *A Treasury of Mahāyāna Sūtras*, trans. Buddhist Association of the United States (Pennsylvania and London 1983).
Lamotte, Étienne (trans.), *La Concentration de la Marche Heroïque (Surāṃgamasamādhi-sūtra)* (Bruxelles 1965).
Lu K'uan Yü (Charles Luk) (trans.), *The Śūrāṅgama Sūtra (Leng Yen Ching)* (London 1973).

Wai-tao (trans.), 'The Śūrāṅgama Sūtra', in *A Buddhist Bible*, ed. Dwight Goddard (London 1956).

**CHAPTER 13. THE LAṄKĀVATĀRA SŪTRA**

Suzuki, D.T. (trans.), *The Laṅkāvatāra Sūtra: A Mahāyāna Text* (London 1932).
Suzuk, D.T. , *Studies in the Laṅkāvatāra Sūtra* (London 1930).

**CHAPTER 14. THE AVATAṂSAKA SŪTRA**

Guenther, Herbert V. (trans.), 'Excerpts from the Gaṇḍavyūha Sūtra', in *Tibetan Buddhism in Western Perspective* (Dharma Publishing 1977), pp.3–35.
Hua, Hsüan, *The Great Means Expansive Buddha Flower Adornment Sūtra*, trans. Dharma Realm Buddhist University Buddhist Text Translation Society. Various chapters issued separately (Talmage CA 1981–.)
Malalasekara, G.P. (ed.), 'Avataṃsaka Sūtra (Hua-yan-ching)' in *Encyclopaedia of Buddhism* (Colombo 1967), vol.1, Fascicle 3, p.345b.
Suzuki, D.T., *Essays in Zen Buddhism (Third Series)* (London 1970), chs. 2, 3, 4.

**CHAPTER 15. THE NIRVĀṆA AND SUVARṆA-PRABHĀSA SŪTRAS**

Chou, Hsiang-kuang (trans.), *The Sūtra of Buddha's Bequeathed Teaching* (Cameron Highlands n.d.).
Emmerick, R.E. (trans.), *The Sūtra of Golden Light*, a translation of the *Suvarṇabhāsottamasūtra* (London 1970).
Sangharakshita, *Transforming Self and World* (Birmingham 1995).
Yamamoto, Kosho (trans. and comy.), *The Mahāyāna Mahāparinirvāṇa-sūtra*, 3 vols. (Uke City 1973).

**CHAPTER 16. THE TANTRAS**

Dawa-Samdup, Kazi (trans.), *Shrīchakrasambhāra Tantra* (London and Calcutta 1919).
Lessing, F.D., and Wayman, A., *Introduction to the Buddhist Tantrica Systems* (Delhi 1978).
Skorupski, Tadeusz (trans.), *Sarvadurgatiparisodhana Tantra: Elimination of All Evil Destinies* (Delhi 1983).
Snellgrove, D.L., *The Hevajra Tantra: A Critical Study*, Part 1: Introduction and Translation (London 1959).

Tsuda, Shinichi, *The Saṃvarodaya Tantra: Selected Chapters* (Tokyo 1974).

Wayman, Alex, *Yoga of the Guhyasamājatantra: The Arcane Lore of Forty Verses: A Buddhist Tantra Commentary* (Delhi 1977).

### CHAPTER 17. COLLECTED EDITIONS

Bunyiu, Nanjio (trans.), *A Catalogue of the Chinese Translation of the Tripiṭaka* (Oxford 1983).

Conze, Edward (ed.), rev. Lewis Lancaster, *Buddhist Scriptures: A Bibliography* (New York 1982).

Cordier, P., *Catalogue du Fond Tibétain* (1909–15).

Mizano, Kogen, *Buddhist Sūtras: Origin, Development, Transmission* (Tokyo 1982).

Religions-wissenschaftliches Seminar der Universität, *Mahāyāna Texts Translated into Western Languages* (Bonn 1983).

Webb, Russell, *An Analysis of the Pāli Canon* (Kandy 1975, and three supplements).

### CHAPTER 18. CONTINUING REVELATION

Chan, Wing-tsit (trans.), *The Platform Scripture* (New York 1963).

Chang, Garma C.C. (trans.), *The Hundred Thousand Songs of Milarepa*, 2 vols. (New York 1962).

Dawa-Samdup, Lāma Kazi (trans.), *The Tibetan Book of the Dead*, ed. W.Y. Evans-Wentz (London 1957.)

Tsogyal, Yeshe, *The Life and Liberation of Padmasambhava: Padma bKa'i Thang*, trans. Kenneth Douglas and Gwendolen Bays, 2 vols. (Emeryville 1978).

Wong Mou-lam (trans.), *The Sūtra of Wei Lang (or Hui Neng)* (Shanghai 1930, revised Christmas Humphreys, London 1953).

Philip B. Yampolsky (trans.), *The Platform Sūtra of the Sixth Patriarch* (New York and London 1967).

In most cases only the date of the original publication has been given. Some of the more popular anthologies and works on Buddhism have been frequently reprinted, many by different publishers.

# NOTES AND REFERENCES

1 Cecil Bendall and W.H.D. Rouse (trans.), *Adhyāśayasasaṃcodana Sūtra*, quoted by Śāntideva. See *Compendium of Teachings (Śikṣā-Samuccaya)* (London 1922), p.17.

2 Franklin Edgerton, *Buddhist Hybrid Sanskrit Language and Literature* (Banaras 1954), p.5.

3 Franklin Edgerton, 'The Buddha and Language' in *The Indian Historical Quarterly* (Calcutta), vol.32, Nos. 2 and 3, p.132.

4 C.A.F. Rhys Davids, *Sakya or Buddhist Origins* (London 1928), Ch.5.

5 *Tamburlaine the Great*, Part One, Act 5, Scene 1. Everyman's Library edition (London 1950), pp.50–1.

6 For discussion and references, see T.R.V. Murti, *The Central Philosophy of Buddhism* (London 1955), p.38. Also K.N. Jayatilleke, *Early Buddhist Theory of Knowledge* (London 1963), and Lal Mani Joshi, *Discerning the Buddha* (Delhi 1983).

7 D.T. Suzuki, *Essays in Zen Buddhism (First Series)* (London 1949), p.20.

8 *Ibid.*, p.167.

9 *Udāna* v.5.

10 C.A.F. Rhys Davids (trans.), *Saṃyutta Nikāya* Part 1 (Sagātha-vagga) 8. §5,6, *The Book of the Kindred Sayings* (London 1950), pp.339–41.

11 Sukumar Dutt, *The Buddha and Five Centuries After* (London 1957), p.99.

12 Sangharakshita, *The Three Jewels* (Birmingham 1998), p.178.

13 Modern Bihar and Uttar Pradesh.

14 *The Buddha and Five Centuries After*, p.91.

15 *Mahāvaṃsa* 33.100–1.

16 See Vidhushekhara Bhattacharya, *Buddhist Texts as Recommended by Asoka* (Calcutta 1948).

17 Sir Charles Eliot, *Hinduism and Buddhism: An Historical Sketch* (London 1921), vol.1, p.286.

18 Edward J.Thomas, *The History of Buddhist Thought* (second edn., London 1951), p.277.

19 *Pali-English Dictionary*, Pali Text Society, Oxford 1992.

20 Maung Tin (trans.), *The Expositor (Atthasālinī)* (London 1921), vol.1, p.33.

21 *Majjhima Nikāya* Sutta No. 123.

22 Csoma de Körös, *The Life and Teaching of the Buddha* (Calcutta 1957), p.25.

23 *The Expositor (Atthasālinī)*, vol.1, p.33.

24 *The History of Buddhist Thought*, p.278.

25 *Mahāvyutpatti* 1385.

26 *The History of Buddhist Thought*, p.278.

27 Edward Conze, *A Short History of Buddhism* (Bombay 1960), p.37.

28 Sangharakshita, *The Three Jewels*, op.cit., ch.17.

29 from the Sanskrit.

30 Quoted Anukul Chandra Banerjee, *Sarvāstivāda Literature* (Calcutta 1957), p.79.

31 See *The Three Jewels*, op. cit., p.199.

32 Quoted in *Sarvāstivāda Literature*, p.79.

33 Ananda K. Coomaraswamy, *Buddha and the Gospel of Buddhism* (London 1916), p.276.

34 M. Winternitz, *A History of Indian Literature* (Calcutta 1933), vol.2, p.68.

35 *Ibid.*, p.35.

36 Goviṇd Chandra Pande, *Studies in the Origins of Buddhism* (Allahabad 1957), p.98.

37 See Sangharakshita, *The Three Jewels*, op. cit., ch.4.

38 Govind Chandra Pande, *Studies in the Origins of Buddhism* (Allahabad 1957), p.181.

39 C.A.F. Rhys Davids (trans.), *The Book of the Kindred Sayings (Saṃyutta Nikāya)*, Part 1 (London 1950), pp.v–vii.

40 A.D. Jayasundere (trans.), *The Book of the Numerical Sayings (Aṅguttara Nikāya)*, Part 2 (Adyar, Madras 1925), p.36.

41 *Ibid.*, pp.82–3.

42 *Ibid.*, p.69.

43 *Ibid.*, pp.127–8.

44 See M. Winternitz, *A History of Indian Literature* (Calcutta 1933), vol.2, p.17.

45 *Udāna* i.10.

46 *Udāna* vi.4.

47 *Itivuttaka* 27 (partly condensed).

48 Hare (trans.), *Sutta-Nipāta* iv.14 (verses 916–20).

49 John Blofeld (Chu Ch'an) (trans.), *The Sūtra of 42 Sections*, 38. (rev. edn. London 1977), p.21.

50 See Sangharakshita, *The Three Jewels*, op. cit., ch.10.

51 T.W. Rhys Davids, *Buddhist India* (third Indian edn., Calcutta 1957), p.94.

52 *Mahā-vagga* x.2(3–20).

53 M. Winternitz, *A History of Indian Literature* (Calcutta 1933), vol.2, p.149.

54 *Ibid.*, p.274.

55 Bhikkhu J. Kashyap, *The Abhidhamma Philosophy, or the Psycho-Ethical Philosophy of Early Buddhism* (Benares 1942).

56 Maung Tin (trans.), *The Expositor (Atthasālinī)* (London 1921), vol.1, pp.1–2.

57 Nyanatiloka, *Guide Through the Abhidhamma-Piṭaka* (Colombo 1938), p.19.

58 See Sangharakshita, *The Three Jewels*, op. cit., ch.15.

59 Anukul Chandra Banerjee, *Sarvāstivāda Literature* (Calcutta 1957), p.62.

60 G.P. Malalasekera (ed.), *Encyclopaedia of Buddhism*: Fascicule A–Aca (Colombo 1961), p.69.

61 Quoted *Sarvāstivāda Literature*, p.66.

62 For a complete analysis see *Sarvāstivāda Literature*, pp.66–7.

63 *Dīgha Nikāya Sutta* No. 27.

64 *Encyclopaedia of Buddhism*: Fascicule A-Aca, p.70.

65 *Guide Through the Abhidhamma-Piṭaka*, op. cit., p.29.

66 Shwe Zan Aung and C.A.F. Rhys Davids (trans.), *Points of Controversy: A Translation of the Kathā-vatthu* (London 1915), pp.344–5.

67 *Ibid.*, p.xlix, note 1.

68 *Encyclopaedia of Buddhism*: Fascicule A-Aca, p.70.

69 *Sarvāstivāda Literature*, p.65.

70 *Ibid.*, p.65.

71 Quoted *Guide Through the Abhidhamma-Piṭaka*, op. cit., p.66.

72 *Ibid.*, p.66.

73 *The Expositor (Atthasālinī)*, vol.1, p.17 (translation revised).

74 Milton, *Paradise Lost*, i.2.

75 Sir Charles Eliot, *Hinduism and Buddhism: An Historical Sketch* (London 1921), vol.2, p.47.

76 M. Winternitz, *A History of Indian Literature* (Calcutta 1933) vol.2.

77 W.E. Soothill, *The Lotus of the Wonderful Law* (Oxford 1930), p.11.

78 N. Dutt (ed.), *Saddharmapuṇḍarīkasutram* (Calcutta 1953), pp.xvii–xvliii.

79 *The Lotus of the Wonderful Law*, p.13.

80 *Ibid.*, p.141.

81 Bunnō Katō, Yoshirō Tamura, and Kōjirō Miyasaka (trans.), *The Threefold Lotus Sūtra.* (New York and Tokyo 1975), p.177.

82 *Saddharmapuṇḍarīkasutram*, p.155.

83 *The Lotus of the Wonderful Law*, p.163.

84 *Ibid.*, pp.196–7.

85 *Ibid.*, pp.200–1. Cf. H. Kern (trans.), *Saddharma-Puṇḍarīka or The Lotus of the True Law* (Oxford 1984), 'The Sacred Books of the East' vol.21, pp.288–9.

86 *The Lotus of the Wonderful Law*, p.201.

87 *Ibid.*, p.213.

88 *Ibid.*, p.224.

89 *Ibid.*, p.230.

90 *Ibid.*, p.231.

91 *Ibid.*, p.235.

92 See Sangharakshita, *The Three Jewels* op. cit., ch.14.

93 Edward Conze (trans.), *The Perfection of Wisdom in Eight Thousand Lines & Its Verse Summary* (Bolinas 1973), p.159.

94 Edward Conze, *The Prajñāpāramitā Literature* (second edn., Tokyo 1978), p.3.

95 See, for example, *Rgan-Drug Mchog-Gnyis* (Gangtok 1962), plate 2.

96 Sangharakshita, *A Survey of Buddhism* (ninth edn., Birmingham 2001), pp.346–7.

97 *Saṃyutta Nikāya*, ii.266–7. I.B. Horner and A. Coomaraswamy (trans.), in *The Living Thoughts of Gotama the Buddha* (Bombay 1956), p.65 (translation revised).

98 Modern Bihar and Uttar Pradesh.

99 *The Perfection of Wisdom in Eight Thousand Lines & Its Verse Summary*, p.83.

100 *Ibid.*, p.83.

101 *Vinaya Piṭaka* ii.10.

102 *The Perfection of Wisdom in Eight Thousand Lines & Its Verse Summary*, pp.83–4.

103 *Ibid.*, p.89.

104 *Ibid.*, pp.90–1.

105 *Ibid.*, p.91.

106 *Ibid.*, p.91.

107 *The Prajñāpāramitā Literature*, op. cit., p.18, note 1.

108 *Ibid.*, p.10.

109 *Ibid.*, p.32.

110 Some modern scholars now believe that this work is to be attributed to a disciple of Nāgārjuna whose name was the same as, or similar to, that of his master.

111 *The Prajñāpāramitā Literature*, op. cit., p.36.

112 *Ibid.*, p.12.

113 Edward Conze, *Buddhist Wisdom Books: The Diamond Sūtra and the Heart Sūtra translated and explained* (London 1975), p.51.

114 'The Diamond Cutter of Doubts', in Lu K'uan Yü (Charles Luk) (trans.), *Ch'an and Zen Teaching (Series One)* (London 1960), p.49 *et seq.*

115 *Ibid.*, p.156.

116 Edward Conze (trans.), *Vajracchedikā Prajñāpāramitā* (Rome 1957), pp.66–7.

117 *Buddhist Wisdom Books*, pp.100–1.

118 *The Prajñāpāramitā Literature*, p.58.

119 Edward Conze (trans.), *The Short Prajñāpāramitā Texts* (London 1973), p.144.

120 *The Prajñāpāramitā Literature*, p.14.

121 Some versions contain twelve chapters and some thirteen.

122 In other versions 'Ratnākara'.

123 'Vimalakīrti's Discourse on Emancipation', in Hokei Izumi (trans.), *Eastern Buddhist* (Kyoto 1924–5), vol.3, p.64 (translation revised).

124 *Ibid.*, pp.138–9.

125 *Ibid.*, p.225 (translation revised).

126 *Ibid.* p.230 (translation revised).

127 *Ibid.*, pp.234–5 (translation revised).

128 Richard Robinson, *Chinese Buddhist Verse* (London 1954), p.22 *et seq.*

129 Cf. Robert A.F. Thurman (trans.), *The Holy Teaching of Vimalakīrti* (Pennsylvania and London 1976), pp.73–7.

130 In some versions this and the concluding chapter of the sūtra form one chapter.

131 Franklin Edgerton, *Buddhist Hybrid Sanskrit Dictionary* (Yale 1953).

132 Aldous Huxley, *The Doors of Perception* and *Heaven and Hell* (Harmondsworth 1974), p.80.

133 Sangharakshita, *A Survey of Buddhism*, op. cit., pp.368–9.

134 Some modern Japanese scholars now regard the *Meditation Sūtra* as being what they term a 'genuine' sūtra (quotation marks theirs), i.e. as a sūtra which, though composed in (as distinct from translated into) Chinese in China is nonetheless fully in accordance with the spirit and the letter of the Buddha's Teaching.

135 J. Takakusu (trans.), *Buddhist Mahāyāna Sūtras* (Oxford 1894), 'The Sacred Books of the East' vol.49, Part 2, pp.167–8 (translation revised).

136 *Ibid.*, p.178.

137 *Ibid.*, p.167.

138 Alex Wayman and Hideko Wayman (trans.), *The Lion's Roar of Queen Śrīmālā* (New York and London 1974), p.63.

139 W.E. Soothill (trans.), *The Lotus of the Wonderful Law.* (Oxford 1930), p.245 (abridged).

140 Edward Conze (trans.), *Buddhist Texts Through the Ages* (Oxford 1954), p.195.

141 M. Winternitz, *A History of Indian Literature* (Calcutta 1933), vol.2, p.306.

142 *Ibid.*, p.307.

143 Garma C.C. Chang (general ed.), *A Treasury of Mahāyāna Sūtras. Selections from the Mahāratnakūṭa Sūtra.* trans. Buddhist Association of the United States (Pennsylvania and London 1983), p.xi.

144 Richard Robinson (trans.), *Chinese Buddhist Verse* (London 1954), pp.28–9.

145 *Buddhist Hybrid Sanskrit Language and Literature*, p.55.

146 *A Treasury of Mahāyāna Sūtras*, pp.152–3.

147 *Ibid.*, p.68.

148 *Ibid.*, p.270.

149 *Ibid.* p.431.

150 Quoted in M. Winternitz, *A History of Indian Literature* (Calcutta 1933), vol.2, p.331.

151 *Buddhist Hybrid Sanskrit Language and Literature*, p.52.

152 Dwight Goddard (ed.), *A Buddhist Bible* (London 1956), p.246.

153 Edward Conze (trans.), *The Perfection of Wisdom in Eight Thousand Lines & Its Verse Summary* (Bolinas 1973), p.83.

154 See D.T. Suzuki, *Studies in the Laṅkāvatāra Sūtra* (London 1957), p.259.

155 *Ibid.*, p.258.

156 *Ibid.*, p.17.

157 *Ibid.*, p.21.

158 M. Winternitz, *A History of Indian Literature* (Calcutta 1933), vol.2, p.333, note 2.

159 D.T. Suzuki (trans.), *The Laṅkāvatāra Sūtra: A Mahāyāna Text* (London & Henley 1978), pp.37–9. This translation differs somewhat from that given in the same author's *Studies in the Laṅkāvatāra Sūtra*, pp.96–8.

160 *Studies*, p.103.

161 *Ibid.*, p.105.

162 *Ibid.*, p.102.

163 *The Laṅkāvatāra Sūtra*, pp.123–4.

164 *Ibid.*, p.169.

165 *Studies*, p.170.

166 *Ibid.*, p.178.

167 *Ibid.*, p.327.

168 *Laṅkāvatāra Sūtra*, p.165.

169 *Studies*, p.330.

170 *Laṅkāvatāra Sūtra*, pp.197–8.

171 D.T. Suzuki, *Studies in the Laṅkāvatāra Sūtra* (London 1957), p.95.

172 Sir Charles Eliot, *Hinduism and Buddhism: An Historical Study* (London 1921), vol.3, p.374.

173 *Ibid.*, pp.283–4.

174 D.T. Suzuki, *Essays in Zen Buddhism (Third Series)* (London 1970), p.71.

175 *Ibid.* p.75.

176 *Ibid.* p.87.

177 *Ibid.*, p.77.

178 Beatrice Lane Suzuki, *Mahāyāna Buddhism* (third edn. 1959), p.95.

179 *Stepping-Stones* (January 1951), vol.1, no.7, p.153.

180 *Ibid.*, vol.1, no.9, pp.209–10.

181 *Essays in Zen Buddhism (Third Series)*, p.90.

182 *Ibid.*, p.110.

183 See Sangharakshita, *The Three Jewels*, op. cit., p.157.

184 *Essays in Zen Buddhism (Third Series)*, p.146.

185 *Ibid.*, pp.146–7.

186 M. Winternitz, *A History of Indian Literature* (Calcutta 1933), vol.2, p.326, note 1.

187 Not in *Aṣṭasāhasrikā Prajñāpāramitā* chapter 16 as stated by Winternitz, *A History of Indian Literature* vol.2, p.326, note 1.

188 *A History of Indian Literature* vol.2, p.327, note 1.

189 Sangharakshita, *A Survey of Buddhism*, op. cit., p.490 *et seq.*

190 The publisher has been unable to trace this quotation, but a similar passage occurs in the *Laṅkāvatāra Sūtra* f.214.

191 *The Sūtra of Buddha's Bequeathed Teaching* (Cameron Highlands n.d.), p.28.

192 The term *mahātta*, great self or great soul, occurs once in the Pali Tipiṭaka. See F.L. Woodward (trans.), *The Book of the Gradual Sayings (Aṅguttara Nikāya)*, vol.1 (London 1932), p.228.

193 Kosho Yamamoto (trans.), *The Mahāyāna Mahāparinirvāṇa-Sūtra* (Ube City 1973), vol.1, p.91.

194 *Ibid.*, p.181.

195 Suzuki (*Studies in the Laṅkāvatāra Sūtra*, p.391) defines *icchantika* as 'those who are destitute of the Buddha-nature'. According to the *Mahā-*

*parinirvāṇa Sūtra* the *icchantika* is not destitute of the Buddha-nature itself but of the 'skilful roots' necessary for its realization.

196 R.E. Emmerick (trans.), *The Sūtra of Golden Light* (London 1970), p.ix.

197 *Ibid.*, p.1.

198 *Ibid.*, p.12.

199 Stanley Frye (trans.), 'Chapter Ten of the Sūtra of Golden Light', in *The Middle Way* (February 1977), vol.51, no.4, pp.151–7.

200 D.L. Snellgrove, *The Hevajra Tantra* (London 1959), vol.1, p.115.

201 Edward Conze, *Buddhist Thought in India* (London 1962), pp.271–2.

202 See Sangharakshita, *The Three Jewels*, op. cit., ch.5.

203 *The Hevajra Tantra*, vol.1, p.114.

204 Sir Charles Eliot, *Hinduism and Buddhism: An Historical Sketch* (London 1921), vol.3, p.282.

205 China.

206 George Roerich, *The Blue Annals* Part One (Calcutta 1949), p.338.

207 More than twenty years later, I am unable to trace the reference.

208 See Sangharakshita, *The Three Jewels*, op. cit., ch.5.

209 Chang Chen-chi, *The Practice of Zen* (London 1960), p.110.

210 W.Y. Evans-Wentz (ed.), *The Tibetan Book of the Dead*, trans. Lama Kazi Dawa-Samdup (London 1957), pp.liv–lv.

211 *Ibid.*, p.xxxvi.

212 Edward Conze, *Buddhism: Its Essence and Development* (Birmingham 2001), p.16.

# INDEX

## Q

The windhorse symbolizes the energy of the Enlightened mind carrying the truth of the Buddha's teachings to all corners of the world. On its back the windhorse bears three jewels: a brilliant gold jewel represents the Buddha, the ideal of Enlightenment, a sparkling blue jewel represents the teachings of the Buddha, the Dharma, and a glowing red jewel, the community of the Buddha's enlightened followers, the Sangha. Windhorse Publications, through the medium of books, similarly takes these three jewels out to the world.

Windhorse Publications is a Buddhist publishing house, staffed by practising Buddhists. We place great emphasis on producing books of high quality, accessible and relevant to those interested in Buddhism at whatever level. Drawing on the whole range of the Buddhist tradition, our books include translations of traditional texts, commentaries, books that make links with Western culture and ways of life, biographies of Buddhists, and works on meditation.

As a charitable institution we welcome donations to help us continue our work. We also welcome manuscripts on aspects of Buddhism or meditation. For orders and catalogues log on to www.windhorsepublications.com or contact:

Windhorse Publications
11 Park Road
Birmingham
B13 8AB
UK

Consortium
1045 Westgate Drive
St Paul MN 55114
USA

Windhorse Books
PO Box 574
Newtown NSW 2042
Australia

Windhorse Publications is an arm of the Friends of the Western Buddhist Order, which has more than sixty centres on four continents. Through these centres, members of the Western Buddhist Order offer regular programmes of events for the general public and for more experienced students. These include meditation classes, public talks, study on Buddhist themes and texts, and bodywork classes such as t'ai chi, yoga, and massage. The FWBO also runs several retreat centres and the Karuna Trust, a fundraising charity that supports social welfare projects in the slums and villages of India.

Many FWBO centres have residential spiritual communities and ethical businesses associated with them. Arts activities are encouraged too, as is the development of strong bonds of friendship between people who share the same ideals. In this way the FWBO is developing a unique approach to Buddhism, not simply as a set of techniques, but as a creatively directed way of life for people living in the modern world.

If you would like more information about the FWBO please visit the website at www.fwbo.org or write to:

London Buddhist Centre
51 Roman Road
London
E2 0HU
UK

Aryaloka
14 Heartwood Circle
Newmarket NH 03857
USA

Sydney Buddhist Centre
24 Enmore Road
Sydney NSW 2042
Australia

## ALSO FROM WINDHORSE PUBLICATIONS

### A SURVEY OF BUDDHISM:

ITS DOCTRINES AND METHODS THROUGH THE AGES
Sangharakshita

'This book remains one of the finest introductions to Buddhist thought and practice in the English language.... remarkable for its comprehensive scope, its sophistication and subtlety, its fidelity to the experience of Buddhism, and its balance in treating the various schools and traditions.' Reginald Ray, author of *Buddhist Saints in India*

Now in its ninth edition, *A Survey of Buddhism* continues to provide an indispensable study of the entire field of Buddhist thought and practice. Covering all the major doctrines and traditions, both in relation to Buddhism as a whole and to the spiritual life of the individual Buddhist, Sangharakshita places their development in historical context. This is an objective but sympathetic appraisal of Buddhism's many forms that clearly demonstrates the underlying unity of all its schools.

'Simply the most complete single volume survey of all the major doctrines and traditions in the development of Buddhism.' *Buddhist Peace Fellowship Newsletter*

576 pages
ISBN 0 904766 93 4
£19.99/$39.95/€39.95

## THE DRAMA OF COSMIC ENLIGHTENMENT:

PARABLES, MYTHS, AND SYMBOLS OF THE WHITE LOTUS SUTRA
Sangharakshita

The *White Lotus Sutra* tells the greatest of all stories, that of human life and human potential. Taking the entire cosmos for its stage and all sentient beings for its players, the sutra illuminates a strange realm indeed, but its parables, myths, and symbols have made it loved and revered throughout the Buddhist world.

In this commentary, Sangharakshita brings these parables, myths, and symbols to vivid life and shows how they relate to our own spiritual quest. The discussions that follow each chapter draw us deeper into the true meaning of the Sutra, the precious significance of our lives.

As befits a tradition of devotion to the Sutra over the centuries, every page is beautifully decorated with lino-cut motifs.

240 pages, with illustrations
ISBN 0 904766 59 4
£8.99/$15.99/€15.99

## THE INCONCEIVABLE EMANCIPATION:

THEMES FROM THE VIMALAKIRTI-NIRDESA
Sangharakshita

Step into the magical, paradoxical world of a Mahayana Buddhist scripture. Mahayana Buddhism, to which the Zen and Tibetan traditions are related, emphasizes the ideal of the Bodhisattva, one who seeks to become Enlightened out of a compassionate desire to help all living beings.

In the *Vimalakirti-Nirdesa* we meet the Bodhisattva Vimalakirti, a worker of wonders, a formidable debater and skilful teacher. Sangharakshita's commentary illuminates this original text, its myths and symbols, and explores the powerful figure of Vimalakirti and the significance of his teachings. By journeying into this scripture we can find the wisdom and compassion that lie at the heart of the Bodhisattva path and discover, communicate and put into action Vimalakirti's message.

168 pages, b/w illustrations
ISBN 0 904766 88 8
£8.50/$16.95/€16.95

**WISDOM BEYOND WORDS:**

THE BUDDHIST VISION OF ULTIMATE REALITY
Sangharakshita

The Buddhist *Prajnaparamita*, or 'Perfection of Wisdom', teachings are unique and extraordinary. To the unwary student they can be dangerously disorienting, offering a fast route to some well-trodden blind alleys – or to the very heart of reality.

In his commentary on three core texts of this tradition – the *Ratnagunasamchayagatha*, the *Diamond Sutra*, and the *Heart Sutra* – Sangharakshita leavens a formidable subject with anecdotes, both humorous and startling, as well as strong doses of common sense. The result is a lively appreciation of the real issues and difficulties experienced by Westerners living in the twenty-first century who want to make use of the wisdom and guidance of traditional Buddhist texts.

304 pages
ISBN 0 904766 77 2
£12.50/$25.00/€25.00

**PUJA:**

THE FWBO BOOK OF BUDDHIST DEVOTIONAL TEXTS
Sangharakshita (compiler)

Our practice of Buddhism must touch all the different aspects of our being. Ritual can help bring about a greater harmony of body, speech, and mind through enriching our imagination, cultivating our emotions, and refining our senses.

Ritual practices within the Buddhist tradition are referred to as *puja*, which means 'devotional worship'. This new, beautifully illustrated edition is an anthology containing a number of such practices in the form of chants, ceremonies, and rituals. Included are the *Heart Sutra* (in Sanskrit and English), the *Tiratana Vandana*, the *Dhammapalam Gatha* and a number of mantras.

64 pages, hardback, with illustrations
ISBN 0 904766 96 9
£9.99/$19.95/€19.95

## MEETING THE BUDDHAS:

A GUIDE TO THE BUDDHAS, BODHISATTVAS, AND TANTRIC DEITIES
by Vessantara

This best-selling book invites us on a vivid and inspiring journey to the magical heart of Buddhist visualization and devotional practices. With Vessantara as our experienced guide, we are introduced to the main Buddhas, Bodhisattvas, and Tantric deities we may be fortunate to meet in that miraculous realm. This unique 'encyclopedia' of the Buddhas and Bodhisattvas in the Indo-Tibetan tradition is an incomparable – and inspiring – resource.

'Attentive reading could become a devotional act in itself.' *The Bloomsbury Review*

376 pages, 36 b/w illustrations, 27 colour plates
ISBN 0 904766 53 5 paperback
£16.99/$27.95/€27.95

## EXPLORING KARMA & REBIRTH

Nagapriya

*Every Buddhist should read it* David Loy
*An excellent introduction* Stephen Batchelor
*Cogent, knowledgeable, and penetrating* Norman Fischer

*Exploring Karma & Rebirth* helps us to unravel the complexities of these two important but often misunderstood Buddhist doctrines. Clarifying, examining and considering them, it offers an imaginative reading of what the teachings could mean for us now. Both informative and thought provoking, above all, *Exploring Karma & Rebirth* insists that, to be of enduring value, these doctrines must continue to serve the overriding aim of Buddhism: spiritual awakening.

176 pages
ISBN 1 899579 61 3
£8.99/$13.95/€13.95

## LIVING WITH AWARENESS:

A GUIDE TO THE SATIPATTHANA SUTTA
Sangharakshita

'Paying attention to how things look, sound, and feel makes them more enjoyable; it is as simple (and as difficult) as that.' Mindfulness and the breath – this deceptively simple yet profound teaching in the *Satipaṭṭhāna Sutta* is the basis of much insight meditation practice today. By looking at aspects of our daily life, such as Remembering, Looking, Dying, Reflecting, Sangharakshita shows how broad an application the practice of mindfulness can have – and how our experience can be enriched by its presence.

200 pages
ISBN 1 899579 38 9
£11.99/$17.95/€17.95

## LIVING WITH KINDNESS:

THE BUDDHA'S TEACHING ON METTA
Sangharakshita

*Just as a mother would protect her only child at the risk of her own life, let thoughts of boundless love pervade the whole world.* Karaniya Metta Sutta

Kindness is one of the most basic qualities we can possess, and one of the most powerful. In Buddhism it is called *metta* – an opening of the heart to all that we meet. This book takes us step by step through the Buddha's words in the *Karaniya Metta Sutta* to consider its meaning, its ethical foundations and its cultivation, culmination and realization. Excellent for beginners and an insightful refresher for those looking for another way to engage with metta.

'will help both Buddhists and people of other faiths to come to a deeper understanding of the true significance of kindness as a way of life and a way of meditation.' *Pure Land Notes*

160 pages
ISBN 1 899579 64 8
£9.99/$14.95/€14.95